THE SHAPE OF THAT HURT

ALSO BY GORDON ROHLEHR

Pathfinder: Black Awakening in "The Arrivants" of Edward Kamau Brathwaite (Tunapuna: Gordon Rohlehr, 1981).

Calypso and Society in Pre-Independence Trinidad (Port of Spain: Gordon Rohlehr, 1990)

My Strangled City and Other Essays (Port of Spain: Longman, 1992; Leeds: Peepal Tree Press, 2019).

The Shape of That Hurt and Other Essays (Port of Spain: Longman, 1992; Leeds: Peepal Tree Press, 2020).

A Scuffling of Islands: Essays on Calypso (Port of Spain: Lexicon, 2004).

Transgression, Transition, Transformation: Essays in Caribbean Culture (Port of Spain: Lexicon, 2007).

Ancestories: Readings of Kamau Brathwaite's "Ancestors" (Port of Spain: Lexicon, 2010).

My Whole Life Is Calypso: Essays on Sparrow (Port of Spain: Gordon Rohlehr, 2015).

"These Collapsing Times": Remembering Q: Afterword to *Victor D. Questel: Collected Poems* (Leeds: Peepal Tree Press, 2016), 181-295.

Perfected Fables Now: A Bookman Signs Off on Seven Decades (Leeds: Peepal Tree Press, 2019).

Musings, Mazes, Muses, Margins (Leeds: Peepal Tree Press, 2020).

GORDON ROHLEHR

THE SHAPE OF THAT HURT

AND OTHER ESSAYS

Man knew Art before he discovered fire.
— Aubrey Williams

May I learn the shape of that hurt
which captured you nightly into
dread city, discovering through
streets steep with the sufferer's beat
— Anthony McNeill "For the D"

PEEPAL TREE

First published by Longman Trinidad Ltd in 1992
This new edition published in 2021 by
Peepal Tree Press Ltd
17 King's Avenue
Leeds LS6 1QS
England

© 1992, 2021 Gordon Rohlehr

ISBN13: 97818452324645

All rights reserved
No part of this publication may be
reproduced or transmitted in any form
without permission

Dedication
for my wife and friend, Betty Ann, in gratitude for the sustaining love, support and laughter over five decades.

CONTENTS

Acknowledgements	8
Author's Preface: Twisting into Shape	9
The Problem of the Problem of Form	15
Possession as Metaphor: Lamming's *Season of Adventure*	68
The Space Between Negations	94
"Assassins of the Voice": Martin Carter's *Poems of Affinity* 1978-1980	126
Three for V.	144
The Shape of that Hurt: An Introduction to *Voiceprint*	156
"Megalleons of Light": Kamau Brathwaite's *Sun Poem*	180
Brathwaite with a Dash of Brown: Crit, the Writer and the Written Life	195
The Rehumanisation of History: Regeneration of Spirit, Apocalypse and Revolution in Brathwaite's *The Arrivants* and *X/Self*	227
Trophy and Catastrophe: Guyana Prize Feature Address	266
Apocalypso and the Soca Fires of 1990	277
Index	335

ACKNOWLEDGEMENTS

My gratitude is again due to my wife Betty Ann Rohlehr for the original typesetting this second volume of essays. Thanks are also due to poet Anthony McNeill whose poem "For the D" provided the epigraph from which the title-essay of this collection derives its name; to Kamau Brathwaite and Longman Group Limited for permission to quote "Kingston in the Kingdom of this World" from *Third World Poems*, 1983; to David Rudder for quotations from "Hoosay"; to the staff of UWI Library, St. Augustine for their cooperation over the years; to Selwyn Cudjoe for "The Space Between Negations" an interview which he conducted with the author.

"The Problem of the Problem of Form" was first published in *Caribbean Quarterly*, Vol. 31, No. 1 (March 1985) pp. 1-52; also published in *Anales del Caribe*, Vol 6 (1986) pp. 219-277. "Possession as Metaphor: Lamming's *Season of Adventure*" was first published in *Journal of West Indian Literature*, Vol 5, Nos 1 & 2 (August 1992) pp. 1-29. "The Space Between Negations" was published as "Talking About Naipaul" in *Carib*, No 2 (1981) pp. 39-65. "Assassins of the Voice" was first published as "The Poet and Citizen in a Degraded Community: Martin Carter's *Poems of Affinity* (1978-1980)" in *Cultural Resistance and the Guyana State,* First Caribbean Conference of intellectual Workers, Grenada, November 20-22, 1982. "Victor Questel: A Homage" was first published in *The Luv Arts Digest*, Vol 1, No 2 (June 1982) pp. 31-35. "A Severity of Seeing" was first published as an Introduction to Victor Questel, *Hard Stares* (Port of Spain: New Voices, 1982). "The Shape of That Hurt" was first published as the Introduction to *Voiceprint*, eds. Stewart Brown, Mervyn Morris & Gordon Rohlehr (London: Longman Group U.K. Ltd., 1989). "Megalleons of Light" was first published in *New Voices,* Vol 11, No 2 (March 1983) pp. 43-64; also published in *Jamaica Journal* Vol 16, No 3 (May 1983) pp. 81-87. "Brathwaite with a Dash of Brown" is the hitherto unpublished text of a paper presented at the Conference of English Departments, UWI, Mona, Jamaica, May, 1988. "The Rehumanisation of History" is an extended version of an Inaugural Professorial Lecture, UWI, St. Augustine, Trinidad, 10 December, 1986; "Trophy and Catastrophe" is the text of the keynote address delivered at the Inauguration of the Guyana Prize for Literature, National Cultural Centre, Georgetown, Guyana, on December 8th, 1987; published in *Kyk-Over-Al* 38 (June 1988) pp. 13-22. "Apocalypso and The Soca Fires of 1990" has been hitherto unpublished with the exception of "Hoosay" which appeared as "Mighty Poet of a Shallow People in a Savage Time" in *Trinidad and Tobago Review*. March 1992, pp. 17-19.

AUTHOR'S PREFACE

Twisting into Shape

"where on the aching floor of where I live
the shifting earth is twisting into shape"
(Martin Carter, "I Come from the Nigger Yard")

The Shape of That Hurt is the sequel to *My Strangled City*[1] and includes most of the author's major essays of the 1980-1990 decade, while *My Strangled City* contains mainly statements from the seventies. While both collections are concerned with the relationship between upheaval and making, the vortex of old worlds going out of, and the turmoil of new worlds coming into existence, *The Shape of That Hurt* is more consistently devoted to an identification of the shapes which have emerged out of the apocalyptic process through which the Caribbean has been engendered.

The title of this collection derives from Tony McNeill's elegy for Don Drummond[2] and suggests, as that poem does, the necessary creative movement both through and out of soul-shattering hurt towards the living sculpture of form. There is a blend of engagement and transcendence in this process, a paradoxical sense of our New World Art as being simultaneously entramelled in "the fury and the mire of human veins"[3] and of having in spirit, if not in fact, moved beyond the immediacy of fury and mire, by either creating space and silence within or above it, or fashioning form through painful confrontation with it.

The essays in *The Shape of That Hurt* are for the greater part about the relationship between traumatic experience and the primal impulse to shape, in the evolution of contemporary Caribbean civilisation. The first essay, "The Problem of the Problem of Form" suggests the difficulty of even conceptualising "form" in a New World situation of flux, historic and psychic chaos, cultural erosion, the complexity caused by the intersection or confrontation of the residues of several truncated cultures, as well as the idiosyncratic nature of each artist's intellectual background, imagination and aesthetic preference. It posits the paradox of a Caribbean, poised between a vanishing but still remembered folk heritage and the ever-changing contours of modernist and post-modernist aesthetics, in which the imagination constantly makes and unmakes the vessels for its containment, builds and dismantles the structures for its habitation.

Focus on individual artists such as Lamming, Carter, Questel or Brathwaite, further illustrates the relationship between social and psychic cataclysms and the quest for shape and structure. Significantly, the image of fire is consistently employed to denote both the interior and the exterior upheavals. Carter, for example, begins "Shape and Motion" with the lines

> I was wondering if I could *shape* this passion
> just as I wanted in *solid fire*. [8]

Lamming in *Of Age and Innocence* signals the apocalyptic ending of the old colonialism and ominous beginning of the adventure of Independence, by a great fire, which destroys a mad house and, at the same time, deepens the racial suspicions and misunderstandings that have bedevilled political unity in San Cristobal.

Season of Adventure, the novel that succeeds *Of Age and Innocence,* advances the exploration of Lamming's great theme of the birthing of New World society. Yet, it is argued here in "Possession as Metaphor", that Lamming's main preoccupation is with shaping the passion that is generated in such birthing. He does this by exploring Haitian folk religion as paradigm, basic deep structure and primary shape, and so gives coherence and wholeness to all the otherwise fragmentary elements of the novel.

The essays on Questel ("Three for V") and Carter ("Assassins of the Voice") flesh out claims made in the opening essay of *My Strangled City* about the "driven" quality of some contemporary West Indian writing: its spareness of word, bleakness of image and severity of seeing; its intense fusion of the political and personal domains and its quest for language, style and form sufficiently skeletal to express the eye's bruised vision.

The central essay, "The Shape of That Hurt" is best read in relation to *Voiceprint*[9] the anthology of oral and oral-related poems to which it is the introduction. As its name implies, this essay is about the relationship that has continued to emerge in West Indian poetry between pain and form. This essay affirms the survival of traditional oral poetic modes beneath the surface of contemporary writing. In a sense, it complements "The Problem of the Problem of Form" in that while that essay identifies the range of aesthetic registers – from folk/oral to "modernist" – that are simultaneously available to the Caribbean writer, "The Shape of that Hurt" discerns the undying shape of the ancestral voice in even the most contemporary writing.

The three essays on Brathwaite, when read alongside "Songs of the Skeleton"[10] seek to update the discourse on the work of that poet begun in *Pathfinder*.[11] They chronicle the shifts in his approach to form; his ceaseless wrestle with the chaos of the contemporary Caribbean "and his stubborn understanding of this pain."[12] They trace his movement towards a growing density and complexity of image and allusion which is, at times, almost the polar opposite of the "folk" aesthetic on which *The Arrivants* and much of the two autobiographical texts, *Mother Poem* and *Sun Poem,* were structured. "The Rehumanisation of History", hitherto unpublished, traces the development of interrelated themes of Spirit, Apocalypse and Revolution over the wide expanse of Brathwaite's work. More than any of these essays, it is about the relationship between Art and Fire; between the creative and destructive aspects of energy, in the shaping of human civilisations.

"Trophy and Catastrophe" sums up the paradox of the entire collection: the dichotomy of Fire and Art, chaos and the creative impulse, ruin and resurrection, hurt and shape. In a real sense, it is the true ending of the cycle of exploration which these two volumes of essays have described; though it seemed appropriate to include some direct commentary on the attempts made by Trinidad's calypsonians to grapple with or evade the implications of the 1990 insurrection, whose fires were real, not metaphorical. The final essay, "Apocalypso and the Soca Fires of 1990", therefore, not only counterpoints those more abstract statements which deal with fire as concept, but also balances "Man Talking to Man", the essay that ends *My Strangled City*, and closes the circle described by these two collections by returning us to the image of a real apocalypse and suggesting the shape of things to come.

Gordon Rohlehr
24 September, 1992.

References

1. Rohlehr, G., *My Strangled City and Other Essays* (Port of Spain: Longman Trinidad, 1992).
2. McNeill, A., "For the D", in Brown, S., Morris, M. & Rohlehr, G., (eds) *Voiceprint* (London: Longman Group U.K. Ltd, 1989), p. 92.
3. Yeats, W.B., "Byzantium", *The Collected Poems of W. B. Yeats* (London: Macmillan & Co., Ltd.. 1961), p. 280.
4. Brathwaite, E.K., "Caribbean Man in Space and Time", *Savacou* 11/12 (September 1975) pp. 1-11.
5. Brathwaite, E.K., "Caribbean Culture: Two Paradigms" in Jurgen Martini (ed.) *Missile and Capsule* (Bremen: Universitat Bremen, 1983), pp. 9-54.
6. Carter, M., "I Come from the Nigger Yard", in *Poems of Succession* (London: New Beacon Books Ltd., 1977), p. 40.
7. Williams, A., in Walmsley A., (ed.) *Guyana Dreaming: The Art of Aubrey Williams* (Aarhus: Denmark: Dangaroo, 1990).
8. Carter, M., "Shape and Motion One", in *Poems of Succession,* p. 55.
9. Brown, A., Morris, M., & Rohlehr, G., (eds) *Voiceprint* (London: Longman Group U.K. Ltd., 1989).

10. Rohlehr, G., "Songs of the Skeleton" in *My Strangled City & Other Essays*, pp. 270-323.
11. Rohlehr, G., *Pathfinder: Black Awakening in **The Arrivants** of Edward Kamau Brathwaite* (Port of Spain: 1981).
12. Brathwaite, E. K., "Krow" in *Black + Blues* (Havana: Casa de las Americas, 1976), p. 66.

THE PROBLEM OF THE PROBLEM OF FORM

The Idea of an Aesthetic Continuum and Aesthetic Code-switching in West Indian Literature

Form involves a number of factors. Firstly, there's the writer's intelligence, temperament and sensibility. Secondly there is the material, the *stoff* on which that sensibility nurtures or famishes itself. This material or *stoff* may include both the given conditions of personal and social experience and vicarious experience: what the writer has read, absorbed, admired or hated, reacted to or against; the world of writing of which what he writes is a part and to which it is, perhaps, a contribution. Thirdly, there's the writer's imagination which shapes experience by means of processes which maybe arbitrary, intangible and unpremeditated. For some writers, indeed, the work of art is its own subject, and tells about itself and the processes whereby it came into being, some of which may be hidden from the artist himself.

Form is the result of the interrelation of these factors and the problem of form is how to appreciate this interrelationship. It involves a sense of process as well as the capacity to recognise structure as the end result of process. The problem of the problem of form is that form thus defined is a different thing for each writer and for each work. Our problem is complicated by the fact that some of our writers have been productive for over three decades and have, naturally, undergone several changes of style and developed very complicated notions of aesthetic. They have been part of a Caribbean which is itself caught up in a vortex of social and political change, whose pressure has been inescapable, and has forced writers to adopt modes and forms which would earlier have seemed alien to their temperaments and sensibilities.

Our problem is further complicated by the nature of the creative person who has evolved over the last fifty years in the Caribbean. This person is usually multi-talented: Norman Cameron: accomplished historian of the pre-colonial era in Africa, mathematician, teacher, essayist, playwright, bibliophile, man of letters; C.L.R. James: novelist, playwright, historian, philosopher, politician, literary critic; Edward Kamau Brathwaite: poet, historian, critic with a seventy-page curriculum vitae; Derek Walcott: poet, playwright, critic, painter with, perhaps, an even longer C.V.; Michael Gilkes: playwright, actor, critic, teacher, chemist and, it has been whispered, alchemist about to find the philosopher's stone; Dennis Scott: poet, playwright, dancer, teacher; Rex Nettleford: choreographer, dancer, political analyst, labour expert; Wilson Harris: land surveyor, poet, novelist.

One can go on like this. My point isn't to celebrate or applaud, but merely to cite these creators as examples of a quite familiar Caribbean tendency; one that, ironically, had to do with the very restrictions of Caribbean societies: the emergence of an intelligentsia which was simultaneously rooted and elitist, and which was willing and able to adjust to the currents of change in Caribbean societies. To read any of our writers at any depth is to be plunged into a thicket of letters. Our writers have themselves read widely, and what they have read has helped determine their notions of form. I'd like to stress, therefore, that my comments in this paper concern only fragments of writers' works, and are in no way final, comprehensive or prescriptive.

One would naturally expect from such multi-disciplinarians a sense of form based not on the notion of a specificity of genre or aesthetic, but on the interrelationship of various art forms, aesthetics and areas of interest. The problem of the problem of form is to understand this compulsive Caribbean drive to realise a complex, multifaceted, flexible sense of shape. Such a multifaceted shape is easily visible in works as different as Lamming's *In the Castle of My Skin*, *Natives of My Person*, and *Water with Berries*; Brathwaite's *The Arrivants*, *Mother Poem*, *Sun Poem* and "Crab"; Harris's *Guyana Quartet* and several works since then; Walcott's *Dream on Monkey Mountain*, Gilkes's *Couvade*, Brodber's *Jane and Louisa Will Soon Come Home*, Clarke's *Douens*, McNeill's *Credences* and Scott's *An Echo in the Bone*. One could, indeed, devote two or three long essays just to trying to account for this remarkable phenomenon; and even then one would not have described all the dimensions of the problem of form, which involves an appreciation of how the Caribbean mind has coped with the rich diversity and contradictions of its experience. So my task here is to produce a positionless paper which will try to outline some of the directions in which we have moved in our various attempts to structure certain aspects of our experience.

The evidence of our writing suggests that we live in late twentieth century societies in which there are memories of villages, but the cities determine the dynamics of change. There is a groping for the pastoral even in writers who criticise other aspects of such yearning when they see them revealed in the work of their fellow writers. There is, conversely, a preoccupation with the worst effects of urbanism: nightmare slums, ecological atrocity, violence, madness, despair and dislocation. Our peoples and our sensibilities have been shaped by both experiences, and we have added to village and town, suburb and metropole. A Guyanese huckster, say, who travels to the bush to obtain raw gold which will be used to buy foreign exchange and bribe officials in any country from Trinidad to Toronto, spans an even wider geography of experience. Our writers have dealt with this movement of people backwards and forwards, and we can recognise predominant and interrelated themes of rootedness and exile, journey and homecoming in a significant amount of our writing.

Recognising this oscillation between geographical and situational opposites as an integral part of our social and psychic experience, I had in "Literature and the Folk" (1971)[1] suggested that we apply the sociological concept of a folk/urban continuum to our literary situation. Continuum theory thus applied allows for both linguistic and aesthetic code switching; for the dialectical collision of opposite tendencies and notions of form in the same writer and between different writers. Continuum theory employed as a tool for clarifying the problem of the problem of form, points us to two poles which have guided our writers in the achievement of shape: the oral traditions of the West Indies and certain aspects of the aesthetics of modernism.

If the oral tradition directs our attention to assemblies of people, the lime, the calypso tent, church, grounation, cult, drum, dance, performance, narrative, song, and sermon, modernist aesthetics highlights the separateness or the alienation of the individual, who is placed or lost in a universe of open possibilities, where he must create self, style and form. Modernist aesthetics may raise problems of void or vortex, chaos or silence, the irrelevance of the individual, the dehumanisation of art and the emergence in an incomprehensible universe of the art object as its own circular self-contained world, exploring itself, echoing itself, and sometimes with enviable, wormlike flexibility, even copulating itself. My point is that many of our writers have been simultaneously attracted to both sets of possibilities, so that the same works may contain the tension between two poles of shaping, as well as two modes of being. In some writers, indeed, the poles are complementary, and curious continuities exist between them.

Let us, for example, examine Martin Carter's statement of aesthetic at precisely that moment when an oral tradition seemed to have lost its relevance in his work. Carter began as our most rhetorical poet, a writer whose work grew out of political polemic and oratory, and was read aloud in the streets by the poet himself.[2] In the twilight period after the suspension of the Guyana Constitution in 1954, he moved from rhetoric to reticence: from a poetry based on oral, and indeed oracular considerations to something cryptic, half-image and half-riddle: the silence when the oracle has lost its message and there is "no voice from Delphi."[3]

It is at this point that Carter writes the significantly titled "Poems of Shape and Motion", the first of which begins with an attempt to conceptualise an idea of form that he briefly entertained on his journey towards an aesthetics of silence.

> I was wondering if I could shape this passion
> just as I wanted in solid fire...
> I was wondering if the strange combustion of my days
> the tension of the world inside of me
> and the strength of my heart were enough.[4]

"Solid fire", a contradiction in terms, becomes his aesthetic ideal. As in Blake's "Tyger" or "The Marriage of Heaven and Hell", art is defined as the giving of shape to energy. An aesthetic of energy is what Carter now seeks; not the obvious and externally directed energy of political rhetoric, but an interior energy which consumes and tears one apart. The idea is repeated in "the strange combustion of my days." Combustion is the explosion taking place within the sealed-off confines of an engine, whereby energy is controlled and converted into movement. Carter's aesthetic in this brief period challenges the idea of void by an act of making in which the poet's self assumes the shape he bestows on whatever he creates. The poet and the poem, self and form, become one:

> and the challenge of space in my soul
> be filled by the shape I become.

Wilson Harris, writing out of the same furious cradle of Guyana, articulates the geological/geographical concept of "implosion" – that eruption of energy beneath the apparently placid surface of a river; an eruption sometimes strong enough to split boulders. "Implosion" is another metaphor for an aesthetics of energy, one which, like Carter's combustion metaphor, reconciles the apparent contradiction of eruption and containment, movement and stillness; giving shape and clean definition to the fluid and catastrophic. As one reads through Harris's *Tradition, the Writer and Society,* one is struck by how frequently words like energy or power appear.

All this is of crucial importance to the emerging notion of an aesthetics based on the oral traditions of the Caribbean. For the oral tradition has always been concerned with matters of energy, its containment in the shaped process of ritual enactment and catharsis. Any aesthetic based on the oral tradition seeks to address itself to these considerations: energy, containment, catharsis. So the oral tradition, far from being a static "folk" inheritance, is proving to be the vital and adaptable source of new exploration. Kamau Brathwaite, grounded at the opposite pole to that which informs Carter's "Shape and Motion" describes how Caribbean and Afro-American oral traditions adapted themselves to the necessities of the social upheavals of the 1960s.

> The art of the Revolution... has been an art, which, in the first place, has moved from the concept of 'art as exquisite object', 'art for art's sake', as

concern of the elite/initiate (art as distance, or as Raja Rao put it at ACLALS, art as 'silence'); into art as energy (Coltrane, Aretha, the Wailers) as force-field (sound-system, soul sermon) emanating from poet or artist but achieving complete meaning only through contact with the audience (community/congregation), who then complete the circuit through response to source; grounation into heat, light, vision, transformation.[5]

Brathwaite in *The Arrivants* is true to this aesthetic of energy in that whenever states of "nothingness" or "void" or "silence" appear, they do so as the dialectical other of an aesthetics of kinesis. One of the "contradictory omens" of our situation, then, has been the fitful dialectic between "art as silence" and "art as energy". It is part of what involves us here in our attempt to define the problem of the problem of form.

Paradigms of the Oral Tradition

The Religious Paradigm
I want to extract from the oral tradition two interrelated paradigms: a religious and a secular. When one speaks of a religious paradigm, one is speaking not of religion itself, but of a shape or trope accessible for aesthetic extension into form. There is a wide range of religions in the Caribbean, occupying different positions along a continuum which stretches between those religions with the greatest non-European (i.e. African or Asian) and those with the greatest European content. Donald Hogg, indeed, applies continuum theory to a range of Jamaican religions.[6] Religion has been one of the main areas in which oral tradition has been preserved. The most African of the religions, those related to Orisha worship, contain an integrated complex of drum, chant, dance, liturgy, shaped ritual, and performance. Every loa has its rhythm, prayer, form of word and movement: its particular pace, tone and vibration.

The movement of ritual enactment is towards climax and catharsis, in which celebrants become possessed and their normal everyday personalities are displaced by a force of extraordinary inner energy. This capacity for movement beyond and beneath the threshold of ordinary surface experience persists even in Caribbean cities, as well as in those areas of the metropole to which Caribbean peoples have migrated. Some residents of Miami have been signalling concern at the presence of vodun and santeria, which have survived the passage across the gulf. In these days of what René Girard has termed "the sacrificial crisis", when religion ceases to contain and cleanse the impulses towards violence and self-destructive chaos, and when West Indian societies are under extreme stress, many people have been impelled towards the more ecstatic and cathartic forms of worship. Black musics of the New World, too, have constantly celebrated and re-enacted on both the sacred and the secular planes, a capacity for movement beyond.

It is only natural, then, that ecstatic religions should have served as tropes for novelists, dramatists and poets, by providing accessible metaphors of a process of descent into the inferno of the Self, which leads to a recovery of the-word-as-energy, electric, kinetic utterance. The process which leads to this moment of possession, is constantly repeated in West Indian and Afro-American literature, which has also realised an aesthetics of energy. It is there in Lamming (*Of Age and Innocence*, *Season of Adventure*) who explicitly points us to his metaphorical interpretation and use of the Haitian Ceremony of Souls ritual. One sees it in Shake Keane's "Calypso Dancers" and "Shaker Funeral";[7] in Brathwaite's "Jah", "Shepherd", "Wake", "Negus", "Ogun"; Dennis Scott's An *Echo in the Bone* and Salkey's *A Quality of Violence,* that remarkable exploration of the connection between cosmic and human violence on the one hand, and the idea of sacrifice as catharsis and containment on the other.

Among Afro-American writers the process which leads to possession by and release of the loas of energy can be seen at work in Baldwin's *Go Tell It on the Mountain*, Toomer's "Kabnis" from *Cane*, and briefly in Ellison's *Invisible Man.* Ishmael Reed has spoken about his "Neo Hoodoo" aesthetic, in which he seeks to make accessible to literature all the mystery and arationality of Louisiana religion.[8] The same impulse is inherent in much Afro-American music: for example, Max Roach's *Lift Every Voice and Sing,* whose "Troubled Waters" and "Sometimes I Feel" are the exact musical equivalent of the Threshing-Floor passage in *Go Tell It on the Mountain;* or Aretha Franklin's *Amazing Grace* and Coltrane's *A Love Supreme*, *Sun Ship* or *Kulu Se Mama.* Such music not only aims to fill one with the spirit, but operates at a visceral level, somewhere between the navel and the solar plexus, where some of our philosophy has wisely anchored itself.

What is remarkable about all of the writers named is that interior descent is not an escape from surface reality into fantasy, but a descent beneath reality into rediscovered rhythms connected with the historic experience of the people. So Baldwin's John on the threshing floor discovers the whole history of his people, and the voices of the chanting sisters become in the subliminal ear, "a sound of rage and weeping from time set free." Toomer's Kabnis, intoxicated, discovers under the face of his daily humiliation a form burned into his soul, that is

> some twisted awful thing that crept in from a dream, a godam nightmare, an wont stay still unless I feed it. An it lives on words. Not beautiful words. God Almighty no. Misshapen, split-gut, tortured, twisted words...[9]

The very face that Brathwaite's Ogun carves when he descends into Self, and the very word-pebbles that Brathwaite himself cracks in *The Arrivants* in his resolve to write "a literature of catastrophe, to hold a broken mirror to broken nature." "That," Brathwaite declares, is my aesthetic ideal."[10]

"Man Entering His Voice": Lamming's Of Age and Innocence

George Lamming was one of the first West Indian writers who openly proclaimed his use of Afro-Caribbean religious ritual as a metaphor of interior descent into the submerged history of his people. First in *The Pleasures of Exile* (1960), then in his essay "The West Indian People", Lamming described the Haitian Ceremony of Souls, a ritual which he had witnessed in 1956, in which the living, through the medium of the houngan, hold with the dead a dialogue that is crucially necessary for the fulfilment of their respective futures. According to Lamming:

> The dead are supposed to be in a purgatorial state of water, and it is necessary for them to have this dialogue with the living before they can be released into their final eternity. The living, on the other hand, need to meet the dead again in order to discover if there is any need for forgiveness. This dialogue takes place through the medium of the Priest or Houngan...
>
> It is not important to believe in the actual details of the ceremony. What is important is its symbolic drama, the drama of redemption, the drama of returning, the drama of cleansing for a commitment towards the future.[11]

This statement illuminates and suggests the fundamental similarity between a number of incidents and situations in Lamming's novels: Pa's descent through dream and trance to an Edenic Africa of the mind in *In the Castle of My Skin*; Fola's initiatory experience in the tonnelle, which sends her on a compulsive quest to recover not only her real past, but her other Self and double; Teeton's encounter with Myra on an English Common, which takes place, symbolically, in darkness. Lamming again points us to the Ceremony of Souls ritual in order to underline the significance of the dialogue between Teeton/Caliban and Myra/Miranda about their common participation in a squalid colonial history, which has tragically altered or shaped both of their destinies.[12]

The most surprising of all these symbolic descents into Self and history, however, is that of Mark Kennedy in *Of Age and Innocence*. It is also one of the most important because Kennedy, through this descent, comes to represent the duality of the Caribbean mind and its ambivalent swing between folk/oral and Euro/modernist aesthetics. Kennedy is, significantly, a mulatto: that is, ethnically he embodies, or is supposed to embody, as does Walcott's Lestrade and Shabine, Denis Williams's Lionel Froad or John Hearne's Mark Lattimer, the dual potentialities of the Caribbean situation. He is theoretically capable of realising a substantial part of the continuum of Caribbean possibilities, but he may also be the desert, the waste and void which Lionel Froad says stretches between Europe and Africa. Mark Kennedy has residual childhood memories of the fundamentalist/charismatic religion of Shephard, and though he has never participated in it, has remained fascinated by Shephard. His "folk" roots, however, never strong, have become almost completely obliterated by his long and rootless sojourn in Europe, the disorienting influence of World War II, and his adoption of, or absorption by a philosophy of alienation similar to the one which in *Nausea* paralyses Sartre's Roquentin. It is with this alienating paralysis that Mark returns to a San Cristobal which is now on the verge of crucial political change, and seems to make urgent nationalist demands on its intellectuals. Mark is, in this respect, a forerunner of Patterson's Blackman, Naipaul's Kripalsingh, Wyck Williams's Ikael Torass, or some of St. Omer's sonambulists.

It is important that we consider Mark's encounter with the primal, since in one important respect, Mark is made to function as the author's mouthpiece. It is he who explains Lamming's problematic approach to form in *Of Age and Innocence;* and despite his normal inability to articulate his ideas in public or even within a closed circle of friends, it is he who through his diaries, makes a constant attempt to explore his innermost feelings. In the process of so doing, he provides us with a clear clue to the problem of form as it confronted Lamming in the mid-fifties. Here we see the novelist wrestle with an elusive and perhaps inexpressible quality in personal experience, which leads to a complex notion of form as a dialectic between language and silence, the constant imposition of order on an experience which constantly reverts to chaos. Mark asks:

> Is this failure to communicate a kind of illness which puts me out of touch with the others? I have looked for it in them, and I am suddenly made feeble by their fluency. I try to find a way which would enable others to enter my secret so that they might, through a common experience, lead me to its source. But my effort moves off the mark. I begin, as it were, from the circumference of my meaning, moving cautiously and with loyal feeling, towards a centre which very soon I discover I cannot reach. Then speech deserts me. I abandon what I had felt to be an obligation, and the result is silence. Yet my silence contains a need to begin again. But the difficulties accumulate. For I have hardly resigned myself to the solitude of one secret before a new enthusiasm entices me. I am once more at the centre of something I must share, and the origins which I seem to understand for myself suddenly disperse into a frantic chaos.[13]

The paradox here, one central to some modernist literary movements, particularly existentialism and absurdism, is that Mark is being both lucid and lyrically eloquent about his inability to reach or communicate his meaning, which he terms his "secret". Kafka, for example, had said it before:

> What I write is different from what I say, what I say is different from what I think, what I think is different from what I ought to think and so it goes on further and further into the deepest darkness.[14]

Or there is T.S. Eliot:

> Trying to learn to use words, and every attempt

> Is a wholly new start, and a different kind of failure
> Because one has only learnt to get the better of words
> For the thing one no longer has to say, or the way in which
> One is no longer disposed to say it.[15]

Sartre's Roquentin and Beckett's protagonists experience these problems of communication and language to a pathological degree.

Mark's paradox, then, is the paradox of writing itself, particularly in the twentieth century, where language has become, not only the medium of exploration, but also the subject explored. This paradox receives its most extreme expression in Beckett's tragicomic novels where over and over again we encounter characters who tell us that they cannot tell us. But in the act of telling us that they cannot tell us, they are communicating. Such art becomes a constant structuring of space, a shaping of nothing, and the investment with fluid form of what the artist has deemed the incommunicable; a paradox whereby order is imposed on non-meaning, non-experience. This idea frequently occurs in Carter's later poems, and is best expressed in his "Proem" (1975), the first poem in *Poems of Succession,* where the elusiveness of experience is beautifully celebrated in an elusiveness of style and idea.

Mark Kennedy, then, articulates a modernist aesthetic which is the polar opposite of one based on the oral tradition, and is equally attractive to Lamming. What Kennedy says bears striking resemblance to Lamming's description of the predicament of the artist in "The Negro Writer and His World,"[16] an essay originally read at the First International Conference of Negro Writers, Paris, 1956. The writer, Lamming declared then, needs to render justice first to the secret inner world of the Self, secondly to his milieu and finally to the necessity for making a universal appeal. The secret inner world is described in terms identical to those employed by Mark Kennedy. It is:

> the world of the private and hidden self, a world which turns quietly, sometimes turbulently, within one man, and which might be only known by others after that man has spoken. Each man who becomes aware of himself as a separate existence shares this solitude; each man has had an experience, momentary or prolonged, of the meaning of being alone. I do not mean loneliness or any similar illness of certain self-important natures. I am speaking of the experience proceeding from the depths of one's being, of existing.
>
> It is a moment marked by silence. It is a moment when man's utterance cannot catch and convey the shape and shade of his thought and feeling. Language, it would seem, has actually surrendered just when his need is greatest. It is then he requires this weapon of words to enter the area of his consciousness, and bring back with it, so to speak, the kind of picture which another's eye cannot conceive.[16]

It is very clear from this that Mark's predicament with language and communication is exactly the same as the primary necessity of the artist as Lamming defines it in this essay, which was written while work on *Of Age and Innocence* (1958) was going on. Mark's strange and sudden involvement in Shephard's political movement and his charismatic experience while on the political platform are really the result of Lamming's need to explore the other pole of his own divided personality. The scene (Part II, Chapter 2) is an extraordinary one and parallels, in its way, Penelope's and Shephard's self-revelation on Bird Island (Part III, Chapter I): and the boys' ritual of self-confrontation, self-discovery, self-revelation and self-concealment in the wood (Part 1 Chapter 7).

Mark, who earlier is shown to be incapable of choosing, now defines politics as choice, and nationalism as

> the source of discovery and creation. It is the private feeling you experience of possessing and being possessed by the whole landscape of the place where you were born.[17]

Unable to speak before, he is amazingly eloquent on this most public of platforms. Lamming explains this eloquence as being the result of the kind of fervour and charismatic frenzy which possesses both politician and crowd, and is typical of Jamaican political life. The meeting takes place, significantly, in Sabina Square. Mark is dizzy from the experience.

> He was struggling quietly to recover from the *awful spell* which gradually possessed him. It increased with the sound of voices until he felt imprisoned by this *hallucination* which now *possessed* his senses.[18]

Here the abstract alienated modernist encounters the immense pressure of the presence of people. His private solipsistic silence is invaded by the sound of voices, his experience thus becoming a paradigm for what has continued to happen to Caribbean writers inclined towards existentialism. Particularly in Jamaica, writers have found their private worlds invaded by the intense violence of the world around them, and by the sound of the reggae voice exploding in testimony or complaint or violent protest. This has led to fascinating tensions in writers such as Dennis Scott (*Uncle Time* and *Dreadwalk*), Anthony McNeill (*Reel from the "Life Movie"* and *Credences at the Altar of Cloud*), Mervyn Morris (*The Pond* and *Shadow Boxing*), Kendel Hippolyte (*Island in the Sun – Side 2*) and Brathwaite (*Black + Blues*). In all of these writers we see the direct impact of social and political pressures on earlier ideas of form, resulting in different attempts to reconcile the two poles of the aesthetic continuum.

Mark, as we can see from words such as "awful spell", "hallucination" and the twice repeated "possessed" is undergoing a charismatic experience in which he is possessed by the demons of futurity. Hence part of his physical reaction to possession is a sensation of heat, a sort of hellfire:

> The weather had turned to a furnace which boiled the sound of voices acclaiming his speech. It was as though a terrible heat had dissected everything, like a plague producing permanent scars over the earth.[19]

He has an Apocalyptic vision of the whole universe disintegrating:

> He was a part of a constant and perceptible disintegration of things: leaves, grass, asphalt, the hooves of the animals which waited, patient and enduring over Sabina Square.[20]

Mark's Apocalyptic vision is similar to Shephard's epileptic one while on the plane, but goes further, acquiring Macbethian characteristics. He sees, for example, a bloody kid:

> in a scarlet mess which the heat slowly turned to pure fire. But he could see the revolting spectacle of its birth.[21]

This is a prophetic vision of the conditions of fire, turbulence and revolt in which the new nation will come to life; just as the slogans "Vote for the Donkey", "Vote for the Knife" suggest the mixture of folly and murder which the first politics of the new nation will include. Lamming was writing *Of Age and Innocence* with the 1953/54 experience of Guyana in mind, and accurately foresaw the tragedy of 1962-64.

Mark's vision, which is almost completely a reordering of the external scene within the inferno of his psyche, ends with a mysterious oracular statement; one that is as compulsive an issue from the subconscious as his earlier speech about nationalism.

> And someone approached with a malevolent face and black eyes, wide open and sightless, and a voice spoke: 'What is the origin of that voice which calls you to freedom? It is life on the level of pure participation. Man, entering his voice.' The blind seer and Sabina Square and the liquid red birth of the animal were one.[22]

The blind seer, not mentioned before, is an issue from Mark's unconscious mind, a fictional equivalent to Virgil's Sybil guide to the underworld; a sort of weird brother and double; an archetype whose propulsion to the surface of consciousness becomes necessary, because his statement epitomises that particular moment which urged its utterance. It is a moment of fearsome awakening throughout those countries which are today termed the "developing nations": hence "the liquid red birth of the animal." The prophet is malevolent and blind because the awakening of San Cristobal is the blind beginning of nothing less than a new world order, which will of necessity challenge the equilibrium of capital and labour, authority and servitude on which the old consolidated Western Atlantic order has been based; and in so doing awaken the malevolence of that established order.

San Cristobal, then, stands for the emerging independent nations of the Third World, whose birth is a manifestation of that instinct for freedom which Mark had earlier defined in his speech, when he said that the instinct for freedom revolts against whatever threatens it. The seer expands on Mark's observation when he declares that the instinct for freedom also seeks positively to fulfil itself "on the level of pure participation." Freedom, then, manifests itself both negatively and affirmatively: negatively in that it says "no" to whatever limits it, by revolting; positively in that it affirms the necessity for participation. It thus runs counter to the alienation and incapacity for communication which have been Mark's life so far. If freedom is "Man entering his voice", its aesthetics can hardly be an aesthetics of silence; its achieved form will of necessity challenge the closed circle of an absurdist or neo-modernist aesthetic.

Such then is the meaning of Mark Kennedy's extraordinary descent into subliminal space, a descent which, as we have seen, Lamming was later to define in terms of the Ceremony of Souls metaphor. Kennedy's failure is that he lacks both the emotional ground and the faith to give his vision permanent shape, and the rituals which might enable him to move towards catharsis, healing, and reconciliation. His experience leaves him more empty and paralysed than before. Tragically, he denies the terror and "awful daring" of having been caught up in a communal moment, by imposing on it a purely solipsistic interpretation:

> He had been talking to himself. His speech was a fragment of dialogue between Mark Kennedy and himself and the theme was his identity.[23]

Affirming Self and denying Other. Mark, that finished product of a modernist aesthetic, retreats from further participation in people or politics, in an act of withdrawal which becomes a catalyst for the catastrophe in the novel.

Lamming, then, provided us since 1958 with a forevision not only of the turbulence which lay in wait for new nations whose freedom would challenge the existing order, but also of the inadequacy of our intellectual drift towards the more nihilistic aspects of modernism. That it isn't only intellectuals who were faced with existential emptiness has become clear in the novels of Earl Lovelace. In *The Dragon Can't Dance* Lovelace provides us with a different version of energy, which lacks a mould for its containment, in the figure of Fish-Eye, the Badjohn. What has damaged Fish-Eye is his loss of that ritual – the stickfight whose link with African manness and warriorhood Lovelace deliberately points out – that ritual which, by providing a container for energy, might have married strength and speed to skill. Work, another means of giving energy direction, is abandoned. So Fish-Eye becomes empty with the emptiness of the city itself, his energy his own enemy.

As a warrior whose energies require iron – he plays the three-note boom and the iron in the steelband – he's Ogun/Shango. But like the tragic youths of Brathwaite's "Springblade", his Ogun energies are all misdirected and wasted in the fratricidal violence of the steelband clash.

> People said he was mounted: a spirit of a warrior was inside him, and
> he couldn't help himself. At certain times he just had to fight.[24]

It is with this energy which has never realised its creative form, its "fearful symmetry", that he enters politics; or politics enters him. His contribution to politics is, inevitably, an energy frustrated into empty gesture.

What we have been looking at so far, have been works which have sought to explore both the identity crisis and particular historic moments in terms of the metaphor of possession, one aspect of the religious paradigm. What the authors of these works have realised is that there is an aesthetic, a trope, a shape locked up in the religion and fully relevant to their contemporary quests. What they seek to do is to discover and release the shape of the hidden paradigm, what Toomer calls "the form that's burned into my soul."

"Soul Thunder": Shake Keane's "Shaker Funeral"

Growing awareness of the religious paradigm has led naturally to an integration of genres which has always been latent in the oral tradition. In Afro-Caribbean religions, drumming, dance, liturgy, chant and sermon are sometimes indivisible elements of the same process. Consequently, poetry written with an awareness of the religious paradigm has tended towards performance. It maintains a balance between introspection and communication with a world outside of the psyche, between Self and Other. It combines the symbolic and dramatic modes, preserving balance between sight and sound and establishing an interrelationship between rhythm or vibration and image, which combine in unique ways to illuminate idea. We have, for example, Senghor's concept of rhythm as image,[25] while Harris has noted in Brathwaite the coincidence of oracular voice and imagistic intelligence.[26]

In the light of what I've just been saying, a little known poem such as Keane's "Shaker Funeral"[27] emerges as our most successful early attempt to capture something of the shape of the religious paradigm. The occasion is a Shouter/Baptist funeral, one of those ceremonies of release whose function is to facilitate the transition of the soul from the realm of the living to the world of ancestors, spirits, *les invisibles*. In the syncretic cosmos of the Shouters, the Apocalyptic imagery of Christianity blends with Old Testament ideas of sacrifice and older African notions of the funeral as purgation and catharsis, involving ecstatic possession. Philip Sherlock had a similar vision in his well-known "Pocomania", but Keane is much closer to the feel of the actual process, and it leads him naturally to broken, violent drum rhythms, nowhere present in the Macbethian incantations of Sherlock's poem.[28] In Keane, as Edward Baugh has suggested[29] in an article which first made me aware of Keane's poem, we find the true forerunner of *Rights of Passage*.

Shaker Funeral

>Sorrow sin-
>bound, pelting din
>big chorusclash
>o' the mourners;
>eyes red
>with a shout for the dead,
>yelling crash-
>ing sadness in
>the dusty tread
>o' the mourners.
>
>>Sweet Mother gone
>>to the by and by,
>>follow her to the brink o' Zion.

The mourners are first heard (din, big chorusclash, shout, yelling, crashing). Their feet keep the rhythm of life and death (dusty tread). Note the short broken lines, the broken words, the alliteration, onomatopoeia and word-echoing. Note also the dual worlds inhabited by the mourners. They begin the funeral with the traditional Christian view of themselves as being "sin-bound", caught up in the trammels of sin, from which they seek to liberate themselves. But their mode of self-liberation, through dance, the counterpoint of call and response (chorusclash), handclap, shout and tumultuous energy, that mixture of affirmation and anguish (yelling crash-/ing sadness) is African in its origin. In the first chorus, which the poet recognises as the funeral comes closer, we learn that it is a leader, a Mother of the congregation who has died. This chorus is a traditional Shouter chant and could easily be sung within the poem. The function of the hymn here parallels that of the ditty or song of Afro-Caribbean folk tales, which flow naturally out of the narrative, and are generally part of the story. The religious paradigm integrates modes, and the hymn is one of its natural forms which enters poetry based on this paradigm either directly or by means of allusion.

>Wave wave
>as they roared to grave
>a drench song –
>soulthunder –
>was aymens through
>the wind, shrieks flew,
>and eyes were strong;
>for 'twas madness gave
>them dirge, that grew
>made thunder.

As the mourners enter the graveyard and surge towards the grave, the focal and dramatic centre of the ceremony, their emotion-charged voices overwhelm. Their voices, like 'Trane's vibrant tenor horn, suggest the primal elements and the tumultuous forces of nature – ocean, thunderstorm, hurricane – as they become possessed with the "madness" or enthusiasm of the "powers" or "spirits". That Keane's use of the word "madness" is not pejorative is indicated by the preceding line, "and eyes were strong." Madness here is connected with inner energy and an intensity of vision inseparable from an intensity of passion. Their ritual descent, impossible without passionate conviction and the urgency of despair, is also a gateway into vision.

> Drums, flags,
> pious rags o'
> robes stenching
> sweat;
> mitre o' tattered
> straw, bamboo crozier
> wagged by wind's clenching –
> deathwind that bragged
> sorrow, smattered
> o' sweat
>
> Saints in blue
> bathrobes flew
> about the ranks
> o' the sinners,
> and froth-lipped virgins
> with powdered skins
> and frocks that stank
> with the slime and the stew
> from the purged away sins
> o' the sinners:
>
> And heads were white
> in starched cloth... Bright
> was the blood from the eyes
> o' the candles;
> and the "horn of the Ram
> of the great I Am"
> spoke hoarse in cries...
> and crowned with the light
> o' the Judah Lamb
> were the candles.

These three stanzas trace the process of catharsis. First we see the frail artefacts of the cult – drum, ragged robes, tattered straw mitre and bamboo crozier, signalling the people's imitation of the vestiges of the plantation Church, which had helped outlaw them in this period. The mourners are caught in the firm grip of death at this point. Yet their robes stenching sweat, and the slime and the stew, are dross to be purged away, as in exorcism rituals. Keane maintains detachment to record the smells and sounds. Yet he empathises with the mourners and understands the process beneath their rituals. More than that, he captures the dynamic feel and movement of the ritual, even as he records the pathetic caste distinctions within the congregation between saints and sinners and "froth-lipped virgins"; the saved, the damned, the possessed, all actors in this theatre of misery, pathos and hope.

Thus the next stanza focuses on the heads of the congregation, and sees them rediscovering the meaning of sacrifice and reconciling themselves to the death of the Mother.

> And heads were *white*
> in starched cloth... Bright
> was the *blood* from the eyes
> o' the candles

The first image suggests the halo, and this is made explicit near the end of the stanza, where the mourners are described as having been "crowned with the light." Vision (eyes) is connected with sacrifice (bright blood). With vision comes ecstatic utterance, symbolised, as in Baldwin's *Go Tell it on the Mountain* by the ram's-horn trumpet-blast of "the great I Am." It is precisely this hoarse-sounding horn that Keane, himself an accomplished trumpeter and flugellist,[30] seeks to express in his poem. Indeed, the poet who so closely follows the wave and curve of the congregation's feeling, who records the vibrations of their "soulthunder", is himself caught up in their discovery of language which is also his own.

> Lord delivered Daniel
> from shame's mouth,
> (o' strong, o strong roll Jordan.)
> Lord deliver our Mother
> gone to the Glory Home,
> gone to the Glory Home, gone to Zion

> All God's brothers
> were loud, and the ten
> holy lampers were
> reeking in smoke;
> and the "valley of sod-
> and-shadow," Staff-Rod,
> was blenched as the canker-
> ing sweat o' men
> and the reeking o' God
> in the smoke.

Ecstatic utterance is followed by a mixture of prayer and song, hymns of deliverance and faith, and the final exorcism of the spectre of death, by a ritual of incense and light. Such exorcism is an attempt to combine the efforts of man and God; to make their energies touch and so reintegrate man with the life-force of the great I Am. So the elders of the congregation who, the gap between human and divine having narrowed, are now "all

God's brothers", walk not only through the Valley of the Shadow of Death, but in a redeeming cloud of incense (smoke), mixing their own "cankering" (conquering?) sweat with God's, in a new Gethsemane and harrowing of Hell, sharing a common travail in the effort to conquer death.

> His willing be,
> Mother gone.
> Jordan deep,
> but her soul is strong.
> Follow her to the brink o' Zion.

And now the grave
was washed in a wave
o' wails and a
city o' stars
that dribbled and burned
in the tears that turned
hot sins, on the smoke-white pillars...
But their sorrow was yells,
and their faith was brave,
as the blood-blemished lambs
piled big on the grave
their city o' wax and stars.

Sweet Mother gone,
King o' Mansions-over-Jordan
O strong...
Leave her safe on the brink o' Zion.

After the climax of the human/divine struggle with death, the poem moves towards a catharsis which never quite includes resignation, despite the hymn and prayer. "His willing be." There is submission, but no final reconciliation with the idea of death. The congregation, spirit-filled with the great "I Am" of affirmation, follow their Spiritual Mother as far as the barrier between life and death permits – "to the brink o' Zion" – releasing her "in a wave o' wails," and placing on her grave the now almost burnt-out candles of their charismatic vision, to create their replica of, and ongoing hope for the heavenly city – "their city o' wax and stars." To the end they are seen as "blood-blemished lambs." Does blemished here mean tainted? Impure? Or does it mean that they have understood the meaning of sacrifice once more? Maybe the latter; for it is the courage of their faith ("and their faith was brave") and their strength in affirmation that the poet commends as the poem closes.

This analysis, I hope, illustrates some of my earlier assertions about the shape of the religious paradigm: a preoccupation with the movement of energy towards climax and catharsis; the emphasis on vigour and even violence of rhythm; the break-up of the lines; the fusion of sound and sight and feeling in the illumination of idea; and the suggested plasticity of a form flexible enough to include intimations of hymn, prayer, chorus-wail, drum-beat, hand-clap, dance and sermon. This flexible, multifaceted form had begun to free itself in the fifties, as man entered his voice.

Sermon, Possession, Testimony

The sermon has been receiving growing attention in Afro-American studies as a special and dynamic form of rhetoric and performance.[31] Both Baldwin and Ellison employ it as a shaping device in their novels. Indeed, the very rhythm of Baldwin's best prose depends on the sermon, and *Go Tell It on the Mountain,* with its alternations of sermon, hymn and testimony, is an excellent example of how the religious paradigm can inform prose fiction. Toni Morrison's *Song of Solomon* is structured on recurring testimonies, which become the basis of flashback illuminations of the past. As far as I know, there is no study of the style and imagery of West Indian preachers, though the Keane poem just examined suggests that our poets have long been aware of the sermon as a potential model, while the force of Bible and sermon has been partially responsible for the austere beauty of Mais's prose. The impact of Bible and sermon is also strong in a great deal of reggae and such works as proceed out of the reggae ethos.

The direct impress of sermon and testimony may also be seen in Brathwaite's "Wings of a Dove", "The Stone Sermon", "Negus", *Mother Poem*, and in the tone of many of his post-1970 monologues such as "Kingston in the Kingdom of This World"[32] which originally was also entitled "Good Friday 1975". In much of Brathwaite's performed poetry there is a curious conflict between Anglican liturgical tones and the Shouter rhythms of the roots Churches. The poet's natural reading voice in the Argo recordings of *The Arrivants* suggests the Anglican pulpit, but it is precisely against this plantation establishment Church, which in Barbados helped destroy Black music and dance and maintain class snobbery and the stupidities of status, that much of Brathwaite's satire in *Mother Poem* is directed. One may conclude that it is because Bajan Anglicanism constituted such a major force in his upbringing, that it is subjected to ironic reduction in his writing.

Brathwaite is aware of the Anglican church as a shaping influence on his rhetorical style and his satire of Anglicanism is the result of his growing awareness of the force of the submerged aesthetic of the roots church. He is thus impelled to dramatise a conflict in style which exists at the very roots of Self and Society. He creatively explores this tension between aesthetics in "Angel/Engine", and we are fortunate to have on tape a detailed discussion of how that poem came into being and what it is trying to do.[33] According to Brathwaite, the carpenter's shop which now houses a revivalist Church, once belonged to his great-uncle. He has transformed this piece of factuality into a metaphor of great potency, which we first see explored in "Ogun". In that Church, as in Ogun's "shattered Sunday shop", Brathwaite observes a layering of movement and ritual gesture, which suggests that beneath the style of Christian Pentecostalism lies something older and closer to the primal, a movement truer to the first and original nature of the congregation.

The woman in the poem, whom Brathwaite says he observed in the process of becoming possessed, is transformed, like some of the other women in the poem, into a persona for the poet. She is his island, but she is also his muse and his consciousness. According to Brathwaite:

> The woman has moved from the ineffective Church of England and she is moving towards the Zion; and when she goes into Zion she is going to enter into possession. The kind of Church that she is going to enter now is an African-based Church, whose worship is based upon motion, kinesis, energy, communal celebration.[33]

Brathwaite too has, in his career from 1950 to the present, made this movement in terms of style and form, from the Church/School of England towards the Afro-American, Afro-Caribbean and Akan oral traditions; so that there is a parallel between the woman's journey to the *chapelle* and his own movement towards an alter/native aesthetic. Curiously, the woman ends somewhere between the two extreme poles, no longer Anglican, but not yet in full possession of the lost iron of Shango/Ogun:

> What is happening to that woman is that she is becoming a train. That is what the possession is all about. And the train is called "Shango". But in the same way that she moves from being unable to say "God" – (she starts off by saying "Praise be to God", but as she becomes possessed "God" sticks in her throat, and she only uses the guttural "ggn") – and in the same way that happens, she is not able to pronounce fully the god, the other god on the other side of the experience, who is Shango, the god of the train. She is able to say "Shhhaaa", and she hears the whisper of that train and the escape of steam, and the scissors; as if it is a scissors cutting silk cloth down the line.
>
> She is not able to identify the god himself because of the nature of the Caribbean experience, which cuts some of our African experience off... There is a deformation of the African culture in the Caribbean, similar to a deformation of the European; so she loses "God" and she does not quite reach, in this poem, "Shango". But she gets very close to it, because she at least understands. She is invested with the power of the train.[33]

So, just as Mark Kennedy's prophetic vision merges with Lamming's, her Odyssey in spirit is the poet's partially successful exploration of the aesthetics of energy and kinesis, and her struggle to build a bridge of sound between the different and equally unutterable pseudonyms for the divine, are also his efforts to reconcile the tension between alternative modes of shaping.

Testimony, or public confession and witness, because it involves an individual's laying bare of the soul, shares common roots with the centuries-old Catholic and Puritan conventions of spiritual autobiography. Even in the seventeenth century, however, one could distinguish between open oral testimony of, say, the Mechanick Churches, and the private written confessions which took the form of minute recordings of one's spiritual state, from day to day. The one type of testimony assumed the group, the congregation of saints, the other, the privacy of the individual conscience in the presence of God. Both types of testimony assumed formulaic shapes. Public testimony placed the individual "I" at the centre of a narrative, which is really a variant of the autobiography of the entire group. Thus public testimony became a necessary ritual in the cathartic process. Private testimony provided the roots for soliloquy and monologue, and after Wordworth's *Prelude* became the basis for a major trend in all literature. After this, the ego of the writer becomes his most valuable resource, particularly in poetry.

Testimony in West Indian poetry assumes the shape of dramatic monologue or soliloquy, though there is public testimony in Brathwaite's "The Dust". In prose it is best seen in the lengthy confessionals such as *The Mimic Men*, *Other Leopards*, *Ikael Torass, An Absence of Ruins*, most of Jean Rhys, John Stewart's *Last Cool Days*, G.C.H. Thomas's *Ruler in Hiroona,* and certain of Naipaul's short stories, such as "Christmas Story", "One out of Many" and "Tell Me Who to Kill". The confessional novel has become a virtual domain for Modernist aesthetic experimentation, and Caribbean existentialists have naturally been attracted to it. There is no space here to discuss the form, except to note that these confessionals may move in opposite directions: towards the reduction of Self and the negation of experience (*The Mimic Men, An Absence of Ruins*), and towards the ingathering of experience in a celebration of memory and a constant becoming (*Ikael Torass, Invisible Man, Other Leopards*). *Other Leopards*, indeed, seems strangely to have succeeded in combining both processes, in that Froad seems simultaneously to absorb and to void new and soul-transfiguring experiences.

Such testimony as is more directly based on the oral tradition tends toward the emergence of a communal eye and I, as is evidenced by poems such as Malik's "Pan Run II",[34] or Carter's "I Come from the Nigger Yard", or Roach's "I Am the Archipelago". The distinction which existed at the start of the tradition between public confession and private spiritual autobiography, still exists between such testimony as is based on the oral tradition, and its polar opposite, the private introspective voice telling its pain to itself. Carter provides illustration of both. The cryptic riddles of *Poems of Affinity* are the antithesis of the extended rhetorical testimonies ("I Am No Soldier", "I Come from the Nigger Yard") of the early poems. Yet the riddle in Carter is still part of a constant effort at self-judgement and self-justification, which are the two related impulses of testimony. So in this matter of testimony, continuum theory is clearly applicable to Caribbean writers. It is fascinating to observe how deeply our need for testimony grows, as the atrocities increase, and the processes of alienation intensify in our societies. If the oracular poet adopts the cryptic silence of the riddle, the hermetic, self-obsessed poet frequently finds it necessary to escape from the prison of Self, to emerge from the closed monadic world of his dry brain, his clean unlighted place.

One of his ways of doing this is by dramatising his angst through the creation of a double, a voice, a Tiresias persona who bears the burden of his testimony and confession. One sees this happening in Questel's poetry[35] (*Near Mourning Ground* and *Hard Stares*). Often the voice that testifies seeks not the cleansing of confession, but a self-justification which is most successfully achieved when one can show the unworthiness of society. This is particularly true when the writer feels that the sincerity of his commitment is being questioned by a younger generation (e.g. Carter's "After One Year", Walcott's "The Schooner *Flight*"). In the latter poem[36] the persona Shabine becomes a distancing device which enables the poet to deal with a personal trauma of guilty recrimination, and at the same time to assume the role of flagellant of an indifferent and corrupt society, and the tones of morally righteous indignation so necessary to the testimony of the "justified". The poet, like Camus's Judge-Penitent Jean Batiste Clamence, has it both ways: as Shabine he simultaneously confesses and condemns, "a shabby prophet for shabby times." One is reminded of Naipaul's use of the Kripal Singh persona in *The Mimic Men*, as well as of the fact that Modernist confessional is usually aggressive, in that it aims to undermine the complacency of society by making lucid, sick anti-heroes its most representative voices. Walcott's Shabine is the distillation of the bitter voices of the latter section of *Another Life*, the post-1970 political poems of *Sea Grapes,* and the enraged persona of "What the Twilight Says".

In both versions of the poem he is a problematic persona who experiences problems with language and tone, because he has to be both a grassroots sailor from Laventille and Walcott's voice. In *The Star-apple Kingdom* version, his speech is given a vibrant calypso lilt, and he is at one point knife-man and bad-john prepared to turn beast to defend his poetry. The poet and his double draw close in this most unrealistic event. For while it is most unlikely that we'd find a real Shabine, a violent vituperative sailor-poet, it is eminently possible that we'd find a poet fully capable of the verbal violence of the streets, seeking and defending power in the word, because he believes that this is the only power possible in his society. Ultimately, Shabine is a thinly constructed mask which easily becomes the face and speaks with the acerbic voice that wears it.

Formally, Shabine represents Walcott's deliberate and tentative experimentation with an oral tradition, on whose unsuitability as a paradigm for poetic exploration, he'd been most bitterly eloquent.[37] He represents the poet's compromise with a model of shaping in which he'd never quite believed, a partial attempt at aesthetic code-switching. He also represents the result of a twenty-year dialectic, the thesis and antithesis of which were first an Anglo-Saxon and next an increasingly Modernist European tradition on the one hand, and the Afro-centred Caribbean oral tradition on the other. We shall examine the details of this dialectic later.

There were several testimonies in Brathwaite's *Black + Blues* (1976), a collection of poems in which he examines the manscape of urban contemporary Jamaica, within a context of international politics and history, with which he has become increasingly preoccupied. As is his wont, he preserves the distinction between himself and his protagonists. Hence the dread voice which testifies in "Starvation" is recognisably that of one of Kingston's sufferers.[38] In "Kingston in the Kingdom of this World"[39] Brathwaite globalises his sufferer, who now becomes a universal spokesman for all who have endured the diabolisation of history, absorbing atrocity, torture, the balance of terror, "the values of whip, values of bomb, ... the culture of materialism..."[40] He is, like Shabine, ridden by history; but unlike Shabine, he cannot shuck this history off by sinking into land or seascape, or retreat like Makak into "the green beginnings" of the world. He is man in prison, bearing the weight of a doom that cannot be dodged through movement or amnesia, since it isn't the static legacy of past catastrophe, but the recurrent and lived atrocity of the present.

Testimony in "Kingston in the Kingdom of This World" is relocated in its religious context, in that the imprisoned voice is an analogue of Christ's, and his historic experience a type of crucifixion. Brathwaite in doing this follows the examples of Mais (*Brother Man*) and Salkey (A *Quality of Violence*). True to the tendencies of Rastafarianism, he endows his sufferer with centuries of humane 'authority', achievement, and rooted naturalness. But it is precisely these pastoral, adamic, green beginning qualities that have been denied and superseded in the development of the material structures of the world and all that these structures have helped elevate: force, repression, destruction, and the perennial threat of nuclear annihilation.

Unlike the debased youth in "Springblade" or Scott's "Apocalypse Dub", the sufferer here is a "righteous" victim who represents the human potential denied, the Muse in chains. He serves as mouthpiece for the poet, in the sense that he dramatises Brathwaite's personal antipathy to society's disintegration. It is in this respect that he resembles Walcott's Shabine, though it is significant that while the Jamaican ethos should have demanded a religious framework for the testimony, the Trinidad ethos should have led ineluctably to the secular contexts of Carnival and the Calypso.

The Secular Paradigm

As the discussion on testimony has clearly illustrated, any absolute distinction between religious and secular is unreal when one is dealing with the oral tradition. There are several points of intersection, areas of interplay between the two modes. A shortlist of forms predominantly employed in secular contexts would include folktales, proverbs, worksongs, calypsos, reggae songs, the steelband; the drum which, like reggae, inhabits both religious and secular domains; riddles, which have surfaced in quite different ways in Carter and Shake Keane (*One a Week with Water*); forms of rhetorical performance such as Tobago Speech Mas, Robber Talk, Carnival word games of all kinds, children's ring games, jokes and speech-making. Since each of these forms generally has a distinctive shape, they collectively represent an almost inexhaustible resource for the writer who is interested in such tropes.

Folktales and storytelling remain alive only in remote villages and rural areas throughout the Antilles. The living storytelling tradition which Daniel Crowley found in the Bahamas during the sixties,[41] today faces extreme pressure from television, video and "the milk of transistors"[42] which feed the Antilles the plastic instamatic culture of America. In spite of this, raconteurs such as Louise Bennett and Paul Keens-Douglas have been fairly successful in popularising traditions of storytelling. Their success signals the closeness of the Caribbean people to conversation, storytelling and the tale. Wordsworth McAndrew during the seventies did readings of well over one hundred stories in his radio programmes in Guyana, while Alfred Pragnell did the same for Barbados. One also remembers with pleasure the fine achievement of Ken Corsbie, Henry Muttoo and Marc Matthews as they performed poems, stories, songs and jokes taken from all over the Caribbean.[43] Matthews's "Eleven O'clock Goods Train"[44] is one of the most powerful of our short stories, demanding of the performer a flexibility of tone and pace capable of conveying its rapid alternations of humour, pathos, nostalgia for a lost era, and the energy of possession by the spirit of the train, which merges with the intensity of a recalled boyhood.

Thus although the lineaments of the original tradition of storytelling are being erased, the tale still exercises a certain power and force. It may be possible to discuss the evolution of the West Indian novel by considering the linkages between street style, storytelling, the short story, and the formal and extended shaping of these things in the novel. While this approach will not tell the full story, it should provide interesting insights into novelists such as C.L.R. James, Alfred Mendes, Selvon, Vidia Naipaul. There is, for example, a clearly discernible link between the early wit of Naipaul's *Miguel Street* which reinforced itself by, and was a comment on the ballad calypso; the grotesque comedy of *A House for Mr. Biswas,* and the confessional absurdism of *The Mimic Men*. Each phase represents a movement along the continuum, from a detached but still participatory perception of the secular/oral paradigm, towards an increasingly abstract, literary and Modernist model.

The Calypso

Of the secular oral forms, one may choose the calypso and reggae as two living forms, capable of self-adaptation to the extreme pressures of contemporary life. Reggae, indeed, has in twenty years internationalised itself in a way that attests to the creative life-force of the ordinary people of Jamaica. Like blues and kaiso, its cousin forms, it has coped triumphantly with the conditions of urban life, exile and rural dislocation. The calypso is older as a form, and has itself evolved through several identifiable stages.

As examples of the secular aspect of the oral paradigm, calypso and reggae offer quite different glimpses of a Caribbean potential. Both contain elements of celebration, conflict, censure and praise, and are related to the history of dance in the New World as release, as alternative to plantation structure and prison, and to puritan censorship of instinct and eros. Commentators on dance in the New World constantly note its compulsive cathartic quality. This has been true whether one was talking about la kalinda of the French Creole societies from Louisiana to Martinique,[45] or of weekend dances in Barbados during the slavery period, or the Harlem "dance schools" of the early twentieth century. The picture that has emerged has been of the dance as secular ceremony, breaking the tedious routine of plantation, factory and bourg.

As with "Shaker Funeral", Shake Keane was one of the first poets to recognise this, and to realise the concept of dance as secular ceremony leading to catharsis. It is this process – already commonplace in the poetry of French and Spanish Caribbean – that Keane seeks to enact in his "Calypso Dancers", whose rhythms do not simply imitate those of the calypso, but become the process whereby, as with the examples of religious enactment outlined above, the dancers as celebrants make their descent into subliminal space. The calypso dance becomes for Keane what the Haitian Ceremony of Souls is for Lamming: a ceremony of re-entry into fossil memories, a transfiguring ritual:

> Men say the earth is a vital graveyard
> of its own history,
> that every fold of rock
> teems
> with imprisoned residues of an exhausted age.
> So is music –
> so is the music of the Calypso –
> centuries of warm compulsion

spinning a woof of fire –
[...]
pulsating aeons instantly unwombed,
charred passions, fossil emotions
cast up in
rhythmic spurts of undulating dance[46]

This was something new in the poetry: an early definition of the aesthetic of energy.

Music has form and colour,
Rhythm has force –
Music is a river,
men are the strengthless stones
swept on and on...

Notice the preoccupation with defining the relationship of rhythm to the music of which it is a part. This is perceived as the relationship of force to form and colour; of kinetic energy, then, to that which contains it and bestows upon it shape and shade. So immediately we have that fusion of sacred with secular; that celebration in both modes of a capacity to move from surface to the realm of the primordial; that preoccupation with an archaeology of the psyche, a geology of the innermost Self; a history of the psyche which runs beneath what we normally term history. Here we have our early connection – Harris was even more deeply involved in this in *Eternity to Season* (1954) – with the world of Paz's *The Other Mexico: A Critique of the Pyramid,* in which a subliminal, archetypal history is seen as existing beneath the surface of ordinary action, to emerge and overwhelm how a people behaves during periods of stress. The point here is that this sort of vision is emerging from contemplation of the calypso as dance, something that, given the normal superficiality of commentary on the calypso, was most surprising when it did appear.

The calypso as it moved through its phases – kalinda, oratorical, sans humanite minor, ballad, single tone, double tone – had always been concerned with language as magic, ornament, sharp cutting satirical tool, and vehicle for a humour of the grotesque. The calypso helped preserve and formalise a certain twist of mind, which I believe helped in the emergence of Selvon, Naipaul and Lovelace. I've elsewhere outlined its possible contribution to the Selvon consciousness.[47] Since Independence (1962), the calypso, faced with a burden of self-definition which the nation itself feels, has grown in complexity, density, and an awareness of itself as a serious form. It now, for example, often alludes ironically to former calypsos, styles of singing and modes of consciousness. Valentino's "Dis Place Nice" contains a critique of Sparrow's "Drunk and Disorderly" (1972), while his "Barking Dogs" begins with a reaction to certain lines in the classic "Get to Hell Outa Here" (1964/65). Black Stalin's "Repainting the Portrait of Trinidad" (1972) explodes all the complacently nationalist clichés of Sniper's well-loved "Portrait of Trinidad" (1965).

As the anxieties of nationhood intensify, the calypso displays a growing capacity for seriously explored metaphor. Delamo's "Apocalypse" (1981) employs the idea of the Four Horsemen of the Apocalypse to signal the nation's distress and anger at the state-approved and corruption-ridden $250 million dollar Caroni Racing project. Its grimness is equalled by Black Stalin's "Vampires" (1981), or "Breakdown Party" (1980) whose puns on both "breakdown" and "party" remind one of the "blow... mind" pun in Mervyn Morris's poem for Don Drummond, "Valley Prince", and Leroy Calliste's poem about San Fernando's deranged trumpet player, Chancellor, "South Trumpeter". Or there is Penguin's "The Devil" (1980), which employs the chant of a traditional Carnival Devil band to redefine the diabolical in familiar secular terms. Then there is Relator's grotesquely and cruelly humorous "Deaf Panmen" (1974), in which Trinidad is depicted as a steelband of deaf-mutes, led by the deaf Dr. Williams in a crazy Carnival masquerade. Williams decrees that only deaf people can join his band. Here then was a painfully comic measure of the non-communication between leader and led, and the resultant national disharmony which ensued from this lack of dialogue or meaningful participation.

What we see reflected in this small sample of contemporary "consciousness" calypsos, are signs of the complex adjustments of a city's young people to its growing chaos. They are attempts to resist the Absurd, part of a quest for order as profound as anything in Naipaul or Walcott. I sense this quest for order in even the cruel reduction of the murder of Gale Ann Benson and her interment under a bed of lettuce to the Ole' Mas caption, "BENSON UNDER HEDGES". What is happening is more disturbing than mere cynicism, and represents something sharp, strong and fiercely alive, capable of offering poet, novelist and dramatist a wide range of stimuli.

How writers have responded to such stimuli has depended on their temperaments and their initial ideas about the viability, or otherwise, of the oral tradition. John Agard, the Guyanese poet, welcomes the evidence of strength in the Calypso, and produces his prizewinning *Man to Pan* (1982). This poem draws heavily on the ideas of Malik's "Pan Run I & II", Keens-Douglas's "Sugar George", Kitchener's "Spree Simon" and Brathwaite's *Islands*. But its technical virtuosity, its elated experimentation with rhythm and shape, are completely Agard's own development, and arise from his close listening to Kaiso and Pan. Agard's *Man to Pan*[48] illustrates the directness and immediacy of the oral heritage, and its accessibility to new types of shaping. Sound poets such as Brother Resistance and the Network group in Trinidad, are also illustrating this potential of the root form for new and extended shaping. Linton Kwesi Johnson is doing the same thing with his reggae dub poetry.

Walcott, Calypso, Carnival, Spoiler

Derek Walcott has also felt the irresistible force of the oral paradigm; but he experiences it as something to be confronted, wrestled with until it is made to justify itself. The long essay, "What the Twilight Says: An Overture", provides ample evidence of this violent wrestling, as Walcott confronts the vigorous new manifestations of the emerging oral paradigm, triggered into audibility by the Black Power movement and the rhetoric of African revival. This essay is itself the testimony of the dialectic process taking place in Walcott's ridden head, evidence of which may be found in his essays and newspaper articles since the early sixties.

Walcott arrived in Trinidad with the elation of one who was attracted to the living oral forms of that country. As he attests in a 1973 interview with Raoul Pantin:

> I think a lot of West Indian writers should experience this society, especially poets. First of all, this is a society that is very verbal... Apart from its music, there is a very strong sense of composition... The dialect for instance, even if it borrows a little too much from the States now and it's got tired in terms of its own originality, is always being refreshed... Now from the time I was a boy in St. Lucia, Trinidad expressions were popular all up the Eastern Caribbean. So there's always this verbal excitement or novelty in the dialect in this country. Let me take a little time to explain this.
>
> When I first came to Trinidad. I had an isolated respect for calypsonians. In other words, I could stand back, I could look at the calypsonians, admire them tremendously and what they stood for and what they were doing and all that because they were working as poets. In a public auditorium with public approval and public booing and that sort of thing. So there they were, entering the arena and taking the blows or taking the praise.[49]

Walcott had already written the first version of *Ti Jean and His Brothers* (1957), a play based on the exploits of the youthful St. Lucian trickster-hero Ti Jean[50] and the pageant *Drums and Colours* with its calypso-influenced prologue. The early years of the Theatre Workshop were also years of subjecting calypso and carnival to a constant measuring. Walcott listened to the calypso closely, and even served in the early sixties as a judge of the Calypso King competition.[51]

One of his earliest comments on the calypso appeared in 1960 when in an article entitled "Popular Poets Are Now Severely Tested", he declared:

> Songs like Melody's "Peddlers" can be read as poems without the accompanying music, and so can most of Commander's or Mr Action; in fact Commander's ballad of last season on the paradox of crime and justice *can stand by Germany's best poet of this generation, Bertolt Brecht, in its irony.*[52]

There is also a positive appreciation of the rhythmic daring of some calypso compositions:

> The usual criticism of calypso composition is that it is too restricted in form to have poetic merit. There are several examples even if a bit dated which show a natural poetic ear in the daring of their rhythmic experimentation.[52]

Two weeks later, Walcott, still on the lookout for what he deemed 'poetic' qualities in the calypso, tells us that Sparrow "knows the effect of a flattened ending, both verbally and musically for comic effect."[53]

Walcott continued to use the term "poet" to refer to calypsonians for the next four years at least, though he was later to repent of such blasphemy when, obviously remembering his own articles, he berated those intellectuals who, finding values in what "they had formerly despised... apotheosised the folk form, insisting that calypsoes were poems."[54] The Walcott of the early sixties felt free to call calypsoes poems and compare them to poems by Brecht and Eliot. Thus in 1963 we read him saying: "If any *poet* has made the concept of the *calypsonian* and the caiso up-to-date, streamlined and contemporary, it is Sparrow himself."[55]

But it is in this article that he begins to distinguish between calypso and poem; or perhaps, to clarify the distinctions which had always existed in his mind. Commenting on Sparrow's "Slave", he declares:

> One admires what Sparrow is after. A dignity and extension of the range of the calypso. But it seems to me to be making the same mistake of formal poets who try the calypso form in poetry. The poetry has to be used, it does not belong to the poet but to the public, and it must be danced. "The Slave", however daring in intention is feeble in lyrics, and sounds more right for the concert-hall than for the open road.[55] (my emphasis)

So here the gap between calypso (public poetry) and formal (private?) poetry is defined. It is even suggested that it is as fatal for the calypsonian to try for seriousness and lament, as it is for the "formal" poet to attempt the calypso form in his poetry. This would appear to be a departure from the 1960 position where, it seemed, that a calypsonian was able to achieve ironies as subtle as Brecht's, although his rhythms and vocabulary were those of his own, presumably informal, oral tradition.

By February 1964, Walcott is describing the calypso as "Our Poetry in Song."[56] This article, however, not only acknowledges the presence of two traditions in the society, but distinguishes between poet and calypsonian, clarifying the distinction between public and private which Walcott had begun to articulate in 1963. The initial sense of rhythmic possibility in the calypso is now, if not denied, at least held to belong only to the calypso. It is non-transferable. Yet there is evidence that Walcott was becoming even more deeply attracted to the "poetic" possibilities of the calypso. In an article of January 30th, 1964 entitled "Cheers for an Insincere Clown", he commented thus on Bomber's calypso, "Bomber's Dream":

> Nobody expects great poetry from calypsoes, but it is after all, a poetic medium and it can come pretty close, no? Compare Eliot's meeting with a master in "Four Quartets"
>
>> He left me, with a kind of valediction
>> And faded on the blowing of the horn:
>
> with Bomber's bidding farewell to Spoiler's ghost:
>
>> the break of day
>> I don't know where he went
>> but he went away.[57]

Fifteen years later we will get Walcott's "The Spoiler's Return", a poem inspired by "Bomber's Dream" and written in the erstwhile non-transferable calypso couplets. Two years earlier (1962) Walcott had written *The Charlatan*, a play whose central figure is a second-rate calypsonian, and for which Walcott attempted to write calypsos as well as other songs.

All of this was taking place in the context of a parallel ambivalence towards the Trinidad Carnival, whose quasi-theatrical qualities Walcott viewed with a similar mixture of hope and antagonism. On the same day that Walcott thought he heard the similarity between the ending of "Bomber's Dream" and Eliot's *Four Quartets*, he was contrasting the "moving stillness" of the great classical Greek plays with the kinetic restlessness of Carnival. He asserted that:

> The masked actors (i.e. in Greek drama) are moved like objects, inexorably, by fate. The Greek arena, bowl-shaped, contained that silence. Timelessness. These Greek classic principles are the antithesis of Carnival. The essential law of Carnival is movement. Restlessness. It is outward, directionless. Its dictum is, keep going, and it does this for three days.
>
> But now, other qualities have entered it which aspire to the conditions of art. It has become more theatrical. It works closer to the concepts of sculpture. It explores the psychology of colour in the manner of the abstract painter. It is heavy with historical research and obsessed with authenticity. Like ballet, its material is flesh for which it has evolved its own orchestra, the steelband, and it works to simple, but rigid principles of music, the calypso.
>
> It will never become art, the way that tableaux vivants, or "the happening" trys (sic) to. It has to be regarded as something apart, as a mass art, an idiosyncratic form of popular expression.
>
> It is now torn between two directions, a visual formality and its true spirit, anarchy.[56]

One recognises immediately the two poles of the Walcott dialectic: Greek stillness and timelessness; Trinidadian kinesis, anarchy and temporality. Nietzsche's Greeks, torn between the Apollonian and the

Dionysiac (*The Birth of Tragedy*) are replaced by the simpler, less humanly complex figures which a conventional classical education has taught Walcott to venerate. Carnival is as much a challenge to his assumptions about theatre as calypso is to his assumptions about poetry. Because of this, Walcott ends his article on a pronounced note of doubt:

> The bands are designed to be on the move, to avoid giving the impression of being art, while using all its skills, dance, design, colour, belief. But all of these elements combine to make the curious force of Carnival its great almostness, its near-poetry from the calypso, its near-orchestra from the steelband, its near-theatre from the bands, its near-sculpture from its craftsmen. It will remain always as close as that, but no one should look on Carnival as art. It is an expression of a people with a fantastic, original genius for the theatrical, who may never produce great theatre.[58]

Just as a gulf had arisen in Walcott's mind between the territories of calypsonian and poet, even so a gulf arose between the domains of masquerader and dramatist. Earlier in the article he had stressed the danger of "the artist" – in this case the dramatist – abandoning his "isolation from the crude, popular forms" to attempt to impose theatrical discipline on carnival's "anarchy". This was a reference to the 1963 Carnival, which had seen the beginnings of an attempt to organise the Dimanche Gras show along theatrical lines. Errol Hill, who had been in charge of that production, was also responsible for the organisation of the 1964 Dimanche Gras affair. The form which this organisation took is described by Hill in detail in his *The Trinidad Carnival*.[59] Walcott was unimpressed by the show, of which he said:

> "Whistling Charlie and the Monster" is the work of a man who has lost touch with the argot of our streets. It is a determination to impose art on a force that is anarchic, artless and restless... I could use my programme and let you know the plot, but I don't think it would help much. This is not the place to discuss Mr. Hill's qualities as a playwright, just as the Dimanche Gras stage is no place for him to display them.[60]

Four days later, in an article on Stephen Lee Heung's "Japan, Land of the Kabuki", Walcott seized the opportunity to advance the Kabuki and Noh theatres both already sanctified by Brecht and Yeats – as potential models for imposing "stillness" and "formal pattern" on Caribbean folk arts.[61] Two positions emerge from these articles so far: (i) No attempt should be made to impose pattern on Carnival itself, since it is too anarchic and restless a force. (ii) The Caribbean dramatist in isolation could/ should employ the formal patterns of Greek, Kabuki or Noh theatres as models for imposing "stillness" or "timelessness" on his own kinetic forms. Through recognition of what the Kabuki have done with their folklore of "devils, thief-heroes, old men, witch-figures and...masks", so similar to the folklore of

Carnival, West Indian playwrights might find ways of creating a theatre which achieves "the powerful simplicity" of traditional dance and gestures:

> The music and dance are waiting to be used so expressively that village audiences can comprehend archetypal figures set in a formal pattern.

After all this, Walcott in 1965 attempted exactly what he had so severely condemned Hill for trying the two previous years: he produced a theatricalised Dimanche Gras Show. The flood of correspondence which followed indicated that it was the worst failure of all three attempts. Errol Hill's review of March 7th, 1965 tells us what happened. True to precept which had become almost instinct, Walcott had imported his Greeks into the people's mas':

> As far as can be made out, in BATAI Mr. Walcott was attempting an historical survey of Carnival based on an article by Andrew Pearse in the Carnival issue of *Caribbean Quarterly* published by the University Extra-Mural Department. The theme is permissible enough provided the production stressed a carnival rather than an ethnological atmosphere.
>
> But Mr. Walcott is obsessed with the life eternal, as achieved through his celebrated verse, and herein begins his tale of woe. For trusting not to the indestructible masquerade spirit of the Trinidadian, which perhaps he does not truly apprehend, to inform the mass movement, the tempo, tone and colour of his production, he delivers himself of a tedious narration which was accompanied by *silence* and *stillness* on the *yawning* expanse of the stage. So that Dimanche Gras suffered at the altar of Mr. Walcott. A Mr. Walcott, that is, buttered up by the culture of Athens. For his BATAI script parades a host of classical allusions that include Aeneas, Dido, Cassandra, Minerva, Juno and Venus, Anchises and a Sybil. Only Narcissus is missing.[62]

Walcott, then, according to Hill, had achieved a kind of "silence" and a sort of "stillness": the kind that breeds boredom.

Hill gave his picong a sharper edge because a few weeks before Walcott had published a withering review of Hill's recently published *Man Better Man,* in which he accused both Hill and Errol John (*Moon on a Rainbow Shawl*), "vigorous young pioneers, however crude and uninformed," of "debasing their gift to alien gods, one the commercial, the other the academic."[63] Hill had altered the prose version of his play into a play of rhyming calypso couplets and rewritten the entire work after a more tragic original version had been discussed by his Yale Drama Class. Walcott's criticism is mainly of what he sees as the inauthenticity of the language which he says "offers slices of American slang, Elizabethan, (there is one character who says "Alas") and some slightly dated Trinidadian". Hill, he claims, is writing a musical with a hope for Broadway production, "winking at the Broadway audience while keeping his face turned steadily towards Tunapuna." He continues:

> Since Mr. Hill is neither a calypsonian nor a poet, but a naturally powerful writer of dialect plays in prose, (see "*Ping Pong*", see the original, wherever it is, of *Man Better Man*) the doggerel that results is very awkward. He has chosen to manipulate a metre that is by its nature lyrical into the dramatic. He employs the four beat line of the calypso, (Villon's metre), but with rhymes.
>
> Because he has stubbornly set himself the useless task of writing in couplets he distorts the language and the feel of the character to find the rhymes.[63]

Walcott had dismissed the play before he had seen it acted. My own experience of a mid-seventies production of it in San Fernando is that the language works quite well on the stage, and does enable Hill to capture the sound and feel of grandcharge, picong, robber-talk, the rapid wordplay and wit associated with the stickfight, the kalinda, and the *sans humanite* picong kaiso. There was flexibility and variety in the use of song, an instinctive correctness in music, which was itself commendable as an attempt to reconnect with the musical history of nineteenth and early twentieth century Trinidad. Hill also handled his new plot well. His folk types, the trickster who is unmasked, the warrior, the coward, the jamette, were never boring. Indeed, Diable Papa's fraudulence and impotence and his fear of relinquishing power were immediately applied by the audience to the case of Eric Williams. The value of the play for them was as a satire on power corruptly exercised, and on authoritarianism become a mask for the impotence of age.

What lay behind Walcott's review was clearly his own theory that the "serious" poet and the "folk" poet are two different people, who write in two different and mutually exclusive and nontransferable languages. The irony in his situation was clearly visible to the Trinidad public after his Dimanche Gras 1965 failure to blend codes which he had hitherto described as antagonistic to each other. Walcott's reaction was to widen the gulf which already existed in his mind between "the people's crude aesthetic" (Twilight) and the sanctified classical models. It is in the post-1965 period that we get a poem such as "Mass Man" which focuses on the difference between the mindless frenzy of Carnival and the anguished howling isolation of the poet who must impose stillness on the directionless energy of the mass/es.[64] Carnival now evolves as Walcott's antagonist, his rival, and a convenient metaphor for all that enrages him about Trinidad. Hence the aggressive tone of both "What the Twilight Says" and "The Muse of History", essays whose positive aspect is the warning that they both issue against ethnic and aesthetic chauvinism, against the closing-off and confinement of the West Indian sensibility, but which, ironically, seek to close off the West Indian sensibility from its own indigenous oral tradition, by presenting it in terms of limitation rather than possibility.

But with Walcott nothing is that simple. Whatever he warns against, he's on the verge of attempting. The calypso, for example, deepened his sense of the necessity for narrative, and despite its banality made him modify his notion of the language of drama. So by 1973 we witness a modification of the 1970/71 Twilight/Muse position:

> Because you come to realise how many bad calypsoes there are, you get tired of hearing the same type of calypso and so on. But what I think began to happen, particularly through the theatre – not yet in the verse or maybe to some degree there too, but particularly in the theatre was, here I was living in a society which was very lively, where this was a vital tradition. Right? You're not joining it because you want to be identified with it. *It's just the momentum of the fact that this is where you are; it draws you into that world.* Right? So I found myself now trying to write songs or getting into the rhythm of the society I was in because that was a root thing. You see what I mean? *You can't be a poet who writes for the theatre and use an esoteric language.* You have to get down into the language. So the influence of the calypso or the tone of the whole area of the calypso is something one has to learn from a theatre person.[65] (my emphasis)

So by 1973, the movement towards a more positive assessment of the oral tradition had begun for Walcott the dramatist. There is also a hint that Walcott the poet had also begun to feel the pressure of the voice. Also, with *The Arrivants* the terms of the debate about aesthetics had undergone a change. After *The Arrivants* (1967-69) poets and playwrights would seek to develop forms from such tropes as were available in their own societies. Hence the growing interest among playwrights in ritual drama (Scott, Gilkes, Maxwell, Walcott, Gibbons, Questel, Creighton). Several poets also emerge who now find it easier to begin from the oral tradition. As had happened with *Man Better Man*, Walcott had nothing positive to say about these.

As had happened with the mid-sixties Carnival polemic, Walcott's 1970/71 derogation of oral poets was accomplished by his recommendation of whatever literature currently engaged his fancy. In the early sixties, his interest in the Greeks, Chinese and Japanese had coexisted with an affection for modernists and Absurdists: Sartre, Camus, Genet, Artaud, Beckett, Grotowski. By the late sixties he'd become attracted to the vitality of various New World voices – Whitman, Carpentier, Césaire, Perse, Denis Williams, Harris, Neruda, Vallejo and Paz. By the early seventies he'd achieved a personal synthesis of the Old World nihilism of the Absurdists and the New World "primalism" of the Anglo-, Franco- and Hispanic Americans. It was a synthesis of dead-end and green beginning, the opposite Legba poles of a Caribbean possibility. It gave Walcott a new freedom with language: the sealed-off crypt of the lyric began to yield to the pressure of narrative, and it became increasingly possible for Walcott to open himself up, not only to the immense achievements of Latin American prose, but also to the steady pressure of Caribbean orality.

Yet even this is too simple a reduction of the dialectic between aesthetic possibilities which continued to take place in Walcott's head. For he converted his personal synthesis of dead-end and green beginning – Beckett and Neruda – into a new orthodoxy of great achievement, which he now used to sharpen his attack on "pastoralists of the African revival" (Twilight), that is, those who had recognised, as he was himself being forced by the pressure of the voice to recognise, the viability of an alter/native tradition. Such "whores and catamites" – the language is as abusive as this – receive scathing and dishonourable mention in *Another Life,* a poem which is itself evidence of Walcott's movement towards orality. The extremity of the abuse, then, is related to that inner reluctance to yield to the pressure of the voice; that fear of experimentation in regions uncharted and unsanctified.

The law of dialectic, so crucial for an understanding of aesthetic code-switching in the Caribbean, makes us confront our imagined opposite which, in the process of trying to negate, we come somewhat to resemble. Thus Walcott is obeying an inbuilt Caribbean necessity when he criticises Hill's use of batonniers in *Man Better Man*, then does the same himself in *Batai* and later in *The Joker of Seville;* when he condemns Hill's play as a Broadway-type musical, and later produces *O Babylon* and *Marie Laveau;* or when he eschews the hybrid language of Hill's rhymed calypso-couplets and goes on to produce equally, if not more hybrid language in the calypso-couplets of "The Schooner *Flight*" and the more successful achievement of a calypso-poem: "The Spoiler's Return".

We noted earlier Walcott's comments on "Bomber's Dream," (1964), We also noted the increasing depth and bitterness in calypso commentary during the seventies and eighties. Walcott's poem absorbs the acerbity of the time, and also contains all of that rage which had characterised his post -1965 statements of aesthetic. Spoiler, like Shabine, becomes the poet's double, the *doppelganger* and ghost of the oral tradition which has haunted and tormented him for such a long time. Alive, Spoiler had never been noted for social or political commentary. His domain was rather the borderland between fantasy and reality, shadow and substance. It is interesting that the idea of the double thrice appeared in his calypsoes. In "My Shadow", for example, he eventually determines to get rid of his tenacious shadow by placing his neck on a railway track. In "Twin Brother" he suffers because of the exploits of an identical twin whom he has to eliminate. He thus dies and they bury his twin brother by mistake. In "Magistrate Try Yourself", a magistrate arrested for speeding is forced to try himself. He cross-examines, sentences and exonerates himself by questioning his image in a mirror. Spoiler also has calypsos on amnesia ("Lost Memories") sleepwalking ("Sleepwalkers") strange personality displacements ("Cat Brain") and the sudden horror of comedy ("Fountain of Youth").

So the real Spoiler actually explored in his weird style, a few favourite Walcott themes – amnesia, schizophrenia, illusion and reality, showing an entire nation its absurdity – while dying from alcohol and tuberculosis. He died in 1961. He'd even grasped the idea of the double and the technique of looking in the mirror to confront one's image, which Walcott employs in "The Schooner *Flight*". In the poem he's given the wide political awareness of some contemporary calypsonians, the immense literacy of Walcott himself, and the retributive menace of the Mighty Shadow, who also wanted to kill the man in his head ("Bass Man", 1974). He's also read the *Penguin Book of Literary Anecdotes,* from which he borrows a joke about the mock-opera composer Sullivan, "I decompose, but I composing still", palming it off as his own – the oral tradition being, one guesses, the common property of all. Choosing satire, he calls on the aid of Martial, Juvenal and Pope, and extends his bedbug activities from biting juicy young ladies, to biting the hardened, unyielding arse of Authority.

Spoiler's satire resembles Juvenal's most in spirit. It is *satura*, the mixed form, sufficiently free to accommodate a wide range of topics and moods. It rails against corruption, employs scatology, anguished sarcasms and grim humour, in a wide-ranging vision of human degradation. Like Juvenal's, it is angry, middle-aged railing, though it retains some of the violated innocence of angry young man satire, typical of John Donne's Satires and early Elegies. Spoiler's targets are similar to Juvenal's which, according to Charles Plumb, were:

> the legions, the luxury, gladiatorial shows, pomp, slavery, triumphs and crucifixions; the gross and tedious overeating; the almost too abundant facilities for natural and unnatural vice; in short, unmitigated and unashamed materialism.[66]

In Juvenal, bacchanal, corruption, authority, power, role-playing and sexual licence, are all scatologically reduced to their constitutive filth. In the face of these abuses, Juvenal declares:

> well it's hard not to write satire. Who's such a man of steel
> as all the imposture of the imperial city not to feel?[67]

Spoiler in similar vein declares:

> When Spoiler see all this, ain't he must bawl
> "area of darkness", with V.S. Nightfall?

It is difficult, indeed to avoid the feeling that Walcott had been reading Plumb's translation of Juvenal's satires while writing "The Spoiler's Return". Concerned with producing a contemporary and idiomatic translation while preserving the vigour of the original, Plumb departs from the heroic couplet format of earlier translators. He explains:

> For this purpose, relying on Juvenal's own express dispensation for latitude, he has made use of the widest possible range of forms, from straight or looser sorts of 'blank' verse, to 'sprung' rhythms, hexameters or near hexameters, and various rhyming schemes, down to the doggerel of the street ballad, where appropriate, and even once the calypso.[68]

Now, Plumb's translator's licence is precisely what Walcott was seeking at this moment in his career: a model for freeing up the line, yet keeping the pointed regularity of the four-beat calypso line. Plumb's calypso translation of Satire VI, Section III employs the four-beat line in a commendably authentic imitation. It is just the sort of "classical" assurance that Walcott, who hears Villon's metre in the calypso, Brecht in Commander and Eliot in Bomber, would have welcomed. With him, all experimentation with Caribbean forms must first be validated with reference to the classical model.

Walcott's Spoiler, leaving one hell for another, foresees disaster for a Trinidad, governed by a parasitical African elite, a new petty bourgeoisie of latrine-fly speculators overseered by a deaf impotent. He rails against censorship, what Carter calls the assassination of the voice, as exemplified by the killing of Walter Rodney in Guyana, where he sees an Amin type regime developing.

> So I sing with Attila, I sing with Commander
> what right in Guyana, right in Uganda

(It is possible, though, that Amin could have learned from Batista, Machado, Somoza, Trujillo or Duvalier). In Trinidad, if censorship is more subtle, it is equally necessary as a means of controlling protest against the reality of corruption in high places.

The corollary of the censorship of real protest is the withholding of real information, which leads to a corruption of the word, a rot of language.

> it has been done before, all Power has
> made, the sky shit and maggots of the stars
> [...]
> until all language stinks, and the truth lies
> a mass for maggots and a fete for flies.

In this atmosphere of decayed language gutter journalism flourishes, the consequence and cause of the absence of real information. For art, there is Scouting for Talent and Best Village where "the audience have more talent than the show." His conclusion is easy to anticipate:

> Is Carnival, straight Carnival that's all,
> the beat is base, the melody bohbohl,
> all Port of Spain is a twelve-thirty show,
> some playing Kojak, some Fidel Castro

Here we have that automatically negative use of the Carnival metaphor to mean role-playing, play-acting, fantasising and waste. This opinion of Carnival, deeply rooted in the society, is partly the result of the Puritan vilification of Eros, that centuries-old religious urge to direct human instinct towards the divine usefulness of production within the established system. Here Walcott's voice, always, of course, behind Spoiler's, predominates. The real Spoiler existed almost completely outside of that productive system; so that the carnival of waste which he now condemns after his two decades of purgatorial fire, is the natural offspring of the sort of Tizzic life[69] which he lived and affirmed and celebrated while on earth. This is the major irony which Spoiler/Walcott as righteous flagellant excludes. For the highest point of satire has always been the point when it turns inward; when Gulliver realises to his horror, that he too is a Yahoo.

This moment never occurs in the poem where, because Spoiler is already the fully fledged and unchangeable conscience of the society, he is incapable of further moral insight. He differs slightly from Shabine here, in that his own deficiencies never become the issue. Of course, they seldom do in satire which, to paraphrase Swift, is a glass in which everyone sees everyone else's face. Thus, after he sees the neglect and dessication of the East Indian peasantry and the painful arrogance of oil-enriched Trinidad, Spoiler retreats to the more organised Hell down below. The poet and his double merge here; for Spoiler presents himself as Cassandra or Tiresias, the neglected, ignored artist/prophet/poet/conscience of the city.

> All you excuse me, Spoiler was in town;
> you pass him straight, so now he gone back down.

This is how Walcott, the fortunate traveller, would like to be seen on abandoning Trinidad. He needs a persona who'd be able to contain that sense of moral completeness necessary for self-justification, that sense of superiority to the world he is condemning and leaving. In a way, the poem reconciles Walcott's ambivalence, his love/hate of the oral model, his acute discomfort, as poet, with the multiplicity of codes available to us. He is able to employ aspects of calypso form to castigate the very people who created it; and he can rightly claim that dozens of post-1970 calypsos have not only done this, but in the process have also criticised, modified, and in a few cases transcended the cliché of their own form.

Rastafari Reggae Dread

> outta dis rock
> shall come
> a greena riddim
> even more dread
> dan what
> de breeze of glory bread
> vibratin violence
> is how wi move
> rockin wid green riddim
> de drout
> an dry root out. (Linton Kwesi Johnson "Street 66")

Reggae as secular paradigm differs from the calypso in that its linkages to people's religion are direct. It thus reveals many of the features of the religion. Its emergence has been part of that immense explosion of energy which occurred in 1954 when the police destroyed the Rastafarian settlement at Pinnacle.[70] They thus made visible hundreds of Bredren who became urban slum-dwellers, where before they had been cocooned in their self-sufficient, communal world of marijuana, charcoal and drumbeat. The destruction of Pinnacle increased the sense of righteous suffering on which the movement thrives, and deepened the Bredren's search for their own alternative righteous forms, as counter to Babylon's down pressure. So it was that master drummer Count Ossie began his camps at which musicians experimented with new rhythms, and Don Drummond, that mighty trombonist, found his direction, one which was to give depth to the emergence of the ska out of mento, rhythm & blues, jazz, spirituals, Pukkumina chanting, trumping and wailing.

What happened in the mid to late fifties, accelerated by the independence drive for a national image, influenced people such as Nettleford and Scott. It provided a counter-pressure of people's *nam* – Brathwaite's name for the irreducible soul or psyche of a person or people – to whatever colonial culture had instilled in the minds of the intellectual. It is out of this that Nettleford emerged from the McBurnie influence to create new forms: "Kumina", "Pukkumina", "Two Drums for Babylon", and that dance I saw during Carifesta '72, "Desperate Silences", the first true kinetic growth out of the new urban form of reggae.

Desperate Silences

In this dance an attempt was made to explore the exploding urban violence in terms of the alternation of sound and silence in rocksteady. The dancers celebrated to the sounds and tore each other apart during the silences, dancing all the while and maintaining a kind of fluid tension, the paradox of rigidity and flexibility which the music embodies. It is significant that "silence" in that dance symbolised alienation, failure of dialogue, the most destructive basis for an aesthetic, while community flowered in song, speech, the release of word and "ridim".

My only reservation about that fascinating experiment was that it separated the music from the silences when, in fact, the best ska and the whole rocksteady/reggae continuum contains its own silence within the sound. Listen to how most of Drummond's timeless solos abstract themselves from the chaos of cymbals, while the rest of the orchestra keeps time, keeps time. Or in rocksteady there is the interplay of bass/silence, bass/silence, which need no separation since they are complementary.

So, while separating fragments of sound by desperate silences was a brilliant idea, my feeling was that complete songs should have been used, and fewer of them. Nettleford would still have been able to depict the history of dread; and within each whole song he might have been able to show something even more difficult than the schizophrenia of his society trapped in its time, and its history of violence and repression, autocratic abuse of power and eternally imminent rebellion. Using whole songs and less extensive silences, he might have been able to show how the heart, breaking under its tension, or the mind driven to frenzy, are yet sustained by both the relentless, timeless pulse and the empty silences which howl and flow around the beat. For it is this which happens in the better of the music in which anarchy, violence and madness are simultaneously celebrated and contained.

Yet, "Desperate Silences" did travel far enough, resembling in its fragmentation an emerging Caribbean idea of form. Much to my regret, the NDTC eliminated that dance from its repertoire, to do the much more straightforward tributes to Marley and Cliff.

Dennis Scott: Crystal and Chrysalis

Dennis Scott was part of the emergence of the indigenised dancing of the sixties; part, that is, of those who were privileged to feel the pressure of the people's *nam* as it cracked through both the older and perhaps outmoded folk forms and the European overlay of Modernist abstraction. It has not surprised me that whatever preference he may feel for the hard, clean, imagistic lyric has been qualified by voice, sound of nam pushing through the poem's crystal. While this was true since *Uncle Time* (e.g. "No Sufferer"), it becomes more central in *Dreadwalk*,[71] where Scott achieves a fine equilibrium between the poem as self-contained crystal and the poem as chrysalis, always about to unfold, to become something other.

The images of crystal and chrysalis and the parallel images of pebble and egg, coral and tendril, emerged in my *Pathfinder*[72] explorations of Brathwaite's poetry. They represent complementary possibilities for the West Indian writer. "Crystal" is contained by its boundaries of hard clean edges. It may let light through and permit one to see inside the poem's self-contained universe. "Pebble" resembles crystal in its hardness and self-contained sufficiency, but it is opaque and defies penetration. Coral is hardened, encrusted, crystalline fossil-reminder of the life it once contained. "Chrysalis", "egg", and "tendril", on the other hand, are always potentially about to unfold; always uncurling, becoming, reaching out beyond themselves towards an otherness that is potentially and embryonically theirs.

Many of our poets have been attracted to the idea of the poem as crystal or pebble, and aim for dryness, hardness, reticence and economy. My argument is that most of them have been compelled to acknowledge quite the opposite tendency in the oral practices of their society: the desire for a poetry which is not its own end; which like the tendril reaches out beyond its space; or like the chrysalis represents a process, a becoming, a movement towards otherness of shape. In Dennis Scott's most recent work, crystal and chrysalis exist as separate entities in different poems, or coexist in the same poems as the complementary elements of a dialectical process.

One is quite accustomed to the imagistic aspect of Scott's poetry (*Uncle Time,* 1973); but only *An Echo in the Bone* would have signalled the presence of a persona such as that which is assumed in "Nightwalk". There the poet becomes houngan and draws his vèvè at the foot of the tree (i.e. the *poteau mitan*), in order to attract the demonic Damballah forces of the unconscious. In other words, "Nightwalk" signals the emerging presence of a fearsome Other who patrols the poet's dream world; an Other whom the poet, like Lamming's Fola in *Season of Adventure,* needs to acknowledge, attract and embrace. This process: acknowledgement, attraction and embrace, occurs, or is suggested in the patterning of several poems in *Dreadwalk.*

Sometimes the Other assumes precise human form. He is one's neighbour. In "Neighbours" we are introduced to this recurring double, one of the impoverished shanty dwellers whose "snackbox" shack is framed in the poet's window of remote vision. A flood washes away the cardboard shanty. Scott doesn't sentimentalise his reactions to this catastrophe. Like Pilate:

> I washed my hands
> and lounged before the television flood report

He shuts out the double; ignores the disaster immediately framed in his window pane and chooses instead to watch the TV's frame, which makes disaster palatable by setting it at a comfortably edible distance.

Scott is, however, drily aware that one pays a price for each failure in compassion towards, or acknowledgement of the Other. One's dream turns into something unpalatable and nauseating as the sensibility becomes gross.

> But miss his cooking fire
> in the evenings now
> I eat my dreams
> raw

Such grossness is suggested in the link between the poet who lunches on disaster and the flood which licks its tongue and belches after swallowing the snackbox shack.

"Lemonsong" is a response to the Other in his most compelling guise – that of revolutionary sacrifice. The scene of the poem is Cuba's War Museum, part of which is housed in what used to be Batista's palatial Havana residence and part in Moncada. Here Scott contemplates Guevara's assertion that "the true revolutionary is guided by a great feeling of love."

> I am crying under the lemon trees at Moncada
> because of death and the hardness of such love

> Is this what we must pay
> to be complete, my son?

The question is directed to his son because Scott is concerned with the implications that Cuba's example might have for a Jamaica where the next generation may be forced to choose between dubious liberty and certain death. Indeed, Scott's recent and bleak play, *Dog*, indicates that such dog days have already come. Cuba deifies and keeps alive the memory and meaning of sacrifice. Yet Scott questions the worth of "such sour sacrifice" and dreams of a less relentless and more flexible freedom, imaged in his Aureliano-like dream act of melting the guns "to small bird shapes, gleaming behind glass." The revolution's "hard love" has no use for such fancies. It is this that Scott fears most. In spite of his reservations, he leaves the matter open and does not preempt his son's right to choose his ideals – love, war, or art – in a Caribbean whose future may well make the hardness of revolutionary choice both necessary and inevitable.

Son, lament, lullaby "Lemonsong" is all of these, and represents a deliberate attempt to counterpoint Latin American languor with Jamaican rigour. It is an opening up to the presence of the voice, which prepares us for "More Poem", "And It's True", "Apocalypse Dub" and "Dreadwalk". "More Poem" recalls the earlier "No Sufferer" with which *Uncle Time* closed, and "No Sufferer" was itself an indication of how far nam had broken through the poem's pebble. It was the people who through reggae ("We a Sufferer" 1968/69) had defined themselves as "sufferers". The righteousness of this definition pre-empted the usual claim of poets to a monopoly of suffering and victimhood. Such poets suddenly discovered that their word stood in dialectical opposition to that of the people for and to whom they still felt an urge to speak. In Scott's case, the pressure of the sufferer's claim has forced a redefinition of Self and responsibility; an acknowledgement of joint participation in humanhood and a shared poverty, strength and violence of spirit.

The dialectic of Self and Other is best resolved in the title-poem, "Dreadwalk", which begins with a dread who walks by, singing in a voice as dry as sand. His voice, then, is the voice of the desert, a harmattan voice; the "cracked gullet crying for the desert" of Brathwaite's "Ogun". His song, is clearly a "song of the skeleton".[73] The poem is a confrontation between "I" and the dread: I-and-I one might say. Ian Smith draws attention[74] to the utter absence of punctuation, which forces the reader to determine who says and does what. This is Scott's way of suggesting the fluid interplay of personae. The "I" and the dread are doubles, *semblables,* Self and Other. Their dialogue, therefore, requires openness, absolute honesty of *interstanding*, a nakedness of spirit and a patience. Scott seems to have been working for this flow – for a form to suggest how this dialogue between.

Self and Other, the poet and his double has been taking place in his mind.

By the time the poem ends, the confrontation/conversation, dialogue/dialectic of Self and double is complete.

>   afraid I
> would not step aside
> then he held me into
> his patience   locked
>
> one
>
> now I sing for the children
> like wind in the quarry
> hear me now
> by the wide torn places
>
> I am walking[75]

Afraid of the Other, the poet/Self yet understands the necessity to confront him. It is a confrontation between fear and love, the possible issues of which are violence and compassion. It takes place in an atmosphere of shadows, because the dread is the poet's Shadow/Self, his dark double. In this case love does prove stronger than fear, and the initially mistrustful dread stays the hand of violence, accepting the poet's extension of love. His next re/action is to arrest – ("he held me") – to force the Self to share in his suffering, his world-sorrow at the destruction of the children. That holding is both compulsion and embrace. "Patience", deriving from Latin "*patior*", "to suffer" is, as in Hopkins, both the pain itself and the quality of one's enduring.

The dread teaches the poet, the Other teaches the Self, that this sharing of suffering, this *com/passion,* must be absolute. This is why they are "locked" in the attitude of the two adversaries who in the biblical dream wrestled for their names. "Locked" also suggests "imprisoned" in an inescapable commitment, though the end result of both antagonism and imprisonment is reconciliation; the mergence of Self and Other which is indeed love. Focus is directed on the absoluteness of the shared identity of Self and Other, by the splendid isolation of the word "one". The result of this coming together in a spirit of "One Love" is that the poet learns the Other's art, the Other's song, and assumes, like that nineteenth century dread, the Ancient Mariner, the journey, pilgrimage and soul-wandering of the Other. Having participated in a tense process of healing, he now journeys to unify and sings to heal "the wide torn places" in his society.

Like all Jamaican writers, or writers who have adopted Jamaica, Scott has had to come to terms with the overwhelming violence of his society – with the mindless and diseased nihilism of the four motorcycle riders of "Apocalypse Dub" and the religious suffering of father figures, such as the dread in "Dreadwalk" and Father in *Dog*. His search has been for a principle of healing, one which already exists in reggae, whose movement as been both external, towards confrontation ("Blood and Fire", "War" "Beat Down Babylon", "Babylon Burning") and internal, towards healing and reconciliation ("Selah", "Jordan River", "One Love", "Satta Amasa Gana" etc.). Scott's "Dreadwalk" moves like a painstakingly choreographed dance in which the dancers, Self and Other, poet and his double, feel their way around mutual mistrust, menace and uncertainty, towards a reconciliation which is neither escapist nor sentimental. The love which he advocates is every bit as hard as the one he fears in "Lemonsong", which is a love circumscribed by the inflexible rigidities of revolutionary commitment.

"Futuriginal": Kendel Hippolyte's Poetry

The theme of reconciliation appeared early in Scott. During the sixties, for example, in a sonnet entitled "Third World Blues", Scott described his mixed cultural heritage and aesthetics, in terms of the metaphor of song and dance.

> I go among the fashionable drums
> trying to keep true my own blood's subtle beat.
> Something of darkness here, of jazz-horn heat,
> but something too of minuet; it hums
>
> cool in my voice, measures my heart, my feet
> strictly. And not all the blues, the concrete
> jungles of this Third World, mine, can defeat
> that pale and civil music when it comes.[76]

As our exploration of Walcott's articles should have indicated, those were the terms in which the question of aesthetic choice was being posed in the sixties and early seventies. The word "fashionable" is pejorative, and suggests that the drum-centred aesthetic is a momentary, clamorous fad. The aesthetics of energy suggested by "jazz-horn heat" is qualified by the implied association of jazz and blues with the jungle (a concrete one, it is true) – as well as with unsophisticated and uncontrolled sexuality. The antithesis is the disciplined, cool, pale and civil minuet. In short, Scott here conceptualises the conflict of the mulatto, whose realm constitutes the Third World, between Black and White, in the most rigid and stereotyped terms. His aesthetic aim is to reconcile these two stereotypes and so do justice to both.

As we have seen, the combined pressures of fashionable drum, voice and dread considerably altered the terms of the dialectic, the notion of what needed to be reconciled. Kendel Hippolyte, a St. Lucian at the UWI Creative Arts Centre from the mid to late seventies, entered Caribbean letters at a time when the terms of the dialectic had already changed. Linton Kwesi Johnson had already published his *Dread Beat and Blood*[77] and by 1977 had, with *Poet and the Roots* pioneered a serious and politically committed "Dub Poetry"[78] which, while drawing heavily on the sound-patterns of DJ's such as U Roy, had moved away from the context of entertainment and celebration within which the DJ's normally operated. Marley and the Wailers had entered into their major phase and become international voices. Jimmy Cliff's *The Harder They Come* had happened, startling us with its naturalness and its truth. Fashionable drums were with us to stay.

Thus Hippolyte, maybe unconsciously, restates the argument of Scott's "Third World Blues" in "The Last Waltz", where no reconciliation seems possible between the indigenous aesthetic of energy and the rigid *"square"* dancin' of the "pale and civil" minuet world. Hippolyte's only question is:

> can the new rhythm ever
> break out of these bars

Here, the aesthetic of the "minuet" which tells us to keep quiet until we have learned "to suffer/in accurate iambics,"[79] is viewed as a jail. Just as the "pale and civil music", not giving up without a good fight, persists in Scott's poem, Waltzing Mathilda insists that she must have the last waltz with the persona of Hippolyte's poem. But Hippolyte's persona is far less welcoming than Scott's.

> No! No! No! Not
> even my feet say no,
> see them stamping?
> they will break her
> if she makes another
> false step, waltz step
> towards me
> they will trample her.
> my steps are earthquakes
> my anger is another rhythm,
> now.[80]

Here the testimony is clear: new vision, energy and anger demand their own forms and rhythms. "Feet" and "steps" in this poem relate to the concept of metre. The new poet, ridden by the loa of his experience, "stamps". He is a person possessed, and later in the poem describes his music and dance. The waltz of Waltzing Mathilda is replaced by the reggae and something beyond and beneath the reggae:

> you dance like a burning bush
> your feet prophesy
> the new ways, and you go
> your movements flowing like
> you always did know how
> you woulda reach
> to where you always know
> you had to go back to...

The old arthritic colonial waltz is finally trampled under the feet of the ancestral loa of energy... "Trampling Mathilda, Trampling Mathilda."

Mathilda, however, doesn't die. Nor does her mate, the vampire. If their attack on Hippolyte's generation has been on the level of aesthetics, their attack on the children is conducted through the futuristic mythology of television. "bed-time story W.I." is a deft clever poem built on constant wordplay, reminiscent of Victor Questel's poetry. Hippolyte in this poem imagines the children in "the living room" watching TV being able to make their illusions reality by entering the dream/nightmare world behind the screen, which he ironically terms the "eye of god". TV, then, is an extension of contemporary folklore and futuristic myth, as well as a projection of America's nostalgia for its lost dream of innocence. Both its apocalyptic futurism and its nostalgia are manipulated by a commercialism, whose target is the children.

Entering the screen's eye, the children become absorbed by its symbolic white light, that is, its vision, its tyrannical control of image. In this grave "new world" they find only wires and electric "transformers", the viscera of the machine which will consume and change them utterly. Hippolyte concludes: "the twentieth century had outfoxed them." Such then, is his condemnation of the post-modernist aesthetic, concerning which the poem is a witty if grim parable. All are consumed by Kellogs Cornflakes except one boy.

> only one boy returned
> into the living room.
> now, alone, he stares at his own vision.

Because the general urge is to conform, even when this means being consumed by what we as consumers consume, the new rebel is alone in his resistance; and though this aloneness earns him the right to exchange staring at television for "his own vision", there is the clear suggestion that the nonconformist has become autistic ("he stares at his own vision"); incapable of any relationship with the world outside of his mind's electronically transformed space.

"Systematomic Hegemoney": Grotesque Satire

Hippolyte's collection contains a number of love poems, but is for the most part, political. One recognises the imprint of Rastafarianism on his vision, which resembles the neo-anarchism of British and American counter-cultures, in its consistent attack on the machine, money and materia. (E.g. "Your Main Street Ends in Soweto".) In "systematomic hegemoney", the very name of the poem suggests the linkage between money, concentrated monopoly power and the Bomb. Hippolyte normally writes with joy, wit and a healthy, energetic humour. In this poem, he lets himself go in his exploration of this linkage, his long lines reminiscent of Ginsberg, though their verbal exuberance – strange when one considers the poem's theme – suggests that a more immediate model may have been Shake Keane's "Per Capita Per Annum: Lesson Five in Seven Studies in Home Economics".[81]

Keane satirises a statistics grown obscenely inhuman and irrelevant in face of the real horror which it purports to tabulate. Compare Hippolyte's grotesque satire with these lines from Keane:

> Number of large heads, spring beds,
>   large bellies, distended guts, percentage
>   of placentas per square-inch of a
>   school-yard; estimate of prostitutes
>   per cubic-centimetre of a candle.
>   Number of beggars, wooden legs,
>   scrunters, hunters, highest-
>   common factor of broken skulls
>   per millilitre of strong rum;
>   of broken hearts per man-hour
>   of gossip, percentage of
>   sheep per driver[81]

Certainly Keane's "Per Capita per Annum", with its immense compilation of absurd statistics – it runs for seven stanzas similar to the one quoted – is a vision of the overwhelming unfitness of things.

One heard it emerging in the poetry since *Islands* (1989) as Brathwaite started to focus on the ghetto town.

> How many islands will be counted in this congress of lepers
> how many fathers will revoke the edicts of their daughters

Yet this isn't as startling or as sustained as Keane's or Hippolyte's grotesque, "dark" comedy. Brathwaite begins to approach the violence of bizarre comedy in *Mother Poem* ("Peace fire") where he imagines a futuristic Bajun revolution:

> the institute of social and economic research
>
> financed by ford, revived by rockefeller
> would begin, until further unless otherwise notice
> a four year development study
> of harp projects and the consumption of ice
>
> in the newer industrial parks of the island
> and the connection (if any)
> between drum-beat and goat-death in the sound-system
> hurt of the city[82]

Here the grotesque satire of a reactionary and irrelevant economics and sociology, revealing its hurt, ends on the reggae note of pain. So the humour, if it is that, barely holds the hurt and bitterness in place, and may indeed be a way of intensifying the perception of disorder.

Such corrosive humour is superbly deployed by Walcott in the trial scene in *Dream on Monkey Mountain*, and throughout *Pantomime*. It flares at the core of Questel's *Two Choices*.

Hippolyte, confronted with the disorder of Jamaica in the late seventies, isn't interested in the poised distancing from anguish. He seeks, rather, to shock the reader into awareness of horror, in ways as immediate as those of Scott's "Apocalypse Dub". If there is a hint of surrealist distortion here, it exists only insofar as the ordinary world has assumed the distorted features of a nightmare. Hippolyte seeks, like Scott, to present the ordinary as nightmarish. He links the deterioration of life in Jamaica to the country's unconditional surrender to the power of the purse.

> Last week John Day committed suicide, slitting his wrist
>   with a five-dollar bill
> Joseph screwed Marianne again, using a rolled up twenty
>   for a condom
> the pound this month went down, the union jack went with it;
>
> the dollar is up on the flagpole conducting the
> national anthem...

So the islands have exchanged British for American imperialism, achieving what Brathwaite has termed, "the return of the status crow".

> but the dollars are whispering — per capita!
> 'nother head lopped off   — per capita!
> whatsa time, whatsa time?   — per capita!
> 'nother fuck? Coming up   — per capita!

Or there is the obscenity of "they are installing slot-machines between the legs of love-lost women." The same sense of the obscenity of money entered Trinidad's calypsos after the 1975 oil-boom. Black Stalin comments in "Money" (1980):

> Money today change up so much life
> Calculators take the place of wife

Hippolyte is particularly concerned – and here we may compare the Walcott of "The Spoiler's Return" – with the debasement of an entire lifestyle. Note how the voice employs the rhythms of children's ring games – ("children, children", – Yes Mama?) or ("Rick, chick, chick, chick" – Congotay) or most likely ("Pay de Devil" – djab, djab), where the devil is both Money and Sex – in order to suggest the perversion of innocence. Earlier in the poem we have the image of the undernourished children:

> it is the children who rose like kites in February and in April hung
> from electric wires like the broken bodies of birds

United Nations' statistics on arms document that it is on such malnutrition, such skeletonisation that what Hippolyte calls the "inter-continental cannibalistic missiles" are built. The pyramid of society, with its rigid class structure, is a tomb for a mummified idealism:

>   the carefully kept
> corpse of the American dream, whose bandages we smell
> in our children's hair

Hippolyte's attack, like Kwesi Johnson's, is more precise in its political focus than Scott's and more all-embracing than Walcott's in *Another Life*, "The Schooner *Flight*" and "The Spoiler's Return". Where Scott explores violence as a property of the human heart, and converts the sacrificial crisis in his society into a psycho-metaphysical confrontation between Self and Other, Hippolyte gives the same violence a face and a distinctly political root. He focuses on that nightmarish amoral universe of international power politics that is so meticulously described and documented by Noam Chomsky and Edward Herman in *The Washington Connection and Third World Fascism* and *After the Holocaust*.

Thus the horrifying catastrophe in Orange Lane where children were deliberately thrown into a burning building, perhaps the very catastrophe which causes the dread such distress in Scott's "Dreadwalk", is traced by Hippolyte's reasoning bredren back to the charnel house of power politics:

> vampires with attache cases
> who break life into stocks and shares
> [...]
> men prattling among bones
> in a white house of the dead

It is another line of approach to the phenomenon, one which is as necessary and as true, if more simple than Scott's or Walcott's exploration of the phenomenon of violence. Part of a generation bred on the grim politics of Independence, Hippolyte recognises the necessity, for locating parochial atrocity in its international context. In so doing he reverses conventional ways of presenting America, whose dream is a mummy. White House is cemetery or charnel house, like Conrad's portrait of Europe as whited sepulchre in *Heart of Darkness* or Twain's sarcastic dismissal of the combination of American capital and European militarism during the scramble for Africa, as a pyramid of skulls and bones.

Hippolyte also suggests that both major political parties in Jamaica have functioned as the accomplices of "Per Capita". The derangement of the sufferer and the birth of the terrorist in "Suburban Footnote" are attributed to forty years of the politics of fracture since 1938, as well as to bourgeois indifference to the cry of the poor. The sufferer, ignored for years, finally recognises the emptiness, the human nullity of the bourgeois Other:

> today he heard

> the space between
> each word; and wondered...
>
> the silence suddenly left his head
> and, just as it exploded,
> he fled inside
> hearing your crazed voice
> on the final sentence.[84]

He becomes the society's double: – here Hippolyte resembles Scott – his madness being the mirror image of their lunacy of indifference. Hippolyte doesn't make it clear what the *explosion* of his silence portends. On the one hand, it may be the literal explosion of a bomb or gun: the exasperated sufferer shoots his complacent, indifferent bourgeois double. On the other hand, the words "he fled inside" suggest derangement, an autistic inability of Self to relate to an Other which it views as "crazed". The word "sentence" on which the poem ends suggests the mutual condemnation in which Self and Other, society and its double participate. Here, however, we have the opposite to the reconciliation that occurs in Scott's "Dreadwalk" and differently in Walcott's *Dream on Monkey Mountain* or Harris's *Palace of the Peacock*: the emergence of an autistic, solipsist, lunatic hermeticism, the aesthetic of the closed system. The final stage in this process is dead-end rather than green beginning. We see it in aforementioned existentialist-type characters such as Lamming's Mark Kennedy, Patterson's Blackman, Naipaul's Beckettian tramp in "The Tramp at Piraeus", as well as Santosh or the narrator of "Tell Me Who to Kill".

The poem of Hippolyte's which best explores the derangement and alienation implicit in "bedtime story W.I." and "Suburban Footnote" is "Zoo Story" – Ja 76". The occasion of the poem is an occurrence which has taken place not only in Jamaica, but also in Trinidad and Guyana. A Rastafarian, mistaking metaphor for reality, decides to test his own lion-like Lion-of-Judah-sponsored courage against the ferocity of a real lion in the zoo. The lion attacks and kills the dread. Hippolyte presents the Jamaican version of the story through the eyes and language of another dread, or one who is thoroughly familiar with dread-talk, its syntactic economy, tautness and leanness. The model is probably Bongo Jerry, whose "Sooner or Later" and "Mabrak" made this sort of poem possible.

As with Brathwaite's "Wings of a Dove" or McNeill's "Ode to Brother Joe", there is the illusion/reality theme. Here, the dread's failure to distinguish one from the other is both comic and tragic. Zion is a necessary illusion if one is to survive the reality of Babylon. But the dread can't attain Bongo Jerry's "I-tyopia" rainbow; not even on wings of ganja. His quest is for the lightning of the blinding vision. Unable to find this sort of revelation among men, he seeks it at the zoo; realising in another confusion of the literal with the metaphorical that both he and the lion come from the "dungle". But even this claim to an environment of the primal shared with the heraldic beast is undercut by the etymological confusion of the "dungle" (dunghill), where the dread lives, and the rhyming "jungle" where the lion originated. So his problem is partly one of language; of dread-talk as a language of pure mask, a self-protective cocoon of shared metaphor which preserves the dread from confronting the literal and lunatic reality of his society.

Ultimately, his leap, from the metaphorical prison of his society into the real cage at the zoo, is made in the name of that illusory freedom of spirit which he at last "sights" through dark glasses. His last illusion is that the fire in the lion's eye is the lightning or the red, gold and green rainbow which he has sought all his life.

> him sight!
> lightning in a lion eye
> flash green-gold-red
> and dis dread
> again now find him rainbow
> so
> him climb dis last bright hill
> down into Zion
> him answer:
> "Rastafari!"
> to the charging lion.

Rhyme suggests that the dread's final mistake is to have confused "lion" with "Zion", just as before he confused "dungle" with "jungle".

Just as the protagonist of "Suburban Footnote" recognises the lunacy of the sane society, the dread of "Zoo Story" perceives the imprisonment of the free world. But both are destroyed by what they sight, the sacrificial nature of the dread's self-destruction suggested by the allusion to "dis last bright hill", though even this brief ennoblement is undercut by the phrase "down into Zion". This is descent into the pit, rather than its opposite. The poet, or rather the neutral tone of the narrating voice, preserves its distance from the horror which it relates. The poet is, in the best modern style, invisible, so that the poem can evoke from each reader a response according to the quality of his compassion. The poem itself teeters on the brink of grim laughter, and yet implies the horror of the process which has deranged the dread. So laughter is circumscribed by a terror out of which it has grown.

"Zoo Story" is an accomplished poem. McNeill has a few which are on the verge of this; but none of them is as close to the actual language of dread talk as this one. Hippolyte is writing simultaneously out of both traditions; out of the starkness that produced Hughes's *Crow* say, or McNeill's *Reel from the "Life Movie"*, and out of the different starkness and energy that has given us Marley, Bongo Jerry and reggae.

His poetry is an articulate rejection of much that modernity implies, even though it is at ease with the techniques of Modernism. While much of it is protest, it does at times suggest an alternative to Crow's "systematomic hegemony." Per Capita, the status crow, cannot, we are told:

> dream the juice of flowers into our life-blood
> cool the sky into our drinking cups, it cannot
> sustain the human *exchange,* will not *supply*
> *the human demand;* it will never draw
> sea-rock-sand-fruit-land-woman-man
> into a futuriginal circle.

The language of the exchequer continues, but it is reversed and employed in a human context which rejects its abstract reductive indifference. The nature of what Hippolyte strives to bring into being is captured in the neologism "futuriginal": a Whitmanesque world, a sensibility, a people, an aesthetic, a form of the future; a totally original and wholesome growth which yet partakes of the cyclic firstness of man's heritage. So runs the dream.

This paper has covered only a small part of the possible ground suggested by such a topic. My attempt to state the problem of the problem of form has led me to a single idea, which I've tried to pursue with relation to a fragment of the work of a handful of writers. The idea, however variously it has presented itself, is that of an aesthetic continuum stretching between forms derived from an oral paradigm, and forms suggested by various aspects of Modernist aesthetics. I've tried to show that while some writers are able to accommodate both extremes with relative ease, others have been involved in an intense dialectic in which the extremes appear as thesis and antithesis. My claim is that the notion of an aesthetic continuum allows us to understand and accept the existence of both types of writer. This paper has been biased in that its treatment of writers operating out of the oral paradigm has been far more specific and extensive that its exploration of the impact of Modernist tendencies. I trust that a number of ideas have, nevertheless, emerged about the latter.

Some time has been spent in describing the various contexts out of which the writing has emerged and in trying to suggest relationships between context, content and imagination, and their combined impact on the emergence of form. I earlier described this paper as "positionless", because it is descriptive, rather than prescriptive. It begins with the writing, the writers and their societies, and moves outwards from there in a series of radial directions. I hope at least to have illustrated the need for flexibility, and the folly of seeking to impose on our restless and varied sensibilities rigid monolithic notions of shaping. Words such as "interplay" and "reconciliation" have recurred in our discussion of art, artists and society. My hope is that this paper has in its form reconciled the various and interwoven

elements out of which it has taken its genesis.
Crick Crack!

First published as a Conference Paper on West Indian Literature, UWI, St. Augustine. May 1983; published in *Caribbean Quarterly*, Vol. 31, No. 1, (March 1985) pp. 1-52; also published in *Anales del Caribe,* Vol. 6, (1986) pp. 218-277.

References
1. Rohlehr, G, "Literature and the Folk", Paper read at ACLALS Conference, Jamaica, 1971. Published as "The Folk in Caribbean Literature", *Tapia*, Vol. 2, Nos. 11 & 12, (Dec. 17&24, 1972).
2. Asein, S.O., "The Protest Tradition in West Indian Poetry from Campbell to Martin Carter", *Jamaica Journal*, Vol. No. 2, 1972.
3. The quotation is from Conrad Aiken, *A Seizure of Limericks* (London: W.H. Allen, 1965). For my discussions of Carter see: Rohlehr, G., "The Creative Writer in the West Indies", *Kaie* No. 11, Guyana (August 1973) pp. 48-77; Rohlehr, G., "The Poet and Citizen in a Degraded Community: Martin Carter's *Poems of Affinity* 1978-1980", *Trinidad & Tobago Review*, Vol. 6, No. 4 (Dec. 1982)
4. Carter, M., "Shape and Motion One", *Poems of Succession* (London: New Beacon, 1977), p. 55.
5. Brathwaite, E.K., "The Love Axe/1: Developing a Caribbean Aesthetic 1962-1974," Cyclostyled typescript. The section quoted has been omitted from the *Bim* version. *Bim* No. 61, (June 1977) pp. 53-65; *Bim* No. 62 (Dec. 1977) pp. 101-106; *Bim* No. 63 (June 1978) pp. 181-192.
6. Hogg, D., Jamaican Religions: A Study in Variation, Unpublished PhD thesis, Yale University, 1964.
7. Keane, E.M., *L'Oubli* (Barbados: Advocate Press, 1950).
8. Reed, I., *Shrove-Tide in New Orleans* (New York: Doubleday & Co. Inc., 1978).
9. Toomer, J., "Kabnis", in *Cane*, 1923, (republished New York: Harper Row, A Perennial Classic, 1969), p. 224.
10. Brathwaite, E.K., Poetry Reading/Discussion, Creative Arts Centre, UWI, Mona, 1975, Chairman, M. Morris.
11. Lamming, G., "The West Indian People", *New World Quarterly*, Vol. 2, No. 2, (1966) pp. 64-65.
12. Kent, G., "Conversation with George Lamming", *Black* World, Vol. 22, No. 5 (March 1973) pp. 4-15 & pp. 88-97.
13. Lamming, G., *Of Age and Innocence* (London: Michael Joseph, 1958), pp. 110-111.
14. Kafka, F., Letter, July 1914. Cited in Bradbury & Mc Farlane, eds. *Modernism 1890-1930* (London: Pelican Books, 1976), p. 328.
15. Eliot, T.S., "East Coker", *Four Quartets* (London, Faber, 1941).

16. Lamming, G., "The Negro Writer and His World", *Caribbean Quarterly*, Vol. 5, No. 2 (Feb. 1958) pp. 109-115.
17. Lamming, G., *Of Age and Innocence*, p. 174.
18. Lamming, G., Ibid., p. 175.
19. Lamming, G., Ibid., p. 175.
20. Lamming, G., Ibid., p. 175.
21. Lamming, G., Ibid., p. 175.
22. Lamming, G., Ibid., p. 176.
23. Lamming, G., Ibid., p. 179.
24. Lovelace, E., *The Dragon Can't Dance* (London: Deutsch, 1979), p. 62.
25. Senghor, L.S., "Image as Rhythm," in Wake, C. & Reed, J. (eds.) *Senghor: Prose & Poetry* (London: OUP, 1965), pp. 87-88.
26. Harris, W., "History, Fable and Myth in the Caribbean and Guyanas", *Caribbean Quarterly*, Vol. 16, No. 2 (June 1970) pp. 1-32. Quotation on p. 27.
27. Keane, E.M., "Shaker Funeral", *L'Oubli* (Barbados: Advocate Press, 1950).
28. Sherlock, P., "Pocomania", *Caribbean Quarterly,* Vol. 5, No. 3 (April 1958) pp. 192-193.
29. Baugh, E., *West Indian Poetry 1900-1970: A Study in Cultural Decolonisation*, Savacou Pamphlet, No. 1 (Jamaica: Savacou Publications, n.d. [c 1971/72]) (Baugh's comments on Keane first made me aware of the poem).
30. Keane, E.M., *Indo-Jazz Fusions,* Joe Harriot/John Mayer Double Quintet, London, EMI Records, 33 rpm L.P. SX 6122 (Keane on trumpet, flugelhorn) also... *Shake Keane with the Keating Sound,* Decca, 33 rpm LP, Mono. LK 4720; also... *Rising Stars at Evening Time,* London, PAMA records Ltd., 33 rpm, LP SECO-30 / NBP - 1000.
31. Lincoln, E. (ed) *The Black Experience in Religion* (New York: Doubleday/Anchor Books, 1974).
32. Brathwaite, E., "Kingston in the Kingdom of This World", in *Third World Poems* (London: Longmans, 1983), pp. 53-56.
33. Brathwaite, E., "Edward Brathwaite's *Mother Poem*: Reading and Analysis by the Poet" (London: ATCAL 1980).
34. Malik, A., (Delano Decoteau) "Pan Run II" in *Black Up* (Port of Spain: 1970). Discussed in a close reading by Rohlehr, G., "My Strangled City," *Caliban*, Vol. II, No. 1 (Fall/Winter 1976) pp. 50-122.
35. Rohlehr, G., "My Strangled City," op. cit, and "A Severity of Seeing", Introduction to Questel, V., *Hard Stares* (Port of Spain: New Voices Publications, 1983).
36. Walcott, D., "The Schooner 'Flight'" in *The Starapple Kingdom* (New York: Farrar, Straus & Giroux, 1979). A substantially different version exists in Harper, M. & Stepto, R. (eds) *Chant of Saints : A Gathering of Afro-American Literature, Art & Scholarship* (Urbana, Chicago, London: Univ. of Illinois Press, 1979), pp. 166-174.
37. Walcott, D., "What the Twilight Says: An Overture", in *Dream on Monkey Mountain & Other Plays* (New York: Farrar, Straus & Giroux, 1970), also: "The Muse of History", in Orde Coombs (ed.) *Is Massa Day Dead?* (New York: Doubleday, 1974). Essay written c. 1971.

38. Rohlehr, G., "Songs of the Skeleton", Part One: "The Poetry of Fission", *Trinidad & Tobago Review*, Vol. IV, Nos. 3 (Petit Careme 1980) & 43A (Divali 1980). Part Two: "A Poetry of Dread", *Trinidad & Tobago Review*, Vol. IV. No. 5, (New Year, 1981) and Vol. IV No. 6 (Croptime Mar/Apr. 1981) This essay contains full discussions of "Starvation", "Springblade", "Caliban" and other testimonies in *Black + Blues*.
39. Brathwaite, E., "Kingston in the Kingdom of this World".
40. Brathwaite, E., Transcribed from tape of a 1975 Poetry Reading Discussion, Creative Arts Centre, UWI, Mona, Jamaica.
41. Crowley, D.J., *I Could Talk Old-Story Good: Creativity in Bahamian Folklore* (Berkeley & Los Angeles: University of California Press, 1966).
42. Brathwaite, E., "Eating the Dead", from *Islands,* in *The Arrivants*.
43. Matthews, M., *Marc-up*, TIE 33 rpm LP record, Barbados, 1978.
44. Matthews, M., "Eleven O'Clock Goods Train", *Kairi* No. 3, 1974.
45. Epstein, D.J., *Sinful Tunes and Spirituals* (Urbana, Chicago, London: Univ. of Illinois Press, 1977).
46. Keane, E.M., "Calypso Dancers", *L'Oubli*, 1950, p. 30.
47. Rohlehr, G., See Reference No. 1, as well as Baugh, E., (ed) *Critics on Caribbean Literature* (London: George Allen & Unwin Ltd. 1978), pp. 153-161.
48. Agard, J., *Man to Pan (A Cycle of poems to be performed with drums, steelpans)* (Cuba: Casa de las Americas, 1982).
49. Walcott, D., & Pantin R. (interviewer), "We Are Still Being Betrayed", *Caribbean Contact* (July 1973) p. 14.
50. Walcott, D., A Trinidad version of the Ti Jean story exists in the Ti Jean Lopez tales of Paramin. See Barbara Wafe, *Paramin: A Socio-Cultural Study via Folk-Tales Collected at Paramin*, *UWI,* St. Augustine, Trinidad, Caribbean Studies Thesis, 1979.
51. Walcott, D., *Trinidad Guardian* (Feb. 7, 1967).
52. Walcott, D., "Popular Poets Are Now Severely Tested", *Trinidad Guardian* (Feb. 14, 1960).
53. Walcott, D., *Trinidad Guardian* (Feb. 26, 1960).
54. Walcott, D., "What the Twilight Says", op. cit. pp. 34-35.
55. Walcott. D., "Alas! The Last Minute Road March Is Gone", *Trinidad Guardian* (Feb. 3, 1963) my emphasis.
56. Walcott, D., "Our Poetry in Song", *Trinidad Guardian* (Feb. 9, 1964).
57. Walcott, D., "Cheers for An Insincere Clown", *Trinidad Guardian* (January 30, 1964).
58. Walcott, D., "Carnival: The Theatre of the Streets", Sunday *Guardian* (Feb. 9, 1964) p. 4.
59. Hill, E., *The Trinidad Carnival: Mandate for a National Theatre* (Austin & London: Univ. of Texas Press, 1972).
60. Walcott, D., "Curious Mish-Mash of Style", *Trinidad Guardian* (Feb. 12, 1964) p. 5.
61. Walcott, D., "The Kabuki: Something to Give to Our Theatre", *Sunday Guardian* (Feb. 16, 1964).
62. Hill, E., "No Tears for Narcissus", a review of Derek Walcott's BATAI, *Sunday Guardian* (Mar. 7, 1965).

63. Walcott, D., "Sangre Grande Tonight: Broadway Next", *Trinidad Guardian* (Jan. 25, 1965) p. 5.
64. Walcott, D., "Mass Man", in *The Gulf & Other Poems* (London: Jonathan Cape, 1969), p. 19.
65. Walcott, D., Same as No. 49 (my emphasis).
66. Plumb, C., (translator) Preface to *The Satires of Juvenal* (London: Panther Books, 1968).
67. Plumb, C., ibid, Satire I, p. 21.
68. Plumb, C., ibid, p. 15.
69. Plumb, C., ibid. For Tizzic, see *The Arrivants*. Tizzic is an irresponsible boozer, father of several illegitimate children, and independent peasant and lover of kaiso and mas, dying like Spoiler, of booze and tuberculosis.
70. Barrett, L. E. *The Rastafarians* (Kingston: Sangster/Heinemann, 1977), pp. 86-89.
71. Scott, D., *Dreadwalk: Poems 1970-78* (London: New Beacon Books Ltd., 1982. See also *Uncle Time* (Pittsburgh: Univ. of Pittsburgh Press, 1973).
72. Rohlehr, G., *Pathfinder: Black Awakening in **The Arrivants** of Edward Kamau Brathwaite* (Port of Spain, 1981).
73. Brathwaite, E., "Eating the Dead", *The Arrivants*, pp. 219-221.
74. Smith, I., "A Dangerous Art", Paper Read at Conference 3, UWI, May 1983 St. Augustine, Trinidad.
75. Scott, D., *Dreadwalk*, pp. 39-40.
76. Scott, D., "Third World Blues", in *The New Ships,* Wilson, D.G. (ed) (Jamaica: Savacou Publications, 1971), p. 50.
77. Johnson, L.K., *Dread Beat and Blood* (London: Bogle-L'Ouverture Publications, 1975).
78. Johnson, L.K., *Poet & the Roots*, 45 rpm LP record (London: Bogle L'Overture/ Virgin Music, 1977, VS 19012).
79. Walcott, D., "Prelude" in *In a Green Night: Poems 1948-60* (London: Jonathan Cape, 1962).
80. Hippolyte, K., *Island in the Sun, Side Two* (St. Lucia, n.d. [c. 1981]), p. 27.
81. Keane, E.M., "Per Capita Per Annum: Lesson Five in Seven Studies in Home Economics", *Kairi*, 1976, pp. 22-23.
82. Brathwaite, E.K., *Mother Poem* (London: OUP, 1977), p. 106.
83. Hippolyte, K., "Orange Lane, the Fire's Light", op. cit. pp. 14-15.
84. Hippolyte, K., "Suburban Footnote", op. cit., p. 19.

POSSESSION AS METAPHOR: LAMMING'S *SEASON OF ADVENTURE*

The tendency to employ ecstatic possession as metaphor of the descent into the unconscious mind of the individual and the group has become quite common in both Afro-Caribbean and Afro-American literatures. Texts such as Brathwaite's *The Arrivants*, Scott's *An Echo in the Bone*, Toomer's *Cane*, Baldwin's *Go Tell It on the Mountain*, Salkey's *A Quality of Violence* and Lamming's *Of Age and Innocence* and *Season of Adventure* illustrate the point. This essay seeks to explore Lamming's use of the possession metaphor in *Season of Adventure.*

The idea of interior descent is one of the most ancient in literature, stretching back to the time when the poet was *vates* or seer, prophet and singer, the strength of whose saying was authenticated by a capacity for being filled with the energy or enthusiasm of the god. Isaiah or Ezekiel or St. John the Divine are poets of this type; while Virgil's guide into the underworld, the Sibyl, needs to become possessed before she can enter the dark and wide-yawning mouth – (*"alta spelunca fuit vasto immanoque hiatu"*) – of the deep cave of ancestors, within which Aeneas converses with dead comrades, lost loves and his father, Anchises, who reveals to him Rome's imperial destiny "to spare the submissive and to demolish the proud by warfare."

Such use of the already ancient convention of descent into the underworld, and its connection to the even older idea of ecstatic possession, strikes the student of West Indian literature with a sense of familiarity. One feature common to both the Virgilian predecessor and West Indian literature is the connection between the ecstatic possession of the poet or Muse and the encounter of an archetypal hero with his and his nation's ancestry and destiny. The hero's descent is simultaneously an encounter with the past and a vision of the future, aided or engendered by a presence who is poet, muse, dreamer and spiritual guide, who is often conceived of as female, (though Dante's guide to the inferno is Virgil, Melville's poet, muse and dreamer is Ishmael, and Harris's an androgynous blend of male and female presences: for example Dreamer and the Arawak woman in *Palace of the Peacock.*

The convention of descent continued through forms such as the medieval dream allegory; the ideas of trance and *exstasis* in Romantic poetry; surrealism and its preoccupation with dream fantasy and the unconscious; and the renewed interest in mind-expanding drugs, extrasensory perception, psychology and parapsychology. Hence the continued interest in such literature as is concerned with doubling, the dialectic of Self and Other, and the notion of a structure of mind which lies beneath the surface of exterior action and suggests the presence of an archetypal history older than and often different from the superficial doings of conventional academic historical record.

II: The Structure of Possession

The purpose of this essay is to examine how Lamming enters this convention of "descent" and "possession". We begin with a description of his conception of possession as a process that is marked by several distinguishing features. We then explore his use of these features as structural elements in *Season of Adventure*.

Possession as it appears in Lamming displays the following features: first, it is inspired by communal rituals through which a marginalised lower class Afro-Caribbean community retains contact with a fading but still latent ancestral past; second, it is accompanied by tension which manifests itself in a rigidity of muscle, a transformation of the facial features and a fixity of the eyes of the person under possession; third, such tension is an extreme psychic burden which seeks its release through the transmission of energy to someone else. It is relayed from devotee to devotee; one person's possession serving as catalyst to another's. Hence, in *Season of Adventure,* Fola is possessed for most of the book, becoming free only when her personal possession is transformed into the communal quest of the society for its energy, spirit and artistic medium, for the affirmation of its voice.

Fourth: the most important feature of Lamming's use of possession is the dialogue between the living and the dead, between the present and the past over their neglect of the dead; the present must settle with the past by performing the rituals of reverence through which the past is laid to rest.

So important is this aspect of possession to Lamming that one may say that it has become the major frame within which he explores the themes of history; the latter-day confrontation of coloniser and colonised; the question of their joint responsibility for the future growth of newly independent former colonies. The idea of a dialogue between the living and the dead, and its concern with confession and reparation, bring into focus Lamming's ongoing perception of a drama that involves the unlocking of shameful secrets of the past, and a cleansing of the psyches of individual and group for a healthier participation in what Brathwaite has termed a refashioning of the future. In Lamming the dialogue between living and dead includes:

(a) accusation of crime, guilt, neglect
(b) acknowledgement of error
(c) confession in public
(d) assumption of the burden of reparation
(e) cleansing
(f) becoming whole

Achieving such dialogue on the level of international politics is a central feature of the humanisation of historical process.

III

We first hear this dialogue between the living and the dead in the Old Man's descent into a memory of Africa and the beginnings of the slave trade in *In The Castle of My Skin*, where subliminal encounter with the past leads to oracular statement about the future. The present generation is warned against the dangers of sentimentalising the idea of a literal return to the ancestral land. Diasporan Blacks should not "force a passage to where you won't yet belong." Like all oracular statements, this one is tantalisingly ambiguous; the "yet" suggesting that there may or will be a time when the breach between diasporan and mainland African will be healed, but that time is not now, not yet. The questions which the oracle leaves unanswered are "when then?" and "how?"

Mark Kennedy's fit at the Sabina Square meeting in *Of Age and Innocence* is another example of Lamming's use of possession as descent into, as well as release of submerged aspects of the psyche. Here, the conjuncture of present, past and future is established through Mark's memory of the Tribe Boys' legend, a story of resistance and heroic struggle in the face of genocide. This legend encapsulates the history of New World conquest, bringing into focus the idea that the contemporary struggle against imperialism is really the most recent phase of a resistance movement which began with the first encounter of conquistador and New World person. Mark's vision seizes on the present moment as an omen of the future apocalyptic encounter of the worlds of metropole and periphery, as the now vocal and visible colonised seek a reordering of relationships between the two worlds.[1]

It is possible to interpret the Teeton/Myra dialogue in *Water with Berries*, and the catastrophic encounter of all the main characters in that novel as an elaborate extension of the Ceremony of Souls metaphor in which Caliban encounters Prospero on Prospero's home turf. In an interview with George Kent,[2] Lamming makes this claim for *Water with Berries* and suggests that even *Natives of My Person* may be related to the Ceremony of Souls. There is, however, a point where the metaphor loses its concrete context, its grounding in any particular ceremony, act or ritual. In *Water with Berries*, though the idea of the Ceremony of Souls survives, the actual ceremony is missing, and has to be mnemonically and melodramatically invoked. One therefore feels justified in focusing on *Season of Adventure* where act and idea, ritual and meaning are inseparably fused, and possession becomes not only metaphor but major structuring device.

IV: Charlot's Possession

Season of Adventure begins by establishing the link between possession and ideas of instinct, naturalness and the capacity to affirm. Possession is the natural property of the poor and pervades their environment, consciousness and creativity just as it is forcibly excluded from the world of a rising but insecure class of new proprietors, for whom "possession" is replaced by possessions. Music is both the vehicle and the corridor by which one descends to the bottom of the ocean of consciousness, makes connection with hidden or suppressed areas of the Self, and begins the journey towards wholeness. The antiquity of this process is suggested in the narrator's observation that:

> It seemed this music had always been there, immortal as the origin of water swinging new soundings up from the sea's dark tomb of noise. And the women's voices chanted the resurrection of two souls from the ocean's deep chapel of skulls (pp. 19-20).

The music is a blend of nascent steelband and vodun drum, that is, a fictional union of two distinctive Caribbean musical forms, one newly-born and the other ancient and ancestral, one secular and the other sacred. Through this fictional union, Lamming dramatises an idea that there is a generic link between the African drum and the steelband.[3] The music needs to be performed with fervour and energy in order to sound the bottom of the ocean of consciousness, and touch "Guinea", the medium of water in which the spirits of the dead reside. This ocean with its "chapel of skulls" is also the Middle Passage in which so many Africans drowned themselves in that first sacrificial act of revolt.

The link between music, ritual, secular or sacred celebration and popular impulsion to revolt was recognised by the ruling class throughout plantation societies of the New World, and led to the inclusion of clauses banning African dance assemblies in all the Slave Codes. Banning started in the French Caribbean on May 4, 1654 when the Conseil Soverain de Martinique issued an ordinance prohibiting African dance assemblies[4] and continued in Barbados, Jamaica, St. Kitts, Maryland, the Carolinas[5] and the Hispanic Caribbean. It became a major feature of post-Emancipation society in Trinidad where a proprietor class, obsessed with the fear of "another Haiti", constantly sought the abolition of Carnival, the Big Drum dances, and African Orisha religion. In Trinidad, the censorship of African cultural practices culminated in acts such as the Musical Ordinance of 1883 which forbade the playing of drums, chac-chac and banza, and the Peace Preservation Ordinance of 1884 in which several acts against African music, assemblies of the poor, Canboulay and Carnival were combined.

Lamming is therefore correct in his identification of the social, political and historical context of the music, whose metaphorical dimension is really a plausible extension of its historical significance. In *Season of Adventure* the music is part of an ancient religious ceremony revived by the poor in newly independent San Cristobal and tolerated by the new bourgeoisie in power. Whereas the old colonial British rulers would have been absolute in their suppression of both the Orisha religion and its music, the new incumbents, culturally and psychically insecure, are ambivalent. The sound and rhythm of the steel drums fascinate them, while the deeper detonations of the Orisha drums are, at the start, comfortably ignored as the harmless, if mysterious practice of an unimportant subculture.

Fola's introduction to the tonelle and her possession by the drums are clear proof that the gap between the arriviste class of new rulers and the subculture of the poor is less than skin deep. Fola – (Yoruba for "with honour") – the flower of mulattitude, begins according to Powell, self-appointed protector of lower-class purity, as a person with two languages and selves, one of which is superficial and educated while the other is real and subliminal.

> She got open-air talk an' inside talk,' said Powell. 'Like tonight she go talk great with the stranger man. Grammar an' clause, where do turn into doos, plural an' singular in correct formation, an' all that. But inside, like between you an' me, she tongue make the same rat-trap noise. Then she talk real, an' sentences come tumblin' down like a one-foot man. Is how them all is.' (p. 21)

Powell has divined the divided consciousness of Fola and her class. Energetic apostle of the natural and genuine, he sees this dividedness as the curse of Fola's entire class, which he hates with a venom. Grudgingly, however, he does acknowledge in the class a buried capacity for genuineness, and his reference to the "one-foot man" in Fola's "real" language is unconsciously prophetic of Fola's imminent possession by Legba, the one-footed cripple – loa of the crossroads and vestibule of beginning. Later in the same scene Fola hears "the crippled swoon" (p. 31) of the voice of a woman in the process of becoming possessed. It serves as a catalyst to her own possession by Legba, the cripple-loa of beginning.

Charlot is Fola's expatriate history-teacher, whose interest in "roots" and self-discovery, along with his unarticulated desire for Fola, leads him to introduce her to the tonelle. He bears nearly the same name (Charlot Pressoir) as Charles Pressoir, to whom Maya Deren refers in *Divine Horsemen* as one:

> who gave so unfailingly of his friendship in so many difficult situations in Haiti, which I doubt would have been favourably resolved without

the presence of his sensitive intelligence, moral support and practical assistance.[6]

In Deren's case, Charles Pressoir is a local helper, guide and friend who facilitates the entry of a white American artist and anthropologist into the religion of the Haitian people. In Lamming's book, the situation is reversed. Charlot Pressoir is a type of the expatriate scholar/analyst who undertakes the task of understanding the folk activity of a totally different culture – that is, of imposing on it his own culture-biassed categories while he remains emotionally aloof from what he observes.

Yet in his own way Charlot finds that the tonelle is almost as traumatic an experience for him as it is for Fola. Representing the liberal consciousness of a well-meaning European patriarchy, he is nevertheless forced into a recognition of his spiritual emptiness and emotional deadness. Afraid of the explicitly sexual terms in which possession is taking place around him (p. 31), "Charlot hugged his jaws and blocked his ears as he stared, unseeing at the ground" (p. 33).

Speak no evil, hear no evil, see no evil is what his rational mind tells him. For all his fascination with the Orisha, they represent an evil which must not be permitted entrance into the consciousness. Charlot is mistaken about the fundamentals of the religion. The loa already reside within the consciousness and seek release by the means of the music and the dance; even though such release of the loa from the depths of the unconscious often appears to be a visitation or entry from outside the consciousness. Charlot's act of denial, then, is a rejection of the Other, the hidden Self and Double he had hoped to find via the music of the drums.

He had gone to the tonelle "because there are things that remind me of myself" (p. 26). But with his act of rejection he disqualifies himself as Fola's potential lover, the bearer of new life. Lamming makes this clear by spending three pages (pp. 36-39) exploring what Charlot remembers under the spell of the drums. A curiously cosmopolitan person, Charlot is a mixture of Spanish Jew, Chinese and French, born in West Africa and educated in England. Yet he seems not to have embodied the potential universality of his heritage, but to have emerged, like Conrad's half-English, half-French and possibly Jewish Kurtz, as a representative of an Old World so dead that even its angry young people are depicted as corpses. For Charlot, who confesses to Fola (p. 26) that he doesn't really like the drums or the ceremony, the season of adventure is a quest for psychic rebirth, for authentic personhood which can come about only if he surrenders himself to all the crucial stages of the inner journey – acknowledgement of past crime, confession and assumption of the burden of responsibility for reparation. Charlot, however, cannot surrender himself to the process of interior "adventure" and does not move beyond a vision or memory of his most immediate and spiritually sterile past. This memory bars his descent into deeper layers or circles of the self, and makes impossible an encounter with and liberating embrace of the Double.

In describing what Charlot actually discovers as he looks into himself, Lamming is giving utterance to his own disillusioned encounter with an England of dead issues, dead voices, emotional and cultural stasis, in which the Arts are, in the bitter words of the narrator, "a patient far gone in cancer." Charlot realises in the tonelle that his New World "adventure" is an attempt to escape the burden of being a corpse in the Old World, rather than an assumption of the awesome responsibility for redeeming time and history.

> Was this a reason for bartering his future to a childish notion of adventure? Was it because the only England he had known was a kind of corpse in future argument with itself, a dead voice bearing witness to its own achievement, passionate in incest with its past? (p. 36)

Foreshadowed here are all the central images and ideas of *Water with Berries*: incest, the corpse and necrophilia, which Lamming employs to pass final judgement on the stasis of Britain's petrified imperialism; her lingering love for the corpse of the past. Charlot, revolted (like Conrad's Marlow) by his role of culture-bearer for a dead world-order which, ironically, still exercises a paternalistic proprietorship over a New World urgently exploding into History and visibility, salvages some honour when he admits his unfitness to be Fola's lover and leaves the island. But he soon relinquishes even such scant honour when he sends Piggott correspondence relating to his private relationship with Fola. Such correspondence can only damage Fola's position at home.

Charlot's departure, like Mark Kennedy's, is Lamming's symbolic way of suggesting that the anti-heroic persona is irrelevant to New World self-discovery. San Cristobal, as a microcosm of that New World, will have to seek the centre of its energies without patronising guidance from the dead Old World that Charlot represents, and to whose greyness he returns. An instinctive coloniser, Charlot still feels "great pride sometimes to think that any achievement of hers [Fola's] in this direction" (i.e. of scholarship and particularly, history, which Charlot taught Fola) may be the result of his instruction. (p. 124) Despite the clear bitterness of Fola's dismissal of him, Charlot still glories in the fact of his past proprietorship over her. Similar patronage will be displayed by the Old Dowager in *Water with Berries*, a novel whose central theme is the power of such patronage as a bond that ties the coloniser to the colonised long after the formal relationship between the two may seem to have evaporated.

V: Fola's Possession
Fola's possession happens in clearly pointed phases. She first becomes aware of Liza, a little girl caught up by possession (pp. 26 & 29). This makes her remember her own girlhood, and in particular her most

terrifying childhood experience: a fear of rats. Fola has begun her descent into the unconscious, and her fear has arisen to bar her further descent. Liza and Fola are doubles of each other, Liza representing Fola at the earlier stage of consciousness which she is trying to re-enter as she journeys towards wholeness. Liza, too, will later imitate Fola and thus underline her function as double.

The next catalyst to possession is the "crippled swoon" (p. 31) of a woman's voice behind Fola. Then Fola is made to drink a mouthful of gin from a bottle proffered by the houngan (p. 32). Alcohol serves the multiple functions of libation, communion, and inducing release from normal inhibitions. Fola as a member of the mulatto middle class begins with the class inhibitions of shame, colour and class prejudice, all of which would, along with her ordinary rationality, prevent her from surrendering to the frenzy of the tonelle. Powell and Crim recognise that the houngan has gone too far in allowing the stepdaughter of the Police Commissioner to participate so fully in the rituals of the cult. Fola, they can see, is about to "panic". While possession comes so naturally to Liza that she virtually dances in her sleep, is gently possessed and returns to her mother, possession for a middle-class neophyte will be a matter of panic. Liza, one notes, is in harmony with her mother while there is a discord between Fola and her mother Agnes, that will be increased by Fola's quest for herself.

So strong are her inhibitions that Fola's impulse is to run. She is, however, riveted by the eyes of Aunt Jane (p. 33), an old Orisha priestess who we later learn has knowledge of herbs, can restore fertility to Fola's stepfather, Piggott, and is variously regarded as witch, obeah-woman, oracle and wise woman. She is the spiritual mother of the tonelle. An essential aspect of Afro-Caribbean religious practice is that the neophyte, upon initiation into the sect or cult, gains new spiritual parents from among the senior members, and is expected to consult the spiritual mother or father for guidance. What Fola confronts when her eyes make four with Aunt Jane's is the immense authority that a spiritual mother exercises in any of these congregations.

On the psychological plane, the device of eyes making four is a conventional symbol/signal of the encounter of Self with Other. Sometimes Self and Other are lovers, as in John Donne's dialectical exploration of the love relationship in poems such as "The Good Morrow" and "The Extasie". Metaphorically, Fola's encounter with Aunt Jane is an encounter with an older Self, a first Self who takes the form of an old woman, grandmother or witch. Fola is caught between Liza, who is youthful innocence, and Aunt Jane, who represents the experience of age. The tonelle experience provides her with a new line of psychic descent to replace the ruptured line between Fola, her mother and her mother's mother.

Fola then helplessly urinates in an act that links her to both Powell (p.

12) and an old woman who appears later in the novel. This act moves her beyond the second emotional barrier to possession: shame, embarrassment. Powell (p. 14) views this shame as a central feature of middle-class life. It destroys "naturalness" or "nature", fidelity to instinct and desire, acceptance of one's body, Eros; replacing them with moral codes, inhibitions, hypocrisy. The Ceremony of Souls reveals that such shame can also be found among the poor. There is the case of the mother whose husband dies from syphilis which he has contracted from her. She grows ashamed and abandons her son who eventually goes mad after years of self-imposed celibacy in which he unsuccessfully searches for his mother. The woman's guilt and remorse are uncovered in the tonelle, and the discussion between Powell, Crim and Aunt Jane (pp. 46-48) again revolves around the opposing qualities of "shame" and natural behaviour. The boy's quest for his mother foreshadows Fola's quest for her father, as well as her incomplete reconciliation with her mother later in the novel.

Breaking through the barrier of shame, Fola becomes aware of "a new identity" (p. 41) and will eventually term herself "Fola and other than". She next experiences a feeling of rigidity and rootedness, a state of being drilled into the ground (p. 43). She is becoming the country, or the vessel of its reawakened spirit. This leads to a disconnection from the familiar. She only half-recognises her hand, that is, her old self, and she cannot call her mother's name though she longs to do so (p. 45). She recognises the need for reconciliation; for a healing of the ruptured line of connection between mother and daughter, but is unable at this stage to connect. "That fearful encounter with her forgotten self" (p. 50) also seals Fola from Charlot in a private silence which he can't penetrate. Though she had in the tonelle envied him his "safety" and his "detachment" (pp. 33 & 34) she now recognises his emotional emptiness.

Fola remains in a state of being possessed for the greater part of the novel, and is released only when she fulfils the pattern of tonelle ritual by transmitting her possession to the entire community. The tonelle experience is the beginning of a journey towards connection with and embrace of the Other, and a corresponding disconnection from the old world of Charlot as well as the unformed but already spurious "new world" of her arriviste parents, where "cultural events" include such trivia as tea parties, cat-and-dog shows, beauty contests and elocution classes, while "social work" is a form of patronising contempt practised by the idle well-to-do against the underfed.

The first phase of Fola's journey begins after she returns home from the tonelle and manifests itself in morning sickness and delirium (pp. 75-76), which signal Fola as a bearer of new life, while they indicate the confused state of her mind and stomach after the drums and alcohol. The first image and memory that surfaces is that of her grandmother, whom one would expect to be the kindly fostering if authoritative presence that the grandmother generally is in the West Indies. Here, however, Fola's grandmother is a witch. Two things are happening simultaneously: Fola is drifting off into a dream/nightmare in which she recalls her moment of childhood terror when her "deranged" grandmother, that "old witch of a mother" (p. 84) frightened her with a dead white rat. On the psychic plane she has begun a process of self-healing; a psychotherapy which involves the raising to consciousness of submerged moments of trauma trapped in the subconscious.

The secretly healing aspect of the resurrected witch/grandmother is signalled by the fact that the hand that holds out the dead white rat to Fola is crippled. The grandmother is as much a Legba figure as the possessed woman in the tonelle, whose "crippled swoon" had catalysed Fola towards her own possession. We earlier noted the grandmother's symbolic connection with Aunt Jane, healer, witch (pp. 111-112), herbalist, priestess and spiritual mother of the community. If at the time when the incident occurred, the grandmother was an agent of malice, here her function is to strengthen Fola's resolve to sever ties with the old world order of Charlot, who is "the dead white rat".

Fola measures her experiences of the trauma of return against his notion of what it involves.

> She recalled the gentle hint of mischief in his voice when he had spoken of his American friends in Europe. Their return to the past seemed the opposite of her visit to the tonelle (p. 92).

She then meditates on the difference between her confrontation with the past and that of white Americans, and she arrives at the fact of slavery and forced migration making her sense of the past more urgent and fevered than that of those who chose to cross the middle passage. She feels that her "history" is more real, personal and tangible than "their world of monuments and important graves" (p. 93). Her inner voice here blends with that of the omniscient narrator. She further recognises that "the aesthetic denial of... blackness" (p. 94) that she has been taught since childhood was

> an insult she had learnt, an insult which all her infancy had suckled like an udder. And the udder was Charlot's history: the essential history of all Charlot's world. (p. 94)

Fola's journey, then, is in accordance with the structure of possession. It involves a profound realisation of the past. Here, Charlot's history, the history of the "Mother Country" is "maternal" – an "udder" that suckles the black colonial mind with the poison of self-contempt. Charlot's history then, is a kind of wicked stepmother, an old witch whose ultimate objective is to devour her stepchild.

Fola's grandmother has reappeared as ambiguous witch/healer, to reinforce Fola in this task of making a break with Charlot's unhealthy historical proprietorship. Originally, the grandmother's malice had been directed against Fola as an illegitimate child of unknown, but probably white paternity, who was being brought up by her brown-skinned mother, Agnes, to scorn blackness. The udder/mother allusion applies to both Agnes's tutelage and Charlot's history. Fola now understands the symbolic meaning of the dead white rat. There can be no compromise with this deadness, and no easy reconciliation of ancestors until the inner truth of historical encounter is revealed, and there is open acknowledgement of guilt, and reparation, as in the Ceremony of Souls.

Recognising this, Fola also identifies her mother Agnes as an agent of Charlot's history. In Fola's dream delirium, Agnes appears as a lost soul who needs to make contact with her daughter. This is obviously an inversion of Fola's own secret wish and need for connection with her mother.

Lamming is, however, not convincing when he ends Fola's dream with a vision of apocalyptic upheaval and destruction in the island (p. 95). Though true to the structure of possession in which the devotee becomes filled with a vision of both past and future, Lamming is being too insistently ominous here. The coming class confrontation in the novel, though fierce, is hardly apocalyptic; and Dr. James-Williams Baako's new and more competent, but still bourgeois leadership emerges at the end of the novel with what appears to be the author's stamp of approval.

VI: Fola and Piggott

Poor, black and ambitious as a constable, Piggott has risen to eminence in the police force by having been the perfect instrument of colonial authority. Early in the novel, we learn from Crim that Piggott has vowed to put an end to the tonelle. Piggott's rise has also been due to the secret he shares with Vice-President Raymond (policeman turned politician after Independence) and Lord Baden-Semper. These two men have risen to eminence by means of a cache of counterfeit money which they discovered during a police search for stolen jewellery, and appropriated for their own advance. The entire political hierarchy of the new republic – referred to in the novel as "the families" of Federal Drive – has been based on counterfeit money, which is Lamming's metaphor of both the materialism and the fakeness of the new ex-colonial bourgeoisie. Lamming is the first West Indian novelist to have focused with such severity on the elite that came into power with Independence; and he did this before Independence. *Season of Adventure*, then, is one of our great prophetic novels, whose thorough exploration of the pre-Independence present enabled it to project its enquiry accurately into the probable nature of the post-Independence future.

Piggott is partially redeemed from moral disgrace when he heeds

Agnes's warning that he should accept none of the counterfeit money. But by keeping Baden-Semper's and Raymond's secret he sins by omission, and partakes of the deep counterfeit that has overtaken their lives. Piggott as police commissioner can only continue the war against genuineness, instinct, fervour and nature that characterised the British post-Emancipation effort to abolish African music, religion and folkways. This campaign gives him a sense of power; perfects the counterfeit authority that he exercises as the repressive instrument of the new political elite.

Piggott the man, however, is a pathetic figure. Sexually potent but sterile, he cannot generate life. His dearest desire is to be a father, and his efforts towards this end have been monumental but fruitless. This personal frustration makes it even more necessary for him to wear the compensatory mask of an authority that is aggressively deployed against the tonelle; that is, against the island's centre of spiritual, cultural and sexual energy. The tonelle is Piggott's double, the suppressed 'Other' within him; and although Piggott perceives this Other in terms of the criminals whom he relentlessly pursues in the tonelle, the tonelle really represents the feminine principle within Piggott's psyche. It is the creative, softer side of him, which his function as hatchet man for the new regime, as instrument of untempered, counterfeit patriarchy, makes him hide, deny and suppress. Significantly, what he seeks and needs from the tonelle is the herb lore and healing wisdom of Aunt Jane, its spiritual mother. It is magic and miracle, witch and mother that he needs; and these are presented in the novel as feminine qualities. Piggott's deep sense of shame prevents him from returning to Aunt Jane and embracing the Other.

Part of Piggott's rise has been due to his marriage to Agnes, the fallen brown woman whose misfortune in bearing an illegitimate child, and then refusing to name a father, has spoiled her own prospects of social ascension by any other means except marriage to an ambitious black man. Agnes has developed "connections" through her beauty and sexuality, which she uses to gain Piggott his rapid promotion. This aspect of Agnes's past is only hinted at by the omniscient narrator, though it has given rise to full-fledged rumours in the society, and eventually becomes a central feature of Fola's quarrel with her mother. Piggott, then, is doubly emasculated in his inability to reproduce, and the fact that his power and authority have been based on his wife's connections – probably her past high-level whoredom.

Piggott compensates for his sexual sterility by exercising an exaggerated paternalism towards Fola. It is the means whereby he evades the fact that his marriage with Agnes has failed, as well as his bewilderment over the power which she exercises over him through her claim to having "made" him. In his domestic situation, Piggott lives the truth that Powell, the Frantz Fanon of the tonelle, repeatedly asserts: that freedom, independence or power cannot be given:

> "if ever I give you freedom... then all your future is mine, 'cause whatever you do in freedom name is what I make happen" (p. 18).

Lamming feels, like Fanon, that one never recovers from an original act of patronage. His exploration of the way patronage inhibits is generally done on the level of man-woman relationships: Piggott and Agnes; Steward and the Commandant and their wives; Teeton and the Old Dowager who exploits the subtle emotional ties which have bound coloniser to colonised even in the post-colonial period; and Teeton and Randa, whose self-sacrifice earns Teeton his freedom. In each case, the man never recovers from the fact of the woman's generosity or self-sacrifice.

By means of these relationships Lamming explores a paradigm of the post-independence relationship of coloniser and colonised, where independence has been given by the coloniser rather than taken by the colonised. Yet even on the personal level he can propose no simple solutions. The giver exploits the fact of having given, using the act of patronage as a vehicle of control over the recipient. The recipient contemplates revolt – Piggott threatens to leave Agnes – but is kept in place by guilt, conscience, gratitude and the emasculating memory that he was once so powerless that he needed the patronage. What might redeem both giver and recipient is true selfless generosity on the part of the former and true humility – the ability to admit need and weakness without feeling self-contempt – on the part of the latter. In Lamming, the marriage of true generosity and true humility never occurs with the individual, and never with the larger unit, the nation or state.

Piggott's paternalistic tenderness towards Fola is partly, then, an echo of Agnes's patronage towards him, and partly a means of forgetting his failed relationship with Agnes, by recreating with the daughter an unconsciously incestuous replica of the idealised relationship he'd like to have with the mother. But by this token, Piggott cannot afford to allow Fola her independence as a woman. Paternalism requires a child but:

> it had come to Piggott as a shock that Fola had acquired the troubled look and liberty of a woman in private conflict with herself (p. 117).

Fola's quarrel with Piggott occurs in a carefully orchestrated scene which, as if to emphasise that Fola and Agnes are doubles, starts with a quarrel between Piggott and Agnes (p. 99). Between the two quarrels which begin the shattering of Piggott's domestic universe, we have witnessed Piggott's self-examination, his doubts as a stepfather; his realisation through knowledge of the contents of Fola's letter to Charlot (pp. 123-124) that she has grown up and perceives herself as a woman. She therefore has a different perception of men, including Piggott. His hopes of bribing her by an expensive present vanish and he has to endure her silence, the failure of the old kinds of dialogue.

After this we see through Fola's eyes. She has been pulling down the photographs of her friends and family from the walls in her room in a first effort to erase the superficial elements from her life. Fola is still under possession, and as such transmits energy through the eyes and the tension of her body.

> He could feel the tension which closed her fists. The tension seemed to burst every nerve in Fola's body, like the night she knelt in the tonelle, petrified with shame by the shock the ceremony had produced on her. Now she saw Piggott as she had seen herself in hiding (p. 125).

At this moment of severance, Fola objects most to being patronised. She wants to know about her past, a need opened up by the Ceremony. Agnes, who has vowed to explain that past to Fola when she "is old enough to hear" (p. 338), is unaware of her daughter's transformation. This transformation widens the rift between mother and daughter who, unaware of the truth of her mother's past, instinctively condemns. Piggott is alarmed at Fola's demand to know her past, since this would mean an examination of his role as her foster-father, and a possible break with the paternalism which he has exercised over her.

Fola possessed becomes unleashed womanhood – a forerunner of today's feminist revolution that Lamming clearly foresaw. Thus she wants to know her story. She becomes a medium for the energy of "naturalness" that the tonelle represents, and thus catalyses Piggott's abortive journey of self-discovery. Just as the "crippled swoon of the woman's voice" in the tonelle had served to transmit the energy of possession into Fola or to release Fola's innate energy, so Fola's almost physical assault of Piggott's emotions catalyses his necessarily false quest for self. The falsehood of his quest is indicated by the collapsed image which he sees in the mirror when he looks at himself without his false teeth (p. 128). Loss of face, shame, is his biggest problem, preventing him from returning to the tonelle as the origin of his life.

Piggott and Charlot function as doubles in the novel. Both are paternalistic towards Fola for selfish ends. Both are sterile, though in different ways. The link is indicated by the fact that it is Charlot's letter that triggers off Piggott's quarrel with Fola. Both men also avoid the "season of adventure", the journey back to firstness of self. Charlot retreats into his dead Old World; Piggott, equally dead because he is untransformed, unrenewed and incapable of new possibility, remains a medium of sterile Old World values and methods. Piggott conceals his personal failure by transferring all his thwarted desire into a bitterly repressive campaign against the tonelle. He becomes like a ritualist whose possession has been interrupted midway in its process. The released energy, uncontained, becomes destructive. Such is also the fate of Piggott's opposite, Powell, whose clean, pure hatred is another example of energy uncontained.

VII: Fola and Agnes

The confrontation between Fola and Agnes (pp. 150-154) is also done in terms of the tonelle/possession metaphor. The fact that it is a confrontation between Fola and her double is emphasised by the fact that Agnes is wearing one of Fola's dresses. Fola's rage at her mother is unconsciously the result of sexual attention that the newly awakened daughter feels should be hers. Like Piggott's entanglement of his dream of sexual fertility with the idea of Fola's sexual innocence, Fola's sexual jealousy of her mother is a wholly unconscious drama. Fola isn't consciously rivalling her mother for men's attention, but she is aware of a closeness between herself and Agnes (Self and Other) which makes her uncomfortable and resentful.

> Tonight Agnes was wearing one of Fola's dresses... She looked beautiful. Fola knew that this would be so; and she was glad. But it was this sense of her mother's nearness to her own way of feeling which embarrassed Fola. She didn't like this feeling which her mother gave of being so near in years and physical attractiveness (p. 139).

The Fola/Agnes scene is the climax of a crescendo of anger which begins when Fola confronts Dr. Camillon (p. 141), a newly returned member of the emerging professional elite whose aim is to acquire vast quantities of land in the shortest possible time. Representative of what is most sinister, empty, rapacious and proprietorial in the new bourgeois ruling class, Camillon regards both Fola and Agnes as "easy lays"; two high class prostitute sisters on the lookout for whomsoever they can pick up. Camillon gets a glimpse of the obsessed Fola – the intense tonelle persona – and retreats before her rage. He concludes that Fola is mad and like Piggott tries to prepare a face to hide his discomfiture. Camillon (chameleon? lizard, reptile) is by far the most unattractive portrait of the novel. He is later revealed as both lecher and abortionist – irresponsible engenderer and terminator of life. His opposite is Dr. Koji James-Williams Baako, who is Lamming's "verray parfit gentil knight", an idealised portrait of a man of culture and learning who eventually becomes head of state on a wave of popular acclaim. The novel leaves the question open as to whether what Baako represents (responsible and competent patriotism) will prevail over what Camillon represents (rapacious and even murderous proprietorship).

The rising current of anger is felt among the steelbandsmen, who smart at the unfair treatment meted out to a tonelle man. There is also Agnes's anger that Fola has embarrassed her by unceremoniously leaving the State Ball, and Raymond's bitterness against the steelbandsmen, one of whom has slipped broken glass into the pocket of his dinner jacket. Thus when Fola confronts Agnes, it is as if she is giving vent to everybody's rage.

> A passionate resentment had released her from this bond of secrecy with her mother. They confronted each other in a similar state of rage, playing

out their wild and spiteful opposition of interest which neither dared express; which neither could, in fact, explain (p. 150).

Since water is the medium in which the spirits of the dead are released for recriminatory dialogue with the living, Lamming presents this possession scene against the background of a rainstorm which Fola interprets in terms of tonelle symbolism.

> She would have liked the rain to free them from this solitude of threats and dead recriminations.

Freedom can, however, be obtained only if there is openness in the confrontation between present and past, and this does not happen between Fola and Agnes. Release and cleansing require confession, admission of guilt and reparation. Here there is little more than bitter accusation on Fola's part and impassioned denial on Agnes's.

Fola also tries to harm or at least violently repulse the Double. In an act of disavowal she strips her dress off her mother. Release can come, however, only on embrace of and final reconciliation with the Double. This is difficult and painful because the Double usually presents itself as opposite to, other than – possessing and projecting all those qualities that we hate in ourselves. What Fola resents right now is her own awakening sexuality as mirrored in her mother's. She is somewhat like Sharon confronting Magda in Harris's *The Whole Armour*; the virgin in resentful accusation of the whore, something of whose experience of the depths of life is necessary to the virgin's maturation.

Fola perceives her mother as "this woman", a whore who only accidentally mothered her and feels

> taken beyond this moment by the nameless futures which were knocking in her head. Like the dead souls in the *tonelle*, Fola was *beyond* her past. She was free; dead to the accidents of her past, dead and free (p. 154).

This is, however, a false epiphany. Despite the lights that Fola madly turns on, she is still going through the dark night journey of possession. She still hasn't heard her mother speak; but the Ceremony of Souls is dialogue – defence as well as accusation. What has taken place represents only one half of the ritual, and the scene ends with Fola (Self) divided as far as possible from Other, Agnes. This is indicated by Fola's obsessive repetition of the command: "Don't you touch my things." Fola has further to travel.

Agnes has so far been presented as a resourceful but somewhat superficial woman, aware of the advantages of her brown pigment, skilled at manoeuvring herself in the rather dubious social circle of Federal Drive. She is contemptuously confident of her ability to control Piggott, but unable to achieve any but a strained relationship with her moody and difficult daughter, who has grown up with the notion that she's been regarded as a burden by her mother, the unwanted child who spoiled her mother's chances.

We will learn towards the end of the novel (pp. 335-43) that Agnes has been the victim of a double raping, first by the son of an English bishop and then by Chiki's brother, the black tonelle youth. She has thus experienced in the flesh something of the tangled brutal heritage of violation that has been West Indian and New World history; and Fola, the product of uncertain and now absentee paternity and violated maternity, is Lamming's representative Caribbean person. Agnes has never considered herself guilty for the circumstances of Fola's birth which, like Caribbean history, cannot be altered, and must be borne with honour. Hence Fola's name which, as we said, is Yoruba for "with honour". Agnes's attitude towards Fola is Lamming's attitude towards the terrible and bizarre history that has created the Caribbean person. Agnes bears with fidelity the burden that has been imposed on her by fate, and clings desperately to a hope that there will be "Justice" somewhere in the universe. There is a strong suggestion that the ambiguous mixture of love, hate, violation, "anguish and horror and delight" (p. 434) which has characterised the conception of Fola, the Caribbean person, has placed Agnes beyond guilt or innocence – beyond normal categories of moral judgement. Though Agnes had once intended to tell Fola the truth, she finally wonders whether "it were better Fola did not see the darkness which her rebellion has so nobly sought to bring into the light" (p. 343). Like some West Indian commentators, Agnes has come to feel that amnesia is preferable to the dark epiphany which knowledge of the intimate details of the Caribbean and New World past will inevitably bring.

VIII: Fola as "Muse"

The new phase of Fola's journey begins almost immediately when she abandons her office job and tries to live in imagination the experience of working-class women of her society. This is, in fact, an indirect attempt by Fola to work her way back to her mother. Her preoccupation is with the meaning of maternity in the context of colonial history. What, for example, were sexual experience and motherhood like during slavery? Are sexual experience and maternity even now a type of slavery? Fola realises that the women in the waiting room of the maternity ward are, for the nurses, nothing more than statistics – B532, A151, C36.

> It is the animal docility of the women which hurts. Cowed and dejected in their waiting, these mothers look strangled by the charity of this room. 'So they are like that!' Fola thinks, as she hears them answer to their numbers in the Maternity hall. They carry the weight of their pregnancy like ordinary food; take their places with the same servile sureness of animals trained to their stalls, and wait for a nurse to announce their numbers (p. 172).

Fola wants first to empathise so totally with the women that she longs to feel "in the natural pulse of her own bowels the life which has increased their size." She, however, soon recognises that she is guilty of sentimentalising their experience. The women's indifference suggests a vast depersonalising force which has so nullified consciousness that they wait, "as though there were no memory to glance this moment back to another time" (pp 172-173). Fola wants therefore, to restore the women's individual personhood, the specialness of each experience, "to rescue each woman from the anonymity of her number" (p. 173).

At this point Fola emerges as Muse, an aroused and sensitised imagination whose quest and burden are the same as Lamming's, the creative writer who as "a historian of feeling"[7] has rescued the faceless from the anonymity of statistics in which both history and much of the contemporary writing in the Social Sciences have trapped them.

> She aches to know the origin of the life which each contains. She forces herself to see without any evidence at all the history of each face (p. 173).

The idea here is that only fiction has the power to release the lineaments of the lived past where there is little documentary evidence apart from statistics. The creator of fictions must also rewrite history.

> She would make her own history, give it life and motive which she herself might not understand (p. 175).

Fola's notion of rewriting history is identical with current feminist rewriting of both history and myth. It is also identical with Lamming's idea of the fiction he is in the process of writing. Like Lamming, Fola is dissatisfied with the history that the people at large have passively accepted as a true version of their experience.

> They had all been deceived by their ignorant habit of knowing (p. 175).

Lamming is through Fola indicating his dissatisfaction with those writers who have accepted superficial and stereotyped versions of Caribbean history and chosen to remain at these well-known surfaces. Like Fola, he intends to create more genuine fictions which they will be unable to recognise.

> She would select the beginnings of a fact upon which she could build any fantasy that might cripple their recognition.

Here the terms of reference are suggestive of the tonelle: "beginnings" and "cripple" telling us that Fola as Muse is still possessed by Legba, the cripple-loa of "beginning", and that Lamming views Legba, the pathfinder to the underworld, as the Muse of Caribbean writing. Legba is Muse of both history and the future, guardian of all journeyings and of all directions.

What Fola describes here is her intention to be different; to be so new in what she creates through the imaginative interplay of fact and fantasy that the conventional reader will not recognise or understand what she is really making. Her aim is to undermine their complacent image of self by moving beyond conventional reality.

> Fola thought that truth would be irrelevant for her purpose, if she could make people respond with the same intensity of feeling to her distortion of any fact. That's how she would begin. She was determined to offer an image of herself that would work like disease on their certainty (pp. 175-176).

That was 1960, year of *Palace of the Peacock* and *A House for Mr. Biswas*. By one of those fascinating coincidences Lamming was, via Fola, outlining Harris's aesthetic achievement. This could only mean that West Indian writing felt itself at the brink of new and strange explorations after the exciting realism of the fifties, whose climax was *A House for Mr. Biswas*. Lamming is somewhere between Naipaul and Harris in his approach to realism; his fictionalising of fact, his bent towards allegory and metaphorical situation.

IX: Fola as Medium and Catalyst

The next phase of Fola's journey requires the transmission of her "knowledge" to society. She has established a clandestine friendship with Chiki, the painter from the tonelle, and spends some time with him puzzling out the meaning of her experience and the problem of vocation. Chiki is the ideal person for Fola's need, since his situation resembles hers. Chiki is the lower-class boy whose education has almost propelled him into becoming one of the bourgeois he despises. Rejecting social ascent via education, Chiki chooses to cling to his tonelle roots. It is, however, not clear how his choice has helped alter the tonelle situation of poverty, crime and violence and Chiki, for all the genuineness of his choice of roots, has achieved little as an agent of social change. Fola's situation complements Chiki's. She is the bourgeois person who hasn't quite rejected being bourgeois, even though she feels the need to embrace proletarianism.

Chiki feels she should become a teacher, which would be one way of translating vision into useful social action. Fola is in the ambiguous position of having recognised the necessity to sever ties with her parents' world and continuing to enjoy the privileges and comforts of that world. It is some time (30 pages or more) before she resumes her journey, the weight of possession by Legba still heavy upon her.

> She felt weakness and shame like crutches under her crippled arms. Yet some unfamiliar need was taking shape inside her; the need to cut herself off from their possessive concern.

Here the Legba imagery (crutches, crippled) is used negatively because Fola has lingered too long at the vestibule of beginning, and runs the risk of remaining fixed in Legba's state of age and crippledom. That is, Fola may be unable to move beyond the stasis of the old order, as represented by her parents and their milieu. She therefore resolves "to sever all loyalties from the past" (p. 244).

Apart from the cripple/Legba image, one has the childbirth image ("some unfamiliar need was taking shape inside her") as well as the image of severing, which suggests the cutting of the umbilical cord that binds child to mother, in order to liberate the neophyte towards his or her own identity. The process of Fola's individuation will involve two apparently contradictory elements: first, separation from a fostering but possessive mother and second, reconciliation, spiritual reconnection with a mother who has herself undergone the transfiguring ordeal of the Ceremony of Souls.

Fola is in the throes of the first phase of individuation: that is the severing of the umbilical cord that links her to her mother. Given Lamming's wider purpose, Fola's urge to sever links with her mother's world may be seen as symbolic of the necessity for the emergent Caribbean mind or consciousness to cut the ties that bind it to the dying mind- and world-order of the imperial "Mother". Fola's final assessment of the world she is about to reject indicates its similarity to Charlot's dead world. Its cultural occasions are termed "intellectual seances"; the word "seances", with its connotations of white people's dead necromancy, being deliberately chosen to indicate difference from the vibrant Ceremony of Souls. The colonial derivativeness and mimicry of this cultural ethos is suggested in the devastating imagery by which the social elite is described: "a self-propelled circus of talking animals deprived of their original voices" (p. 246). Fola links them with the dead souls of the tonelle who can remember their past, but have no power to choose a future. Such choice is both the burden and the responsibility of the present, which she represents.

Her moment of true decision arrives during a police raid on the tonelle led by her stepfather Piggott. He is looking for the murderer of Vice President Raymond, father of Fola's best friend Veronica, and though they lack evidence, the Police assume that a tonelle man is the culprit. This brutal reality of the police raid forces Fola to move beyond sentimental identification with cultural roots into political commitment. This necessitates confrontation with Piggott, not as her uncertain patriarchal stepfather, but in his public role as Police Commissioner, the incarnation of sterile power, who transfers his aggression to the yard that bred him, and thus compensates for his sexual sterility and social inferiority. At this crucial moment Fola chooses to identify with the tonelle and life rather than with Piggott and Raymond and death.

> Fola had been restored to that freedom which now ordered her to put an end to Piggott's authority.

Here Fola and Piggott are incarnations of two eras, two states or structures of mind, and two types of authority. Her confrontation with Piggott closes the cycle of her encounters with the Other in its two guises as double and opposite, and releases her from her possession. The authority she gains from choosing correctly is immediately evident. She becomes a type of Aunt Jane (p. 274) and focuses Piggott with her eyes[8] in an act that severs for good her links with his dead patriarchy. Piggott's last contact with Fola will be later that night, when he at last becomes "possessed" in the sense of going berserk, and beats her murderously in a final transference of frustrated sexual aggression.

There are two other features of Fola's public emasculation of Piggott which merit notice. One: when she appears, the women who had gone indoors as the police advanced, reassemble in the yard. Fola's entry signals the emergence and liberation of the woman. Two: after the confrontation, she at last experiences a need for her mother.

> She wanted to coil herself to an infant's size, and nestle calm and forgetful in her mother's arms (p. 282).

This is less a moment of foetal regression to the womb; less a rejection of the harsh demands of maturity, than a desire to reaffirm the bloodline between mother and daughter, severed since her grandmother evicted Fola's pregnant mother.

> Some old and dormant bond of blood had come alive. The darkness showed everywhere some promise of her return to her mother.

We never see this reconciliation, though it will clearly be the climax of Fola's personal journey. When we see Agnes for the last time, she too is longing for reconciliation.

X: Politics and the Waning of the Muse

Fola's public role is fulfilled in her planning and implementation of the revolt of the drums against police prohibition. It is her final act in putting an end to her stepfather's authority and affirming the tonelle as the centre of indigenous creative spirit. Though the focus in this scene is more on Gort than on Fola, it is the logical and lyrical climax of the novel, in that it brings together the major actors in the drama, Fola and the tonelle, in an affirmative act of defiance of the old order, and in a movement which acknowledges and releases the latent power of the people. What Fola has discovered through possession – a firstness of Spirit – has been transmitted, or rather, given back to the people.

It is, however, precisely after this climax that the novel, which has been working excellently on the levels of metaphor and complex allegory falters and denies the logic of its own structuring. Fola, bearer of the novel's poetic meaning, Muse and container of the new illumination, is allowed to fade into the background until she finally disappears from the last few pages of the novel.

Her importance, indeed, has been reduced since her confrontation with Piggott at the tonelle, and dwindles even further after she narrowly escapes being murdered by Powell in Chapter XIV. Even when she leads the revolt of the drums, she fades into the crowd, and the focus is, rightly, on Great Gort, who is high priest of this festival. Her role in the novel is supplanted by Dr. Kofi James-Williams Baako who comes to political prominence on the crest of the tide of revolt released by Fola's defiance of Piggott's authority. Baako's formulae are sufficiently plausible to be attractive as a manifesto. He advocates intellectual commitment to change. The university must "assume the burden of the bush" (p. 322). He recognises a political function in all activity: art, science or education. The old religion of drum and energy needs to be both remembered and transcended.

Since he also believes that "it's bad to pass on dead memories to the generation coming after us" (p. 325), it is no surprise the Orisha faith wanes early in his regime (presumably as a dead memory); the steelband music and the drums continue to exist but, detached from the ritual function they had performed in the novel, lose their pristine fervour. Chiki the artist is in a state of paralysing despair. Loss of energy is the apparently inevitable result of the transition from the primal vision of ancestral communalism to the secular rationalism of the new age.

It maybe argued that Lamming is simply being a realist here. After all, almost every detail of popular experience in the novel may be traced back to a source in the social history of the Caribbean peoples. For example, the regeneration of the Ceremony of Souls ritual and the tonelle happened in Haiti immediately after the Haitian Revolution and several times in the twentieth century. The story of vodun is a story of continued resistance to both official religious and secular structures of authority. The people's resistance to the prohibition of the drums and steelbands resembles that of the Trinidad people during the century after Emancipation. The bloodless removal of a corrupt regime and spontaneous acclaim of what seems to be an enlightened, honest and capable leader, has happened on a number of occasions in the charismatic politics of the Caribbean. Even the petering out of revolutionary fervour into despondency and disillusionment is a well-known Caribbean phenomenon, too frequent to need illustration.

The question, however, is not whether the anticlimactic ending is true to fact, but whether it is true to fiction, that is, "true" in terms of the particular fiction that *Season of Adventure* has been presented as being: a partly symbolic, partly allegorical rather than a wholly realistic drama.

Why are symbols – tonelle, vodun, the elaborately developed Ceremony of Souls ritual, the steelband, Fola's interior adventure in spirit – which have been so carefully established and so poetically affirmed for nine-tenths of the novel, so suddenly devitalised and drained of their meaning to be replaced by the dry panacea of Baako's "scientific" politics, technology and liberal-minded agnosticism?

There are a number of possible explanations for this. The first relates to the fiction Fola invents to protect the tonelle from Piggott's rage. In this fiction, Fola identifies a face in one of Chiki's paintings as being that of her father who, she says, has murdered Raymond. Since Chiki's paintings are mainly about the tonelle, the portrait resembles the houngan, who panics and goes into hiding. Fola has inadvertently destroyed both her stepfather and her spiritual father, who never recovers his self-confidence or authority, and sees his failure to attract the loa as punishment for his desecration of the shrine, through permitting outsiders, Fola and Charlot, to its inner chamber. When the tonelle fails the entire community feels the loss in spirit. Great Gort whose music was a corridor for the ascent of the loa ceases to be chief acolyte at the Ceremony of Souls and shrivels to the stature of pan-instructor of an increasingly defunctive sound. This is the logical result of Fola's unintentional destruction of the houngan. Her honourable lie destroys what it was meant to protect.

But if Fola's season of adventure has meant the end of both honourable (the houngan's) and dishonourable (Piggott's) patriarchies, Lamming is unable to make it mean something positive and enduring in and of itself. He is thus forced to replace whatever Fola's journey may mean for the Caribbean future with yet another optimistically benevolent patriarchy, that of Baako, who, after his first presidential speech subsides into silence, his enlightened agnostic tolerance bored with the people's simple faith and honest energy.

Another explanation of the novel's anticlimactic ending is that Lamming, for all his engulfment in what Shephard in *Of Age and Innocence* terms self-redefinition through politics, is as fascinated as Naipaul with Sartrean states of acedia. Paralysis is the other side of politics. Mark is Shephard's double. Vortex may mirror void. Thus one finds recurring in Lamming either the paralysed protagonist (Mark Kennedy, Roger Capildeo) or the politically committed man (Shephard, the Commandant, Teeton, Chiki). The problem arises when political commitment encounters personal trauma – guilt, emptiness, loss of motivation. Then one is faced with a central hopelessness that undermines an earlier energy of affirmation.

Chiki's despair at the end of the novel may be his response to the limitations of his artistic medium: paint, whose capacity to express the fervent soul of the masses can never rival the energy of Gort's tenor pan. But it is also due to Lamming's gloomy tendency to counterpoint commitment with paralysis, vortex with void. The artist's mind becomes in Lamming a trysting-place in which the collision between these mighty opposites takes place. In *Season of Adventure* the tonelle is the centre of life and movement and may be seen as the generator of the community's vortex of energy. It is so magnificently realised that it conceals its double, the other and more shadowy side of the Lamming spiritual universe. It may well be that Lamming stresses affirmation through a character such as Fola because he recognises the possibility of greyness and negation.

XI: The 'Author's Note'

When Fola's role in the novel is almost complete, Lamming presents us with the 'Author's Note' (pp. 330-332) in which a narrator who claims to be Powell's half-brother offers an explanation for Powell's transformation into a murderer who nurses an obsession to exterminate the new ruling elite. The "author" of the "Author's Note" disagrees with the explanations offered by historians or other novelists and poets, who view Powell as either an uncompromising rebel for whom freedom is an absolute and pure ideal, or as one who has nostalgically idealised and tried to grasp an unreal past, as for example, some Black nationalists have done.

The "author" rejects these interpretations for one that is closer in spirit to the drama of Self and Other that has been the central concern of *Season of Adventure*. Powell is his half-brother and double. They are exactly the same age and have had exactly the same primary education. The "author", however, wins a scholarship at the age of ten and grows away from the tonelle, in much the same fashion as Chiki or "G" in *In the Castle of My Skin*. Unlike Chiki, who abandons the prospect of joining the educated elite when he drops out of high school, the "author" embraces the privilege of the entirely different lifestyle which his intellect has opened up to him.

> I forgot the tonelle as men forget a war, and attached myself to this new world which was so recent and so slight beside the weight of what had gone before. Instinctively I attached myself to that new privilege; and in spite of all my effort, I am not free of its embrace even to this day (p. 332).

This separation from roots causes a division between Self and Other, the "author" and his double. It creates a sense of class alienation through privilege on the "author's" part, and a feeling of having been betrayed on Powell's; and is the real root of Powell's hatred of the new bourgeoisie.

Unfortunately, the novel can offer no way out of this dilemma in which education as an instrument of upward social mobility leads to the creation of a new uncertain class, guilt-ridden at having abandoned an old way of life, but unwilling to abandon the new one for which, after all, they've worked. If we consider the various "journeys" of the educated people in

Season of Adventure, we'd see why the novel ends in an ambiguity almost like paralysis.

Chiki, who like the "author" of "Author's Note" has won a scholarship to secondary school, and for some years receives the specially privileged treatment of one earmarked for liberation from the tonelle's ghetto, recognises betimes the sterility of the new world of privilege and returns to the tonelle. This reaffirmation of the grassroots helps neither Chiki nor the tonelle, and part of Chiki's despondency towards the end of the novel is related to the sense of stagnation that comes from his not having fulfilled his intellectual potential. Is Chiki's choice of returning to the tonelle a nobler or better one than that of the "author" of "Author's Note", who remains in the "new world of privilege", but empathises sufficiently with his grassroots origins to be able to tell the story of the tonelle people?

How does one define "intellectual responsibility" in this post-Independence period of startling transition, where the brilliant ghetto person is caught between such contradictory urges? One may, like Baako, opt for enlightened change and obliterate what the "author" of "Author's Note" terms "the weight of what had gone before" (p. 332): the emotional and spiritual genuineness and primal vision of the tonelle. One may, like Fola, seek to rediscover and empathise with the tonelle, to sever links with an original life of privilege, and to commit oneself to action, awakening and leadership. Fola's role is the fullest and most hopeful, though even she is left with a dilemma of how to employ her education in the quotidian situation of change. As we have noted, too, her intervention catalyses the destruction of the tonelle, and she's ostracised by Gort and bitterly blamed by Powell for intruding into their world. Only Chiki, whose ambiguous situation as we saw earlier, resembles hers, sympathises with Fola.

No stance, it seems, is entirely satisfactory, though commitment is held up as a nobler option than indifference. Commitment involves the possibility of being misunderstood. It contains a sacrificial element, and may take the form of "bearing witness", which is what the fictional "author" does in his "Author's Note". One may say that for the "author", writing *Season of Adventure* has been such an act of "witness"; the process of creation being its own Ceremony of Souls, in that it involves recall of the past life of an Afro-Caribbean grass-rooted origin; confrontation with the guilt of having abandoned those origins for a more superficial life ushered in by educational success; and reparation by means of the act of bearing faithful witness through telling the "history" of the tonelle.

As in the Ceremony of Souls, the novel also seeks to suggest what future may emerge out of the dialogue between present and past. It is at this point that options lose themselves in despondency, and the tension between Lamming's equally powerful drives towards affirmation and negation leaves us with the ambiguity of vortex and void, commitment to action and "disinclination". It is not certain that this ambiguity is what Lamming means to convey. He has termed his novels "open-ended",[9] which seems to mean that the writer does not prescribe or impose an appropriate ending. He leaves the options for the future "open".

Lamming's futures are, however, generally foreshadowed by catastrophe: fire, madness, murder and Shephard's death in *Of Age* and *Innocence;* madness, moral disgrace and the deaths of the officers in *Natives of My Person* where, in a typically Lamming situation, the women waiting in their grotto of new beginning declare they are a future that their men (who are, unknown to them, already dead) must learn. Catastrophe in the present renders the future far less "open" than the unresolved issues at the end of each novel may suggest. Such catastrophe is present even in the closing pages of *Season of Adventure,* Lamming's most triumphantly affirmative novel. The tonelle is destroyed by fire. While the perspectives for the future are not utterly closed off, the omens are far from reassuring.

(Paper presented at the Conference of English Departments, UWI, St. Augustine May 23-25, 1986. Published in *Journal of West Indian Literature,* Vol 5, Nos. 1 & 2 (August 1992) pp. 1-29.)

References
1. See Rohlehr, G., "The Problem of the Problem of Form" for discussion on Mark's vision.
2. Kent, G., "Conversations with George Lamming", *Black World,* Vol. 22, No. 5, (March 1973), pp. 4-15.
3. Elder, J.D., *From Congo Drum to Steelband* (Port of Spain: U.W.I., 1969).
4. Epstein, D., *Sinful Tunes and Spirituals: Black Folk Music to the Civil War* (Urbana, Chicago, London: University of Illinois Press, 1977), p. 27.
5. Ibid., pp. 58-60.
6. Deren, M., *Divine Horsemen: Voodoo Gods of Haiti* (London: Thames & Hudson, 1953), p. 13.
7. *Express,* Friday, Jan. 18, 1985, p. 13.
8. Lamming, G., *Season of Adventure* (London: Michael Joseph, 1960), p. 271 cf. p. 33.
9. Kent, G., op. cit.

THE SPACE BETWEEN NEGATIONS

Gordon Rohlehr interviewed by Selwyn Cudjoe, 6 May 1980

Cudjoe: Yesterday we began to talk about the fact that the West Indies seemed to produce a lot of severe critics. Could you please expand upon this theme?

Rohlehr: What I was saying is that a number of factors account for this. First of all, there has been a traditional narrowness of educational opportunities which has produced a certain type of person in the West Indies; the man of letters who sees it as his duty to be involved in virtually every sphere of literary activity. He is politician, maybe he writes a novel, a play, some poems or literary criticism. Sometimes he may even criticise music. Now this kind of figure exists in a situation where he is definitely one of a small group – you might call it an elite: Du Bois used to speak about a talented tenth – and where he suffers from what I would call a "crampedness" of intellectual space. That is, the same fellows who may be writing creative works may also find themselves serving as critics. The fact is that they are operating in a situation where they normally know each other, where they are pretty close to each other and where they meet on the same occasions. Under such circumstances it is very easy to get on each other's nerves. I think in addition, that there has been a concern for high standards and an awareness of one's colonial status has meant that one wanted to make it in terms of whatever the metropole might have determined to be the international standards. This has encouraged us to judge ourselves very harshly from time to time.

Cudjoe: V.S. Naipaul as you know is now receiving quite a lot of accolades from the press, particularly in the United States and England. Would you say that V.S. Naipaul is necessarily the best Caribbean writer? If he is not, how would you compare him with other Caribbean writers? As one of the serious critics of the area, how would you compare writers like Naipaul, Wilson Harris, George Lamming and others?

Rohlehr: This is not normally the kind of question I like to answer. Simply because normally my approach has been to take a particular writer on his merits; to find out what I would call the intellectual hinterland of the writer (that is, the experience which his writing reveals, what lies behind and beneath the writing), and to find out, given where he is starting from, what he is saying about his society. Quite often the writers are zeroing in on the same features of the society but from quite different angles, depending on where they start and what they imagine their individual position in that world is. Now, if we take a writer like Wilson Harris who comes out of a particular experience, there is the Guyanese environment, the forest and the fact that he was a surveyor for several years. There is also the question of who he conceives himself as being – ethnically mixed, composed of four or five different races – and the fact that Harris has asked the question: What kind of image would emerge of the West Indian person, the Caribbean person or maybe the New World person if we took seriously the question of cultural diversity? So in Harris you get an attempt to look for points of intersection of various mythologies, ways of looking at the world, concepts of religion, concepts of self and personality. And more than that we have also (and I don't know if it has appeared in any study of Harris yet), a kind of Guyanese intellectual hinterland. If you look at the TIMEHRI journal which was being published in the nineteenth and well into the twentieth centuries, one of its focal points was its anthropological concern with the Amerindian tribes which are there in Guyana. There has been consistent work on these people. There is this Guyanese preoccupation with history. A preoccupation with the past. Now I'm saying that landscape, the experience in the bush and the intellectual world at the time helped to produce Harris and to make him the kind of writer he is.

Then, there are his own concerns with theology, theosophy, philosophy, Hegelian thought, Marxism, which have intersected and been included in his writing. What I am saying then is that a variety of influences have combined to make Harris the kind of writer he is, and to give him the kind of preoccupation which he has. More importantly, it is becoming more and more evident that Harris is tackling intellectual problems which are of a very contemporary nature. For example, the question of writing about what he called "the diminished man", while at the same time giving some kind of hope, a sense of possibility, and sense of human capacity to people is the most important thing about Harris. The actual people that Harris deals with are derelicts of one kind or another but he attempts to see within these people their human possibilities; which suggests that human possibilities lie within a person and not in external things such as political power, the capacity to manipulate people, material wealth and external success. In Harris these latter things do not count for much because these kinds of achievement are very fragile. It means therefore that he is running counter to the tendency to see political success and political power as the be-all and end-all of life.

When we come to Naipaul, a phrase which keeps recurring in the more recent Naipaul is: "There is an absence of possibility." In *Guerrillas* he speaks about this Caribbean island – I don't think he wanted to give it a name – as a place which has exhausted its possibilities. It is not he who says this, but the character Jane who makes this observation. Naipaul, however, says it himself in a number of other places, in his essays and non-fictional work, so that character, Jane, is simply articulating something which he himself feels. Very clearly, he defines possibility in terms of material structures which places him in a situation that is diametrically opposed to Harris's position. Thus their assumptions about what are human possibilities are totally different. Naipaul would say that Harris is a fantasist: that derelicts are derelicts whether you are talking about rum guzzlers, pork-knockers or criminals going up a river or living in a savannah. Naipaul would argue that if this is what you are talking about, you should talk about it and give it its full dimension of squalor. They are dealing with two different worlds. Harris is dealing with an interior world all the time. In his novels the external world is generally subjugated to the importance of the interior world.

Cudjoe: You said that the question of human possibilities is to be seen within the context of material structures in Naipaul. Would you say this characterises all of his works or that it seems to have taken on much more importance in his later works?

Rohlehr: Well, I suppose it is wrong to make as absolute a statement as I have, but in a novel such as *A House for Mr. Biswas* possibility is defined in terms of creating or even just acquiring something of one's own – that is, in terms of property and the acquisition of property which is given an almost spiritual dimension. In a way it is like *King Lear*. I made this point in 1964. I said there that human significance is measured in terms of the acquisition of property. Lear begins with property which he wants to give up, is stripped of it and his personality crumbles when he no longer has it. Mr. Biswas starts without it and the acquisition of it becomes somewhat of a fetish in his mind, something that will somehow fulfil him so that the achievement of that external thing acquires an almost spiritual significance. Now in a writer such as Harris, you work in the opposite direction. The man who begins with material things often has to lose those external props or trappings before he begins to recognise an internal potential. Harris constantly strips his people naked of material acquisitions which, as far as he is concerned, are the husk and the shell and have nothing to do with the kernel of the real self.

    Naipaul on the other hand, takes the opposite position. He attempts to measure the political potential of small countries, small people and what he would call "the powerless". He has to find some way of measuring achievement and success, and the only way he can measure them is in terms of political or material power. So that the powerlessness of small places like the West Indies in the political or material sense becomes a symbol of the absence of possibilities and human potential of its peoples. In one of his statements he says that he wished he was born in a more important place since he would have something to write; meaning, I suppose, that being born in a place like this doesn't offer the writer the possibility of a wider range of things to write about.[2]

Cudjoe: You say that Harris has been fashioned by his particular environment, his particular concerns, and the multiplicity of his origins and that when the material aspects go the whole being seems to disintegrate...

Rohlehr: No. I said that Harris deliberately makes divestment of the material a precondition of the emergence of the true self. An apparent crumbling or disintegration is usually the first sign that divestment has begun.

Cudjoe: To what degree does Naipaul's other being, that is, his East Indianness and his Hinduism affect his concept of the self?

Rohlehr: This is a hard one, both because of my inexpertness at what Hinduism or East Indianness means, and because my notion of these things has been partially shaped by my readings of Naipaul's work. A novel such as *A House for Mr. Biswas* or one like *The Mimic Men* explores this area in some depth. Ralph Ranjit Kripal Singh, the protagonist in *The Mimic Men*, experiences a loss of wholeness and coherence, which is presented as a violation of purity. Naipaul's Brahmin background comes in here. Violation is a word that he uses over and over again in that book. Contrast Naipaul with a writer such as Kamau Brathwaite in whom the loss of wholeness is conceived as producing a state of fragmentation or a splintering, but in whose work you will hardly find the word "violation" occurring. The connection of the concept of wholeness with that of purity and fear of human touch, a terror of contact, is something which Naipaul seems most certainly to have received from his Brahmin background. A shrivelled, vestigial Brahminism must have left that conception of life with Naipaul.

    What we have therefore to ask ourselves is this: "What happens to this presumably whole Brahmin personality, this whole psyche, this whole self when it comes into contact with the Creole society in the West Indies and the entire Western world in which the Creole society of the West Indies is placed and of which it is also a part?" In other words, what kind of education does that psyche and that personality receive when in the end it becomes entangled, as I suppose we all are caught up, in the sense of loss and decline prevalent in the Western World? Whether this decline is real or imagined, the point is that a notion of decline has been very powerful for most of the twentieth century. The writer whether he is East Indian, African, or of mixed origins, receives an education which acquaints him with this sense of decline. Now what happens to the writer when he begins consciously or unconsciously with a notion of the purity of the psyche? This is the problem which Naipaul will always encounter – a problem of emptiness or void which we see raised in existentialist writing, but to which he brings something that is quite peculiar. It is true that a concept of void exists as a central part of quite a number of Eastern philosophies. But it is a void for which one consciously works. It is a space and emptiness which one is able to acquire after years of training, discipline, asceticism, and denial; years of what one may call studied negation and the divestment, of oneself, of all material things. Therefore, Naipaul brings something peculiar to literature because we have what I have called in another context,[3] a man caught between voids. A man like Kripal Singh turns out to be neither the Western existentialist hero, although he resembles him, nor the Eastern ascetic saint who has negated and divested himself of the material and who has achieved a state of emptiness or nirvana. He is neither. Because part of the Western response to the sense of void, which I think has been a result of the sense of Western decline and decay, is a kind of heroic defiance. In other words, there is energetic resistance to the notion of void within existentialism. In fact it would seem that for a writer like Camus, for whom Naipaul has more than once expressed admiration, the sense of the absurd exists not simply in the presence of void, but in the lucid perception of void and in the energy generated in the struggle against the void. In *The Myth of Sisyphus*, Camus speaks about a number of hero-types in each of which there is this almost classical Grecian quality of heroic defiance.

Naipaul's Ralph Singh lacks the energy of heroic enthusiasm. He succumbs to the void but does not make a positive choice of divestment.[4] In other words his negation is neither Eastern nor Western and this is where his crippledom lies. It is in this state of being in a limbo between two types of negation that we will find something of Naipaul's Hindu background or his perception of what has happened to the Hindu personality in the Caribbean outposts of the Western metropole.

Cudjoe: In comparing Naipaul with some of the other Caribbean writers, you argued that Naipaul stuck to his limits, that is, in terms of technique, way of seeing, etc. Can you expand upon this point somewhat?

Rohlehr: By limits I mean that he has set himself up to do a certain kind of thing. I think that what unifies the late and early Naipaul is that the eye of the writer functions as a very selective camera which severely chooses its images and what it is going to photograph. In an early novel like *The Mystic Masseur* there is a character called Ramlogan who is a shopkeeper. Wherever we see him we see a dirty case in which he keeps a bun or two on which there are flies. We see him hawking and spitting and he possesses a greasy handkerchief with which he rubs an equally greasy forehead. These images are repeated about ten times in the novel. We find this same technique in a writer like Dickens who, like Naipaul, is fascinated by the notion of the grotesque. Caricature often implies a perception of a certain incompleteness of character – it may be the extension of an incompleteness in the writer, for all you know – and a desire to reduce the character to the gesture or the thing. This is one of the limits that you will find in Naipaul from his earliest works. He has a particular idea or notion of a character or a society and goes about looking for evidence to support his idea, Everything radiates from that central idea and very little else is allowed to get in.

In a late novel like *Guerrillas* the basic idea is one of dereliction and abandonment, and the central characters are derelicts whether they are European or Caribbean. The land is derelict; it is in drought; and people cast off things that they don't want into the rubbish heap. That T.S. Eliot cliché, the wasteland, is applied to the landscape on more than one occasion. Then we discover that the people are derelict and the fellows in the commune are either orphans or they have lived with no one who has been concerned about them. So that you have a central idea around which everything is built (that is the characterisation, the landscape and the season in which you place the novel). Beginning with this fixed idea you then select your images for photographing. Added to this is the futile political or pseudo-political activity of the people. All their activities conform to the single theme and in a way one might argue that it is a good, skilful way of writing. But I think that there are limits there.

If we take a writer like Gabriel Garcia Marquez who comes from these parts and also writes about a land without history and the complete human waste of potential, we find that one does not get this sense of the simple organisation of detail which is designed to satisfy a simple central preoccupation. Although it may be possible to point out a kind of coherence in his writing, there is something that is different, wider, and bigger in his work. Marquez covers a much wider area of human sensibility and examines more layers of human experience. His is not the reflection of a single vista. In Naipaul's *Guerrillas,* one does not have to read beyond twenty or thirty pages to learn virtually everything that it has to tell one. The same is not true with the works of Marquez.

Cudjoe: Can you speak about the lack of experiment and exploration which one finds in Naipaul's work?

Rohlehr: I won't say a lack of experiment because one can see him trying a variety of different things. The form of *The Mimic Men* is quite different from that of *A House for Mr. Biswas.* I am also interested in a type of development which has been taking place in the Naipaul short story, where the monologue-form in a story like "Tell Me Who to Kill" or "One Out of Many" is quite successfully employed to explore the loneliness, the complete loss of context, country and background of the central characters. And this is one of the things which has been happening in the modern short story where it is becoming a lyrical form, almost as intense as poetry. Indeed, some writers feel it is a better form for exploring the kinds of complexity which entangle the isolated individual mind, because it is short, spare and requires skill, economy, and a great deal of finish. I think that Naipaul's skill and finish come across more effectively in some of the later short stories, than in some of the longer novels. No, I won't say that there is a lack of experimentation in Naipaul's fiction. I'd say that I've grown used to his ideas and his ways of treating them, and that for me he has become predictable even when he is experimenting.

Cudjoe: The role of the Bible is very evident in both Lamming and Vic Reid. Do you have any such influence you could point to on Naipaul, biblical or theological?

Rohlehr: I don't know. There is the possibility that he has used the *Ramayana*; but I don't know how he is using it, because I don't know the work. I do know that Mr. Biswas is more than a little sceptical about the Tulsi approach to Hinduism, and sees himself as a reformist. In the middle of his breakdown in the storm he instinctively returns to traditional Hindu prayers. But I am not too certain about whether or not this kind of influence functions consistently under the surface of Naipaul's fiction. I would suspect that it would, although, given Naipaul's tendency to satirise ritual of all types, if it does exist, it exists as something which people are either not living up to or are departing from. It exists therefore as something which heightens the satire just as Kripal Singh's dream of this mythical horseman in *The Mimic Men* deepens the fantasy which surrounds his life. In other words, he is miles away from a world in which that kind of myth seems to make sense. Where Naipaul will possibly find some point of very clear resemblance with other writers is not in his shaping of any theological influences, but rather in his denial of a mythic capacity to the West Indian people. There is a very strong tendency to deny a real mythic capacity and this is bound up with the state of Western sensibility and thought in the twentieth century. For example, you have a writer like Derek Walcott saying, "All the Gods are dead anyhow, and to attempt to resuscitate them is to lie at a more profound level."[6] Even though I think he is very busy trying to create certain kinds of mythology of his own he would deny very strongly the mythic capacity.

Cudjoe: Naipaul in one context says, "Style, I don't know what style is." How do you interpret that statement?

Rohlehr: Well, he seems to admire a very clean, plain style which is suited to recording the bare bones and skeleton of realism. I think he is committed to this plane of realism. He does, however, attempt to invest the real with the symbolic capacity, but the real must always remain the real. In other words, you must authenticate the experience on the surface level before it can stand for or point to anything else; and there is in this method a very twentieth century mistrust of the symbolic. He hasn't gone quite as far as, say, a modern French novelist such as Robbe-Grillet who in his *For A New Novel*[7] is totally against any type of connection between inner and outer worlds: that is, between inner and outer realities. He attempts to write a literary version of phenomenology, where you pick out images, each of which is as important or unimportant as the other. Nothing is accorded symbolic weight. Naipaul by contrast works from image to leitmotif and seeks to make surface reality suggest a metaphorical dimension.

He resembles Conrad in this respect and is, like Conrad, caught halfway between the traditional and the modern; the nineteenth and twentieth centuries. Conrad would pick a single image like darkness, or decay, or the silver in *Nostromo*, and repeat it ad nauseam. He would take a single detail about a character, or he would give him a name or a tag which, like Dickens, he'd repeat every time that character appeared. The character Nostromo, for example, is sardonically termed, "the magnificent capataz de cargadores." But every time he appears, the irony which is meant to make us recognise the distance between Nostromo's illusions about himself and the hollow reality of his inner life, becomes a little more heavy-handed and tiresome. Naipaul still tends to do this. The method is most insistently employed in *Guerrillas*, a novel which owes something to both Conrad's *Heart of Darkness* and *The Secret Agent*.

Cudjoe: Since you have done a study on Conrad, how much of Conrad is in V.S. Naipaul?

Rohlehr: How much is very difficult to say. In *Heart of Darkness*, Conrad has produced probably one of the major modern mythologies. The book talks about the decay of a civilisation and the illusion and lie of history. It even talks about the breakdown of symbolism, because although it is such a symbolic novel, it takes symbolism to such an extent that the symbols almost seem to lose meaning. If one reads *Heart of Darkness*, and Naipaul clearly read *Heart of Darkness*, it is very difficult for that novel not to function beneath one's consciousness. One can hear the obvious echoes in Naipaul's late novels as he attempts to write about Africa. Yet Conrad was stronger, bigger, more profound and his African experience caused a far deeper trauma. Naipaul, by contrast, writes like an unusually literate tourist who is not really involved in what he sees except at a calculated cerebral level. For Conrad the experience was so traumatic that even in his Malay novels, *Almayer's Folly* and *An Outcast of the Islands*, one finds the darkness, the fear of the forest, the wonder at what the European was doing in an alien environment, the implicit critique of imperialism and the decay of adventure. *Heart of Darkness* is also a critique of the genre of adventure fiction which was in its heyday. It was the age of Rider Haggard, Rudyard Kipling and Robert Louis Stevenson, whose writings Conrad saw as an added distortion or a trivialisation of the actual brutal realities of imperialism. It is, finally, a critique of the entire sensibility of a civilisation, one of whose major myths – the descent to hell – is employed to give depth to the political fable.

Naipaul was aware of Conrad's immense presence when he travelled to both India and Africa. *An Area of Darkness* echoes the name *Heart of Darkness*. Naipaul may also have been aware of Andre Gide's[8] journey to the Congo in 1925, which was prompted by his friendship with Conrad, and his fascination with *Heart of Darkness*. He may also have remembered Graham Greene's *Journey Without Maps*, a travelogue about Africa whose technique could have influenced sections of Naipaul's *The Middle Passage*. In Graham Greene's novels one finds the same burnt-out, useless European in Africa who reappears in Naipaul's *In a Free State*.

The differences between Conrad and Naipaul are as striking as the similarities. Conrad had a much wider range of primary experience because of his two vocations: sailor and writer. His response to experience, too, resonates more deeply, is more profound. His response to landscape is more genuine than Naipaul's and he retains a capacity for wonder and beauty which seldom, if ever, surfaces in Naipaul. Maybe in the Guyana section of *The Middle Passage* you get a fairly effective response to landscape; but Naipaul largely excludes his response to landscape from his novels or he gives us very specialised aspects of this response. Like Graham Greene, Naipaul travels around the world looking for experiences to write about. A lot of his recent work has a kind of journalistic finish. It is journalistic. He goes to a place where he can take notes and tries to shape the scraps and odds and ends of a tourist experience into material for fiction.

Cudjoe: What is the reason for his wanting to scrape together these odds and ends of experience. Has he lost some sort of centre?

Rohlehr: I suppose when you have written for as long as he has you begin to repeat yourself. I find I virtually know what he is going to say long before he says it. There are things which repeat themselves – types of analyses, types of character, types of detail, types of gesture – and this happens to any writer after a certain amount of time. I think you run out of your primary experience which you have actually lived and you have to find other things to write about. What happens then is that the writer includes a greater number of ideas in his writing. When a writer is at the start of his career there are more things happening, more raw experiences, shaped, as a writer must shape his experience, when you write out of that primary experience. When that primary experience goes you begin to depend more on pure intellect and ideas and to depend more on literature and other things you have read. You begin to echo other writers, to become derivative and to try to filter your voice through theirs. All of these things have happened to Naipaul. He is very much the professional writer. When he describes his routine he says he sits down and he writes – good or bad he sits down and he writes for so many hours. There's a kind of heroism as well as a kind of absurdity in this sort of routine: this necessity to go on at times when you don't have anything to say: going on because you have to go on. A very Beckettian situation there. Crippled on his sick bed, Malone writes because he has to write, unsure of whether he can achieve even death.[9]

Cudjoe: You said that *Heart of Darkness* is a critique of the sensibility of a civilisation at the particular point in time. Naipaul in "Conrad's Darkness" says the following: "Conrad's value to me is that he is someone who sixty or seventy years ago meditated on my world, a world I recognise today. I feel this about no other writer of the century. His achievement derives from the honesty which is part of his difficulty, that scrupulous fidelity to the truth of my own sensations." In what sense do you think Naipaul feels this tremendous identification with Conrad?

Rohlehr: In writing about Conrad, I met with something which I felt too. Here is a guy who is writing about Malaya, but I can recognise the tropical forests, the lives engulfed by that forest, the seedy colonial types, what's happening to the people there, and the tremendous gap between how the Europeans see that world and how it really is. I can see Conrad struggling, with only partial success, to get inside the Malay sensibility. His Malays are often technicolour natives, unreal, like Naipaul's Africans in *In a Free State*. They have exceedingly complicated political intrigues and are working out their own problems in a way which the Europeans don't see and which they largely ignore. European adventurer types like Tom Lingard imagine themselves to be rescuing the Malay world from itself. Like Graham Greene's quiet American in Viet Nam, they are profoundly ignorant of the reality of that world, and many tragic misunderstandings arise from this ignorance.

Exploring the ironies of primitive colonialism is part of Conrad's aim in the early novels. Such exploration is taken one stage further in *Nostromo*, which deals with what we would now call the neo-colonial Third World by taking a Latin American situation, one generation after Independence, and looking at the chaos of dislocation from the Spanish empire. Features of this chaos are the scramble for power, the impotence of the Spanish Creole gentry which has catch phrases, rhetoric and an admiration for British institutions, but has no way of translating this admiration into any sort of reality. This class, the best-educated and most ambitious for rulership, are totally divorced from a plural and fragmented proletariat who are themselves the tools of semiliterate, self-seeking leaders. There is also the cynical young intellectual, Martin Decoud, a kind of fictional Naipaul who has been educated abroad, has contempt for his origins, and analyses the issues with great lucidity. Conrad shares his sceptical vision, but is sufficiently guilty about his own detachment from the Polish cause to punish Decoud for his lack of a sense of roots or commitment.

What I suspect is that Naipaul would be attracted to the negative elements in Conrad; to what V.S. Pritchett calls his "incipient nihilism". There are several points of similarity between Naipaul and Conrad. Conrad as an exile from Poland, then a partitioned "colony" of Russia, Prussia and Austria, was made to feel a terrible sense of guilt by the Poles. He was regarded as a betrayer in much the same way as Naipaul has been regarded by some West Indians. Conrad's was a similarly traumatised personality whose way out of its situation was one of necessary exile. His father had been sent to Siberia for his political activities and it was almost certain that had the son remained he too would have been sent there. Naipaul claims that flight was also a necessity in his case; though fleeing from the imagined, nightmare of Trinidad is a far cry from having to evade the persecution of Czarist Russia.

There is in Naipaul a perception of anarchy and an obsession with order that is similar to the vision of Conrad's *The Secret Agent*. Both writers seek out the elements of sham in "revolutionaries" and deal with the ironies which accompany revolutionary "success" and "failure" alike. It is, indeed, sometimes impossible to say which is which in their writing. There is, on the other hand, an energy and a capacity to identify with human wholesomeness in Conrad which counterbalances his vision of the grotesque and horrible. In Naipaul, this countervailing agent is usually delight or astringent wit; but it has been largely absent from his more recent work. Nor does Naipaul share in Conrad's admiration for the physical, or the elemental. There is no figure in Naipaul like Conrad's Singleton who is a powerful, elemental old man; the kind of person that one can sometimes see in our society. Naipaul is more attracted to the grotesque, the cripple, the weakling, the fraud, the man with a bad stomach. Physical and spiritual dyspepsia are his favourite themes. Such dyspepsia is often complemented by a repeated horror at touch and a nausea of taste, which are the histrionic and mechanical extensions of Naipaul's "Brahmin" upbringing.

Cudjoe: Why did you select Conrad for your dissertation?

Rohlehr: He was a writer who had fascinated me since school, where I had read most of what he had written, as I had read Graham Greene and the evolving Caribbean novelists, Mittelholzer, Selvon, Naipaul and Lamming. I recognise now that I had been unconsciously attracted to writers dealing with colonial situations. I might have chosen West Indian literature had there been enough of it in 1964 when I graduated from UWI, Mona, Jamaica. But most of our poetry then existed in scattered journals, and the novel was in a state of relative infancy. There was almost no critical reflection on our writing, and the research student would find himself as isolated as the artist.

Conrad turned out to be a good choice. He was a stylist, whose every novel engaged one in different aesthetic and formal problems. Studying him gave one a sense of form and style, and many of Conrad's experiments went far beyond what had been happening in our own literature. There is, for example, still nothing in Naipaul which compares with, or is even vaguely close in terms of experimentation with the novel form, to the fragmentation and miraculous control of time and incident in *Nostromo*. Maybe Lamming's *Natives of My Person* is the closest our novel has come to the total control of a vast structure. Wilson Harris's work is comparable to the mytho-poetic aspect of Conrad, one of the dimensions which has not attracted Naipaul.

Cudjoe: Naipaul argues in his work "Conrad's Darkness" that, "most imaginary writers discover themselves and their world through their work. Conrad, when he settled down to write, was, as he wrote to the publisher, William Blackwood, a man whose character had been formed." Do you think that Naipaul forms himself; or discovers himself and his world through his work? And if this is so, does his writing become an almost obsessive necessity to discover his world and his being?

Rohlehr: You like to ask hard questions. Naipaul has set up very rigorous standards; a very rigorous set of necessities for himself as a writer. There is physical isolation. He goes somewhere outside of London, somewhere in the country. There is physical isolation of an almost absolute kind when he is writing. There is the necessity he feels to write a certain amount every day; producing five hours of sustained writing per diem. Out of all this rigour grows a certain bleakness, the asceticism of a writer who is trying to say, "I don't need anything like a community, I don't need any props, I don't even need people around me. I need myself, my pen, my theme." Clearly, then, in such a case, writing will be self-discovery. For example, out of *The Mimic Men* emerges an image which is a very modern absurdist image of the writer in isolation somewhere, trying through his writing to make a clearing, an arrangement and an order in the face of chaos. We find the suggestion of such a figure in Camus; the idea of writing as an arrangement, an organisation of chaos, and a making of space. This is certainly true for Naipaul who sees writing as an organisation of chaos which he perceives in the world around him; not simply in the colonial situation, but wherever he goes. That organisation of chaos constitutes a discovery of whatever his self or his world is. But then it is quite normal in the twentieth century for the writer to see himself as somebody devoid of personality, somebody drained of self. It is quite normal, then, for his writing to become an exploration or adventure, at whose terminus, or in whose process lies the possibility of self. This is part of the whole existentialist phenomenon and the diminishment in twentieth century writing which extends to the writer himself and to his characters.

Cudjoe: Are you saying that V.S. Naipaul is very much a part of the contemporary world, writing very much about the same kind of contemporary problems as the contemporary novelists?

Rohlehr: Oh yes, I have absolutely no doubt about that. Naipaul is attracted more to existentialist/nihilist influences than to the two other major streams of this century – the Freudian stream with its emphasis on Eros, and the Jungian, with its stress on Myth, Archetype and the Collective Unconscious. It is easy to place *The Mimic Men* in the genre of confessional novel; novels like Camus's *The Fall* and virtually everything that Beckett has written. But perhaps Naipaul in *The Mimic Men* derives most from Ralph Ellison's *Invisible Man* where Ellison describes a process of self-discovery in which the psyche of the major character has been maimed by the school which he had attended. Through a series of traumatic stages the protagonist discovers fragments of a self which he thought had disappeared. As he moves through the novel he gets closer and closer to reassembling a past, a self, and a face. He has an entire hinterland of music, blues, speech, rhetoric, etc., to reclaim. Most of Ellison's formal experimentations in that novel have to do with the excitement of rediscovering an entire milieu which the black world had already created through music and rhetoric. This is why Ellison's invisible man cannot be placed in categories, and why when Brother Jack attempts to place the invisible man into a slot with his doctrinaire Marxism it just doesn't work. Characteristically, Brother Jack has a glass eye which prevents him from seeing straight. Ras, the Exhorter, attempts to place him in another kind of category, the black nationalist thing – which also doesn't work because there is a certain variety about him and a richness of self which he constantly is in the process of discovering. Even though he is invisible there is so much of him to learn that the book ends with him in hibernation. Even though Ellison has taken the man from Booker T. Washington's South, through the Harlem Renaissance to the pre-world war situation of the late thirties, he could hardly predict what form the visibility of this fellow would take when it surfaced. The form it took, of course, was the Civil Rights marches, the Black Power movement, and the riots of the ghettos. This is what surfaces after his hibernation.

Naipaul is dealing with a counter-process involving constant loss and a divestment of whatever the memory seeks to recover. Kripal Singh's hinterland of associations evokes shame, terror, nausea and self-disgust. He doesn't relate to any particular music except once – to a sentimental song which echoes his distress. He has no tradition of speech, ritual enactment or humour – all of which are patently present in the Caribbean community. When he does dream of an ancestral archetype, that dream is presented as groundless racial nostalgia and fantasy. So much for Jung. When he does cohabit, he experiences violation or a lack of enthusiasm or even comic detachment from the act. So much for Freud.

Because nothing has been accorded validity, nothing affirmed, experience is resurrected to be shucked off, and Kripal Singh is left with that void of which we spoke earlier; a void which is neither Eastern nor Western, but a kind of neuter space between the two. Naipaul, it would seem, is moving in the opposite direction to Ellison. Thus, where Ellison's narrator seems to be more solid, richer and fuller, Kripal Singh is always in the process of losing experience, and ends up seeking the final emptiness in his exile in London. While Ellison's narrator is simply in a state of hibernation before he emerges again, Kripal Singh says that he has lived through all his cycles which, of course, is also a joke. Whereas in the real ancestral situation, one chooses consciously to live through these cycles, Kripal Singh doesn't make that choice and things which happen to him are imposed on him from the outside, there being no inner choice on his part.

Cudjoe: Is there any direct evidence that V.S. Naipaul had read Ralph Ellison?

Rohlehr: Any direct evidence in the novel? I'd say yes. There is a scene in Ellison, which one can possibly call the "dispossession scene",[10] where all the worldly belongings of the old couple are thrown out of an apartment onto the pavement in the snow. Compare that passage with what Kripal Singh remembers when he goes into Brown's house,[11] and the items listed are almost exactly the same. What is completely different is the reaction. Kripal Singh sees in these objects a symbol of the prison of spirit in which Brown lives. These are not possessions in any real sense as far as Kripal is concerned. Brown's intimate household objects are objects of shame which point to the same spiritual dereliction that is Naipaul's obsession. The narrator in Ellison's *Invisible Man* recognises these objects with a kind of warmth and they trigger off a series of quite irrational, emotional reactions in him. They make him political in a very unconscious way. It is the sight of those objects which makes him decide to address the crowd and which makes him start a demonstration on behalf of the couple. Without his actually intending it, the reaction comes from somewhere deep in him because he identifies positively with those objects. They are not just simply a symbol of the prison of the spirit. They are his household objects, they are his past, and they are his history, and it is in the reclaiming of these things that he becomes political. Kripal Singh cannot reclaim Brown's household objects because they are not his and he already has a ready-made stereotyped way of seeing and interpreting these things. Naipaul makes Brown as much a self-scorning cripple as Kripal Singh, so that Brown does not go through any traumatic process of self-discovery that would have enabled him to invest these objects with some kind of significance. The pictures of Joe Louis and Haile Selassie in Brown's house were there because Joe Louis was an icon of a particular quality of struggle. Kripal Singh can't give that kind of thing any weight. For Naipaul that is just racial nostalgia. I think that these are some of the real differences between *The Mimic Men* and *Invisible Man*.

Cudjoe: You spoke of Naipaul as a very contemporaneous writer in that he is concerned with the question of dispossession and void to some degree. Now if we look at Beckett and the others from the existentialist school, we'll find that at the basis of their art is the notion that life itself is absurd and that condition of absurdity generates their fiction in a way. If we look at Ellison's *Invisible Man* and the whole tradition of Afro-American literature, we could see that their position of being exploited and made "things" by the dominant white culture, in a way is responsible for the reclamation which Ellison in fact makes. In light of this what would you say generates Naipaul's fiction?

Rohlehr: I think it is his sense of being a displaced person within his own home society. He sees the Indian as a displaced person, he speaks of the Black and White as having a private patois – master and slave still talking some kind of language which presumably they both understand. Kripal Singh says that he is the outsider, the exotic Asiatic, which of course is a stereotyped role which he often decides to play. Because of this Kripal Singh has this sense of being an outsider within Creole society. Given all the other things that Naipaul has written, this is very much how Naipaul himself feels. He is an insider and yet an outsider in a Creole world which has rendered the Indian an "invisible" man, in very much the same way as Ellison's minority black person becomes an invisible man within white society. But Naipaul's invisibility has given him that sharpness of insight and that willingness to attack and hurt which Ellison's protagonist has described as being one of the advantages of seeing without being seen or acknowledged.

The sense of being invisible is a very contemporary thing. If you look at T. S. Eliot's Prufrock or James Joyce's Leopold Bloom, who is a Jewish outsider in Irish society, you will see that the "invisible man" pervades modern writing. Bloom's humour, the satirical sharpness of some of his observations about the Catholic Irish, the quality of his irony, are all aspects of his position as invisible man. They are also a function of Joyce's position of insider/outsider; the characteristic position of the colonial writer in exile. Conrad, too, we must remember, was both colonial and outsider, whose irony was a function of his inability to identify with any base or cause or people, and his own guilt feelings about this incapacity. His minimal sense of human possibility was qualified by endemic unhope.

The World Wars caused a sense of displacement which Blacks had already known because the Middle Passage was their first World War. Europe experienced a sense of displacement, dislocation and diaspora through which Blacks had already lived. Colonial situations, then, are extremely contemporary and universal modern situations, insofar as they are situations of cultural loss and shock. Blacks have lived in a very active and concrete way the existentialism of which Sartre writes, which is why Sartre can take up the colonial cause and write about it with a certain clarity, and also why a number of Black or colonial writers are attracted to existentialism. The colonial man has become an icon of the displaced modern man. This is the point where Naipaul easily joins the mainstream of contemporary literature, down to taking up all its poses: the writer in isolation, the inability to affirm anything, the void, the negation and the sense of meaninglessness of life which are the favourite poses of the contemporary writer.

Cudjoe: You spoke of Naipaul's perceived indifference of the Creole community and the Indian's invisibility in the society which makes me recall the charge of racism which has been made against V.S. Naipaul. We know that when Naipaul began *The Middle Passage*, the thoughts of James Anthony Froude (a disciple of Thomas Carlyle who authored the "Occasional Discourse on the Nigger Question") were ever present. What influence do you think Froude had on V.S. Naipaul?

Rohlehr: In reading people like Froude, Anthony Trollope and Charles Kingsley, all of whom travelled to and wrote travelogues about the West Indies, Naipaul recognised these writers as his literary ancestors. They were tourist-historians and although he was born in the West Indies he returns and views the society with that insider's/outsider's eye. They say things that fit into Naipaul's deterministic vision of Caribbean history and, like them, he becomes something of a tourist-historian. What Froude said in essence was that the failure of the West Indian plantation economy resulted from the emancipation of the slaves. The black slaves just wouldn't work, he said. Like Carlyle, he was saying that a return to slavery or some other kind of coercion was necessary. Since 1956, Elsa Goveia has dealt with people like Froude and others in her *Study on the Historiography of the British West Indies*[12] where she identifies them as being simply apologists for the plantation system. She argues that theirs was a long tradition where they had to find justification for everything that was associated with the system, that is, chattel slavery, child labour, certain attitudes towards people and, of course, racism, which knitted the whole complex together. She makes it clear that Froude, Trollope and others were pretty extreme for their day.

Now the important thing about these people is that they measured the Caribbean through the eyes of outsiders with a concept of the good life and culture drawn from the society which produced them; a society of which they would give a fairly idealistic picture. But the point is that they had norms against which they measured the West Indies. It is clear that Naipaul admires and adopts those norms although I think that he begins to question them in his later books. The most interesting feature about Naipaul's choosing to see the nineteenth century West Indies through the eyes of these writers is the fact that there were other writers who did not present quite that kind of biased picture, which said that the West Indies were useless backwaters where nothing had been created, and which dealt with certain racial stereotypes. For Trollope the salvation of the West Indies would be in a racial mulattoism, by which he most likely meant the offspring of white men and black women. I don't know if he meant that, but he certainly saw the mulatto in the very stereotyped terms of the late and mid-nineteenth century, where whites would supply intelligence, and blacks would supply brawn, and between them you would almost get a super race. And he saw this marvellous genetic arithmetic as a possible future for the West Indies. A cultural extension of the mulatto myth – the mulatto as the salvation of the society – is some thing which has resurfaced in some of our writing.

What I find fascinating, though, is that Naipaul read those guys and there is no obvious evidence that he has read a writer like Sewell, *The Ordeal Of Free Labour*,[13] or a writer like Underhill,[14] who gave a totally different picture, because he had lived and worked in the West Indies. He quotes Froude, but at no point does he mention J.J. Thomas[15] and C.S. Salmon,[16] but again we have been talking about Naipaul's selection of evidence to make a particular point. I won't call him a racist because I think the issue is bigger than that. It's a kind of profound dishonesty in which the documents of history are made to serve the narrow obsessions of the mind that observes or reads these documents. So in Naipaul what is excluded is just as important as what he includes and this is where the fraudulence comes out. This is a fraudulence which I am prepared to accept when it appears as a narrowness of focus or a particularity of concern in a fictional work where it might even be a sort of advantage. If you want to present the Caribbean only as a wilderness and to choose images of drought and so on, that is your privilege as a writer of fiction. If you are writing satire in which the aim is to distort in order to define, I can understand your game. But when you are writing something which is attempting to give me an insight into the history of the place, and you exclude a dialectical presentation of the material, that is, a two-sidedness which is not a simple matter of black answering white (for both Underhill and Sewell were white men), I say that is a kind of intellectual dishonesty. In other words, within the white historians you had a variety of approaches to the West Indies. Why pick only those who make the kind of point you want to make when the history of the place, poor and impoverished and derelict as it is, still has more facets than that?

Cudjoe: This also brings another point which I guess I am trying to make also. That even Naipaul's non-fictional works cannot be seen as being unproblematic. In fact they are problematic, and must be looked at in the light of the concerns of intellectual dishonesty, that is in the selection of material, etc.

Rohlehr: Well, the point is that he often is writing the nonfiction to explain or counterpoint the fictional world. There are points where you get almost whole paragraphs, virtually repeating themselves and clearly one cannot simply divorce one from the other. They are both issuing from a particular kind of sensibility. This is how I read Naipaul or any other writer. I try to read a writer in toto. If you have written criticism, I want to see the whole thing and put it all together and see what comes out: whether there are contradictions in what you might say as a playwright and what you might say as a poet. You take somebody like Walcott who seems to have almost opposite notions of the playwright's and the poet's function, the kind of language they can use, the kind of situation they can talk about and who states these opposite things with a great deal of passion. He accepts these contradictions and states them with a great deal of passion and conviction. You put them together and you say surely a man who says he wants to build a drama on folklore, folk forms, etc., ought not to write with such hostility about the presence of such things in poetry.

Similarly, I try to relate Naipaul's non-fictional works to his fictional work. But I draw some distinctions between the different categories in that I'd ask myself: "What do I require of a man who says he is going to write something which he calls a history of the place and who excludes so much?" I'd want to ask that question. I would feel that part of your duty if you are operating in a non-fictional genre would be to do as much justice as possible to all the evidence on which you could lay your hands. If you are not doing this, you're lying. You are giving a specialised kind of picture which is lying or intellectual dishonesty.

Cudjoe: What do you think accounts for V.S. Naipaul's recent popularity, particularly in places like the United States?

Rohlehr: Well, I don't think his popularity is recent. I think that he has always been very popular. First, I think that his popularity has to do with the clarity with which he writes, which makes him easily accessible. He is a good craftsman because he has worked hard at doing a particular kind of thing which he has perfected. He is like a batsman with one or two strokes. Whenever you come down the offside he hits you for four. Don't bowl him on the legside because he can't play any balls in that direction; or if he plays those he will do something to hit them to the offside as well. But he does that brilliantly and people applaud. Second, his being published in Penguin, which has probably one of the widest paperback circulations in the world is very important. When you get published in Penguin you become visible in a way that lots of other things don't become visible. I think many of our other writers have suffered from having their books go out of print for several years after the first edition, while some of them never got into soft cover. So that they have a limited readership, people don't even know about them. America has discovered a lot of West Indian literature very lately. In discovering the literature, you discover the literature which is available, easy to get and which can be ordered quite readily for college syllabi. In that respect Naipaul is readily available.

Third, Naipaul is what I call a blamer of the victim. I've taken the phrase from William Ryan's excellent work: *Blaming the Victim*.[17] In what he has to say about the Third World, whether it is about Africa, India or the West Indies, even though he tries to tell you that these imperialists were here and this is what they left, Naipaul is really more concerned with the actual state of decay and dereliction than with asking who caused this situation. By contrast, Lamming, like Conrad, always asks what are the implications for the coloniser's civilisation. In other words, if we look at what he has done to the colonised, what he has left, how he has performed, what does it tell us about the man? What are the implications? Does it have any repercussions in his own world? Does it erode his position morally, or in any other way? Does it produce a certain kind of person? Does it affect the way his civilisation sees itself? Does it drain some of the moral energy of that civilisation? Can the sense of wasteland, the sense of meaninglessness, the sense of absurdity, the sense of void, which is so much part of the contemporary Western worldview be attributed in some way to the performance of that civilisation abroad? Has the colonisers' civilisation in the twentieth century awakened to what it has done or is it simply unable to face the horror of its own face, as is the case with Kurtz's European fiancée in Conrad's *Heart of Darkness?* In other words, when a writer like Lamming is handling the imperial theme, which he is always doing, you are never allowed to forget that colonisation eroded the coloniser maybe as much as it eroded the colonised, although in a different way. Similarly, with Harris, in the presentation of a figure like Donne (Donne, protagonist of *Palace of the Peacock*, conquistador, coloniser, plantation owner, frontiersman) you are never allowed to forget this. In Naipaul's *The Loss of El Dorado* you get some such picture, and there are suggestions of it throughout all his writing, yet the major focus is on the colonised to the point where we get a sense of the impotence of the colonised; and a sense that what the colonised have lost is somehow the fault of the colonised. For me this is just the blaming of the victim. Naipaul feels that colonised peoples escape from their incapacity by blaming history and insists that we focus rigorously on the deficiencies of the present. Nothing is wrong with this except that in the process Naipaul somehow deprives himself and his colonial peoples of a genuine historical context. This makes him popular. Wouldn't America like a picture of Viet Nam which somehow is able to blame the Vietnamese? I think that any writer who is able to do that in excellent prose will find no shortage of supporters, because it will give America a moral "out".

Cudjoe: So you think that by blaming the victims Naipaul is giving the colonisers and the imperial powers a way out of their own dilemma and provides a justification for their cruelty?

Rohlehr: I don't think that this is his intention. I think that as a satirist he is dedicated to identifying the flaws of any society under examination. When his target is a "half-made" colonial society, he usually locates its deficiencies in a pseudo-historical context. But I don't think he is consciously seeking to justify imperialism. In fact one can pick out several passages which are a direct critique of imperialism. But I think the overall effect, the thing which makes him pleasing to read to these people (apart from his style, his lucidity and all the other things), is the fact that he gives them a "moral" way out and their civilisation emerges with a relatively clean face. Imperialism can now sit back and say, as Carlyle and Froude said of the post-emancipation West Indies: "Look what has happened to all those backward peoples since we left!" Only recently Naipaul has become preoccupied with decadent European types, who are so unimportant and so detached from significant political action, that their decadence is illustrative of nothing. Lamming has a different approach. He wants to castigate the coloniser's civilisation; to get to the very centres of power with his picture of a decay and psychic incompleteness at the core of the imperialist experiment. It is not surprising, therefore, that it took Lamming years to get *Natives of My Person* published. Eric Williams had similar problems with *Capitalism and Slavery*. C.L.R. James's *Mariners, Renegades and Castaways,* that lucid interpretation of Melville's *Moby Dick*, where it is convincingly argued that Melville had, through his presentation of the relationship between Ahab and his crew, divined an authoritarianism and a Nazi-like potential for totalitarianism at the very core of American democracy, has not featured very prominently among mainstream American approaches to that novel. Mark Twain's *King Leopold's Soliloquy*, a satire on both European barbarism and American capitalism in the Congo, was ignored for years. *Heart of Darkness* was regarded as macabre and unreal because it shattered the illusion of adventure fiction and revealed the true face of imperialism. Conrad gained a reputation for being a rather grim, sadistic writer when in fact all he was doing was looking at the ordinary sadism of how Europe performed in the colonies, and making inferences about the nature of European civilisation uncongenial to England in the age of jingoism. What I am trying to say is that writers who have come from a certain angle, have often not been popular.

Cudjoe: You said that when Conrad tried to shatter the image that Europeans had of themselves that he was termed a grim, sadistic writer by a particular type of critic. In looking at the works of Naipaul, do you think it's wise to differentiate between the vision of First World critics and Third World critics? Do they see Naipaul's fiction in a substantially different way?

Rohlehr: I would say that people who write from within the colonial situation are going to have more important things to say because they see the man more closely; they know the man in a more profound way and they know where he is coming from. Because it is my situation he is dealing with, there is no "First World" critic who could write about anything here with the intimacy with which I can write about it. As they say in America, "It's my stuff." So that while Naipaul can write about us with a certain kind of intimacy, Graham Greene writing about Haiti in *The Comedians* will not register as authentically as a Naipaul writing about Isabella in *The Mimic Men*. Naipaul, who in that novel is incapable of getting "inside" the world of Blacks, is nonetheless at home in depicting the strange metempsychosis of the Hindu psyche in the Caribbean outpost of the Western world. That is the advantage of writing about one's own situation, whether as novelist or critic. Recently Chinua Achebe has written scathingly about Conrad's inability in *Heart of Darkness* to treat Africa except as a stage on which Europe displays its sores. He attacks Conrad's cartoon portraits of Africans which he sees as a major deficiency in the novel.[18]

One of the things that I've found is that when one writes about Naipaul with the kind of rigour that Naipaul employs to write about our world, one is then accused of chauvinism. I remember how Edward Lucie-Smith in reviewing *The Islands in Between* in 1968 spoke of my doing an injustice to Naipaul and accused me of envying Naipaul's talent, saying that my critique of Naipaul was characteristic of the kind of envy West Indians feel for Naipaul because he is successful, popular and so good.[19] I thought that it was an unjust and cockeyed assessment of what my article was about because I thought that I was enthusiastic about Naipaul where he had balanced things to say about the West Indies. I have always been enthusiastic about *A House for Mr Biswas* because it has a kind of balance about it. Mr. Biswas is grotesque but he is a recognisable Caribbean struggler and a positive weight is given to his struggle, however petty it may seem at points. And I thought my enthusiasm for this kind of thing came across.

Cudjoe: Have you had other such responses?

Rohlehr: I really don't know how people have reacted to what I have written because there is precious little reaction to it in any case. There is a mention of one or two of my articles in Walsh's book on Naipaul[20] which he sees as critically deficient in some kind of way. Kenneth Ramchand responded in the same way to "The Ironic Approach".[21] Sylvia Wynter, on the other hand, commended it in her "Reflections on West Indian Writing and Criticism",[22] and Kamau Brathwaite was enthusiastic in his "Caribbean Critics".[23] Apart from these responses there has been the usual silence.

Cudjoe: Is there a struggle for hegemony between the First World and Third World critics in order to determine who speaks authoritatively about Caribbean literature? Do you discern such a tendency?

Rohlehr: If there is such a struggle it cannot be important. Neither what you term the "First World" nor the "Third World" critics form a coherent group. At present the field of Caribbean criticism is relatively new and open, and there is too much work to do for one to be involved in an absurd question such as who should speak for Caribbean literature. I'd repeat what I said above the advantages of writing from within a situation; with the caveat that this does not of itself make one a competent critic. Nor does writing from outside the Caribbean situation necessarily invalidate a sensitive expatriate response.

I think a far more serious issue than this is the scattered nature of our critical responses to West Indian literature. I have written about forty critical articles, but have been unable to get any selection of these published. I know of several good academic theses lying dormant in university libraries. Publication lags behind research by ten years, so that one gets little chance to see what either "Third" or "First" World critics have been producing. The struggle here, then, is more for visibility than hegemony. The latter struggle will materialise later on.

Cudjoe: The Indian publication *Mukdar,* published by some of your students, argued that there was a dichotomy between the way the Indians and the Africans saw the works of V.S. Naipaul. There was also a kind of struggle to establish a kind of primacy of V.S. Naipaul, presumably the hero of the Indians, and C.L.R. James, presumably the hero of the Africans, and the argument was made that the Africans were jealous of Naipaul's international success.

Rohlehr: First we have to locate those students in their particular context. Most of those students came into the University in the late sixties and left in the early seventies. Nineteen-seventy cut across their university career. Nineteen-seventy was a traumatic time for the society in that it had to assess where it stood and work out its position on many issues. If you look at newspapers after 1970 you will find that many people, who didn't normally write or comment in public about our society, now thought it their moral duty to do so. The issue of race was one which was most frequently ventilated, and at the centre of that issue was not the white / black confrontation, but the far more important and insidious Indian / African rivalry. That rivalry has assumed the most absurd proportions since Independence. Any thing which makes for the cultural, political or economic visibility of any one group is regarded as a matter of envy by the other. This may well be a paradigm of behaviour in culturally diverse societies, where the masses of the major ethnic groups, dispossessed and under the control of elitist oligarchies, are pitted against each other in the dog-fight for the crumbs of political patronage. Naipaul, indeed, noted this growing rivalry in *The Middle Passage*.

His return in 1975 to give the feature address at the First East Indian Conference must be placed against the background of the cane-farmers' strike in the sugar belt. This was the rural/Indian-based counterpart to the urban/African-based Black Power movement of 1970, and it was recognised as a high-point in Indian militancy. It was into this charged situation that Naipaul walked. In spite of his having said a number of negative things about the Indian community, he is regarded as one of the means whereby the group has gained international visibility. He thus has become a fetish object for an insecure Indian middle-class, whose neuroses he has already laid bare. This insecure Indian middle-class is seeking visibility in very much the same way as the Black middle-class has been seeking and still is seeking visibility.

What is disappointing about *Mukdar* was that it could only react, and react in a most hollow and inauthentic fashion, to what Black critics had said in their examination of Naipaul. The insider, Indian approach, which should correct the alleged prejudices, did not emerge from the pamphlet. This was a pity. One was left with a piece of simple propaganda, written for that particular moment, by a group who were using the Naipaul occasion to celebrate their new-found visibility, their elation at having been identified as inhabitants of Hanuman House. It was weird, and can only be seen in the context of "outsider" politics as a cry for attention. The 1970 Black Power movement, though officially declared dead, had affected the Mukdar group traumatically and convinced them that what was needed was an Indian nationalist movement which, in obedience to the paradigm of behaviour in plural societies mentioned above, was compelled to seek its identification in reaction to the now invisible Black Power movement.

Cudjoe: It seems as though Naipaul dismissed the piece saying that one ought not to seek either glory or solace in one's particular identity. Was this a reflection on Naipaul or on the group?

Rohlehr: Naipaul saw through the group whose motives were embarrassingly transparent. He saw that there was a preordained role which they intended for him to play and he reacted to being placed in a position of articulator of Indian values and Indian nationalism. For a writer who has worked for years to get rid of the epithet "West Indian writer", it is unlikely that he would naively accept any such role or slogan. As a consequence, I think Naipaul saw what was required of him and decided not to play the role.[24]

Cudjoe: At the end of Eric Williams's book *From Columbus To Castro*, he endorses Naipaul's position that all of us in the Caribbean are mimic men. What does this say about Naipaul's and Williams's position in the society? Are they speaking about their particular kind of alienation which they have generalised and made into the condition of the masses of people?

Rohlehr: First of all Naipaul's concept of the mimic men is not what many people think it is. He is dealing with a situation which he calls "cultural violation" and the consequences of such violation in which there is loss of self, an inner-self whose loss robs his people of the will or the energy to act. The people, Naipaul believes, do not act from any authentic ground or self because colonialism has shattered this inner ground. It is this emptiness which makes his people susceptible to all kinds of external notions of who they are and what they ought to be. Hence you adopt whatever role is imposed upon you from the outside, which is the case of Kripal Singh. People tell him what he should be, what he should wear, how he should behave and from those notions he forms a series of poses out of what people expect of him. Naipaul seems to be saying that you need to have some inner core to interpret the impulses which come from outside and you need to be able to be yourself in a really deep way. Because colonialism has deprived us of this capacity we are unreal on two planes: the private and the public plane: the internal and external plane, and it is this that constitutes the mimicry and places us in a trap where we can become Americans or whatever America wants us to become. We have nothing nor any ground from which to resist.

Now I'm not too certain that Eric Williams has such a complex or profound concept of mimicry or of anything. Naipaul's perception is a profound and true perception about a certain phenomenon. It is true that the colonial experience has robbed people of all sorts of things and in every sort of way, material and spiritual. Where I disagree is in that I believe that people have always been resisting that process, or have always brought some internal quality which has enabled them to interpret that process and to make something of it. I don't accept, for example, that a Black American has simply become or has been a product of the white mainstream and that he has not been creative within the context of that system. There is so much overwhelming evidence of ongoing creativity that the formula that colonialism just simply shatters and converts somebody into a nothing, a blank, seems to me to be totally unreal and I don't think it is true of the West Indies either. It is just that Naipaul denies and can give no positive weight to the little things which signal the stubborn persistence of this inner self. Four thousand folk songs were discovered in Jamaica, a few thousand more throughout the West Indies, they plus the ongoing oral traditions in song and performance signal the presence of a world which has always been there. Daniel Crowley goes to the Bahamas and finds them still an amazing storytelling people.[25] All over the West Indies you can pick up these fragments and signals of the subterranean life which has always been there, and which has always tried to make sense of the colonial or plantation experience.

So I don't fully accept Naipaul's notion of mimicry because I just don't think our people are like that. I think that his is a very intellectual notion which holds a theoretical validity but it is not totally true. We adopt what America sells, not simply because we have a void which we have to fill but, as Naipaul himself knows, because of the vigorous marketing policies of capitalist America. And it is not only we who buy their culture products. German television translates Sesame Street into German and a Japanese wins the world disco competition. Small islands under the shadow of that energetic and aggressive continent have done well so far just to be able to retain a few of the things which we have.

Eric Williams says that we move in a vicious circle because we are not liberated culturally and have no sense of who we are. So when we are faced with the necessity for choice, we make choices which reaffirm and strengthen the political or economic shackles in which we are placed. Williams is a politician who has been in a position to make history in the West Indies. What choices has he made in the direction of cultural liberation in his multi-ethnic society? Where are our archives, our historical publications, our records which could make possible a sense of continuity; our school of music, folklore, research, ethnomusicology? The fact is, Williams has simply succumbed to the culture of Carnival and Best Village competitions – Best Villages for easy votes, Carnival because it is the anodyne that the society feels it needs in order to escape from itself and its face, and because it brings in the tourist dollar.

Cudjoe: Could you explain what a Best Village Competition is?

Rohlehr: The Prime Minister's Best Village Competition is an annual contest in which villages compete with one another in song, dance and dramatic skits. It provides temporary exhibitionist visibility and functions as a palliative against governmental indifference over roads, ecology, public transport, health, agriculture, drainage and all the things which could make life in villages or town more bearable. Unprotected from the multi-company land speculator who has escalated the price of even rural land beyond everyone's reach, the villager finds consolation in an annual song-and-dance act. Best Village is thus no more than a political circus without the traditional bread.

Williams, then, has simply succumbed to the economics and the politics of our situation and has not really done anything to liberate the culture. Not that I am saying that culture can be divorced from economic or political considerations, but insofar as he has spent any money on culture it has been for the superficial areas and aspects of culture. And, if we are still in that kind of vicious circle, it is so because there remains an absence of action if not an absence of vision. I am saying that, within whatever limits we have as a society, Williams and his Party[28] have had considerable power to act in order to transform that condition.

Cudjoe: But isn't it a sort of class-position? Isn't it precisely because these guys have gone abroad (and we are not exempt, I suspect) and have been exposed to the dominant culture that they find themselves fractured and/or violated by that dominant culture that they then attempt to call their condition the condition of the masses? And, if it is true, as you say, that there are thousands of folktales which have been found and many other forms of mass-culture, could we then argue that these folk (Naipaul, Williams and others) simply generalise their conceptions and notions of society and then call these perceptions the perception of the masses?

Rohlehr: Yes, but with qualifications. One must distinguish between the independent, sceptical intelligence of the writer and the paralysed cynicism of the politician, even when both end in the same impotence. Politicians control the word and the media, and in places like Guyana their control is absolute. So that they control what is called cultural policy and, even though there is a subterranean thing that doesn't really bother too much with foreign influences, in itself it is very much open to the high pressures of marketing from America. The psyche is daily losing a hinterland for maroonage. Hence the impact of disco on the mass-culture. To view the masses as if they exist in a vacuum of purity in which they are immune to the erosive or corrosive effects of American capitalism is incorrect. They are open to these things also. So that I don't want you to get away too easily with the notion that Naipaul and Williams are only articulating their own impotence. They are also articulating an impotence which can very well be the future of the society if people like them continue to control the word and lack a vision beyond paralysis. Williams will argue that he has attempted to liberate folk culture, but he attempted to do it for political ends and in a way in which its stagnancy becomes evident almost every year.

Cudjoe: You wrote in *The Islands In Between* that only when one reads *The Middle Passage* one realises how much Naipaul has opted for anarchy and chaos as a vision of society. Do you still feel the same way or do you want to add anything to that prescription?

Rohlehr: That was written in a particular time, for even though the article came out in 1968 I had finished writing it in 1965; so that Naipaul hadn't written much besides the early novels, *The Middle Passage* and *An Area of Darkness*; *The Mimic Men* hadn't come out yet. I would say that Naipaul certainly has been consistent in these two areas (anarchy and chaos) since *The Middle Passage*. Virtually everything he has written since has affirmed the notion of the West Indies as chaotic, anarchic, unfinished and a sort of outpost in which you find the dregs of whatever Western civilisation has tried to do or be. These are areas which have remained in his writing. But I'd make the qualification, though, that what he is losing slowly and surely is a base from which to make such statements. A question he must ask himself is: "What place is not anarchic?" This is why the murder of somebody like Gale Ann Benson in Trinidad was a serious letdown for Naipaul. What was such a nice girl doing in a place like this? The point is that nice girls like her do come to places like this. Some of them come down here to the garbage heap to be screwed. In other words, people like them are not necessarily nice people. He has to begin to accept the decadence that he has been talking about as being a total human condition in which we are not particularly different from anybody else. It is this that is really happening to Naipaul: the loss of a base from which he can measure Caribbean decadence; the loss of an easy sanity. It doesn't exist in the twentieth century anymore and twentieth century writing has been saying this for the longest while. It doesn't exist. What is left is what Ezra Pound called a "botched civilisation, an old bitch gone in the teeth"[27] – either a universal sense of waste and dereliction or a kind of nihilism: a paralysed anticipation of Apocalypse. Therefore, Naipaul is left with the question of what to do when these standards no longer exist, if they ever existed at all, and when they have lost their currency. What do you do? You turn your satire towards that world as well and the only way you can do this is to produce a gallery of devitalised whites who act in counterpoint to a gallery of black anancy figures and frauds such as James Ahmed in *Guerillas*. So now you have two types: blacks who are either crazy, dishonest, anarchic or disturbed (mentally or otherwise) and whites who are decadent and impotent, homosexuals going through Africa, fake Cinderellas lost in the bush. Naipaul chooses the weakest and least heroic types to represent the white world in order to record his dismay at its failure to sustain the illusions which he had about it, and because of his inability to create really powerful people capable of what Tillich termed the courage to be.

Cudjoe: Could you say then that the kind of literature which Naipaul is now producing has simply become irrelevant both to the Third World societies and to whites who are trying to understand their own condition?

Rohlehr: I don't like to use words like irrelevant. What one deems irrelevant will depend on what one considers relevant, and there is no simple answer to that question. Naipaul is skilled at diagnosis, and the half of the truth which he illuminates is generally presented with great accuracy and penetration. We will continue to need such accuracy and penetration. Therefore I can't dismiss his vision as being irrelevant. When I want wonder, delight, affirmation, wholesomeness, positiveness and celebration, I'll simply read other writers. Here Naipaul is of limited use.

Blacks and Third World peoples are going to have to look for the centres of energy and affirmation in their own situation. They are always going to have to address themselves to the question: "What are we to do and how are we to solve our problems?" We will always be confronted by the necessity for willed choice in situations where we don't control the options. Naipaul's later work from that point of view is a dead-end because it begins with the defeatist conclusion that "the place had exhausted its possibilities." There is no point asking him that kind of question. He will answer like Roche in *Guerrillas*: "Perhaps it's a dead end for me. But I don't know why you should want me to hold out hope."[28] If nothing is possible one might as well as do nothing. That is a hopeless position, and one shouldn't expect countries caught in the real problems of choosing to accept it, however brilliant one's analysis might be. So that while I would not simply call his work irrelevant, I would say it would not serve our purpose if we wanted to understand what we have to do. It might serve the limited purpose of helping us to foresee certain types of pitfall, which is an objective Naipaul at times accepts. I would not say for one moment that we should not look out for pitfalls, but we have to look out for them in the context of action and problem-solving, not from a position of stasis and paralysis, which is the only position that Naipaul allows us.

(Published as "Talking About Naipaul" in *Carib,* No. 2 (1981) pp. 39-65).

References

1. Rohlehr, G., "Predestination, Frustration and Symbolic Darkness in Naipaul's *A House for Mr. Biswas*", *Caribbean Quarterly,* Vol. 10, No. 1, (1964) pp. 3-11.
2. Naipaul, V.S., in a BBC radio interview with Ronald Bryden, in April, 1973. The interview is reported by Hugh Lynch in "Mr. Naipaul and His 'Barbarous Background'", *Express* (Trinidad), 27 April 1973, p. 11. See also, Mel Gussov, "Writer without Roots", *New York Times Magazine,* 26 Dec., 1976.
3. Rohlehr, G., Guest Lecture on *The Mimic Men*, delivered to the English Department, UWI, Mona, Jamaica, 5 Feb. 1980. (Unpublished).
4. See also Rohlehr, G., "Man's Spiritual Search in the Caribbean through Literature", in Idris Hamid, ed. *Troubling of the Waters* (Trinidad, 1973), pp. 187-205.

5. Naipaul, V.S., *In a Free State* (London: Andre Deutsch, 1971).
6. "What the Twilight Says: An Overture" in *Dream on Monkey Mountain and Other Plays* (New York: Farrar, Straus & Giroux, 1970), 3-40.
7. Robbe-Grillet, A., *For a New Novel: Essays in Fiction* (New York: Grove Press, 1965).
8. Gide, A., *Travels in the Congo* (Berkeley: 1962; originally published Paris, 1927).
9. Beckett, S., *Malone Dies* (London: Penguin, 1958).
10. Ellison, R., *Invisible Man,* Chap. 12. (Penguin edn., pp 216-226).
11. Naipaul, V.S., *The Mimic Men* (London: Deutch, 1967), Part II, Chap. 4, pp. 177-180.
12. Goveia, E., *A Study on The Historiography of the British West Indies to the End of the Nineteenth Century* (Mexico: 1956).
13. Sewell, W.G., *The Ordeal of Free Labour in the British West Indies* (New York: 1861).
14. Underhill, E., *The West Indies: Their Social and Religious Condition* (London: 1862). Republished by Negro Universities Press, Connecticut, 1970.
15. Thomas, J.J., *Froudacity* (London: 1889). Republished by New Beacon Books, London. 1969.
16. Salmon, C.S., The *Caribbean Confederation, a Plan for the Union of the Fifteen British West Indian Colonies* (London, n.d.)
17. Ryan, W., *Blaming the Victim* (New York: Random House, Vintage Books, 1971).
18. Achebe, C., has made this kind of observation on *Heart of Darkness* in various places. See, for instance, his "Viewpoint", *Times Literary Supplement*, (1 Feb., 1980), p. 113.
19. Lucie-Smith, E., "West Indian Writing", *London Magazine,* Vol. 8, No. 4 (July 1968) pp. 96-102.
20. Walsh, W., *V.S. Naipaul* (Edinburgh: Oliver & Boyd, 1973).
21. Ramchand, K., "Concern for Criticism", *Caribbean Quarterly,* Vol. 16, No. 2, (June 1970), pp. 51-60.
22. Wynter, S., "Reflections on W.I. Writing and Criticism", *Jamaica Journal,* Vol. 2, No. 4 and Vol. 3, No. 1, (1968-69). See also Sylvia Wynter, "Creole Criticism: A Critique", *New World Quarterly,* Vol 5, No. 28, (13 July 1975).
23. Brathwaite, E., "Caribbean Critics", *Critical Quarterly*, Vol. 2. No 3, (Autumn 1969), pp. 268-276. Also published in *New World Quarterly,* Vol. 5, Nos. 1 & 2, (1969), pp. 12-34.
24. Rohlehr, G, "An Interview on V.S. Naipaul", *Tapia,* Vol. 5, No. 27, (6 July 1975) and Vol. 5, No. 28, (13 July 1975).
25. Crowley, D., *I Could Tell Old Story Good: Creativity in Bahamian Folklore* (Berkeley & Los Angeles: University of California Press, 1966).
26. The People's National Movement, led by Prime Minister Eric Williams (from 1956 until his death in 1981), is the leading political party in Trinidad and Tobago. Eric Williams, a leading international scholar, was the author of the famous work *Capitalism and Slavery*, as well as of *From Columbus to*

Castro. Gordon Rohlehr reviewed the latter in Orde Coombs, *Is Massa Day Dead* (New York: Doubleday/Anchor, 1974).
27. Pound, E., "E.P. Ode Pour L'Election de Son Sepulcre", Section IV.
28. Naipaul, V.S., *Guerillas*, Chap. 13.

"ASSASSINS OF THE VOICE":
MARTIN CARTER'S *POEMS OF AFFINITY 1978-1980*

When I first met Martin Carter in December 1980 – I'd known his work for twenty years and taught it for ten, but had been living outside of Guyana for nineteen years – I could hear these poems in the way he spoke. He seemed to be trying to communicate the urgency and meaning of a horror which he had seen. He was spasmodic of utterance, cryptic and fragmented, as many of these *Poems of Affinity* are, yet electric and warm and able to make the fragments cohere, as many of these poems do. It was only six months since Walter Rodney's death, the culmination of a series of violent political events, some of which Carter had witnessed, once in the intimate capacity of a victim.

In June 1978 Carter had been attacked and beaten while he was demonstrating against the referendum, by which the People's National Congress (PNC) in Guyana sought fifteen additional months in office, the time necessary to draft a new Constitution which would bestow on its leaders absolute dominion and eternal life. He had also been in the July 1979 demonstration when the Roman Catholic priest, Fr. Bernard Darke, was murdered in broad daylight, an incident which gave rise to his poem "Bastille Day – Georgetown", and to his "Open Letter to the People of Guyana", where he defined his role as citizen in a degraded society. The cameras of Trinidad and Tobago Television focused briefly on his shell-shocked face during the funeral of Walter Rodney, where Lamming in his oration quoted Carter's bitter condemnation of the regime as "assassins of the voice".

Carter's "Open Letter to the People of Guyana" provides the perfect context for his latest collection of poems, *Poems of Affinity* 1978-1980, a slim, stark volume which, along with those courageous Working People's Alliance (WPA) newsletters, provides us with depressing testimony as to the quality of life in the Cooperative Republic. Carter writes in the "Open Letter":

> Like all other regimes of similar character, the PNC's main preoccupation is self-perpetuation. In principle the preoccupation with self-perpetuation is understandable, since it accords with the fundamental idea of self-preservation. But while a truly democratic regime would try to ensure self-perpetuation by acting in a way such as would make it acceptable

and needed by people, what does the PNC, which poses as socialist, actually do?

> The PNC's method of ensuring self-perpetuation consists of indulging in a deliberate policy of degrading people. And the reasoning behind this is that degraded people are incapable of effective resistance.

Carter then proceeds to cite examples of such degradation: the rigging of elections, the reduction of honest people to a norm of cheating and lying, the regime's rigid control of

> mass media in which the very language used is perversion; facts falsified; threats against individuals and groups openly advertised; internal events of significance ignored; local events of significance suppressed; all contributing to the whole process of assault on moral and intellectual honesty, one end of which is to make mental independence a crime, and mental subservience to the regime the highest qualification in the land.[1]

The result of this Carter defines as "warp of personality and degradation of spirit."

Two questions are posed by this context where perversion of the word leads to perversion of thought and deed, and ultimately to subservience and degradation of spirit: (i) what perspectives for political action and involvement does Carter perceive in a scenario of growing absolutism and (ii) how does the Muse, the spirit of poetry, sensibility and honest utterance survive in such an environment? The relevance of these questions is, of course, by no means limited to the Guyanese scenario.

Carter in the "Open Letter" answers the first question by suggesting two necessary lines of political action: (i) "Resistance to the brute fact of degradation itself. Resistance to the exploitation of this degradation by the regime" which should take the form of "individual repudiation and civil disobedience." (ii) Exposure of the regime's "ideology of self-perpetuation." Carter's answer to the second question has involved a definition both of the situation of the artist and of his active responsibility in a context of both political and existential exigency.

In a statement entitled "The Location of the Artist", Carter describes art as a form of "negative productivity (which) presupposes a process of positive productivity as its environment". He goes on to explain what he means:

> The first consideration to be dealt with concerning art and the artist has to do with satisfaction and fulfilment. This satisfaction and fulfilment has to do with the development of self-consciousness. Self-consciousness itself is an issue, itself subsumed by the issue that subsumes all issues: human fate. The artist cannot change the nature of this fate: all he can do is endure it. At the same time it is his society which has to provide the conditions that make this fate endurable. It is in these senses that art is described as negative productivity and positive productivity suggested as the required environment of the artist. Where there should be interaction of negative and positive productivity we find instead only the contiguity of two negative productivities, one seeking to retain its integrity through

independence and autonomy, the other attempting to assimilate this independence and autonomy into a system which, since it does not have the requirements of positive productivity, is not in a position to offer co-existential status.[2]

The artist's responsibility in this context is defined again and again in *Poems of Affinity*. These poems are often about politics, and do offer a perspective of "resistance" and "exposure". But they are also about time, endurance and people's unfulfilled abuse of their grim time. If politics is constant degradation of peoples' sensibility, a diet of decaying language, and ultimately an assassination of the voice, time is neutral process in which all life is caught. If resistance to corruption of the word and its corollary, clarity of utterance, are a political imperative for the citizen, resistance to the riddle of fatality, time and death through constant exploration of Self in Cosmos and Cosmos in Self[3] becomes the existential responsibility of the artist.

"Our Time", the first poem in the collection, explores both the political and the existential situations. Here Carter notes the failure of people to create their "time".

> The more men of our time we are
> the more our time is. But always
> we have been somewhere else.

"Time" here means a particular historic moment People create their time by investing their historic moment with the energy of effort. Meaning and identity are connected to, and grow from the quality of creative sensibility, the fineness of our response to our moment.[4] "But always we have been somewhere else." Here, as elsewhere in the collection, time and place are equated, and the word "place" could easily replace the word "time" in the first two lines.

In order to illustrate our abject failure to create our time, Carter employs an image drawn from the Guyana landscape: that of the crab holes[5] which become visible when water drains out of canals, and ooze slime and muddy bubbles as the crabs emerge or hide. Thus, the people who should articulate their resistance loud and clear are heard:

> Muttering
> our mouths like holes in the mud
> at the bottom of trenches

The corruption of the voice, the rot of the word, is suggested in the phonic similarity between "muttering", "mouths" and "mud". Our failure to be people of our time is related to a failure in articulate statement, here given an implied quality of putrescence and suppuration. And this failure is the result of a failure in resistance.

> Badly abused
> we fail to curse. Our fury pleads.

Carter returns to this theme later in the collection in "Our Voice Betrays", where, "Caring too little", the people surrender their birthright to a parvenu regime – symbolised by a voracious stray dog – and blindfold themselves rather than face the truth of what they have become. The fact that Carter there says "Everything blindfolds", rather than "Everyone", indicates that the people, "caring too little", have reified themselves, or allowed the regime to reify them.

The consequences of apathy and self-evasion are explored in the next poem, "Playing Militia". Carter in his "Open Letter" had cited as an example of degradation:

> the militarisation of the people in which poorly fed children are made to march in the sun like soldiers, playing militia at the expense of their lessons; in which paramilitary forces enjoy a spurious social prestige at the expense of the rights of their fellow citizens; thereby putting a premium on authoritarian bullying in clear mirror image of the behaviour of the leaders of the regime; all serving to bring about in the consciousness of people and their children that parading is more important than learning, and uniforms more important than a respect for law.[6]

In "Playing Militia" Carter presents the various military and paramilitary groups as examples of a loss of individual personhood. A people has acquiesced in its own degradation and pays the price in a devaluation of their uniqueness. He also notes that the children are being robbed of their childhood and of their innocence ("girls unbreasted, boys ungamed"). Loss of uniqueness is presented as being contrary to the very spirit of nature which allows each object, leaf, flower or fruit, its originality and distinctness. Even in the cemetery where things are equal, they are also separate. The Guyana regime, then, has actually outdone Death; they have succeeded in making an entire nation indistinct, an undifferentiated mass of faceless uniforms which can scarcely conceal the inner festering.

> the sleeves
> of uniforms droop
> like the wet feathers of a crow's wing
> over secret carrion

Here the scorn is conveyed by a power and precision of image. "Droop", for example, captures both the ill-fitting appearance of the uniforms and the jaded spiritless exhaustion of these children, whose tiredness is the nation's. "Secret" captures the very quality of the regime, who have made accomplices of these cruelly misguided children. It is a quality of suspicion, a secretiveness out of which flowers scandal.[7] At the centre of each secret is decay.

There is also the beginning of a kind of wordplay, extreme in poets such as Brathwaite and Questel and frequently evident in Walcott, though absent from earlier Carter.

> the phalloid needles of sewing machines
> have sown a new drill

"Phalloid" is overdone, but it does imply the rumour that sexual exploitation of young women has occurred in National Service camps. True or false, such allegations are a natural result of the secretiveness with which much is done in Guyana. "Needles" suggests that the people are being innoculated with some loathsome serum or sperm. One notes, too, the subtle shift in spelling and meaning from "sewing" to "sown", the latter word definitely implying the mechanical insemination of the people by water and the word, semen and propaganda. Then there is the more obvious wordplay on "a new drill" where "drill" is both the green khaki of uniforms and the military exercises of these fake soldiers, as well as the monotonous catechism of State propaganda, by which children and adults are made ready for the new life. Such wordplay enables the poet to explore several layers of meaning at the same time and in an economy of space.

The counter-poem to this is "Let Every Child Run Wild", and it comes very late in the collection. In this moving exhortation, Carter reveals a Blakean sense of the sanctity of childhood, whose destruction evoked the bitter "Playing Militia". "Let Every Child Run Wild" has a freer movement and is less laconic than most of the poems of affinity. The wild freedom of children in the rain suggests the elemental, the primal, the ancestral.

> Rain is a cousin
> of air, the blood of parents

The children's freedom, endorsed by the poet's imperative "Let every child!" suggests guitar music.

> Let every child run wild, or stop,
> or stop the way men journey
> through the earth's loop, the freedom
> of a guitar

The alternatives are to permit the young the joy of their youth, or stop the wild guitar melody of their freedom by entrammelling them in the noose of the adult world.

It is for having done the latter that Carter condemns the regime, and the poem leaves us with a vision of freedom curtailed:

>   the still air
> of a child's wild guitar
>
>   shuddering in the silence
> of parents

"Shuddering" is powerfully suggestive of the sudden terror which overtakes the children as their parents interrupt their game in the rain. As in

Blake, the parents represent experience, authority and the inhibitions imposed by centralised authoritarianism. The "parents" are the regime's censorship of peoples' freedoms, a censorship which is exemplified by their attempts to commandeer even occasions for celebration, depriving them of the spontaneity which gave them point, and imposing on them the rigid paramilitary monotony of the State's "new drill".

Carter frequently asserts the need for vigilance or active rebellion.

> In this foul age of a new
> and recurring despair, I
> keep working for a storm, some
> kind of fury to write new dates
> in our vile calendar and book.
> ("Some Kind of Fury", p. 53)

Here the connection between assertive rebellion, the act of making and the redemption of debased time is made explicit. What, however, is the fate of those who aren't obviously in step with the regime?

"Paying Fares" provides us with the answer. Here Carter describes the results of that loss of uniqueness and individuality noted in "Playing Militia". People who have so abjectly acquiesced in their own depersonalisation lose the capacity to value the uniqueness and survival efforts of others. In this poem, we see the people waiting for the bus of collective deliverance, the poem taking place between their waiting and the bus's arrival.

> Waiting for the bus
> they see him, the powerful crab
> edging sideways through the silt
> of their lives.

If in "Black Friday" the crab was a symbol of the brief triumph of the citizens' rebellion before the high tide of repression obliterates them, here it is a symbol of survival, cunning retreat, aloneness and a saving instinct for resistance. The crab's triumph here is to have remained itself in a time when everyone is expected to jump or be coerced into jumping on the collective bandwagon.

The shell of the crab, the armour of irreducible personhood within which and behind which the poetic vision dwells, the shuttered "flags" of his window blinds which allow him to see through the regime without being seen, are the targets of the system's instinct for destruction. The word "flags" mocks the State's anthem-and-flag nationalism. The questions

> What, they wonder
> does he eat, and who
> his obeahman?

are grimly humorous. The first refers to the regime's tendency to victimise its opponents by denying them employment. The crab survives such spiteful meanness and menace. The second refers to the legalisation of obeah in Guyana,[8] by which the State sought to appropriate one of the survival mechanisms of those driven to desperation by the extreme psychic distress which life in the cooperative republic has inflicted on people. The powerful crab is agnostic and lives without such a prop.

Carter fully understands that to live without the moral muck and silt of the regime's patronage is to invite its reflexive viciousness. Nor are the people on the poet's side. They are more likely to turn in fury and spite on the isolated rebel whose courage is also the measure of their own cowardice, and whose independence of spirit becomes a symbol of the fineness which they have denied in themselves. Rather than bear the shame of admitting this, they adopt a victim-making psychology, and willingly become henchmen and assassins for the regime. They plan to set his house afire:

> but cloth
> can burn, they mutter, paying fares

There is, it should be noted, an almost opposite line of interpretation of "Paying Fares". In this simpler, but quite feasible analysis, "the powerful crab" becomes Burnham; his "edging" and oblique movement would then be the menacing secretiveness of his relationship to citizens whose material and moral existence he has reduced to muck. The citizen as lesser crab wonders about the private life of his leader. Does he indeed, as it is rumoured, savour the finest of local and foreign cuisine while reducing their diet to silt? By what mysterious necromancy has he sustained his relentless grip on power? The "flags" of his curtained windows could then be the tawdry nationalist sloganeering to which political vision and public understanding have become reduced; while the final bitterly muttered threat "but cloth/can burn" would then be the people's as yet unarticulated resentment as they reluctantly pay yet another pay hike for goods and services which, like the mythical bus, never arrive. "Paying fares" can refer generally to the price the nation has been paying for the ride on which their leaders are taking them. Carter itemised this price in the "Open Letter" quoted above. One notes, however; that in Guyana, "fares" is the name given to a prostitute's fee. Carter may be implying that those who do the regime's dirty work are undergoing a most peculiar whoredom, in that they pay the very regime which has reduced them to a prostitution of spirit, for reducing them to such prostitution.

The daylight murder of Father Darke was the most glaring example of such prostitution of spirit. Carter's witness of this barely credible crime led him to the bitterest condemnation of his people.

> I have at last started
> to understand the origin
> of our vileness, and being

> unable to deny it, I suggest
> its nativity

His use of the word "nativity" is an act of deliberate desecration, by which Carter seeks to convey his perception of the murder as a kind of monstrous birth, a reversal of the Incarnation in which the Word was humanised, the diabolical genesis of "vileness".

The title "Bastille Day – Georgetown", is bitterly ironic, since its aim is to locate the Guyanese struggle in a context of international proletarian revolt, thereby exposing the former as a nauseating insult to the history of the working class. Guyanese sans-culottes don't rise up against an aristocracy of corruption; they murder for a mess of pottage ("a pot of rice"). Yet Carter declares, hope issuing out of the depth of such hopelessness,

> In the shame of knowledge
> of our vileness, we shall fight

Shame can indeed be a source of revolutionary defiance, since it requires the consciousness of a sense of limits, the recognition of a point beyond which behaviour ought not to be allowed to deteriorate. Carter holds open the barest perspective for the rebirth of consciousness and conscience out of shame, and with consciousness/conscience, the will to fight.

But the will to fight is only the beginning. The real issue is whether the confrontation between the people and the regime will result in the positive transformation of the society. For that to happen, both the people and the regime must experience shame, a sense of limits and sanctions leading to a rebirth in consciousness. If shame can result in a strengthening of people's will to struggle, it ought ideally to result in a recognition by the regime of the necessity for compromise and imaginative flexibility in its dealings with people. Compromise will involve here what Paolo Freire termed consciencisation: a recognition of the people's right towards participation in defining both their objectives, and the means of deploying their energies and labour in the attaining of those objectives.

The picture of the regime which Carter has painted in *Poems of Affinity* includes no evidence that it is capable of shame, or will recognise any sanctions except those which it has itself imposed on the people. Nonconformity, as we saw in "Paying Fares", is greeted with ferocious recrimination which, more than any absence of shame or conscience, is what keeps Guyanese apparently passive, and positively afraid of the active and visible defiance which Carter advocates. Their resistance tends to be passively subversive – as in the peasant who deliberately underproduces, hoping thereby, obscurely, to starve out the supporters of the regime – or escapist, as in the thousands who have migrated to the West Indies, Suriname, the USA and Canada, some of whom have been seeking the status of political refugees in the countries of their adoption. Thousands of highly skilled people whose unmolested existence in Guyana the regime couldn't permit, have revolted by leaving, the stories of their escape providing lively testimony of the real ingenuity of the people in sidestepping degradation at the hands of the regime. Hundreds of smugglers, hustlers, hucksters, are part of an alternative subsistence economy which, in fact, challenges and undermines the regime's rigid economic sanctions, but ultimately at the expense of the proletariat, who have to pay hugely inflated prices on the black market for commodities which the State can neither afford nor supply.

Carter never acknowledges the quality of passive resistance which the Guyanese people have revealed. It is, in his opinion, not a means of fighting for transformation, but a type of evasion, a being "elsewhere" ("Our Time") when our historic moment calls for confrontation. But he is aware of the possible consequences of the people's confrontation with a regime that has time and again signalled its preparedness to employ the various military forces at its disposal against the people whose "fares" have paid for those forces. Carter's response to the State's potential for recriminatory overkill is verbal defiance, a bitter scorn which, while it conveys resistance, also implies political impotence.

This scorn is communicated through his application of feral imagery to the regime. In "In a Certain Time", he contrasts the regime's abuse of the mouth – "old jaws and a toothless snarl" – with his own use of language as resistance and vigilance.

> But as an owl hoots
> to startle the vile eye of a toad
> and initiate its own defiance of dark:
> I also speak. Having despised
> all fangs, I neither have nor want
> a time to bite.

If this sounds a bit extreme, like an echo of the 1953 Carter, it is worth pointing out that soon after this poem was written, the regime acknowledged its own saurian nature when it adopted as part of the insignia of the Guyana presidency, the cayman, a particularly voracious black crocodile.[9] No shame there at all; no capacity for consciencisation; only the persistent signalling through word and symbol, of a potential for naked ferocity; only a perversion of language and sign which deepens in proportion to the degradation of consciousness.

II

As we have already seen from our examination of "Our Time", the political poems of this volume are generally about other things besides politics. One of those things is time. In "I Still Stare" we have a characteristic poem on this theme. The poet emotionlessly stares at his future (death) through the window of vision. His unillusioned stare "beyond a pattern of stars" is in no way connected to earlier dreams. "Pattern" suggests that the future has been prearranged and astrologically fixed. Beyond the pattern is impenetrable void in face of which the act of writing becomes a motiveless reflex.

> Our hands have
> written. They will continue to write
> always the same.

Everything, including his writing, will be absorbed in "the time beyond sundown." "Being Always" is a similar sort of poem. It begins,

> Being, always to arrange
> myself in the world, and the world
> in myself, I try to do both.

The strange syntax – a characteristic of these poems – suggests Carter's preoccupation with the ontological/existential problem of the nature and implications of being. "Being" involves (a) perpetual location, what Carter calls "arrangement" of Self in Cosmos and (b) constant "arrangement" of Cosmos in Self. The word "arrange" suggests falsification, fabrication, the deliberate invention of otherwise nonexistent relationships between things which are utterly "other", totally separate.

Such fabrication is, of course, second nature to the poet, particularly to the twentieth-century post-romantic, post-symbolist, post-everything poet. But Carter takes no comfort in what he arranges, because he feels that life itself is an arrangement in which men are time's puppets:

>   time's
> doll house of replaceable heads
> arms and legs

to be assembled or discarded like the world itself, when its time comes. Ultimately, both ontological and existential questions, as well as aesthetic ones, lose their point. Here we are as far as possible from Carter's passionate avowal of the necessity for political confrontation.

There are less hopeless and more complex poems on the same theme. "As New and as Old" and "As New and as Old ii" or "With That Loan" posit a far more complicated relationship between man and time. The first of these begins with a riddling statement:

> Every day is as old
> as a new day is

"Old" and "new" mean the same thing in the neutral process of time. Night and day are twin illusions, the one ruled by stars, the other by the sun. But the difference is false, since both are manifestations of time as neutral process. Writing too is illusion; but it is also an act of desperate and utterly necessary faith in a time and place of crawling things and people.

The last lines of the poem pose some difficulty since initially they seem unrelated to the rest of the poem:

> Having betrayed
> old gods in an old day, we seek
> now to betray new ones
> in a new day

They suggest that the avowal of faith and the reality of betrayal are, like everything else, part of a fixed pattern. Carter seems to be questioning the strength of his political commitment in the face of his existential despair. Full of self-recrimination and self-doubt, he discloses a nakedly honest, driven, unillusioned and unhoping self beneath the political one. This self, caught up in the neutral process of time, experiences what T.S. Eliot in *The Dry Salvages* described as:

> the trailing
> consequence of further days and hours,
> While emotion takes to itself the emotionless
> Years of living among the breakage
> Of what was believed in as the most reliable –
> And therefore the fittest for renunciation.[10]

Carter is, if anything, bleaker, more "emotionless" than Eliot in the grip of the succession of new/old days, and his sense of man's continual betrayal of his faiths.

The second poem entitled "As New and as Old ii" starts with nearly the same riddle, one that could have been taken from *Ecclesiastes* whose theme is the cyclic sameness of time, and the unnewness of things under the sun.

> This morning is new, but the sun
> that made it is old

There is a connection in both of these As New and as Old poems, between the sense of being ridden by a vast impersonal process, time, and the development of (i) a stoical toughness shot through with anguish (ii) a sense of the undifferentiated sameness of all things – good/evil, happiness/grief, truth/falsehood, faith/betrayal; (iii) a capacity to affirm and negate in the same breath, or to negate what one has affirmed. So Carter listens to "the world's great grief" which, like his confessed tendency towards betrayal, is both new and old.

> a kind of music we listen to and hear
> when the toil of silence builds
> our house of language in this wind's
> throat, the grim larynx

The "music" Carter listens to and hears, is of a decidedly starker quality than Wordsworth's "still sad music of humanity"; for the things in which Wordsworth had faith – Nature, harmony, a process of reconciliation, the consolation of philosophy when elation waned – are all, despite "Let Every Child Run Wild", more normally rejected as impossible props in Carter's vision of the world. Carter suggests both the inner ordeal of making ("toil of silence") and the fierceness of external stimuli ("this wind's throat, the grim larynx") against which his voice must assert itself. This dialectic of introversion and extroversion, elsewhere illustrated by the extreme tension between existential and political concerns, gives the poem its severity, its fiercely affirmative quality.

As with the first of these poems, the final focus is as much on society as it is on the poet. The "our" of the penultimate line assumes a communal quality which it did not have earlier in the poem, even though the "We" is still the poet.

> A green leaf
> on the branch of a tree fingers
> our time's disgraceful space. We
> are its measure.

"Our" here refers to society; the word "disgraceful" makes this clear. "Disgraceful" and "vile" have become favourite words with Carter for describing Guyana. The "green leaf" here is not the symbol of explosive rebellion that it was in "Death of a Comrade",[11] it is, rather, an example of renewal in Nature, an illustration of the cyclic movement in life, the naturalness which in "Playing Militia" Carter describes his society as having insulted.

We emerge from this poem with two notions of the poet's commitment: (i) in the very process of making he listens to, shapes and defies the cold neutrality of time and (ii) when he looks outside of himself at his society, he measures the degree of its disgraceful abuse of the wide waste of its time.

In "With That Loan", Carter begins with an even more puzzling riddle, whose relationship to what follows isn't immediately obvious.

> A tick on the flank
> of a beast is also
> a beast; as every answer
> creature of a question

Its implication is that everything is generically related to its apparent opposite: the parasite to its source of nourishment, the victim to his oppressor, the answer to its question. The poet's relationship to time is that of a lesser parasite to a greater. He derives nourishment from a process which is slowly devouring him. The poet, then, is simultaneously trickster-hero and inevitable loser, Anansi, the web-spinner of riddles, himself caught up in time's snare.

>   In
> this world   time is a snare
> and I am masticated
> by its jaw. All I could have
> and have done was to borrow
> its tongue. With that loan
> I have gained a mastery
> of the language of our negative yes.

Kamau Brathwaite[12] correctly sees this poem as being representative of the spirit of the entire collection. Carter's universe, abandoned by old gods and new becomes, like Eliot's, subject to time. But whereas Eliot struggles to relocate God at the centre of his universe and so redeem time and resolve paradox, for Carter time remains eternally present and unredeemable. The result is that, for Carter, each act of affirmative faith is also an act of negation; and each act of choice returns him to the opacity of a neutralising process which confounds both lucidity of vision and the faith implicit in all choosing. So that he says "yes" and "no" in one and the same breath.

This results in a poetry of constant paradox, which is characterised by what I have termed the "riddle". The riddle is an attempt to give concrete shape to a perception of ambivalence. It depends on a correspondence between an image and its "meaning". We must be able to move from an image – often one that describes the "behaviour" of an animal, plant or object – to some human or general situation. The riddle here is like the proverb in traditional African folk tales, with the difference that the proverb is a condensation or concretised summary of the story which precedes it, while with the riddle we have no elaborate tale, only the crystallisation of paradox, of trick, of spell, of rune. What Carter does is to present us with imperfect riddles; riddles in which the image doesn't quite correspond to the idea which it seeks to convey. This gives many of his later poems a cryptic quality, even an incoherence, since at times the reader is confronted with a succession of apparently unrelated images, or of images unhinged from their suggested "meanings".

In "Rice" the peasant, like the poet, is caught in time's and nature's riddle, the apparently pointless alternation of seasons, neither of which fulfils hope. Here again we have the vision of *Ecclesiastes*: son succeeds father, new moon full moon; but nothing changes: The cycle is unhallowed by any ritual which might give meaning to its implacability. What replaces the circle of meaning is paradox, whose archetypal form is the riddle or the rune. Hence the poem begins with a riddle as the poet/peasant seeks words which will, at least, describe the trap of time. Borrowing time's language of paradox where yes and no complement each other, the poet becomes, like time, an equivocator.

The peasant, caught in what is really the same paradox waits in drought for rain to grow his "harvests of wind padi" – itself an image of unfulfilment

– a harvest of grainless husk, analogous to the poet's futile harvest of time's language. The peasant, like the poet, questions not only his own waiting for rain, but the whole process of time. His first question/statement is a simple riddle, to which he supplies a simple answer.

> What is rain for, if not rice
> for an empty pot

One notes, though, that the suggested answer to the first riddle is itself stated in question form, and leaves open the possibility that rain might well be for something else – flood, for example. It could be a destructive as well as a regenerative force, as Carter noted in early poems such as "University of Hunger" and "Not Hands Like Mine".

The second riddle, though, asks "What is the use of a pot when there is no food in the village?" This is the question for which we were being set up. There are no illusions here about a fostering Nature or a loving Providence; only a sense of trap and pointlessness. So the peasant, like the poet, imitates time. He too becomes trickster, Anansi, master of the riddle.

> In his calculations
> his yield was the share he would reap
> when he cheated, like the moon and the sea.

The riddle, then, is the form which man creates when he perceives paradox and his helplessness in the face of cosmic incongruity. The trickster emerges when he pretends an illusory mastery over a fickle universe.

In "Beans of God" the poet assumes the peasant persona. Society is as indifferent to the poet's toil as Nature is to the peasant's. The poet works in an indeterminate twilight between the sunlight of reality and the moonlight of a waning illusion, just as the peasant is caught between and mocked by the twin seasons of drought and flood.[14] The poet also works in the poorest of ground – the hard, blank foot-trodden concrete pavements of the city, in whose cracks only the toughest weeds survive. He is planting, of all things, the beans of God.

> On the pavements
> of the feet of cripples I plant
> the green pods of the beans of God.

Glowing and alive, these are the most affirmative lines of the entire collection. They attest to the sacredness of the poet's role, despite its apparent futility. Beans don't grow on concrete and even if they did, could scarcely survive the trampling, crippled feet of his society. Yet the poet – no longer trickster but the related figures of magician and wise fool – plants, his song a challenge to the system's concrete.

We end this essay with an examination of three poems, "Our Number", "Bent" and "Ground Doves", each of which offers a different clue as to how

Carter perceives his role and responsibility as poet in a degraded society. "Our Number" is an attempt to connect image and idea in a less riddling manner than, say, "With That Loan" or "Too Much Waiting". The scene is the foreshore at low tide. The focus is on a shrill-tongued fishwife counting shrimp. One of the ideas that emerges is that the people are shrimp in the hands of their leaders – the abusive fishwife – and have been born out of "a way of counting", an economic and totally materialistic system. "Census", the penultimate poem, wittily connects this "way of counting" with rigged elections.

The poet responds to and transforms the objects which he perceives outside the cranium's bare space. One notes an extreme compression of syntax which includes the use of adjectives and nouns as verbs ("irregular" in line one or "denizen" in line eight) and the omission of words ("the tide has gone [and left?] them bare"). This last image is most certainly a reference to Carter's poetry in which the language is for the most part pruned of rhetoric and bare and clean. The fisherman, who in "Till I Collect" had served as an image of the poet as dreamer, has here brought home a meagre catch.

The poet is resigned to both the barrenness of imagination and the squalor of politics. Yet there is still the effort at defiance. He shares in the seagull's and the seawife's desperation, in their querulous struggle for food and their defiance of "the tide that naked skins us." Tide here is both abstract process of time and the political regime which flays (skins) us and leaves us naked. The fishwife who, with relation to the shrimp, may represent the power of authority to falsify the accounts and census lists, is herself fragile and helpless in the grip of time and tide.

In "Bent", what strikes one immediately is the stark clarity of the image, the naked brilliance of light in which it is seen:

> On the street, the sun
> rages. The bent back of
> an old woman resurrects
> the brimmed bucket of this world's
> light and insupportable
> agony. A damage of years

Here there may be the faintest echoes of "The Fabulous Well" sequence from Harris's *Eternity to Season*,[15] though Carter, it must be stressed, normally displays little of Harris's interest in the mythic, the ancestral, the primal, or his sense of the possibility of reconciliation. The old woman is the Muse. She has endured in spite of the "damage of years" and has something of the eternal quality of Wordsworth's Leechgatherer, as well as his bent hoop-like shape, "feet and head/Coming together in life's pilgrimage."[16] The Muse as fetcher of water resembles the slave of antiquity, yet her servitude brings light, and her task is a redemptive one. She is Carter Agonistes, the artist/victim whose agony is "light" in both the adjectival and the nominal senses, because he has willingly chosen to bear it, and because he seeks the halo of illumination which it bestows.[17] But the agony is also "insupportable" because the burden is cosmic. It is "the world's light", the sun reflected in the circular mirror of the full bucket of water, which she "resurrects." This connects her with Apollo, sun god and patron of music and poetry, Atlas the world-bearer, and Christ the resurrected son/sun of God. The word "resurrects" is itself ambiguous, and reconciles the paradox of intolerable Sisyphean ordeal and transcension, because it can mean both "lifts again and again" and "rises again from the dead". The second meaning also accords the Muse victory over injurious time.

The impulse towards art is a driven need, an incredible thirst in the spirit, the primal necessity for grace (water). It is

> the crushed cloud
> of an incredible want

which has drawn the aging, crippled Muse, Legba's sister, out into the sun's inferno. In that fierce heat and stark light, she's both caught and apotheosised, and enduring, partakes of the cosmic. The eternal sky, "blue and ever", imitates her, shares her curved state and perhaps her blues. She is finally both the victim of a hostile cosmos and a paradigm from which the universe devises its own curvature and bent. This is, perhaps, the poem in which Carter best reconciles the two responsibilities which he outlines in "Being Always", that of locating Self in Cosmos and Cosmos in Self, or, as he states it elsewhere, that of going through the open-ended process of becoming that identity is: "a process and becoming in which even without a conscious intention on the part of the human agent, the objective world is humanised and the human world objectivised."[18]

In "Ground Doves", the Muse, here imaged by the doves which in Guyana are known as God-birds, seeks refuge from "our time's new wind." Here, as in "Bastille Day – Georgetown" and "Bent", the imagery is religious. Grace, holiness, the Word of God, the Paraclete, here associated with a quality of sensibility, faces asphyxiation in an atmosphere of the perverted use of language and sign. Our degradation begins with the corruption of the Word. Attempting to escape, the doves, who are anima, irreducible spirit, seek their element, the air. But then, tragically,

> On electric wires
> which stretch from nowhere
> to somewhere, they perch to perish
> with singed feathers

The refuge which the doves seek is dislocated in space, rooted nowhere and stretching towards an indefinite somewhere little different from that nowhere. Those stretched high-tension wires have featured in several twentieth century poets[19] as an image of neurosis, the mind's short-circuit. The choice offered is to live in and through the foetid swamp of society and politics, or alienation in a nowhere region where the soul's electricity short-circuits, and the mind snaps under its hypertension.

There is a faint suggestion of hubris and fall, but this is outweighed by the presentation of the doves as true though fragile souls. They are ordinary and average, identifiable as "you and I". They are, in fine, the attainable goodness of the average person, which becomes fugitive in an oppressive ethos. The poet, part of their community of fear, advocates a duty of compassion.

> We shall have
> to pick them up. And burn our hands.

The victims' lives can be given meaning, their efforts to preserve humanity rendered more than a dead letter, if those of us who once shared in their timidity participate in this final act of retrieval. The price of such participation is vicarious suffering – imaged by the singeing of the hands – sustained in an act of rendering meaning to our pain: in an act of com/passion, a consciously chosen fellow-suffering which is absolutely necessary, if we are collectively to survive the broken wind of unchange in our "swamp of vapours".

Carter, as poet of a society which he considers degraded, frequently finds himself in the dilemma of the anti-hero of modern confessional fiction: how to castigate a society for a degradation which one often recognises within oneself. His position is that of Camus's Judge-Penitent of *The Fall,* Jean Baptiste Clamence, who assumes the role of his biblical namesake, John the Baptist, but modifies it considerably by describing himself as a shabby prophet for shabby times. Carter summarises his problematic position in a phrase from one of these poems: "Accursed, I curse." Clamence's claim is that he is conscious of his own degradation and that it is this which earns him the right to castigate his supine brethren. Carter redeems and justifies the poet who "makes a victim of himself",[20] not only through his social role of resisting the regime's perversions, but also in his existential role as one who achieves apotheosis through the painful shaping of his meaning and his moment out of the neuter waste of time.

(First published as 'The Poet and Citizen in a Degraded Community: Martin Carter's *Poems of Affinity* (1978-1980) in "Cultural Resistance and the Guyana State", First Caribbean Conference of Intellectual Workers, Grenada, November 20-22, 1982).

References

1. Carter, M., "Open Letter to the People of Guyana", in "Guyana's National Poet Calls for Resistance", *Caribbean Contact* (Sept, 1979) p. 9.
2. Carter, M., "The Location of the Artist", *Release*, Vols. 8 & 9 (1979), pp. 3-4.
3. Carter, M., "Being Always", *Poems of Affinity* 1978-1980 (Georgetown: Release Publishers, 1980).
4. Carter, M., *Man and Making: Victim and Vehicle*, The Edgar Mittelholzer Memorial Lectures (Georgetown: National History and Arts Council, October, 1971).
5. Carter, M.. Compare "Black Friday 1962", *Poems of Succession,* (London: New Beacon, 1977), where a similar crab image is used.
6. Carter, "Open Letter to the People of Guyana", ibid.
7. See e.g. the scandals which have surrounded the People's Temple, or the House of Israel.
8. See newspapers of November 1973. Also *Man and Making* reference(4) above where, anticipating the regime's action, Carter suggested a bond in charlatanry between politician and obeahman.
9. See *Caribbean Contact* (November 1980).
10. Eliot, T. S., "The Dry Salvages" in *Four Quartets* (London: Faber, 1959).
11. Carter, M., "Death of a Comrade", *Poems of Resistance* (London: Lawrence & Wishart, 1954).
12. Brathwaite, E.K., "Martin Carter's Poetry of the Negative Yes", *Caliban*, Vol. IV, No. 1 (Fall-Winter 1981) pp. 30-41.
13. Eliot, T.S., "Burnt Norton" in *Four Quartets.*
14. Carter, M., "University of Hunger" in *Poems of Succession* (London: New Beacon Books, 1978), first published 1954.
15. Harris, W., "The Fabulous Well", *Eternity to Season* (London: New Beacon Books, 1978), first published 1954.
16. Wordsworth, W., "Resolution and Independence".
17. Carter, M., "Man and Making" (See reference No. 4.).
18. ibid., p. 5
19. Walcott, D., "Laventille" in *The Castaway and other Poems*; Brathwaite, E., "Robin", *Bim* Vol. 10, No. 39 (July-Dec 1964) & "Ogun", *Islands* (London: Oxford UP, 1969); McNeill, A., "Notes on a September Day", from *Reel from the "Life Movie"* (Jamaica: Savacou, 1972).
20. Carter, M., *Man and Making.*

THREE FOR V
1949-1982

I: Victor Questel: A Homage
We met some months before he entered UWI in October 1968, at a gathering of young writers, and what struck me then about Victor Questel was his sense of the haphazard nature of living and dying in this society. This he recorded, at times almost with gusto, but after 1976 with a mixture of anguish and starkness, and with growing intimations of exhaustion. His poetry and plays were imbued with this sense of the aimlessness of living and dying, which he countered by bringing to his own life direction and an extraordinary energy of dedication. Because he perceived aimlessness, waste and void all around, and sometimes deep within himself, he strove tirelessly to create and affirm, working his way through wildernesses of words towards the simple truths of faith and love.

The fruit of this creative activity was a curriculum vitae, nineteen pages long in 1981, and excluding some of his writing. His interests were enormous – poetry, radio, interviewing, painting, literary criticism, theatre, the novel and short story. His short adult life was filled with a restlessly energetic activity. He was a teaching assistant in the English Department of UWI for five years (1971-76), and he also designed and taught a programme on Creative Writing for the Extra-Mural Department. Always in tune with the current and relevant, he conducted a "Radio School" series of sixteen programmes for CXC English Literature students in 1981. Before that, he had done countless radio programmes for the Government Broadcasting Unit's *Focus on the Arts* series, between 1972 and 1980.

A major problem which faced him as a critic was how to bring all that he knew into central focus. He didn't succeed. There was a febrile, fragmentary element in much of his work, particularly in the forty or so book reviews. Yet he did succeed marvellously well in his voluminous thesis on Derek Walcott, which contains a study of the poetry from 1948 to 1976, the plays up to *Dream on Monkey Mountain,* a history of the Theatre Workshop (the only one of its kind); and a classification and analysis of Walcott's 500 articles and reviews.

But it didn't stop there. Questel became interested in the relationship between what Walcott read and the shape of his writing, and included in an earlier draft of the thesis indices of the writers and painters whose works have influenced Walcott, as well as perceptive discussions on how these influences manifested themselves in the poetry. Miraculously, he was able to make his thesis cohere: an encyclopaedic work which took seven years, and could have, with revision, become the major reference text on Derek Walcott. As it stands, the section on the Theatre Workshop has been revised for publication by Yale University Press, while a collection of essays entitled *Critical Perspectives on Derek Walcott* has been edited for publication by Three Continents Press of Washington D.C.

He was grounded, rooted here; barely knew Barbados, got ill on his first visit to Jamaica and on return became subject to the very haphazardness against which his own work had been an assertion. I'll remember him for his gentleness, humanity and compassion; for his thoroughness as a student and teacher, the warmth of his humour and his constant growth in depth; and I shall miss the wry dry laughter with which he constantly illuminated the daily absurdities of our existence and filled the interstices between scepticism and faith.

II: The Splitting Image

> Finally
> an act of trust was
> rewarded with a violence of language
> that is still burning
> within his skull,
> kept alive by its own organic growth
> separate from his will
> (Victor Questel: "Scarecrow")

Victor Questel's poetry was an unflinching testimony of one person's quest in an inner universe which he perceived to be other, bleak and haphazard. It was cerebrally dry, skeletal and probably impenetrable except to those familiar with the situations out of which it grew. It was further complicated by the poet's habit of allusion, and a wordplay informed by a sense of the arbitrariness of language, the unanchored instability of the word which could illuminate multiple fragments of meaning, but might obey no single unifying principle.

This sense of the arbitrariness of language was reinforced by a vision of social anomie, which threatened to engulf him, and in whose despite he struggled for the faith to continue working. Commitment, he discovered, was its own reward, the poet or critic sending words out into an echoless void, deriving little sustenance from society, the language "within his skull, kept alive by its own organic growth." Writing about his Uncle Simeon, a Baptist Shepherd, Questel is, in fact, discussing his own dilemma, and that of most writers:

> Yes he saw it all.
> There is no gratitude there. No
> imagination. Nothing to capture,
> but nothing. He
> saw that blank early and fled.
> Things still seem strange
> and pointless
> explanations too simple;
> but at these cross roads
> he will speak. Ashes,
> water and tempered steel
> can't seal his fate.
> There is a meeting here tonight.
>   ("Scarecrow")

The poet, however bleak the landscape of the spirit, remains Legba, god of the crossroads, crippled, crucified yet potent. So that if in an earlier poem, "Ash Wednesday", the poet had complained:

> But that's what this country is about,
>
> the burning of flesh and cane; the ash
> of effort.
>
> Find me that voice which
> cried
> "Land, Bread and Justice"
>
> Find me that voice which
> cried
> "I come out to play"
> and Today
> I will show you
>
> the splintered halves
> of your twisted
> self-
> mockery.

he slowly works his way back to a faith "in spite of", an acceptance of the role of the artist as man at the crossroads and man on the cross. There was nothing self-righteous in this vision of self and role. In fact, the extent to which Questel understood his role to be a common and communal one is revealed in several poem/reviews such as "Couvade", "The Weather Eye", "No Pain", "For Real" and "Seagull", where he indicates his sense of belonging to a shared landscape of sensibility.

    Many of his poems, moreover, are informed by the notion that his personal situation simply mirrors the stasis in which the nation has found itself. Their demoralisation ("Wreck"), directionlessness and degradation ("Sea Blast") are inalienably his. In "Wreck" (June 1971), the central image is that of a ship becalmed in the doldrums, while "Sea Blast" employs the image of the *Federal Maple*, moored, like the idea of Federation, its purpose long forgotten. The first poem depicts the nation after the Black Power revolt of 1970, drifting from masquerade to tragedy (ole mas and half mast). The poet is both fool figure ("Jack of all Spades") and independent consciousness ("mastered by none"), mamaguyed by neither the self-justificatory speeches of the regime, nor the rhetoric and harboured hatred of its opponents.

Yet he cannot avoid the fate of disillusionment, the dreadful pointlessness of his society, like whom he is in the doldrums. There is no escape in love, lust or alcohol. The ribbed shadow of the palm suggests not the touristy comforts of the beach-party, but a spider-web of entrapment. The last line, "Hitting the bottle my faith splinters" completes a stream of wry puns, all of which thinly mask the tragedy of a process whose result is the jetsam of splintered faiths and shattered minds. The society drugged and incensed ("needled") by rhetoric at the beginning of the poem, enters the doldrums at the poem's centre, and succumbs to alcoholic stupor at the end.

Such devastation obviously raises the problem of language and making, and their relationship to the question of faith. I've already posited that punning and wordplay are Questel's method of creating a language as splintered as his faith; that wit and humour are for him the most appropriate masks for a vision of the tragic. "Wreck" illustrates this. "Coconut", a poem of the mid-seventies, is an attempt to show the face without the mask of humour. "Coconut" is about cracking-up; its suddenness, its violence, its irreparable destruction of the psyche, and the privacy of its pain. Mental seizure or attack is depicted as part of a violent process in which the poet, in the grip of some uncontrollable force, is shattered, as one cracks a coconut with its three eyes on stone. This is the cruellest and most violent statement in Questel's poetry of the alienated vision in an opaque, blank, impenetrable universe of stone.

Yet the poet suggests that the cracking of the skull and the bruising of the eye are necessary for new vision. The water which pours out of the dry nut is symbolically stale. It is the no longer nourishing or palatable water of the old vision. Soon after this the coconut image shifts to that of the water-coconut vendor in his donkey cart, returning home with his cargo of now empty nuts. The focus here is on his dogged and certain journey home. He becomes for the poet a persona that suggests the quest which he has to make in the face of fragmentation and emptiness. Nowhere in Questel is this quest sentimental or predictable. Nor is any refuge sought in conventional ideas of the artist as one who reconciles the splintered fragments of experience. The woman who makes a broom from the coconut palm and sweeps out the fragments of broken shell is not wife but Muse. The branch which she chooses suggests not the triumphal acclaim of Palm Sunday, but the crucifixion which followed that ceremony of homecoming. The branch must be symbolically stripped by the broken nails of the Muse.

The act of sweeping, so reminiscent of Afro-Caribbean and older West African funeral and sanctification rites, is a ritual act of purgation in which the spirit of the dead is dismissed, is laid to rest, and the dwelling place purged so that the living might reconcile themselves both to the fact of death and the necessity for their own continued existence. Questel's Muse, then, does not restore what has been shattered. She prepares the house of the psyche for the task of going on, by sweeping it clean of the ruins of the past. But she is a thoroughly Trinidadian Muse, who cleanses her own house, then dumps the garbage on the road. So the fragments of shell are revealed to "the dazzling ray of sun/ stroke." The function of the Muse is to make the poet's anxiety public, even as he transcends the actual occasion of his mind's splintering. Yet even in the act of exposing his hurt to the public, the poet retains a certain mystery, an element of the dense and a certain distance. He keeps himself "a stone's throw away/ from everyone," "so that no one is clear about the broken pieces of skull/ in that dazzling ray of sun/stroke."

Maybe so, maybe so. But sufficient is said for us to be able to empathise, and the dazzling ray illuminates rather than obscures the fragments of what, with a characteristic pun, Questel terms in the poem "Lines", "the splitting image."

III: A Severity of Seeing

Hard Stares Victor Questel's final collection of poems, contains a number of severely shaped portraits of domestic and political life. The anthology is divided into four sections: "Looking", "The Glare Hurts", "The Eye Explodes", and "Cast a Cold Eye", and is about the connection between vision and pain. The glare which hurts is both the furious look that the poet aims at the world, the family and the Other, and the hard hurt of blinding light which the world directs at the seer. The relationship between Self and Other is dynamic, starkly reciprocal and mutually hostile.

"The Eye Explodes" suggests that vision is fission, and returns to an experience of mental collapse, as it measures the mind's capacity to remain "together". "Cast a Cold Eye", Yeats's famous epitaph, indicates Questel's attempt at stoical indifference in face of life and death. While the names of the four sections suggest some form of progression, and the placement of each poem is carefully done, all the sections are informed by an inexorable severity of seeing. A cold eye has been cast throughout the collection. We see it in the hardening vision ("Dirt"); the quest for detachment ("Downstairs", "Pa"); the dispassionate anatomy of political fraud, futility and decomposition ("Footfalls", "Coup", "A Prime Minister's Address"); the constant and stoical encounter with states of interior and exterior chaos ("Downstairs", " Severity", "Numb"); and in the bleak and uncompromising stare at death ("Aunt", "Pathway", "Accident").

The title-poem, "Hard Stares", is about the encounter between vision and the opacity of the universe, where history is irrecoverable or, embedded in rock, recoverable only with the utmost difficulty. The present, too, is characterised by a tough unlovely modernity, imaged by the ribbed red clay brick which this entombed past has begotten. Hard stares are applied not only to history, but to literary theories ("Judge Dreadword"), domestic life ("Housework"), religion, love ("Sheets", "Absence"). Each scrutinised experience reveals its holes.

> myriad holes surface like your toast
> fixed taut by an electrical flame.

The "electrical flame" is the searing glow of perception, the particularity, exactness and severity of seeing. Its effect in "Hard Stares" is the same as that of the sun in "Dirt". Things harden under the heat of vision and reveal their perforations. Questel achieves here, and throughout this collection, an ability like Sylvia Plath's, to invest the banal domestic image or situation with a latent terror.

This is well illustrated in "Absence", a moving poem which begins with the image of soiled clothes, and then moves on to suggest ideas of collapse, disembowelment, torture (the wringer), death, healing and resurrection. There is also blessing and anguished embrace.

> Let me
> put my hands in those spaces –
> The holes you have vacated

"Playroom" reveals similar qualities. On the one hand, it rhymes and jingles along, suggesting the possibility of delight and the atmosphere of the nursery. On the other hand, the toys named are all broken or "cracked", projections of inner disorder. The cracked doll, for example, resembles those deranged people who sometimes undress and stroll through the city. The Mickey Mouse games parody more adult exercises in annihilation, which will receive particular attention in "Coup" or "Taking Orders".

The most obvious of these domestic poems is "Downstairs", where Questel encounters under his mother's house, the discarded paraphernalia of three generations – objects immured in dirt from those times when families threw nothing finally away, and obsolescence occurred at its proper unplanned pace. If there is any nostalgia in encountering the rusty past, it is dry. Downstairs, the light is uncertain, and the stares have to be hard. The word "downstairs", indeed, is a pun on "down" "stares", and suggests a looking downwards into the gloomy pit and abyss of the Self.

Each object recognised seems not only a reminder of the life it once had, but an omen of death.

> Propped against six feet of raw earth
> is a spade without a handle. To the left of this
> is an English typewriter frozen in dirt.

This spade without a handle next to a mound of dirt and the English typewriter frozen in dirt, together suggest the death of the two sides of Afro-Saxondom, neither of which can help one to spell one's name ("handle"). The "shorthand of modernity" is both the planned obsolescence of this age and the cryptic difficult poetry of contemporary times, which Questel has generally found to be more appropriate to his own self-definition than the easier traditional verse.

The ice tongs (tongues?) suggest lockjaw, his own inability to speak, as well as his grandfather's death. One notes, too, the words "collapsed" and "depression", references, surely, to Questel's own period of depression and collapse, when he returned home. So his grandfather's rusting, stiff tongs are an image of his own frozen incapacity to speak, just as his mother's failed adventure as a stenographer is an intimation of his own sense of the failure inherent in the different and more difficult shorthand of poetry.

Similarly, the "wooden man with a broken hand for letters" is Questel's *alter ego*, his double whom he encounters, significantly, "further in". Only the eye of the *alter ego* is alive, and "stares piercingly at you out of the darkness." Downstairs, then, is really a metaphor for the Id, or whatever dark region of the soul Questel had entered. He intuited that there was a strange if frightening creative potential in the state of schizophrenia – the release of something terrifyingly real and blinding, which he sought to contain, to know, and maybe command to speak. One can see this endeavour throughout his earlier collection, *Near Mourning Ground*. In "Downstairs", he stares into that frozen moment when he had known collapse, linking it to the scattered objects of a past accumulated beneath his mother's house.

The last segment of the poem, in which he identifies his condition, makes this clear.

> I live below (temporarily) and it's my link
> with civilisation. Recovering from nervous exhaustion
> levelled by junk and objects that define upstairs
> I, a rusting dog-chain and crawling memory hold downstairs together.

Here he's like Ellison's invisible man, whose link with the world above, electricity, he shares. But there's more here. "Below" is within the infernal regions of the psyche, whose link with the Superego – i.e. the rational order of "civilisation" – is rather reluctantly maintained. Ironically, though, "downstairs" is simply the obverse of "upstairs"; for if the world of upstairs is ordered, it is also sterile, frozen and inhibited. This is why its most appropriate metaphors are the dirt-stiffened, rusty and dead objects which clog downstairs. The two strata of the psyche complement each other and are electrically linked. The poet is confident of his ability to keep things and himself together, though his implements are frail, collapse always imminent, and the effort demanded of him, extreme.

Section Two, "The Glare Hurts", begins with an intimation of the terror of breakdown, the carefully crafted "Numb", but is on the whole, far more concerned with the themes of dissolution and death. Self-pity and self-indulgence are absent from these poems, where subjective experience is objectified to such an extent, that in addressing Self, Questel frequently acts as if he is addressing Other. "I" thus often becomes "you" and "he".

Another method of achieving detachment from obsessive and traumatic personal experience is to recognise Self in Other while preserving the apparent detachment of the observer. This method is put to good service in "Pa", where Questel describes the retirement of his father from his job as a sailor. One notes how often the figure of the doting, dying sailor has occurred in his poems. In *Near Mourning Ground*, one saw him in "Sea Blast" and "Father". If in "Sea Blast" the captain of the *Federal Palm* slipping into dotage, silence and obsolescence, strongly suggested Eric Williams and his generation of political impotents, in "Father" the aging sailor is Questel's father and an omen of the future which lies in wait for his son. The father's petering out provided the son with a personal vision of the power of time, and an intuition of the futility of human effort, which he sought to defeat by means of a frenzy of activity.

Constant work which initially was a means of postponing the threat of obsolescence, ultimately became an end in itself. Work thus lost its point and became another function of that rubble of experience on which it sought to impose order and clarity ("Housework", "Downstairs", "Severity"). Questel understood this trap, felt the circle of absurdity close around him, and saw his marvellous humour metamorphose into bitter mirth. His father's slow dying became for him a metaphor of time's trap of futility. As he wrote in "Father":

> now I circle
> the fears that
> encircled you

He circles those fears in the sense that he skirts them, is detached from them, even though he too is on the verge of entering them, and records their surfaces, which is all he knows, his father never having openly articulated the source of his terrors. But beneath the poet's apparently detached and fragmentary record of the externals of decrepitude, lies his own fear of being encircled and engulfed by a fruitless future.

It is this which leads him to paint yet another portrait of Pa, one from which he carefully excludes any hint of his own reaction, whereas in "Father" he'd made explicit the parallel between his father's condition and his own. This effort at detachment, characteristic of *Hard Stares*, indicates not increased distance between the poet and the life he observes, but rather his deeper recognition of similarity. It is because of this that the lines of the portrait are bleaker and harder, that no softness is allowed to mollify the severity of line.

The son, "conceived/ in the cracked mind of an outcast sailor" ("Numb") recognises his own image in every feature of the father's portrait. The father's posture of impotence, "huddled over scrambled eggs", is an ambiguous one, suggesting at once helpless emasculation and an instinct for protective warmth. Questel, as we have seen, was also accommodating himself to the tedium of a domestic life. A later poem, "Severity", depicts the violence of his inner struggle against the tedium of an household routine which constantly thwarted the manic frenzy of his drive to work.

The "silent rage" of his father's "broken posture" is also the son's. Father, like son, now sits at the centre of an encircling amnesiac void – ("Blanks circle him") – the father, a memory away from his sailor's days "when he rolled and pitched/ the seas with the best", the son similarly separated from his own boyhood, his marble days when he too "rolled and pitched" with the best. Both stand at the centre of the same circle, reeling from recall and thought. And although Pa remains to the end almost a stranger – he is still referred to as "the aging man" – although the son retains his distance, there is recognition and embrace. For surely the words "almost bent double" convey two distinct meanings. There is the visual portrait of the old man, a living hieroglyph of the life's cycle which he has almost completed. But this aging man is also the poet's "almost bent double," his *alter ego,* the father whose predicament the son silently shares. The tie between father and son is finally affirmed in the poem's last words: "he's anchored to his eggs", which not only return us to the image of the domesticated sailor, but indicates the father's secure rootedness in the nest of a family which he engendered.

Part III, "The Eye Explodes", is largely satirical. It examines the fevered politics of the contemporary Caribbean, focusing its hard stare on Guyana ("Footfall", "In Memory of Walter Rodney", and "A Prime Minister's Address"); Trinidad, ("Shop" and "Taking Orders") and Jamaica ("Coup"). Questel is aware of the dreadful degree to which local politics are the result of external manipulation ("Coup") and of the helplessness of the individual in the face of the contradictory pressures of the international Cold War. He is also aware of the part that the artist plays in an age of ideological polarisation. In "Judge Dreadword", his satirical stare is levelled at the purifiers of the dialect of the tribe, the enemies of indigenous oral tradition, those who would impose on the West Indian writer a burdensome apprenticeship to foreign models. Patterning the poem on Prince Buster's "Judge Dread", Questel makes a crucial link between imperialist aesthetics and imperialist exploitation. Judge Dreadword tells Rude Boy Q:

> This court is a product of a proven tradition
> of oil and its related cultural benefactors –
>
> B.P., CIA, IMF, IOU, the UN, PNM – letters that matter
> in the world. You want to destroy all that? Hush up

The fruits of exploitation are employed in the metropole to subsidise an art that says the correct things, eschews political confrontation, berates and demoralises the victims of imperialism, and challenges nothing. Literary honours are under the control of a multinational Mafia, whose colonial commissar in the world of letters is Judge Dreadword. Dreadword sentences the deviant young writer to four hundred more years of colonial servitude, in the same way that the multinationals entangle the economies of small powerless states. (IMF – IOU). He is, in fact, working for the kultur of the Corporation, earning his grubstake.

A product of the old plantation West Indies, Dreadword is authoritarian and contradictory. Absolutely no different from the old generation of politicians, he brooks neither silence nor dialogue in his court. He accuses and passes sentence in the same breath, and his final punishment is crucifixion. Yet he is irrelevant, and this is proved by the fact that he is being ignored by the youth, who with elation do and affirm their own rooted thing. Rude Boy Q takes delight in his crime against language ("I have language in a vice of my own") and will continue committing atrocities against both the foreign model and its local apologists.

The same spirit is present in "Footfalls", a poem inspired by Burnham's TV performance on the occasion of Rodney's murder. Burnham tried to outstare the camera which, however, revealed much more than he could have wished of the callousness and spiritual bankruptcy of his regime. Questel's final portrait of "the Kabaka" suggests that the uncompromising stare of the camera has both revealed guilt and passed sentence. The politician's revolving chair becomes an electric chair.

> A dictator is *turning* to ashes in his chair
> while trying to outstare
> both a camera
> and the sad truth of murder

The camera has become the public eye and tribunal, revealing the cracks in his case. This quiet poem does not mourn or lament. It warns and defines the mood of dread and grim resolve, alive in the Caribbean for decades, but heightened by Rodney's assassination. Out of that moment has grown the possibility of what Brathwaite has termed many "murderous tomorrows."

In "A Prime Minister's Address", the decaying patriarch is seen amidst the ash of ironies, justifying and condemning himself with each sentence. There is just a hint of sympathy in the suggestion that he has been the victim of fate.

A huge vision corrupts, when the race is against time.

This, however, disappears when it is revealed that Burnham's only race has been "The need to get there ahead/ of the next race." The final stanzas envisage the maximum leader afraid of his guards who, according to Questel, "also have a destiny to mould". The leader is now unable to see behind the people's "iron stares", because the people have for some years been trained only to echo the given opinion of the leader, and to become amnesiac whenever they are forced to look him straight in the face. The last two lines: "regular blackouts/ when they see the whites of my eyes", are double-edged and may apply to several Caribbean leaders. The "blackouts" are the electricity cuts which the people are often forced to endure, but they are also the automatic failure of memory to which the people pretend, as they passively accept or reject the system. The "whites of my eyes" suggest that the Prime Minister is as colonial in vision as the whites whom he has replaced, and who have for many years underwritten his corrupt regime. The last two lines make it clear that the political meeting, which the people have no doubt been coerced into attending, is an occasion for mutual non-communication between the politician and his(?) people.

Part IV, "Cast a Cold Eye", begins, inappropriately, with "Severity", a poem which derives something from Walcott's "The Brother" (*Sea Grapes*, pp. 23-24), and is a furious rejection of everything – hypocrisy, love, a noisy neighbourhood – that frustrates Questel's quest for silence and inner space. Here, more than anywhere else, one recognises the desperation behind his drive to work, and the violence of his efforts to escape into "a forest of paper".

The last two poems in the collection, "Tonight's News" and "Calm" make it clear that this section has been misnamed. The cold eye has not been cast. What one has, instead of indifference, is resignation and ironic reconciliation. "Tonight's News", like the earlier "Downstairs", is about interior descent. Tonight's news is news from and about the night journey; news from a region beyond memory or self-advertisement. The writing is on the wall of the cave of self, the omens of death unmistakable.

The future
is beneath this sheet. Stare

The last two lines, however, interrupt this vision of the blank of death with the sudden scream of a gospel singer, whose voice is, presumably, one of hope and affirmation, though it may just as well be one of hysteria. Significantly, the singer too is entrapped: she screams "from the dust jacket of her disc." She too is caught up in circles, and enclosed in her envelope of dust – that is, the body, the flesh, these mortal coils. The fact that her voice penetrates beyond the poet's future does suggest that it is part of the eternal energy of life itself.

It is not this energy, however, that the final poem "Calm" celebrates. "Calm" is about convalescence after inner turmoil, not affirmation. It ends on a whimsical note of reconciliation to the tedium or menace of domestic life.

> Automatically
> he jumps as his Furelect shoots
>
> the morning toast at his head

We've completed a circle with this comically reductive image of assassination. In the title poem "Hard Stares", the toast, perforated with holes, is an image of experience fixed taut by searing vision, and of the mind, brittle, dried-out, and on the verge of collapse. There is, finally, no escape from the terror of downstairs, or from the necessity for a poetry of naked, unflinching honesty, informed by a severity of seeing.

(Part I was first published in *Trinidad & Tobago Review*, Vol. 5 No. 9 (High Season 1982) p. 3.

Part II was first published in *The Luv Arts Digest* Vol. 1, No. 2 (June 1982) pp. 31-35.

Part III was first published as an introduction to *Hard Stares* (Port of Spain: New Voices, 1982).

THE SHAPE OF THAT HURT
AN INTRODUCTION TO *VOICEPRINT*

It is only since the 1970s that the term "oral tradition" began to be consistently used in connection with certain developments in West Indian poetry. Before that decade, the debate concerned the viability of "dialect" as a medium for poetry, and was an extension of the troubled issue of the nexus between education, speech, class, status and power. Creole dialects, many held, were the restricted code of the semiliterate, and entrenched both the social crippledom of those who spoke them, and the political hegemony of those who controlled the official level of verbal communication. To argue as some linguists did/do that Creole is simply another language, neither better nor worse than any other, was to ignore the social and political nature of language. To speak about the vitality and expressiveness of Creole was to sentimentalise warm folksiness without wanting to share in the anguish of its decrepitude, and to display the contempt of a complacent and uncommitted intelligentsia, who secretly wanted to reinforce their superior social status by keeping people uneducated.

Nowhere has the dialect versus standard polemic been more bitter than in the question of whether a serious poetry can grow out of a dialect base. Since it was widely believed that dialect was a restricted code, incapable of expressing abstract ideas, sublimity or complexities of thought and feeling, the functions permitted dialect were those of drama and energetic folksy humour. While West Indian novelists had from the twenties onwards begun to reveal the widening possibilities of Creole dialects as flexible literary languages, West Indian poets, with a few notable exceptions, made relatively little use of the vernacular. A visible gap also existed between quasi-poetic folk forms such as the mento, chant and calypso, and the formal poetry of the schoolmen. The debate about the status, nature and potential of dialect did little to close this gap, serving rather to harden the prejudices at either side of the chasm.

One useful concept, however, did emerge, which influenced the direction of literary criticism: that of a continuum stretching between Creole and Standard English, from which speakers naturally selected such registers of language as were appropriate to particular contexts and situations. The notion of a continuum made sense of what West Indian novelists had been doing for some time: that is, exploring the whole range of language and speech registers open to them. The poets too needed to recognise that alternative registers, tropes, modes and moulds for shaping were accessible to them and to liberate through an openness to all available voices such word-shapes as these voices might suggest.

If continuum theory illuminated an openness of linguistic possibility, the concept of an oral tradition made immediately accessible a virtually limitless range of prosodic, rhetorical, musical and sonic shapes that inevitably became the basis of new making. Roughly parallelling both the folk/urban and the Creole/Standard continua was an aesthetic one:

> stretching between forms derived from an oral paradigm, and forms suggested by various aspects of modernist aesthetics... while some writers are able to accommodate both extremes with relative ease, others have been involved in an intense dialectic in which the extremes appear as thesis and antithesis... The notion of an aesthetic continuum allows us to understand and accept the existence of both types of writer.[1]

Voiceprint is partly concerned with poetry based on an apprehension of the oral tradition. The inclusion of selections from Claude McKay, Louise Bennett, Philip Sherlock, early Arthur Seymour and Shake Keane, illustrates the experiments with voice, fable and rhythm that had been taking place five decades ago. These experiments increased in the sixties, gaining sudden depth with the publication of Kamau Brathwaite's *Rights of Passage*, *Masks* and *Islands* (1967-69). Brathwaite's trilogy, later to be published in a single volume as *The Arrivants* (1973), absorbed and improvised on earlier efforts at orality ranging from Akan traditional drum-poets, through Caribbean pioneers, Afro-American musicians and poets, and the Beat poets. Out of this web of ancestors Brathwaite wove a network of sound-skeins, in which the full folk/ modernist continuum was included.[2]

After the appearance of *The Arrivants*, the terms of the aesthetic debate had to change. On the one hand, the issue hardened into an absolute struggle between two supposedly irreconcilable camps, on the other, one became aware of the range and versatility of the oral tradition as a source of tropes capable of creative extension into new poetic forms.

II:

The oral tradition is a heritage of song, speech and performance visible in such folk forms as the litanic work songs, chants, battle songs, queh queh songs, hymns, thousands of calypsos, mentos and reggae songs, sermons of both the grassroots and establishment churches, riddles, jokes and word-games. Societies such as Guyana and Trinidad, with their large East Indian communities, possess at least two alternatives to the European models enshrined in the education system. A few calypsos and several songs which blend Hindi and English, suggest that an inter-creolisation[3] process has been taking place between African and Indian folk elements. The potential of this blend has not been recognised by either community, even though nearly two decades ago musicians such as Joe Harriott, Shake Keane, Coleridge Goode and the Johnny Mayer Quintet, had already illustrated the possibilities of fusing Indian classical music and Black people's classical music, jazz.[4]

Music, because it has been the means of preserving linkages between the Caribbean and a non-European sensibility, has become the container of a wealth of alternative rhythms, a few of which have begun to inform the poetry of the Caribbean. Songs were our first poetic shapes, though for a long time, our apprehension of what was accessible for poetry remained limited to the standard ballad shapes of the Anglo-Scottish tradition. Hence Claude McKay's *Constab Ballads* and a great deal of Louise Bennett were patterned on the iambic tetrametric quatrain shapes of hymnals and Burns's ballads. Prosodic achievement here had to be confined to the tension created through the counterpoint of Jamaican Creole speech rhythms and the fixed metric cage of the stanza. It is in the heightened dramatic situations of Louise Bennett's street poems ("Candy Seller", "South Parade Peddler") with their "tracings" and aggressive performance, that the interplay between voice and metre is greatest.

An illustration of the virtual tyranny of the quatrain is seen in the work of Antonio Jarvis from St. Thomas who, in 1935, published a small collection of verse entitled *Bamboula Dance*. This title would have led one to expect the shaping influence of the bamboula drums, of Congolese origin, with their warlike rhythms, which were known throughout the archipelago both before and after Emancipation. One might also have expected Jarvis to draw on the bamboula songs, whose function in St. Thomas had once paralleled that of the kalinda chants and satirical banter songs of mid to late nineteenth century Trinidad and Martinique. This is not the case. "Bamboula Dance" is standard hymn-book stuff, whose culturally biased content explains its formal limitation.

> Can I in pride mock sad buffoons
> Who ape ancestral circumstance?
> My fathers, too, these thousand moons
> Cavorted in some tribal dance.
>
> I can still feel, when drumbeats call
> The pulsing blood new rhythms take
> As garment-like refinements fall
> Unconscious longings spring awake.
>
> My honoured sire now would say,
> For all his solemn high degrees
> That drums recall Nigerian play
> And drown out later dignities.

Few naked tribesmen yet remain
To dance the sacred dance for rain.[5]

The poem is a sonnet in iambic tetrameter, and though it speaks of an African heritage which is still sufficiently powerful to produce the "pulsing new rhythms" of the St. Thomas bamboula dance, and awaken the "unconscious longings" which lie beneath the flimsy cloak of "refinements", that heritage of sound, rhythm and orality contributes nothing to its making. Despite its subversive power, the alter/native tradition is recognised negatively as the misguided and nostalgic concern of "sad buffoons/Who ape ancestral circumstance." There is a genuine confusion and contradiction in how "heritage" is perceived.

Jarvis identifies his father in this poem as a spokesman for Western Atlantic education and civilisation, whose "solemn high degrees" are drowned out by the older Nigerian heritage. Western dignity is defeated by the childishness of an engrained savagery. In another little poem entitled "Atavistic", Jarvis describes his "alien sire" as "Nordic", and himself as the meeting point of contradictory ancestral tendencies.

I whose dark ancestors played
Where the Nile's first drop was laid
Have within me Nordic blood
Pulsing like the tide at flood

Dowered by an alien sire
Is it strange my tropic fire
Often cools to virtuous fear
When nice brown girls venture near?

The epithet "alien" which he applies to his father suggests that the heritage of Nordic blood, here depicted as powerfully alive, is also strangely cold and distant. It represents "virtue", but it also represents inhibition, the death of Eros, which is illustrated by his inability to respond to the beauty of women of his own ethnicity.

Jarvis perceives in terms of stereotypes which had been established in the European mind centuries before the twentieth[6] and are still present in the Caribbean today. Africa equals drum, naked tribesmen cavorting, play, passion and backwardness: Europe equals refinement, culture, education, intelligence, virtue, self-control. According to the rigid mathematics of such stereotyping which climaxed in the mid-nineteenth century with Arthur de Gobineau's *The Inequality of Human Races*, the psyche of the person of mixed racial heritage became a battlefield of conflicting elements. Since the African aspect of a mixed colonial heritage was under constant official and personal censorship,[7] the "mulatto of culture" was faced with the choice of either total negation of, or subversive self-identification with the black ancestor. Since progress, thought and enlightenment were thought to be exclusively Western and "Nordic", and colonial education entrenched and reinforced such prejudice, the Caribbean mulatto of culture was programmed to accept and strenuously affirm the white ancestor.

The affirmation of the white ancestor and denial, negation or degraded perception of the black one, was most visible whenever the question of an aesthetic arose. The rigidly stereotyped terms of perception described above lay beneath the bitter polemic concerning West Indian poetry as late as the 1970s. If in 1936 Jarvis could censor the "new rhythms" engendered in the "pulsing blood" by the call of drumbeats, with the argument that the New World mulatto had moved beyond the naked tribesmen whose "sacred dance for rain" had lost its meaning, Eric Roach would bitterly condemn the emergence of these new rhythms in the poetry of the 1970s, employing the same terms as Jarvis.

> Are we going to tie the drum of Africa to our tails and bay like mad dogs at the Nordic world to which our geography and history tie us?
> We have been given the European languages and forms of culture in the traditional aesthetic sense, meaning the best that has been taught, said and done.[8]

Roach wasn't alone in the sentiments he expressed, nor in his declaration that, "To be a Caribbean English language poet is to be aware of the functions and structure of English verse." Nor was he singular in his ambivalence towards the "cultural dominance" of English literature, which he advised the young post-Independence West Indian writer to both "revere" and "disdain". His ambivalence was that of the 1930's mulatto of culture, and like Jarvis's involved the negation and scornful caricature of the African aesthetic presence, and the reverent acknowledgement of the European presence, along with a contradictory resentment at the cultural hegemony which the European presence had historically exercised over the colonial person. Roach's position was rendered even more painful by the anguish, which he felt and expressed as a black poet, at the degradation in which black people in Africa, America and the Caribbean were existing. His political position and bitter ethnic loyalties were in harsh conflict with his cultural and aesthetic preferences.

III:

If Roach had remained the aesthetic creature of the colonial era, West Indian poetry had not. The alter/native tradition, alive enough throughout the colonial period to have required constant censorship by law, pulpit and school, had since independence become the medium of a whole new group of artists, for whom it provided the basis of an indigenous sensibility. The self-censorship of the pre-independence generations had been the product of, as it had been reinforced by, the legalised censorship of a variety of folk forms. A cardinal principle of plantation and colonial society, censorship in its various forms drove the folk tradition into maroonage: stickfighting and Orisha to the provinces, the Baptists to the hills and bushes on pain of prosecution and police harassment,[9] herblore and magic to the underground; the dark telluric gods to Catholic and Calvinist versions of hellfire; waist movement and buttock-ripple to Dungle, Behind-the-Bridge, Back-o'-Wall penumbra of jamette, wahbeen, robust man and jagabat.

Censorship took serious toll on the folk-consciousness of Trinidad, where even among grassroots preservers and developers of folk tradition, one could observe curious gaps in sensibility. Shango or Spiritual Baptist worshippers, outlawed by the Shouters Prohibition Ordinance of 1917, were generally presented in the calypsos of the 1930s as indulging in laughable or exotic rituals. In other words, the grass roots absorbed and disseminated comic caricatures of their own image, which they had derived from the country's ruling elite. There were, of course, a few exceptions, such as the Growling Tiger who in "Yoruba Shango" acknowledges the power of the Orisha and the rooted strength of the tradition. But even Tiger, an extraordinarily conscious calypsonian who accurately defined the race and class situations of his time in compositions such as "Workers' Appeal" (1934), "Money is King" (1935), "The Gold" (1936) and "Let the White People Fight" (1942), derided the Baptists in "What is the Shouter" (1939).

> We have Roman Catholic, Anglican and Salvation
> But what is the Shouter band?
> If it is a religion do tell me please
> I am tired with the nonsense: give me an ease.
> The unknown twang on River Jordan
> Is the thing I can't understand.

The Shouters are viewed as devil-worshippers, "With candle and a cross and cycle bell/ Invoking Lucifer in hell", and ultimately as "a disgrace to my native land." Not surprisingly, Tiger applauds, as Louise Bennett's folk persona in "Pinnacle" was to do in the early forties, the police action in brutalising the Shouters (Rastafari in the case of "Pinnacle").

> I read at Mount Hope the other day
> They had to chase some shouter away
> With their head tie in white, with some long night gown
> While the police had them surround.
> In the height of the feast they began to moan
> Five mile apart you could hear them groan.
> A fellow said he came from Carriacou
> They burst his head with police butoo.*   *(i.e. baton)

Here we also have an intolerance of the migrant from Grenada, Carriacou, St. Vincent and "dem small islands." The Shouters, a part of Trinidad for decades, are still being viewed as the purveyors of an alien religion, a style of worship vastly different from that of the respectable "civilised" – Tiger uses the word in the calypso – Anglicans and Catholics. Governor Sir John Chancellor and his 1917 law had done their job well. Propaganda against non-European styles and customs had permeated the society at every level, so that the keepers of the tradition were themselves ambivalent about its deepest aspects, and could deal with it only on certain superficial planes. Even the recognised spokesmen of the people, calypsonians, when describing folk religions often assumed the essentially bourgeois role of the frightened or fascinated interloper describing quaintly excessive behaviour.

If the folk themselves had learned ambivalence, the natural reaction of the educated was to abandon folklore, folk music and religions and, seeking nineteenth century versions of the sublime, tune their poetry away from the sounds that were most familiar and the rhythms that were most available. Hence the disconnection between poetry and the oral tradition, poetry and the indigenised folk self. The growing nationalism during the thirties and forties resulted in attempts throughout the Antilles to rehabilitate the idea of the "folk", and each territory possessed its people who were in the forefront of the movement to document and make visible the beleaguered culture of the people. Hence the importance of people such as Louise Bennett, Ivy Baxter, Lennox Pierre, Beryl Mc Burnie, Edric Connor, Olive Walke, and later Jacob Elder, Wordsworth Mc Andrew, Rex Nettleford and Errol Hill. Along with the work of these West Indians was that of anthropologists such as Melville and Frances Herskovits, Andrew Pearse, George Eaton Simpson, Daniel Crowley and Roger Abrahams, whose efforts ensured that the West Indies approached Independence with a clearer notion of the breadth and potential of their folk and oral heritage.

There was in this rediscovery the inevitable question of how to accord the folk tradition an everyday normalcy and wholeness, when for so long it had been regarded as both esoteric and eccentric. As George Lamming was to recognise in *Season of Adventure,* the line between bourgeois adventure into the folk world and adventurism, is exceedingly thin. Fola's rediscovery of the folk results in both the transformation of her own life and the destruction of the authenticity of the folk religion, when the houngan feels he has betrayed the gods by permitting infidels into the inner chamber of the tonelle.

The problem was whether a genuine folk heritage was still available for anything except anthropological enquiry. Mulattoes of culture who had had doubts before restated them now. Anthropological findings, according to Derek Walcott,[10] were signs that the folkways had become fakeways, and the order which anthropologists placed on the remnants of folk behaviour was abstract and unreal. Poets should be careful to avoid the "pastoral" simplicity of an idealised and abstract folk world, lest it lure them away from their real "adamic" task of "naming" without nostalgia a unique new world, whose ancestral roots had become inaccessible, unnecessary and irrelevant. It wasn't that Walcott had not himself once believed that he could and should undertake:

> the forging of a language that went beyond mimicry, a dialect which had the force of revelation as it invented names for things, one which finally settled on its own mode of inflection, and which began to create an oral culture of chants, jokes, folk-songs and fables.[11]

but that he believed everyone else's attempt to do the same was spurious. He also noted how after Independence, folk culture had been exploited politically by both the local bourgeoisie come to power and their fake-radical opponents of Black Nationalist persuasion. It had thus become both the basis of a thinly strident cultural nationalism and a burgeoning tourist trade. In this respect, the very disconnection of the pseudo-folk idiom from lived reality was its greatest attraction. This did not mean that Walcott had anything positive to say about such poets as had begun to speak directly out of the lived reality of the now urbanised folk. In a 1973 interview, he dismissed these with as absolute a condemnation as he had in 1970 berated practically everybody: poet, politician, anthropologist, actor, critic, mas man.

Walcott's major criticism was that in writing "immediate poetry", the poet does not listen to his "inner ear." He is conscious of an audience, and produces a sort of easily communicable theatre, which for all the immediacy of its relevance "leaves out the most exciting part of poetry, which is its craft."[12] Walcott admitted that the new poets were "trying to reach closer to the root rhythms of the speech", but felt that they knew little about crafting the poem. He contrasts the oral poets with poets such as Dennis Scott, Anthony McNeill and Wayne Brown.

> Now if you look at the better poets of the younger generation, there are three particular poets who are very fine and permanent poets. That's Wayne Brown, Anthony McNeill and Dennis Scott. They have the same power of impulse that the young polemic-type poets have. Their feelings are the same anger, the same drive. But when you read these poets, they are not using a language which is a platform language that can be delivered over to a waiting public. The intensity of their feeling is making their anguish extremely complex. In these poets, the language that is being used is not the "down with the honky", a language of the people who consider themselves to be the revolutionary poets.
>
> They are not using a platform language because the revolution is being enacted inside of them. You mustn't trust revolutionary poets who can do a poem on a typewriter or a drum quickly, because when the Government changes, they'll turn out another one just as fast for you. You know. It's no sweat. It's like editorial policy. Tomorrow it may change.[13]

In this interview, Walcott makes his usual clean distinction between the theatrical and the poetic; one which he'd made earlier between the public nature of the calypso and the private nature of poetry, and which he'd maintained between his roles as poet and playwright. The problem with such a clean distinction, when applied to West Indian poetry, is that it conceals the dialectical relationship between what Walcott presents as two opposite and irreconcilable poles. It also fails to recognise that a poetry based on the oral tradition would require, seek and create its own crafting; would release the paradigms and shapes implicit in the various aspects of the tradition on which it was based. What the oral tradition demanded, then, was an alter/native notion of crafting, one that Walcott, an updated version of the old-time mulatto of style, needed to resist because it ran counter to the models he had studied.

IV:
The lived reality of post-Independence proletarian youth was one of even grimmer ghettos than their newly uprooted peasant forebears knew. They faced in Jamaica a political reality of grim factional encounter between new alignments of the agricultural, commercial and intellectual elites scrambling to control a neglected peasantry and their migrant cousins, the urban dispossessed. Out of this tussle emerged the twin tendencies of reward via political patronage and bitter internecine violence among ordinary people, whose creativity in music and verse would become a means of coping with, understanding, giving utterance to and even celebrating the violence of their world. The tragic immediacy of this violence and the interplay of their own folk-urban culture with that of the similarly marginalised cultures of Afro-America and Black Britain, together fused to engender the culture of the youth which, in the seventies, spread throughout the Antilles and beyond.

The state throughout the West Indies was caught between impulses to market "dread beat and blood" and to censor its subversive nature. Hence in Jamaica and Trinidad, the really penetrating political song has tended to receive little or no air-play on the state-owned media, while the appeasing or purely entertaining song has been promoted. Wise singers and songwriters understand the message and produce for the market, rather than for the parochial community. In spite of such stricture, a number of reggae singers, dub poets and political calypsonians have emerged determined to speak from within the ghetto reality of their world. Those who recoil from the naked and unadorned realism of the word and sound-portraits which they paint, should reflect that they provide not only a window into, but a voice crying from the wilderness, one which we certainly would not otherwise have heard.

These are hardly voices that the State, concerned with appeasement, the tourist trade and the eagle's grin of the Yankee dollar, can afford to foster. Thus Malik (Decoteau), Lasana Kwesi, Wayne Davis, Syl Lowhar and

Efebo were all political detainees in 1970 Trinidad. Leroy Calliste, a gentle poet, hanged himself. Wrongfully imprisoned, Jack Kelshall, an old time Marxist, wrote poems from prison. The disillusioned Eric Roach looked hard at the ghetto, wrote a score of post-1970 poems which contained a fierce clean bitterness, drank poison, cast himself into the sea and killed himself. Oku Onuora served several years in a Jamaican jail. Don Drummond, the shape of whose hurt inspired Anthony McNeill, died in the madhouse to which he had been committed for the murder of his partner. Harold Simmons slashed his wrists and bled to death. Mikey Smith was stoned to death. Walter Rodney, not hearing or heeding the warning poem that Wordsworth McAndrew addressed to him since 1976, in which he implored Rodney to leave an incorrigible land which could find no use for his academic skills, became the occasion for further poetry when he was blown into fragments on June 13, 1980. McAndrew himself, Guyana's best folklorist and an accomplished radio personality, was himself forced to leave Guyana, because his superiors hated his style of dress and his forthrightness of speech.

No. The state could not foster such voices. Where necessary, they imprisoned or muzzled them, and under extreme circumstances, they assassinated the voice. What the state did with great efficiency was to promote carnivals and festivals throughout the region. The most significant of these, from the point of view of the arts, has been Carifesta, which was sponsored in Guyana in 1972, and has since occurred in Jamaica, Cuba and Barbados. State policy, despite its obvious political pragmatism and its habitual brutality, has been beneficial to both folk and oral traditions, raising to the surface what had in the colonial era been submerged. Today, the oral tradition is alive both in its decorative aspect and as the vehicle of the passion of urban youth, concerned with creating shapes out of the grim immediacy of their situation.

V: Legend, Tale, Narrative, Folk Song
The new wave of writers is not as easily divisible into distinct categories as Walcott has supposed. They have approached their heritage with a freedom rarely found in the pre-independence era, seeking all available metaphors, sounds, rhythms and levels of speech and prosody. The either/or approach of the colonial era, which had promoted English verse-paradigms and marginalised Caribbean orality, was gradually replaced by the both/ and approach, in which, as the situation demanded, writers varied freely along the continua between folk and modernist, creole and standard, oral and scribal; the poem as uncurling tendril reaching out towards the Other, or self-sufficient pebble, total in the opacity of its own waterless universe; the poem as unfolding chrysalis or transparent hard inert crystal. The mixture of qualities which Walcott

sees in Scott, Brown and McNeill is in fact to be found in Brathwaite, Questel, Malik, Goodison, Phillip and Mordecai. Walcott himself has yielded consistently to the pressure of the voice, his late work including several instances of the same orality that he had criticised in other poets. Perhaps the difference lies in the crafting.

Voiceprint is meant to illustrate not only the wealth and range of the West Indian oral tradition, but also the relationship between this tradition and a large body of writing which contains a certain orality even though this may not be immediately evident. It is important at this point to distinguish between folk and oral traditions. Though the folk tradition of the West Indies and perhaps of most places is largely oral, the oral tradition contains both folk/proletarian and middle-class elements; both "black" and "white" aspects of style. The sermon of the Anglican and Catholic, or other establishment churches, is as much part of Caribbean oral tradition as Baptist shouting, Zion Revival "trumping" or Rastafarian "reasoning". Calypsonians of the oratorical period (1900-1920), listened to the orations of lawyers and bishops, according to Atilla the Hun. High-flown tea meeting speeches are as much part of traditional style as sharp grass-rooted "tracings", or the clean razors of picong. The music of diaspora peoples ranges from complex jazz to folk-song and nursery rhyme.

The important link between each element is that of "voice". The poems chosen here all contain voices. Voices signal the constant presence and pressure of people, and the steady challenge of abstraction by the pure uncerebral force of lived life. So while our poets have at times expressed an admiration for such well-known modernist trends as dryness, hardness, hermeticism or a monadic aestheticism in which poem, novel or play becomes a closed, self-contained system, there isn't one who hasn't responded to the immediacy of people.

Our first oral category, Legend, Tale, Narrative & Folksong, includes both pre- and post-independence examples of how these forms have influenced the shape of West Indian poetry. Seymour's "The Legend of Kaieteur" is an obvious example of legend. It tries for a speaking voice, employs dialogue at points and has a clear story-line. Mc Andrew's "To a Carrion Crow" contrasts nicely with his celebrated "Ol Higue". While both are dramatic addresses to an unanswering Other, "To a Carrion Crow" is free verse and employs devices such as internal rhyming and metaphor. It not only invents a legend of the crow, but hints at an interpretation, the poet seeking meaning behind the plot's metaphor, in much the same way as the crow in hubris and wonder seeks meaning behind and beyond the sky's empty curvature. "Ol Haig", transcending earlier excursions into the vernacular such as the efforts of McTurk, is the first significant Guyana Creole poem. Addressing the "Ole woman wid the wrinkled skin", Mc Andrew recreates the legend of the Ol Haig. Dramatic and incantatory after the style of Macbeth, it however breaks its lines and rhythms towards the end. Together, the two poems illustrate the point about poets who are comfortable at both "poles" of the continuum.

Narrative becomes increasingly complicated in both plot and structure as one approaches contemporary times. Important landmarks in the progression of storytelling in West Indian verse were Scott's "Uncle Time" and Walcott's fine voice portraits, "Tales of the Islands". Concretising the abstract concept of Time, "Uncle Time" obeys the allegorical impulse of the folk tale, and employs not only a folk voice as narrator, but recognisable folk-tale characters and situations – the warmly avuncular but dirty and sinister old man, whose sexual play means blight, poison, bitterness and the withering of love; the legendary sly mongoose of one of the best known West Indian folk-songs, scurrying through the undergrowth; and most familiar of all, the deceitful anti-hero, Anansi, who in folk tales is a blend of libido, trickery and survivalist intelligence. Like Anansi, time is a shape-shifter capable of rapid metamorphosis, from apparent and beguiling stasis to sudden and swift movement; from old man to sea-wind, to hill, to mongoose, to spider whose functions also change from love-play to poisonous separating gossip, to ensnarement and finally, death-touch. The poem's major achievement is to have said all this in a folk-Creole voice which changes fluidly in pace and tone as Time changes his masks.

The sixth tale of the islands, "Poopa, da was a fete", betrays in its flawed first line the studied care of its crafting of the voice. When the true Creole speaker begins with the intensive and interjectory "Poopa" and "Mooma", he usually seeks an even greater intensity by omitting the indefinite article in whatever follows. The line should therefore read, "Poopa! da was fete!" with rising stress and pitch on the word "fete". A small point, which does not affect the poem's stature as the initiator of a line of oral poetry in which the voice recalls a kaleidoscope of passing sights, sounds and disconnected fragments of gossip, conversation and trivia. In "Poopa" there is disjuncture between the seamless fluid connectedness of the line which, like the drunken scholar's monologue, doesn't "let a comma in edgewise" and the disconnectedness of the information contained in the line. This disconnectedness is the poem's real subject matter; the disjuncture between the jump and jive and the anguish it conceals; between awareness of pain, horror and tragedy and the attempt to drown it out by means of drunken stupor; the recognition of the vital subterranean presence of a folk tradition, and the recoil from its more negative and frightening aspect: its secretion of a destructive, sterile malice.

This disconnectedness will recur later in Victor Questel's "Down Beat", where the moral emptiness of the street limer is expressed in terms of the equality of importance which he accords to cricket scores, rape, his sweet mas', pan music and prison. Questel's impulse here is essentially comic. The pun, the joke, are the cornerstones of his aesthetic. But even here the joke is juxtaposed to the possibility of derangement. By "Pan Drama" (included in another category) the narrative voice has already withdrawn into its loneliness. The persona there, as in Paul Keens-Douglas's "Jus Like Dat" is commenting on the masquerade after Carnival. Keens-Douglas's voice is that of a reveller awakening stale drunk on the pavement on Ash Wednesday morning, wondering how he got there, and piecing together his haphazard drift "jus' like dat" from vacancy through masquerade to dereliction and vagrancy. His story is the country's central fable and journey to which its poets and novelists and calypsonians continually return; its major myth: the passage from mas' to mass, or "from ole mas to half mast" as Questel puts it in his variation of the national pun.

The narrator of Questel's "Pan Drama", like that of Walcott's "Mass Man", has never been a participant; and thus has not even the memory of fantasy to sustain his reverie. He is well on the way to becoming the wry intelligence behind a poem such as "Wreck" or that bizarre tragicomedy of vagrancy: "Two Choices". The pan man, "attuned to the base tenor" of his daily ghetto existence becomes the poet's double, because of his skill at creating harmony and attunement out of the unrelated fragments of existence. It is interesting to listen to the calypsonian Relator work in "Deaf Panmen" with the same image of the pan man. Only here, the deafness of the pan man is related to that of the country's political leader, while the disharmony that ensues from the pan man's deafness is related to a fragmented society in which everyone is going in his own individual direction. Calypso too had moved towards metaphor over the years of its emergence from the kalinda and bel air.

Questel as poet generally works with unrelated images, the odds and ends of experience. This tendency is fuelled by, as it strives to explore, a fear of fissures within the psyche, an awareness of chasms of madness, blankness, void, the black hole of breakdown. His poems and plays display the two sides of Trinidad's famous "schizophrenia", not as separate halves, but intermixed, or so closely juxtaposed that in one half – the gaiety, the brilliance and the laughter – lies the ever imminent possibility of the other – the break-up, the breakdown. Hence his commitment to the pun, not as irritating ornament but as driven necessity. For in the pun lies the doubleness of vision, the duplicity of meaning and possibility which he sees in life, as well as the means of transcending the despair of the condition. "Hitting the bottle, my faith splinters."

The fragmented narrative is taken to even more desperate extremes by Mikey Smith in "Mi Cyaan Believe It", and Jean Binta Breeze's "Riddym Ravings", both of which present kaleidoscopes of the city's derangement. Smith shapes narrative fragments into sharply dislocated and rapidly changing impressions of voice and image. In a sense, the narrator is similar to that of Questel's "Down Beat", save for the menacing grimness of what is recalled: the struggle for existence alongside "cockroach, rat an scorpion", Anansi "politricks" in which the yout' are pitted against each other in sacrificial waste; prostitution, recurrent pregnancy; the casual pointlessness of violent encounter on the streets; that horrible Orange Lane fire in which children and mothers were fed to the flames by gunmen. That incident recurs as tragic nightmare in recent Jamaica poems (e.g. Scott's "Dreadwalk", Brathwaite's "Poem for Walter Rodney", Hippolyte's "Orange Lane: The Fire's Light"). It climaxes the list of incredible events and images which provide Smith's narrator with her now famous refrain: "Mi cyaan believe it."

Jean Binta Breeze's mad woman represents a further development of the fragmented fable. She's Slade Hopkinson's Madwoman of Papine, Roger McTair's deranged prophetess of "Ganja Lady", the mother who "gleams from the ghetto" in Brathwaite's "Springblade", and who will throw the first stone to which even now her claws of fingers are irreversibly hooked. The difference between the voice-portrait and the monologue/narrative is that in the latter the voice speaks from within the experience. "The Madwoman of Papine", Walcott's "Laventille" and McTair's "Ganja Lady" are voice-portraits. The voice describes a situation which is clearly seen from outside. Malik's two "Pan Run" poems, Mikey Smith's "Mi Cyaan Believe It", Questel's "Down Beat" and "Pan Drama", Binta Breeze's "Riddym Ravings" and Mutabaruka's "A Sit Dung Pun de Wall" are monologues which take us inside the minds of the narrators.

Binta Breeze's madwoman is telling the story of her derangement. It begins with her movement to the alienating city, continues with her eviction, prostitution, pregnancy and subsequent vagrancy, and climaxes with her obsession that within her head there's a radio with a DJ constantly playing a reggae refrain:

> Eh eh
> No feel no way
> Town is a place dat a really kean stay
> Dem kudda – ribbit mi han
> Eh – ribbit mi toe
> Mi waan go a country go look mango.

But the healing journey back to country, to land, ground, family, community and endless fruit – which is a recurring theme in Jamaican literature, from Mais's *The Hills Were Joyful Together* and "All Men Come to the Hills Finally", through Barrett's *Song for Mumu,* Brodber's *Jane and Louisa* and Senior's *Talking of Trees,* especially "Reaching My Station", and *Summer Lightning* – never occurs. The cleansing bath which she attempts one day at a city sidewalk standpipe is interpreted as a further sign of derangement and she's taken to the madhouse where the doctor and the landlord, the two evil geniuses of her world, try to remove the radio from her head. This obsessive sound, her song and lament, is at once the sign of her derangement and her last point of connection with her first world and her story. So pregnant, abused, but existing in a strangely happy space within her cracked head, she clings to the lifeline of her radio, her story, her refrain, tricking the doctor and the landlord by reconnecting whenever they disconnect her from her dream.

Other extended narratives include Pamela Mordecai's "Southern Cross" and James Berry's "Chain of Days". These are, however, more connected – as the metaphor of a chain of days suggests. The narrators here have an autobiographical sanity, a nostalgic security of untraumatic memory of rural childhood, which even now seems attainable. Binta Breeze's narrator, by contrast, lives for a past she'll never regain, but which she has made her sole and obsessional reality, negating the dislocation and mental shock of urban experience.

Binta Breeze's "Riddym Ravings" recalls Shadow's calypso "Bass Man", where the narrator is plagued by a monstrous double named Farrell, who controls his creative impulse by constantly pulling the strings of his bass. The bass man is his muse, the source of the driving new hypnotic rhythm which Shadow brought to the calypso in 1971, the year when in "The Threat" he threatened to bring water to the eye of Kitchener, the Road March King. But the Bass Man is also a fixed obsession, a demon of rhythm, the monstrous double of imagination of which Shadow seeks to unburden himself, the Other whom he feels an urge to kill: Shadow's Shadow.

> Ah went and ah tell Dr. Leon
> I want a brain operation
> A man in me head
> Ah want him to dead
> He said it's my imagination
> But I know I hearing the bassman
> [...]
> I don't know how this thing get inside me
> But every morning he driving me crazy
> Like he taking me head for a panyard
> Morning and evening like the fellow gone mad
> Tim Tom – And if ah don't want to sing
> Tim Tom – When he start to do he ting
> Ah don't want to, but I have to sing
> Tim Tom – And if ah don't want to dance
> Tim Tom – He does put me in a trance
> Ah don't want to, but I have to prance

The "Bass Man" electrified Trinidad in 1974. "Shadowmania" became a new Trinidad word by 1975, as the society recognised its dark double of creative obsessional energy in the earth of Shadow's harsh-sweet tones.

VI: Elegy/Lament

The elegy has become a predominant mode in West Indian poetry, perhaps because St. John Perse's "tristes tristes tropiques" still produce much that can evoke lamentation. Here the elegies are for the society itself, for its myriad failures and victims. These laments explore every register along the speech continuum, and include Linton Kwesi Johnson's beautiful "Reggae for Radni", and Malik's haunting "Fireflies... for Beverly", of which "Fireflies" is an elegiac lullaby for lost girlhood, as well as a warning that the blood of Beverly Jones, shot down as a guerilla in the seventies, will eventually be redeemed by "fireflies". The other half of the song/poem, "for Beverly", is spoken against the background of the song.

Other laments are for the general state of things, (e.g. Eric Roach's "Hard Drought"), for the failure of some great moment (Salkey's "Maurice" Johnson's "Reggae for Radni"). Roger McTair's "March-February Remembering", included for its cool dreaming narrative voice in the first section, also belongs here. These categories are not meant to be exclusive: many poems belong to several of them. Many of these elegies are also praise songs, which seek to celebrate the qualities of the person who has died. This is particularly true of those which are dedicated to artists, poets and musicians. Harold Simmons becomes for Walcott "the fervour and intelligence of an entire island." Drummond becomes for McNeill his guide through dread city and the dark places of the heart.

VII: Dread Talk: Warnings: Dub: Sermon: Prophesaying

Dub poems are poems which have grown directly out of the speech and music rhythms of reggae and Rastafari. They represent an extension of the much older toaster tradition, which in Jamaica involved the DJ talking smart, slick and often silly jingles into the microphone, either in introduction of a tune or in the spaces between the music. This was happening with ska in the early sixties, and developed further with rocksteady, a music with wider spaces, in an attempt to fill which DJ's such as U-Roy developed, until their voice became even more important than the bumpy rhythms over which it rode.

Technological change in the mixing of music, the advent of the 16-track tape and easy over-dubbing, the development of the synthesiser, intensified the DJ's role as manipulator of sound, juggler of gimmicks, controller of rhythm and pace, exhorter of the audience, who would be soldiered into jumping, prancing, raising their hands in the air, wining, grinding, and jamming, getting up or getting down to it. The DJ became high priest in the cathedral of canned sound, fragmented discotheque image projections, broken lights, and youth seeking lost rituals amid the smoke of amnesia.

Dub poetry is at its worst a kind of tedious jabber to a monotonous rhythm. At its best it is the intelligent appropriation of the manipulatory techniques of the DJ for purposes of personal and communal signification. As I said earlier, the dub poet speaks from within the ghetto experience, clarifying the confrontation between the lumpen youth and the entrenched system. Of all the poems included here, the dub poem needs most to be heard, and there are excellent recordings of Linton Kwesi Johnson, Oku Onuora, Michael Smith, Binta Breeze and Mutabaruka. Space does not permit a full discussion of these poets in performance. A few notes will have to suffice. The very nature of reggae, heavy bass-line and space between voice and "riddim" with horns or synthesiser muted in the middle range, generally means that one can hear every word of the performance. Sound is stripped down to the skeleton of riddim, with the superimposition of the flesh of voice in performance. In dub, one runs less risk of the voice having to compete against its accompaniment than frequently happens with calypso in performance. There are, however, instances when dub poets have complained about the competition between voice and accompaniment.

One danger that dub poets face is to believe that riddim can or should be allowed to become the sole foundation of the dub poem's appeal. The better poets avoid this pitfall, first of all by making subtle variations in tone, pace and heaviness of the beat. The heavier the beat, the more "dread" the emotion. There is a whole vocabulary of tone and feeling contained in what Linton Kwesi Johnson has identified as "bass culture". Apart from variation in how a regular bass-line is employed, there is the technique of breaking up the poem, so that it varies between unaccompanied monologue and those sequences where the voice follows the contour of the beat. In "Reggae fi Dada", Johnson employs this technique in order to vary the mood of the poem between sorrow for his father, relief at his release from the stony asperities of Jamaican life and bitterness at the fact that the country could have offered no more than this mean, unchanging bareness.

Sometimes the poem is for unaccompanied voice. This type of poem usually allows the performer greater freedom, since the bass-line no longer controls its movement. The unaccompanied voice is particularly effective in Mutabaruka's "Sit Dung Pun De Wall", whose theme is precisely that of the menacing silence which exists between the terrified passerby and the vagrant, society and its double. The poem has a freedom of voice and contains a certain humour of the grotesque, oddly similar to that of Kendel Hippolyte's "Zoo Story".[14] In both cases, the deadpan tone of the narrating voice conceals the horror of what is being narrated, a tragic and unnecessary accident in the case of Mutabaruka; the fatal encounter between dungle dread and jungle lion in the zoo's symbolic space, in the case of Hippolyte. Binta Breeze's performance of "Riddim Ravings" also employs the relative silence of the unaccompanied voice to convey the rational irrationality of a woman who, pushed beyond the threshold of pain, no longer feels anything. Here, too, there is the mixture of humour and horror, as the madwoman sanely talks about the radio inside her head.

The narrator of Mutabaruka's "Sit Dung Pun De Wall" is a street dweller whose only connection with the well-dressed, faint-hearted passer-by is through the silent exchange of glances – neutral on the part of the narrator, wary on the part of the passer-by, whose peace of mind depends on there being absolutely no alteration of the position of the vagrant, or of the visible space between them. As soon as the vagrant changes his normal position, the self-affrighted passer-by panics, runs into the path of a passing car and is killed. A menacing, tantalising poem, it provokes speculation as to its hidden meaning. Is it a parable of the society's movement closer to its time of terror, whose measure is the deteriorating condition of the vagrant?

Oku consciously tries for a menacing tone in poems such as "Pressure Drop". His style blends chant and statement, with the guttural voice expressing at times a great sadness, at others a great indignation. There is sincerity and fervour in the voice as the poet tries to transcend the written word and become himself the poem. Oku defines this ordeal precisely when he declares:

> I am no poet
>   no poet
> I am just a voice
> I echo the people's
>   thought
>   laughter
>   cry
>   sigh...
> I am no poet
>   no poet
>
> I am just a voice

The aim of the dub poet, then, is to submerge identity in voice. Mutabaruka makes a similar claim in "Poem". This does not mean, however, that these poets really abandon their individuality. Mikey Smith's performances are absolutely individual. His use of voice, his honing of voice to stark sheer scrape of sound; his prolonged "Lawwwwwwwwwwwd" cannot be imitated. Of the dub poets, he was probably the most flexible, the one who had the greatest impulse to abandon the beat and allow the voice to establish its own rhythm.

Dub poetry, and indeed, much of the aesthetic of the oral tradition, employs repetition as a cardinal technique. Malik's elegy for Mikey Smith, "Instant Ting", employs a technique found in some folk ballads, where each stanza advances the plot by one idea, inching it towards its climax. Mikey is simultaneously recognised by both his admirers and his enemies. His admirers recognise him as hero/king: "swift as a hawk/with a hop and drop walk." His enemies instantaneously recognise him as target for the stone. It is as if he draws their menace upon himself, by his too visible and defiant independence of spirit. The poem limps on its hop-and-drop Legba rhythm towards the menace of the stone, its muttering bass varying by semitones.

VIII: Calypso; Rapso; Pan; Parang; Hosay

Dub poems are heavy with testimony, warning and prophesy. So too are many post-1970 calypsos, a few of which have even incorporated reggae rhythms and dread themes. The calypsos selected here illustrate a range of themes, concerns and styles. The eloquence and wonder in the word inherited from the oratorical period are clearly seen in Atilla's "Graf Zeppelin". Tiger's "The Gold" helped arouse public opinion in Trinidad during the Italian invasion of Abyssinia. The strong narrative quality and the often bizarre humour of the calypso are illustrated in Kitchener's "Take Your Meat Out Me Rice" and Spoiler's "Fountain of Youth". Protest, complaint, satire and wisdom may be seen in the calypsoes of Relator, Stalin, Sparrow, Valentino and Chalkdust.

Always strong in sexual metaphor, calypsos gradually expanded their metaphorical range, and in the period after 1970 began to reveal an admirable control of image and idea. Penguin's "The Devil" (1980) redefines evil in secular and political terms, employing the vocabulary and rhythm of the old-time devil band. This is a calypso which develops a single image, providing several illustrations of the devil theme, throughout its length. It ends with an ironic twist typical of the decade when it warns the society:

> And if you praise the wrongs men do
> Well then you is a devil too.

Society is diabolical because it has permitted the devil to exist. Calypsonians, after a decade of assigning blame to politicians for the ills of society, had begun to turn their scrutiny upon the nation itself. Even Valentino, dubbed "the people's calypsonian" after 1970 because of the sincerity and plaintive strength of his songs, focuses a withering irony on the people in his magnificent "Dis Place Nice".

> We live in a land
> The better part is owned by the aliens
> We fill the pockets
> Of Portuguese, Chinese and Syrians.
> Trinidadians is who should own land
> Now is the time to make the land your possession
> But their sense of taste could just trace
> To all them fancy showcase.
> So the businessman, he blow their mind
> And his dollars they have to find.

> Trinidad is nice for men like Sabga,
> Kirpalani, Maraj and Y. De Lima
> Chorus: – Trinidad is nice
>   Trinidad is a paradise
> Amoco and Shell, business going swell
> On your oil those foreign parasites dwell
> Chorus: – Trinidad is nice
>   Trinidad is a paradise

Here, the coherence of the calypso depends on a constant exposure of the old calypso cliché "Trinidad is nice/Trinidad is a paradise." This cliché had become one of the stockphrases of the patriotic calypso, and it had become fashionable in post-1970 calypsos to comment ironically on rooted attitudes and catchphrases. Chalkdust, for example, rejected the "smutty calypso" in "Why Smut" and "Juba Dubai". Stalin turned Sniper's "Portrait of Trinidad" inside out with his "New Portrait of Trinidad".

The calypsonian has emerged, then, as a critic of consciousness, and the calypso has become aware of itself, its formal potentialities and limitations, its confused and ever-changing aesthetic. This suggests that the calypsonian has begun the journey towards an inclusion of the full range of human emotions in what used to be a form where only certain types of feeling or mood – celebration, praise, censure, erotic desire, ridicule – were admitted. Stalin's "Make Them All Right" (1984) approached anguish and compassion, while Delamo's apocalyptic condemnation of human limitation in "Sodom and Gomorrah" (1982) and "Armageddon" (1984) is, if hopeless, still a genuinely anguished cry from the heart.

Included in *Voiceprint* is Delamo's "Apocalypse" (1981), a calypso that illustrates the development in the poetic use of language in calypso. Social commentary, the anguished concern for the state of the nation, the phenomenal development of image and allusion, the use of mask and allegory, and the perfect blending of lyrical and musical content together constitute the poem's strength. Delamo's mask is that of the prophet or apostle of the Apocalypse. Like St. John the Divine, he is given a dream/vision of the end of the material world; or the world of materialism, the Trinidad of money, financial complexes, wildcat investment and super-fraudulence. This Trinidad has its most appropriate symbol in the proposed Racing Complex in Caroni which cost the nation hundreds of millions of embezzled dollars. Around this complex run the four horses of the Apocalypse. The spectators are "ministers, businessmen, even a president," who "kneel down worshipping this horse as if it was the day of judgement," and who "ignore the son of man" though he was there. Line by line it flays the government for its moral decadence, and its failure to foresee the disaster and collapse which are symbolised by the fourth horse – a mangy grey ridden by a skeleton and headed for the Lapeyrouse

Cemetery. This mangy grey horse has its double in a real Trinidad racehorse of the late seventies named "Beheaded". The "headless horse" of the final stanza, Beheaded, was entered in a major race in Venezuela, and ran last. This event is regarded as symbolic of our headless state, our visionless, directionless, decapitated leadership sallying forth into the economic big time and trailing behind better equipped organised countries.

The calypso, then, captures a delicate balance between the plainest and the most metaphorical speech. Drawing instinctively on the religious base, it yet understands that it must secularise myth if myth is to make any sense in an agnostic age. The growing dimension of the calypso inspired Derek Walcott to attempt a long satirical and narrative poem in a simplified version of the calypso rhythm. In this poem, "The Spoiler's Return", the ghost of one of the most famous calypsonians of the fifties returns from hell to denounce Trinidad for its myriad failures. The Spoiler functions as persona for Walcott himself, and the poem, like "The Schooner *Flight*" is meant not only to lacerate, but to justify the poet's belated self-exile from a country which had increasingly evoked in him feelings of helplessness and rage.

Also worthy of note in this section are the "rapso" poems of Brother Resistance. A development of the "talk-songs" (my term) of Trinidad musician Lancelot Layne (e.g. "Blow Way", "Bringing Off", "Ghetto"), Jamaican dub, calypso and Afro-American rapping songs, rapso's themes are essentially those we've already discussed in our discourse on dub – blackness, poverty, ghetto culture, vagrancy, Africa, "the struggle", apartheid. Like dub it is a performed art, very much in its infancy and developing. I haven't yet seen the development in narrative for which I've commended a few of the dub poems, or the growing command of metaphor which we've seen in the calypso. Brother Resistance, a UWI graduate, represents a new type – the grassroots intellectual for whom the very world and word of the intellectual is an abstraction that needs to be resisted, lest it direct vision away from the immediacy of social reality. Just as Walcott instinctively resists the pressure of the oral tradition, making concessions to it only when it has, through its own efforts, gained in depth and dimension, Brother Resistance struggles against the treacherous voids which underlie the world of "Book" ("Book so Deep"), measuring as did Lamming's G., the price which he has paid in being educated beyond his reality.

The "pan" poems, which have their counterpart in a large number of calypsos about the steelband, usually derive their metaphors from the steelband, whose rhythms and idioms they may try to imitate. The most significant of these are Malik's monologues, "Pan Run I" and "Pan Run II"[15] and John Agard's *Man to Pan*. There are also the lyrical prose pieces of Marc Matthews ("Rass Pan") and Paul Keens-Douglas ("Sugar George").

Agard's *Man to Pan* pays homage to its predecessors, the poems of Brathwaite, Malik, Kitchener and Keens-Douglas, and is a sustained experiment with shape, rhythm and metaphor. Its climax is a roadmarch whose narrator is Spree Simon, one of the fathers of Pan.

IX:

The other poems included in *Voiceprint* fall into familiar categories. The monologues chosen range from Louise Bennett's "Me Bredda" to McNeill's "Strange My Writing to You". As in the other categories, a wide range of linguistic registers is represented. Brathwaite's "Nametracks", a poem originally included in the anthology, actually employs an imagined language, the transitional pidgin of Caliban, who is caught between his broken mother tongue and Prospero's half-understood language of individualism, power and greed. Caliban invents words, working from sound and syllable towards his meanings. Brathwaite seeks to capture the flux of his transitional "making-up and breaking-up" (Harris) language, while he notes Caliban's inner assurance that the name given him by his mother will survive Prospero's efforts to devour it.

"Signifying" is a term borrowed from Afro-American streetlore to describe the tendency of black men towards heroic self-identification. This tendency was also strong in the West Indies, and once formed the core of the oratorical or sans humanité tradition in the calypso. In *Voiceprint,* the term is applied to poems of self-identification, particularly those that locate the individual in the political or historical moment. Not all of these, however, are expressions of heroic self-confidence. There are also many poems which express a brooding self-doubt or a qualified pessimism (e.g. Walcott's "Codicil" or Questel's "Wreck").

Praise songs, prayers and incantations are also included. These are the opposite of tracings, curses and warnings, for which the islands are renowned, and which are well represented here. Political manifestos and satirical pieces are also included. Satire here involves parody of revolutionary rhetoric ("Shaka's Cycle"), statistics, and the manipulatory language of officialdom, (e.g. Keane's "Per Capita Per Annum" and Sharma's "Government Memorandum").

"Word Songs" constitute an unusual category; but it was felt that the considerable body of poems about music, or poems which capture the lilt of song should be represented here. Even here there is voice. Collymore's "Hymn to the Sea" is a kind of monologue, as is Roach's "Transition" and Goodison's "Mulatta". McNeill addresses his ecstatic music poems to the unanswering void that he terms "Ungod", Christine Craig to a saxophone player. Several other poems, located in other categories, might fit here.

The selection ends with a number of poems about poetry, statements of aesthetic. These vary considerably and contain affirmations of both public and private modes. Wayne Davis, for example, whose "Prison Blues" (not included) is the most naked and direct protest, indicates in his tribute to Miles Davis, "Miles Beyond", his preference for an art which has transcended the horror of its origins. Black artists have, he believes, been denying themselves their human fullness. Miles Davis has moved:

> ...miles beyond
> The common rush and sometimes
> Hysterical, splintered sway,
> Of the common, troubled, black propagandist way
> In art or music
> And in that crystal calm
> Where silence is stretched thin
> Like the blue membrane of the sky,
> The pointed arrows of your blues
> Is each man's historically tragic cry
> But only more calm, more assured
> And more elegant
> Graceful, classical, in its stripped simplicity,
> And therefore more deadly.

The statements of aesthetic counterpoint each other. Taken together, they illustrate the point of this collection of poems: that a West Indian aesthetic will embrace all ways of saying, all language registers, however contradictory some of these may seem to be; that each type of saying requires its particular skill for shaping voice; that "Man must chant as man can, 'gainst night."[16]

(First published, London, Longman Group U.K., 1989.)

References

1. Rohlehr, G., "The Problem of the Problem of Form: The Idea of an Aesthetic Continuum and Aesthetic Code-switching in West Indian Literature", *Anales del Caribe* Vol. 6, 1986, pp. 218-277.
2. Rohlehr, G., *Pathfinder. Black Awakening in* The Arrivants *of Edward Kamau Brathwaite* (Trinidad: 1981).
3. See Brathwaite's *Contradictory Omens* (Jamaica: Savacou, 1974) for the term "inter-creolisation".
4. Joe Harriott/Johnny Mayer et al., *Fusions*, EMI records, SX 6122 & *Indo-Jazz* Suite, Atlantic, SD 1465.
5. Jarvis, A., *Bamboula Drum* (St. Thomas, V.I.: The Art Shop, 1935, in Krauz Reprint, Germany, 1970).
6. Curtin, P., *The Image of Africa: British Ideas and Action, 1780-1850* (Wisconsin: University of Wisconsin Press, 1964).
7. Rohlehr, G., "Calypso Censorship: Historical," in *Seminar on the Calypso* (UWI, Trinidad: ISER, 1986).
8. Roach, E., *Trinidad Guardian*, 14 Jan., 1971. See also Rohlehr, G., "Some

Problems of Assessment", *Caribbean Quarterly,* Vol. 17 Nos, 3 & 4 (Sept-Dec., 1971) pp. 92-113.
9. See Lovelace, E., *The Wine of Astonishment* (London: Deutsch, 1982).
10. Walcott, D., "What the Twilight Says: An Overture", in *Dream* on *Monkey Mountain and Other Plays* (New York: Farrar, Straus & Giroux, 1970).
11. Ibid., p. 17.
12. Walcott, D., Interviewed by Raoul Pantin in *Caribbean Contact*, Vol. 1, No. 7, (July 1973), pp. 14-16 & Vol. 1, No. 8, (August 1973), pp. 14-16. Quotation from Part 2, August 1973, p. 14.
13. Ibid.
14. Rohlehr, G., See "The Problem of the Problem of Form", where Hippolyte's "Zoo Story" is discussed.
15. Rohlehr, G., "My Strangled City", *Caliban* Vol. 2, No. 1, Fall/Winter, 1976.
16. Scott, D., "More Poem" in *Dreadwalk* (London: New Beacon Books Ltd. 1982), p. 3.

"MEGALLEONS OF LIGHT":
KAMAU BRATHWAITE'S SUN *POEM*

"The sun made patterns on the water that gave birth to children"
(*Sun Poem*)

The Arrivants (1967-69) located the Caribbean islands and their present inhabitants in a broad historical context involving settlement, disruption, catastrophe, movement, exile and reconstruction, and viewed Caribbean sensibility as a process and an issue of this history. *Black + Blues* (1976) intensified Brathwaite's focus on the contemporary diasporan person in the Caribbean and America. In that collection one perceives an emerging secular eschatology in which historical process increasingly creates the possibility of apocalypse. The omen of apocalypse has been predominant in Brathwaite's poetry since the mid-seventies, and has led him to review the grim history of the contact of Western Atlantic civilisation with the civilisations of the New World, and to trace the arc of the vulture of empire as it has swung from feeding ground to feeding ground.

The vision of apocalypse has, however, been counterpointed by "our calm histories" – the largely autobiographical *Mother Poem* (1977) and *Sun Poem* (1982). In those works Brathwaite has tried to trace the coral's growth of the history of his "mother", Barbados, and the tension is between the poet's sense of belonging to landscape, sun and sea, and his awareness of the country's dislocation from both an ancestral past and the sort of education necessary to self-perception. *Mother Poem* portrays and meditates on the lives and fates of a number of women, who in soliloquy define their lot and ultimately rebel against the roles which have been imposed on them. The poem owes its dimension and structural coherence to the fact that the "mother" is identified with the island itself, the sea surrounding it, the limestone caves of subterranean water beneath it, and all of these are metaphors for anima and muse. The "mother" is, ultimately, a principle of renewal and rebirth, an aspect of universal law which counterpoints the apparently irreversible entropy of the apocalyptic poems.

Sun Poem unites three distinct themes. There is the autobiographical "Son" poem. There is, secondly, the historical theme in which Brathwaite tries to project into visibility Bussa, the leader of a nineteenth century slave revolt, to suggest ways of rewriting the history of the catastrophic collision of Africa with Europe, and to describe the island's loss of myth and a sense of the meaning of the hero-archetype. The third poem is "sun" poem in which the microcosmic histories of both Adam, universal man, and Barbados, the earth and sea which he has been given, are placed in a framework of cosmic principle, in which movement is simultaneously towards the waste and void of entropy, and towards the sunlight and rainbow of renewal.

The autobiographical "Son" poem is a lyrical description of a boyhood in sun and sea, with all the rituals peculiar to boyhood: the initiatory fights, the acquisition of beach and sea skills, dreaming, falling in love. The portrait of boyhood has the authenticity of experience intimately felt, of sensation faithfully rendered; though it should be noted that autobiography is set at a distance by Brathwaite's choice of the name Adam – first man, father of the human race and Son of God – for his protagonist. Adam becomes a little like Wordsworth's primal child, a representation of childhood itself, where immediacy of sensation transcends meaning. It is age and growth that expose Adam to the meaning and pattern which have emerged from his experience.

Part of this poem was written twenty years ago. "The Return of the Sun" (Section IX, pp. 73-83) first appeared as "Christine" in *Bim* Vol. 8, No. 32 (Jan-Jul 1961) pp. 246-50. In that excerpt, the boy's name is also Adam, though the girl, who is to become *Esse* (Being?) in *Sun Poem*, is called Christine. The two versions are nearly the same, except that in the poem the dialogue is in italics and the story is split up into intervals or movements and has a number of interpolated new passages. Esse is given a lisp which Christine lacked.

Frank Collymore, in his introduction to *Bim* 32 quoted Henry Swanzy:

> A propos writers from Barbados he [Swanzy] observes: "A talent that almost equals his (George Lamming's) is that of Edward Brathwaite, a Cambridge graduate with some remarkable poems of Europe, and at least one unpublished novella, *The Boy and the Sea,* obscure but brilliant."

One suspects that most of the purely autobiographical element of *Sun Poem* has derived from that unpublished novella. A great deal of *Sun Poem* is narrative or descriptive prose, sometimes, though not always, controlled by a certain rhythmic regularity patterned, I think, on the movement of waves. In *Mother Poem* there is a continuous sea-surge and cadence which can be heard even in passages that don't treat of the sea. In *Sun Poem* there is less sea-swell, but more lilt and ripple of waves in the boyhood sequences. The reason for this is that the sea in *Mother Poem* is the major presence through which the perpetual ongoing movement of the life-force is conveyed, while in *Sun Poem*, this function is performed by the sun, the sea becoming a stage on which the drama of boyhood is enacted, its movement a dance which parallels the pure sensation of youth.

The autobiographical element extends into a portrait of the island's sons and fathers, paralleling the portraits of the women in *Mother Poem*, and ending with the grandfather's death where *Mother Poem* had closed with the grandmother's. Among the sons are beach boys who grow up with their fishermen fathers and "land boys" who also grow up on the beaches, but come from more conventional homes. Brathwaite accords the beach boys of memory an almost legendary stature, through his portrayal of Batto and the folklore of repeated narrative, passed on from generation to generation of beach children, which surrounds him. Batto is a beach hero and bully, a kind, of amphibian boy-god, honoured by the poet with the emblems of sun and sea.

> his skin which on the beach was hard and rough and was spotted with salt
> till it flaked like scales was smooth in the water and tight in the wind...
>
> and the sun was a medal on batto's chest (p. 17)

Batto, who looks forward to a manhood when "proper prison" will fulfil the short sojourn he has already served at a boy's reform school, is mixture of angel of light and snake. There isn't only the reference to "scales", but later in the same passage we are told of his "glittering weight", and there is the reference to "the fallen star". Adam's underwater wrestle with him is a rite of passage, a do or die struggle with the lucifer of the beach.

It is not surprising that intimations of the fall from this boyhood paradise come immediately after Adam's encounter with Batto, when the boys' consciousness begins to alternate between the mythology which grows naturally out of the marriage of sun, sea landscape and the people whom they know, and the alienating archetypes of a foreign folklore, which they enact in their games. They will eventually pay for this in an incapacity to generate hero-archetypes patterned on the fathers that they know.

> the games we *paid* had little meaning

Those which retained their African form had lost their significance and were, indeed, never recognised as having been African. The others, from Robin Hood to Monopoly and Monte Carlo, already celebrate the ethos of romantic fantasy and vampiric capitalism which will prey on their adult lives. The constant absorption of Euro/American norms and image-ideals results in plastic, undead people, grinning a white celotex welcome to tourists.

> when strangers passed and said hell
>
> o: we let our eye
> lids down and slowly un
> dead: grinned (p. 20)

Brathwaite is later to reflect on his own poetic role in the image of

> the lighthouse distant beyond distance beyond fields
> now silvery like nerves in darkness like quixote with
>   his lance of light
> searching for salt for dead souls for
>
> we were dead: the us/not us: the dust: blood
> spilled: green branches of the family bone cut off
> from root and rib and culture (p. 92)

The image of the lighthouse beam searching for dead souls appeared earlier in the "Mid-Life" section of *Mother Poem*. The task which the poet sets himself, then, is to illuminate dead souls, to resurrect the ghosts of the past for the enlightenment of the undead, so that a reconnection with root and rib and culture might occur. It is a task which, predictably, many have deemed futile or impossible, the undead not lacking voice or point of view, or pride in their undeadness.

The Adams and Bussas are due to become the fathers of "Clips", whose grey or histrionic lives are measured against the sun's arc. The first father is "your secular bourgeois family man of the property owning class," who begins with a sense of responsibility, lapses into fornication and ends in eclipse, vainly awaiting fulfilment in the society's recognition of his talents. Impotence and obsolescence are his lot as he experiences

> the afternoon of fathers going grey
>   soft in the head
>   in the belly
>   in the heart
>
> and where it hurts him most (p. 66)

In *Mother Poem* ("Moth Air") we have the aging wife reflecting on the noon and afternoon infidelities of this husband with tired resignation, because their life together has become part of the menage of work, sweat and joyless effort, the tedium and flatness of the daily round to which she has dedicated her life.

The second type of father is middle of the middle, the good Christian paterfamilias who differs from his secular brother only insofar as he has more property and respectability, and sexually exploits the maid at home rather than going outside "the four white walls of moderation" for his amours. His afternoon fate, a judgement passed by time upon this hypocritical preserver of the old plantocratic skin trade, is natty dread children who hate his guts and seek to enter the world of explosive youth culture with the urgency of those who, born to privilege, imagine themselves to have missed something by not having been poor enough, black enough or roots enough. The results of the children's choice of blackness – pop, anarchism or leftwing activism – have already been dramatised by Brathwaite in "Dred" (*Other Exiles,* pp. 47-48) where the judge in passing judgement on the dread rapist suddenly sees in the condemned his son, his double and image; his own dual life, in short, and the emptiness of his soul which the wig of dead caucasian hair, so different from dreadlocks, can scarcely conceal.

The third "version" of fathers – the word "version" warns us – are the real dreads, the makers and products of reggae culture. Despite his affirmation of the music and creativity of this counter-culture, Brathwaite is critical of its deficiencies. Its energies are as misplaced and wasted as those of the youth in "Glass" (*Black + Blues*) those pathetic "angels of the fix". Almost outside of any system, they seem to avoid being exploited in the labour market, but at the hustler's price of living a life at the behest of chance and "skull". Responsibility is outside their vocabulary, and their fatherhood comes early.

> the thrilldrens here are feathers in a hat-
> trick or medals upon
> idi amins chest
> no more no less (p. 69)

Children, the products of the thrill of the second, are regarded as a trick or trap by these gun-children, whose deification of Rhygin and Amin suggests a debased machismo which crowns itself as casually with murder as it does with offspring. This "version of fathers" is, of course, indigenous to the debased politics of Jamaica in which they have achieved status as gunmen for both political parties. They were part of Duvalier's Haiti, Gairy's Grenada, and have since surfaced in Guyana. They seldom live to see their afternoons.

The portraits of fathers end with a monologue which is the counterpart of the wife's reflection in *Mother Poem* on what the system has done to her man ("Twine", *Mother Poem* pp. 6-7). The man's lament concerns his having become dispossessed of sunlight and the rainbow promise of boyhood. The father, in his afternoon, watches his son growing bigger towards his noon, with the envy and muted bitterness that normally characterises the father's reaction in an Oedipal situation:

> is only i gettin smaller. somethin squeezin i head like a sorringe.
> uh drink it an dry. is the sun dyein out of i vision. no man i never
> did own it. cause a man cyan be faddah to faddah if e nevvah get
> chance to be son/light (p. 71)

Implied here is the father's realisation that his son has replaced him in his wife's affection, and has thus become the real "father" in the house. We saw this happening early in *Mother Poem* (pp. 12-14). Now that his wife has started working "to make enns meet" and begun to establish the meagre basis for an independent income, the father feels his manhood to be doubly eroded, regarding her independence as his own diminishment. Now he returns to an empty house in which he is a stranger, "a dry stick stickin up lonely". It is in the context of his own diminishment and sexual sterility ("a dry stick") that he envies his son his youth, even as he laments his own eclipse.

Though, as we have observed, his soliloquy parallels the woman's in *Mother Poem*, tragically, neither woman nor man understands or speaks openly in the presence of the other. Misunderstanding of each other's loneliness generally takes the form of quarrelling; a constant loveless bickering on the part of the women and a bitter resigned silence on the part of the men. The women, who move in a world of religiosity, are generally more able to ritualise their sorrows, and their laments sometimes are given the strength and depth of song. Thus in *Sun Poem* the wife, faced with dispossession and destitution after her husband's death,

> sang the hymn without tune without words with long
>   hot pregnant pauses
> chugging the milk into butter
> hugging its warm animal mutter closer and closer and closer
> and
> *amen* was all she could say
>   to the back and the break and the breeders of strife
> *amen* to the wind and the fish and the cool of the knife
> *amen amen* to their love and the men in her life

The song issues forth like the spasms and contractions of pregnancy. But it does issue forth, this tuneless, wordless, heartbreak hymn, and with it there is a faith to continue, a quality of stoicism different from the men's bitter hopeless pride and eventual resignation to life's planned obsolescence.

II

The second major theme concerns the consequences of a society's continued disconnection from its past. We first see it in the absence of an indigenous hero-archetype on which the boys can pattern their games (pp. 19-20). We see it next in their rapid loss of a capacity to dream; a loss so extreme that they have no room for the dreamer or for the poetry of their own inward growing.

> Bubbles of the world
> sky blue moonlight
>
> the sons of earth ignore dreamers
>   faced with bone iron steel in their pillagers
>
>   they work long lines of rock cutters
>
> harrowing steps up the steps of the cit-
> adel terracing fields to the factory (p. 37)

The divorce between the worlds of work and dream is absolute for those who are chained to a self-renewing system of exploitation in which the factory's ancient treadmill and Henri Christophe's citadel are two millstones in the same old grind.

The dreamer, out of step with the treadmill rhythms of reality, seeks to relocate his experience in time, history and myth; to roll away the boulder in the back garden under which history is interred. This history, as in the harmattan poem "Crab" (*Black + Blues*), is imaged by the crab who "knew ancient histories/ old harbour cartegena tenoctitlan." The poet dreams of becoming reconnected with the submerged histories of the peoples, which have never been taught on his island. He sees omens of that history in the ordinary actions and work of his people. The stone-cutting gangs replace the slave gangs. The sea-egg hunters, for all the clarity and beauty of light and wave which surrounds their work, are conquistadors and treasure hunters, "rippin an robin an rapin the ripenin blue egg blackeyed summertime sea." They reenact an ancient piracy in which both landscape and people are raped of gold, pristine fertility and vision.

> the blue black boats blazed with the white living
> > white waving light
>
> of the heaped-up sea-egg shells and they cracked the egg through
> > its one black
> watery eye and their spoons raked the gold core clean. (p. 24)

The centre of *Sun Poem* is preoccupied with the consequences of the split vision of the already half-blind, one-eyed colonial. The transition from lyrical boyhood to the moment when the eye was cracked is smoothly accomplished in the "The Crossing", which is on the surface a description of a Sunday school trip to the eastern side of the island, but soon becomes invested with metaphorical significance. We are prepared for the crossing by a vision of the island from off the west coast. The land seems to vanish as one travels further west. Here we have, unobtrusively, the connection between the diaspora and amnesia. The poet shifts in his seat to look back because the vision is a disquieting one of slow obliteration, engulfment and the loss of enlightenment. Here then are intimations of both personal and communal loss:

> how the land that you loved like your mother
> seemed to sink under dark choppy water
> that was ringing you round like a wall

Eventually, only the tallest trees, (the poets? the rebels? a handful of exceptional people?) still remain visible.

> but they were losing their colour
> but they were closing their names
> they didn't toss light anymore (p. 41)

Consequent upon this erasure of name and vision and heritage is the distortion of the image of Africa in the popular mind. The eastern side of the island, the side of the sun's red rising, is associated with a terror of Ogun/Shango turbulence. The Atlantic coast facing the middle passage is metaphorically that suppressed area of the diasporan psyche, associated here with that area of lost history, of suppressed, submerged identity, which resurfaces in the society's exaggerated dismay and terror at the emerging Rastafarian movement.

> and the sea over there was a giant of i: ron
> a rasta of water with rumbelling muscles and turrible
>   turrible hair (p. 42)

These schoolboys, perfectly at home with the white horrors of barnabas collins and dracula in whose images they have remade themselves, convert the iron of Ogun into the panicky Bajun "i : ron" – flight from face. The journey from west to east coast thus becomes an unnecessarily fearful rite of passage. It is worth bearing in mind, however, that Brathwaite believes that the journey can and should be made, and that he does present us with a vision of the emerging land, and the possibility of reinvigorated powers of recall, as we begin to travel eastwards.

"Noom", a blend of noon and doom, is Brathwaite's version of this suppressed history, what he has elsewhere termed the "alter-renaissance". Prospero's history and historiography are filtered through Caliban's ironic eyes. Racists of the Long-De Gobineau-Froude-Carlyle school are caught in the ironic glare:

> there were tribes of scarecrows
> hunters of heads who ate humane bones
> crink skull and cavicle
>
> big buttock women who preferred to mate with baboons

The superstitions of history are invoked to be deflated by Caliban's vision of Prospero's heroes of civilisation:

> and worshipped the devil like
> henry viii, like leo x, like francis i, like pope joan
> of arc, like baptists, like Jesuit   priests, like ni-
> collo machiavelli like the niggers they were (p. 48)

Precisely when Europe is experiencing its Reformation and everyone in sectarian Christianity is defining everyone else as the devil; precisely when Europe is in the middle of its witchhunts and Inquisition, it is also encountering Africa. It is, in other words, a Europe well grounded in atrocity that shaped the image of a diabolical Africa. In this way they were able to justify the slave trade to themselves, and establish the ideal foundation for the further atrocity which a significant part of their history since then has been. Brathwaite's point is that many Black people have accepted and internalised Europe's distorted image of Africa, and prefer it to the challenge of really knowing. He views this divorce from a healthy image of oneself as one of the major problems of Caribbean social history; a problem which in *Sun Poem* lies at the roots of the psychic dispossession of the male.

III:

As in *Islands*, Brathwaite is driven to understand "this death/ of sons, of songs, of sunshine", and this leads him to the third great theme of *Sun Poem*: the sun itself. *Sun Poem* has as its central metaphor the arc which the sun seems to describe from east to west as the earth spins. It is one of the most conventional metaphors of man's life, and is employed by Brathwaite consistently throughout the poem in this way.

The sun is presented as a source of mythology, and as one reads one is aware of Dahomean, Akan, Egyptian, Dogon and Judeo-Christian creation myths underlying the poem. Brathwaite's major task is that of unifying the Sun and Son poems. The Sun poem suggests a cosmic dimension which runs counter to the autobiography. Even the language in which each theme is presented differs, the language of the autobiography being warm, conventional, essentially prosaic and totally accessible, while that of the Sun poem is frequently obscure or choric.

Brathwaite attempts to overcome this dichotomy by suffusing the many narrative and descriptive sequences with light and colour. Adam, recently arrived from the country, awakens to the "sudden green sun", the light of the sun on the sea, after having left behind in the Edenic country, "the shower of green light around the gooseberry tree" (p. 5). Mouse is seen against this light.

> her dress looked very white
> and her skin against the gooseberry light
>
> was smooth and bright
> as if it had a life of its own
> that lived in her skin that was black (p. 6)

Batto, though presented as a fallen angel of light, is honoured with the sun's medal on his chest (p. 17) and Adam and Esse are similarly crowned by the sun which illuminates their love (pp. 73-83). The Muse of poetry and dream is made to resemble both Mouse and Esse:

> there is a girl at the window
> her flesh of cheek reflects the sheen of shadow
> green tangerine young black
>
> but the sons of the earth ignore dreamers (p. 37)

The land and its tallest trees, its poets, its artists, temporarily forgotten in the amnesiac drift westward ho, disappear from the eyesight. Reclaimed, remembered,

> they were suddenly green and sharp and alive again
> into the dream   of the water
> into the dream   of the world
>
> till the sun and the sky and the whirl where they were
> was one with the spot where they were (p. 42)

At such moments, "sudden in a shaft of sunlight" as Eliot might have put it, the Sun poem, the Son poem and the themes of history, memory and rooted belonging merge.

The sun theme provides the autobiography with a kind of circular cosmic frame or ring of light. Significantly, it is most predominant at the very beginning and the end. *Sun Poem* begins in Brathwaite's heraldic style. The theme is genesis, the primal age "when my songs were first heard in the voice of the coot of the owl" (p. 1). It is a time of reconciliation of the primal elements, earth, air, fire and water. The Sun here is the sun of all creation mythology: he is simultaneously Apollo in his chariot (hence "wheels of the sky") and Ra in his sun ship (" the keel of the blue"). Ra is the son of Nu, the primeval water "who gave birth unto himself"[1] and then became inert, surrendering his energies to Ra. Ra thus became a father and progenitor as well as the sun/son who emerges from Nu the ocean. It is in this respect that the "son of my song" is also the "father-giver."

The mention of "*sunsum*" alerts us that this poem will be about spirit and essence transmitted, as the Akan believe, through the fathers, and becoming part of the bloodline of family and nation. But Brathwaite's contention is that the conditions of the African diaspora resulted in an attenuation of the bloodline and a wastage and drying up of the male essence. This drying up, this dessication of spirit, is enacted in the poem's centre and symbolic noon ("Noom"), where the Dahomean Loa – most likely Legba, who in Dahomey was the Sun – dies on the Barbadian Cattlewash coast. Fallen, cast out from Africa with the Slave Trade, the loa, who is also the Dogon Nummo, first feels "his body lose its shining" and at noon, "gazing full at the sun that was beating tormenting drums in his head," cries out to the Sun which he once was, but from which he has become separated.

> and his cry grew greater as the pain of the world grew black for him
> (p. 52)

Here the Dahomean Legba and Dogon Nummo are equated with the hero of Good Friday in his experience of the Passion. He is the God in exile, all the Gods who died and resurrected themselves. It is this dying of the sun which is alluded to from the very beginning of the poem in the lines where the "sun/sum"

Walks the four corners of the magnet, caught in the wind, blind in
the eye of ihs own hurricane (p. 1)

Diasporan, the African "sun/sum" wanders to all points of the compass, trapped and without vision, drifting in a void of its (or "ihs") own making. The use of "ihs" rather than "its" preserves the link between the Dahomean Legba and Christ, who is represented by the letters "IHS" (Iesu Hominum Salvator) in Roman and Anglo-Catholic churches. The eye of the hurricane is a void, though the hurricane itself suggests the potential fury and energy of the Caribbean self. It is what the sons need to recognise and realise within themselves. At present they inhabit only the void of themselves, a hollow centre which Brathwaite elsewhere attributes to an absence of "sunsum" ("Springblade" in *Black + Blues*).

In the next lines we are provided with an alternative to this vision of unrealised potential:

and the trees on the mountain become mine: living eye of my branches
of bone; flute
where is my hope hope where is my psalter

There is hope in the claiming of new indigenised roots. The eye of reduced scarecrow man – the image and idea have been borrowed from Harris – need not be blind. The hope which springs out of the new rootedness which Brathwaite felt on his return to the Caribbean, and particularly during his sojourn in Barbados (1972-73), is the theme of his psalm of praise ("psalter"), and the prevailing spirit of both *Mother Poem* and *Sun Poem*. *Sun Poem* is the flute which Brathwaite has fashioned from the skeletal, hollow branch of diasporan existence, in order to celebrate his indigenisation and proclaim the muse and good news ("mews") of his origin. Our dried-up intellectualism, he suggests, has still largely ignored those areas in which we are most vibrantly alive: "brain corals ignite and ignore it." It is these sun spots of life, however, which the poet will affirm and celebrate.

Towards the end of the first sequence he refers to the time "when the sky first spoke with the voice of the rainbow." This is in one sense simply boyhood, in which the sun is described as a rainbow-coloured kite (p. 9), and the radiance of life is expressed in the image of "de singin angel kite in me hann already ablaze wid de rainbow a heaven" (p. 71). On another level the rainbow, born of the marriage of sun and water, represents phases in the sun's life from the red blood of its rising, through the orange and yellow of morning, the green and blue of afternoon and the indigo and violet of evening. The rainbow-image provides Brathwaite with a structuring device on which *Sun Poem* is erected.

The rainbow is also related to the creation mythology which is the subject of the poem. In Dogon creation mythology, the Nummo or life force assumes the form of a ram.

> He moved about the high clouds leaving a track of four colours from the earth shaken off his hooves. His left forefoot made a black track, his right a red track, the two others one green and one yellow. That four fold track was called 'the Nummo's track'. It is the rainbow.[2]

It is along the arc of the rainbow that the Nummo sent the stolen fragment of the sun to earth in order to create fire.[3]

By coincidence, perhaps, the four colours of the Dogon rainbow, are also the colours of Rastafari, and Brathwaite mentions three of them in naming the symbolic colours of his life, those sunspots or areas of his being which make possible a flowering of creativity:

> black spot of my life : jah
> blue spot of my life : love
> yellow spot of my life: iises
> red spot of my dream that still flowers flowers flowers (p. 2)

He also claims that these four colours are North American Indian sacred colours, though he doesn't identify the nation. One knows that his concern with the tension between the primal and non-primal visions of life, has often led him to explore parallels between mythologies. In "Shango" (*Black + Blues*) the submerged primal visions of African Meso-American and North American Indian are resurrected and confront the materialistic structures of the genocidal West at the moment of apocalypse.

The voice of the Sun in the second movement of the poem is the voice of the non-primal vision, the voice of the son/sun of empire, the Prospero counterpart to the poet's Caliban. He is uncomfortable with the circle or arc of universal and natural law, which he seeks to replace with the mad forward rectilinear drive of the "loco/motives" of a technology employed to dominate human and natural life. He yearns, in spite of himself, to embrace the dark primal Other whom he has "wracked", the Black who has become his ego-trip back to the romantically primitive, the nigger of his narcissus, the shadow of his sun. He is, however, chained to his own loco/motives, caught in his missile thrust towards holocaust or void, nuclear fission or black hole. The primal demands an entirely different sense of both movement and time, the idea of a cyclic curve back to a past which is also the future.

This forward movement into the past is what East Africans have termed *zamani*, and is the result of a cyclic notion of time in which one's life is regarded not as a rectilinear movement away from birth and towards death, the end of the line, but as a curve backwards to the ancestors, towards a future which is also the past, since the ancestors have already lived. This notion of time is resisted by the European who has, indeed, stigmatised it as an example of the African's supposed inability to break out of the closed circle of traditionalism in which the ancestors retain supreme authority, and to progress in the sense that the European understands the term. Brathwaite is concerned with the implications of the Caribbean man's almost unconditional acceptance of the rectilinear perspectives of the "missile" culture, and his corresponding resistance, and at times hostility, to the idea of the primal. The consequence of this is both the death of the hero-archetype and the violation of the Muse, as well as that indifference to both past and future which grows out of a constant erasure of history, that blind forward movement without point of reference. Since Brathwaite sees that forward movement as having its terminus in catastrophe, he is finally concerned with the reclamation of the cyclic vision of *zamani*, which alone can move him beyond a terminal gloom of apocalypse.

It is therefore with a reassertion of the cycle that the poem ends. This is first seen on the microcosmic plane, in the treatment of his grandfather's death.

> and i looked up to see my father's eye: wheeling towards his father
> now as i his sun moved upward to his eye (p. 93)

The lives of grandfather, father and son describe similar arcs, one flowing into the other. There is a certain comfort in this sense of ordered movement, a mature acceptance of the human subordination to cosmic principle. In *Mother Poem*, it is the sound and movement of the sea and the inward and outward movement of the stream which reassert the cosmic principle: "closing her eyes. he can hear the breakers breaking in her bleak of bone." (*Mother Poem* p. 115)

The penultimate sequence strengthens the parallel between the fates of suns and sons. "Suns don't know when they die." They store up "megalleons of light" which make them appear to be vigorously alive when seen from our vantage point of light years away, even though the death of ice has already overtaken them. The word "megalleons" is one of those happy Brathwaite coinages, which suggests both the ideas of "medallion" and of the sun as an enormous ("mega") ship ("galleon"), Ra's sun-ship preserving its light during the twelve hours in the underworld. If the "mega" in the word also suggests the megaton, then the idea of resurrection, after the post-historic chaos of nuclear fission, of reestablishing the cycle of life which man has sought to violate, is also there.

As with suns so with sons, who remain sexually immoderate even when they have lost fire ("though their intemperate i: ron has already wrinkled to rust.") A principle or arc of ascent, tumescence, zenith and flaccid shrivel governs the lives of both suns and sons. And it is this principle which Brathwaite invokes to explain the life-movement of the males in his world:

their blaze of boyhood, guttering at noon, and despairing attempts to arrest detumescence, the inevitable slide down the sinister side of the arc. There is no renewal for the individual but for the species, the next generation of sons. The individual faces a future in which passion is only remembered, and finally attains a distance more absolute than that of Yeats's disdainful starlit dome in "Byzantium", in which all human entanglement and intercourse are reduced to "that howl and hammer", as the sons and suns each seek the separate voids of their black holes.

Brathwaite, however, whether his theme is history or the *sunsum's* progress through time and space, generally ends with a reaffirmation of the cycle of life. Hence the final movement, based perhaps on the Egyptian myth of Ra's progress through the underworld of night, has as its first stage the graduated uncreation of the world, leaving only darkness. Then there is the divine happening:

> and out of this dark came nam
> nameless dark horse of devouring morning (p. 65)

Nam is Dogon Nummo or life principle, Akan Onyame or irreducible divine *sunsum*, which is neither created nor destroyed, but propels itself along the cycle of birth, life, death and rebirth to resurface again in its emblem, the Sun. Nam is a "nameless dark horse" because of his firstness, his originality, his arrival into an empty universe without names. In the Babylonian account of the Creation, the stage of genesis is described as "when no name had been named, no fates had been determined." Nam is a dark horse because he's an African creator god and therefore both obscure and nameless in a Caribbean context of divorce from self and image. He's also equated with Greek Apollo who drives his horses across the sky. He devours the darkness and, like countless other such life forces, either emerges out of, or sets in order, or marries with and fecundates the murky waters of primeval Chaos.

Nam fills the void, saturates all non-being, all "absence, darkness, death: things which are not."[5]

> until there was nothing there
> until there was no nothing there

Here we have the central crux of all creation, the primal mystery: the calling into being of a world *ex nihilo*. The first thing Nam creates after his abolition of "nothing" is "meer", the sea, the "mother of water" of "Dawn" in *Islands*. This water is different from the dark waters of Chaos, since it has been called into being after the light. Water is also the Dogon life-force:

> and the light grew
> and opened the eye of its flower
> they say

Literally this is a reference to the sun emerging over the horizon and sending out rays in all directions to form the sunflower. The "eye of its flower" may also be a concealed reference to "iris", which is both the pupil of the eye, a flower, and the Greek goddess of the rainbow. She would be an appropriate presence at this moment of marriage of light and water. However, it is Isis, the Egyptian goddess, who successfully sought equal power with Ra, the Sun god, who is named. Isis is associated with the sun and with the spreading of civilisation and the rebirth of Osiris.

The brazen sheen of light on water which will crown both Adam and Batto, first man and fallen sun-ship (batteau) of the beach, is the first voice or colour of the sun, the red copper of its rising. So the light spreads, "beating its genesis genesis genesis genesis" [...] "and the water coloured the land with ihs hum." One notes the use of coloured rather than covered. The colour of light passing through water is that of the rainbow. Its voice suggests the Om, Ah, Hum the sacred breaths and first words of prayer in the discipline of the Mandala. A creation myth such as this is almost certainly a description of the poet's own discovery of voice and breath, his achievement of music and first word. It is in this sense that this final movement is appropriately entitled Son, the Cuban kaiso-like form of celebration.

Out of the sea emerges coral, the "Rock/Seed" with which *Mother Poem* begins. *Sun Poem* has thus described a circle back to the genesis of its progenitor, *Mother Poem*, and the children who rise up with the new sun, the adams and esses, are also his poems and the creativity of the region at its renaissance.

(First published in *New Voices* Vol. II, No. 2 (March 1983) pp. 43-64; also published in *Jamaica Journal* Vol. 16, No. 3 (May 1983) pp. 81-87.)

References
1. Van Over, R., *Sun Songs: Creation Myths from around the World* (New York: Mentor, 1980), p. 255.
2. Griaule, M., *Conversations with Ogotemelli* (London: OUP, 1965), pp. 107-108.
3. Ibid., pp. 42-43.
4. *Sun Songs*, p. 175.
5. Donne, J., "A Nocturnall upon S. Lucies Day, Being the Shortest Day".

BRATHWAITE WITH A DASH OF BROWN: CRIT, THE WRITER AND THE WRITTEN LIFE

> and alone, my hand following
> the crab's poem, stalked
> the inheriting ghosts
>   – E.K.B. "Crab"

I: Carray

At the end of the original jazz poems,[1] Brathwaite, anticipating crit, produced a satirical portrait of the listener who "fits on his new/ wide-angled ears" and sets up "his newfangled electronic kit/ to listen." Unfortunately, the listener, who is also critic, approaches jazz with theories born out of an aesthetic developed for the appreciation of a different music, "heavenly melodies/ celestial and thin." His critical equipment, however "new-fangled", is not attuned to the dissonance and discord, of the new thing. The poet concludes:

> It is a pity
> That his theories
> Dictate his joys
> Because he hears
> Not heavenly melodies
> Celestial and thin
> But highly refined dissonance
> And noise...[2]

Brathwaite later reworked and rearranged the six poems, which appeared as "Octet" in the *Sunday Gleaner* during the latter half of 1964, and as "Jazz Portraits"[3] in Stewart Brown's *Now* (1973).[4] "The Listener" was retitled "The Critic", to clarify Brathwaite's intention of providing the reader with an ironic portrait of himself as incompetent critic of an emerging poetry based on what Brathwaite was soon to call "the alternative tradition" of "the jazz aesthetic". The poem was then omitted from subsequent editions of the jazz poems.[5]

It however came to mind after I read Michael Dash's review of *The Visibility Trigger*,[6] a selection of Brathwaite's poems, and *Jah Music,* an expanded collection of both new and old music poems. Both of these collections appeared in 1986, in the wake of his prize-winning Casa de las Americas collection of essays, *Roots.* "The Listener" or "The Critic" also seemed to apply to Beverly Brown's "Mansong and Matrix: A Radical Experiment".[7] Both articles were written by critics with "new wide-angled ears" and "new-fangled" critical equipment: Dash's modernist/existentialist, Brown's feminist. Both, too, were a result of listening more closely to the equipment than to the music. In addition, Dash's distortions were due to his very closeness, as a colleague, to the distraught post-September 1986 Brathwaite. Brown's were due to her failure to consider *Mother Poem* in her assessment of the quality of Brathwaite's depiction of women. In answering Dash, this paper will attempt to raise the issue of the relationship between Brathwaite's life, the act of poetic making, and the frequent masking of autobiography in his poetry. In answering Brown, this essay will seek to establish *Mother Poem* as the most appropriate text, so far, on which to base any enquiry into Brathwaite's notions about the female experience in the New World. Since *Mother Poem* is based substantially on autobiography, this essay will seek to explore the processes whereby Brathwaite has transformed the raw material of personal experience into a complex and idiosyncratic vision of history and landscape.

II: Brathwaite

> "I have been becoming my own poem to Mikey Smith"
> — E.K. B. 22 Nov. 1986

Jah Music was launched as "a new collection of poems by Edward Kamau Brathwaite", on Friday 21st November, 1986, on the Mona Campus of the University of the West Indies. The occasion of its launching was Brathwaite's first major public appearance since the death of his wife, Doris Brathwaite, on September 7, 1986. After reading at the launching of *Jah Music,* Brathwaite went home to Irish Town to pen an intensely emotional letter[8] which was subsequently circulated to members of the Mona campus community, and particularly to those who had attended the launching of *Jah Music.* The letter accused the campus community of "brutal and frightening neglect from all those who seem(ed) so close before that date." It sought to disabuse them of any impression that his performance at the reading might have conveyed that he was coping with his wife's death and his solitude. It stated instead, that

> I am really lucky to be still here. The violet emotional internal hemorrhage which has been going on is now black clotted & massive and it is this I was referring to when I said that I had been becoming my own poem to Mikey Smith.
>
> & fills my blood
> with deaf my bone with hobble. dumb
> & echo . less neglect neglect neglect neglect

The letter decried what Brathwaite saw as an absence of "remembering communion." It also reflected Brathwaite's belief that he was being deliberately punished for having been a sort of recluse for so many years.

> now you is being punish far being a recluse/far shutting yuself away from us writing poems poems poems poems (when you shudda been one a de boys in de Coffee Room or SCR Bar or at parties parties patties.

Here then, we have defined what is perhaps the central irony of Brathwaite's life as a poet: that for all the critical acclaim or rejection he'd received as a "public poet", he was, in fact, the most private of persons, who needed to retreat from a community in order to create. The "public poet" needed to detach himself from the audience. He thus manifested the monastic nature of all researching, and the essential solitude of the creative act. Since most of his colleagues, by the very nature of the vocation, feel a similar need for private space in which to work, the campus has become that well-known paradox: a community of isolatos, each, despite socialising institutions such as the celebrated SCR, with his or her own private life and agenda. Brathwaite was demanding from Mona far more than it could ever have given: a support system of continuous concern and caring, that is possible only within the warmth and immediacy of a family.

And Brathwaite had lost his.

*

Retreating from the crowd has been a tendency not only in his life, but in his poetry, where personal experience is often hidden at some distanced centre beyond the voice of the multiple personae. This once led Winnifred Risden to conclude of *Masks* that

> The small private moments when the conscience is shattered through contact to (sic) new perceptions are excluded by the poem's very nature. Brathwaite's success is to have endowed a familiar theme with the dignity of public ceremonial. He offers no message to the heart.[9]

I've argued[10] that Risden is wrong here; but I understand her problem. She wants to know who speaks from behind the masks; "which face is his among the strange and terrible."[11]

Even in an early poem such as "Arrival"[12] which is one of the few poems to hint at Brathwaite's personal reaction to Cambridge, a satirical tone serves to conceal the trauma of adjustment to an alien world. The comic description of the sequenced arrival of feet, guts, fingers, arms and brain of a robot-like persona, masks the bewilderment of accommodating to a strange landscape.

> when the brain arrived, safe-
> ly transported, telescoped and raped

> he unpacked the wired apparatus of his eyes
> so that he could assess not only surfaces
>
> but doubts and coils, unreeled perspectives
> could distinguish lies from solid ground
>
> and his recorded mentums oiled like wheels
> soon he would play his part
>
> all he awaited was his heart

"Telescoped" is an image of the real narrowness of the colonial mind, which arrives already "raped" by colonial education. Such scepticism as he learns at Cambridge teaches him to question the packaged deal of the curriculum. Yet his development of a discriminating intellect, simply completes the process of dissociation which began at home. The protagonist's final state is that of the assembled, expertly programmed and functioning robot, where originally he'd arrived as the dismantled and imperfectly programmed colonial robot. His now perfected schizophrenia is suggested in the final image of the zombie – a creature divorced from the actions it's been commanded to perform, because its heart and soul have been captured by an evil sorcerer.

> soon he would play his part
> all he awaited was his heart

This is the final enigma of arrival.

The tone of this clearly autobiographical poem, semi-comic and wryly self-mocking, masks with dryness its bitterly disillusioned core of feeling, and establishes a pattern in Brathwaite's "written life" whereby autobiography is presented through distancing metaphor, and the ego is masked and protected at its shattered centre.

"Clock",[13] first published in *Other Exiles* and reappearing with changes in *Jah Music* [14] dedicated to Albert Ayler, is one of the few places where this central implosive shattering is directly explored. Yet even here the poet distances himself from the protagonist who is presented in the third person. The trauma of the experience is conveyed through intense and at times difficult imagery, in disjointed phrases whose visual separation from each other suggests the implosive shattering of the psyche.

> At last   that night   the pounding
> in his dark released a flower
>
> electricity of nerve a blue
> serrated fire   the scent
>
> blooming with tears of glass
> rounded him   he
>
> unfolded e-
> rect a wrecked

> calyx   what disasters unhinged
> from his growing   what
>
> impinges of pain

Here, the anticipation of the poem takes place in a state of extreme tension, even terror. The "pounding in his dark" recalls the dark night of the soul in Donne and Hopkins. Creative illumination is a state of being charred, electrified and seared by jagged pentecostal lightning. The inner flowering, alluding very probably to David Murray's piece "Flowers for Albert", is also a shattering of the mind's mirror, an implosion within the psyche causing intense stabbing pain ("impinges of pain") and a sense of derangement. ("wrecked calyx"; "unhinged"). Brathwaite is treading here on dangerous ground – the interstices between mental breakdown and the creative act; between catastrophic shatter of brain-cell and a kind of growing. Later, Tony McNeill and Victor Questel will traverse this painful ground again and again.

"Clock" reveals what lies behind the poised self-mocking laughter of "Arrival". There is no mask of laughter here to defend the shattered centre. What saves and stabilises is a sense of rootedness.

>   ... he stood
> still   still
>
> unable to move   his roots
> moored in water mirrored
>
> through mud   anchored him

Here, the strongly external quality of this image of mangrove growing out of swamp suggests Brathwaite's perception of the artist's need to maintain balance between traumatic internal processes and the gross but fertilising material world outside the psyche's electrified space. This perception is conveyed through the image of the mirror, where the muddy water of swamp or foreshore provides mirrored rootage for the unhinged mind.

This state, however, does not last. The rest of the poem presents the creative talent beset by time which, as in Dylan Thomas's "The Force That Through the Green Fuse", simultaneously nurtures and destroys. The artist is a driven man, playing for and against time, which undermines his embryonic skill before it can mature, and spreads disease in blood and bone. This time-haunted state yields its own grim vision, a dark flowering and birth, signalled by the feminine images of moon and menstrual blood.

>   an eye
> opened on the
> moon

> tides of darkness
> flowered flowered flowered
>
> corp
> uscles clicked
>
> from the three
> corners of the room

Where the first shock of creative energy "rounded" the creator, here the triangular room is an image of the waning or narrowing consciousness. The perfect primal shape of the circle is lost. Circles, as contrasted with angles and straight lines are major features in Brathwaite's iconography, and have been employed in his work as symbols of primal as contrasted with modern consciousness, or of "capsule" as contrasted with "missile" cultures.'[15] This second phase of creative vision dies with what seems to be a loss of the feminine principle, the closing of the moon's eye, the departure of the Muse. After this is the time of stones: hardness, dryness, cerebration and disintegration.

> when the eye   closed
> the
>
> clock
>
> stopped   and the rocks of his skull fell down.

"Clock", then, enacts the full process of the creative mind in its journey from the blinding flash of first seeing, through moored rootedness in external society, towards the darkening of the word – what Dylan Thomas called "syllabic blood" – and final failure of vision and disintegration. The revised version of this poem in *Jah Music*[16] is dedicated, as noted above, to the 1960's avant garde jazz saxophonist, Albert Ayler, "who died in 1971 at the age of 34. (His body was found in New York's East River after he had been missing for 20 days.)"[17] The effect of this dedication to Ayler is to place further distance between Brathwaite and his double, the protagonist of the poem. Ayler, both avant gardist and traditional, neo-modernist and rooted in the mud of the Mississippi delta, becomes Brathwaite's double in the poet's quest for a form that is simultaneously rooted in "folk" culture and "capable of exploiting the extremes of contemporary sophistication" – a "living, active expression on easy terms with all the world."[18] Ayler's career, like Parker's or Dylan Thomas's, is cut short by the clock, against whose persistent beat he lived and played with urgency.

Time's victory is indicated by the insistent ticking of the clock, which in the second section intertwines itself with Ayler's saxophone solo.

>   it threw rick
>   ets into the
>
> blood.   it flew
> crick
>
> ets into every quar. ter
>
> &
> quaver   till an eye
>
> O
>
> pened on the moon
> &
>
> blue notes flick.
> ered   flick.
>
> ered   flick.
> ered   from the three
>
> corners of the womb

In both versions, the sound of the poem suggests the ticking of the clock of doom. Here we have "rick", "crick", "flick", "flick", "flick". The later version connects "the blue serrated fire" of the original psychic shock, with the flickering blue notes of Ayler's dying solo. It also replaces "blooming with tears of glass" with "blooming through years of glass." Glass is the medium of unProspero, against which Ayler created. In the later version, the flash of vision does not round or complete; it wounds. Also, the identification of the creative act with the feminine principle is more specific, as the contracting "three corners of the room" becomes "three corners of the womb."

One of Michael Dash's complaints is that Brathwaite has been recycling old poems in a fashion which, while it provides "a seemingly inexhaustible stream of publications",[19] in reality represents the opposite: a desperate clinging "to the word in order not to surrender to silence."[20] While the charge of recycling old poems is true, equally true is the fact that the new context modifies the meaning and alters the impact of the poem. "Clock", when dedicated to Ayler, becomes a little less personal – more suggestive of the poet's involved detachment; his control over that inner demonic implosive process; his poise in the face of the clock of doom; and his recognition of his creator-self in a creative other.

In *The Arrivants* and even in the more obviously autobiographical *Mother Poem*, *Sun Poem* and *X-Self* (Brathwaite's intellectual autobiography as a New World historian), autobiography is set at a distance as the ego is filtered through multiple voices that become the conduits through which the tangled experience of the Caribbean and the New World flows. Brathwaite in "Timehri"[21] calls this process of filtering the self through multiple personae in order to achieve distance and dimension, and to articulate an "awareness and understanding of community, of cultural wholeness, of the place of the individual within the tribe, in society," egolessness, an aesthetic of "the self without ego, without I."

It would, however, be a mistake to believe that the quest for "egolessness" in the major work meant that in real life the ego had been buddhistically transcended. In his letter to his colleagues of November 22, 1986, Brathwaite wonders whether the academic community

> that harbours books, gives lectures on our poetry, writes crit, creates models, talks of paradigms, has & has had several of our poets/ people with us & among us / artists and writers / those who create the crits... ever stop(s) to think of where those metaphors come from / how they come from/what source & sauce of energy[22]

Whatever "detachment" or "egolessness" the poet might achieve in the poem, the critic should be sufficiently sensitive to recognise the driven and anguished source of metaphor and the ordeal of making. The Brathwaite of "Clock" was very much alive behind the multiplicity of masks. Dash's review recognises this fact, but asserts that Brathwaite has now arrived at the final phase of the creative process, where the moon's eye of inspiration begins to close, the blood ceases to flow, the rocks of sterility tumble in avalanches of dry sound, and Time emerges as the grim medium against which man must desperately create.

Brathwaite's letter was not only an accusation, but a plea to his colleagues to understand that what was taking place was not only literature, but life. Life and literature, indeed, were doubles of each other and had begun to exchange faces; the written life and the lived life, the poet and his sacrificial double – Mikey Smith, Albert Ayler, Charlie Parker, Billie Holiday, and the enchained prophet and Nummo of "Kingston in the Kingdom of this World" – had begun to merge. "I am becoming my poem to Mikey Smith".

Similarly, the Campus had become for him a microcosm of the wider community which, since "Wings of a Dove" and several of the urban poems of the seventies (e.g. "Starvation", "Springblade", "Dred", "Manchild" and "Kingston in the Kingdom of this World") and the staggering violence of the eighties, had all but destroyed the sense of community that he'd affirmed in the sixties, as the most valuable bequest of his encounter with traditional Africa. He ends his letter:

> I am only one symptom of what is happening to our society: we are so bombed out, burnt out, raped out, knifed out, shot up, robbed out that I wonder if we are still a society at all/ whether if called on to defend ideas, ideals, structure, family or dreams/nations? we'll be able to do it Or have we not found ourselves, without perhaps knowing it, into another Babylonian Captivity (lock stock & prison): but one now without the

ships & the physical bars/ scars: a psychological wasteland: victims of the 21st century as we have been victims of the 18th, 19th & 20th And victims because we have been too passive and too passive because we haven't had/ or lost the heart to love each other/ caritas[23]

Viewed in the context of his poems and essays since the mid-sixties, Brathwaite's letter becomes a text that illustrates the mergence of literature and driven life, without mediating mask; the anguished coming together of the artist and his double.

Brathwaite's accusations, though by far the most extreme that I've read, are not at all the only ones to be made against the Mona Campus. Walcott in "Gib Hall Revisted"[24] associates the campus with the emergence of an elite whose repeated cyclical achievement has been to betray their early vows to transform the society that they've inherited from Prospero. A decade later in "The Star-Apple Kingdom"[25] he presents us with a fingernail sketch of the campus: as a world shut off from the imaginative perception of the islands' landscape as mystery and wonder.

> and he climbed from that submarine kingdom
> as the evening lights came on in the institute,
> the scholars lamplit in their own aquarium,
> he saw them mouthing like parrot fish, as he passed
> upwards from that baptism, their history lessons,
> the bubbles like ideas which he could not break:

Here there is almost resignation at the divorce between the visionary life of poetry, and the campus as narcissistic prison, a generator of fixed formulae and stereotyped vision. The ISER has never recognised culture as part of the business of social research and, imprisoned in statistics, lives on another planet from the poet and dreamer, the sleepers of the tribe.

Garth St. Omer in *Shades of Grey* and Slade Hopkinson in "The Mad Woman of Papine" both point out its propinquity to madness, St. Omer employing the Campus as the landscape where his terribly empty and guilt-ridden people bring to fruition their home-bred neuroses. George Lamming alludes bitterly to it in both *Water with Berries* and *Natives of My Person* as a place of incestuous gossip and character assassination. The SCR bar is described as the Mona Crematorium, where reputations are cremated. Erna Brodber's *Jane and Louisa Will Soon Come Home* contains a wickedly satirical portrait of the SCR crowd turning always to the right on their stools; while her portrait of the activist left, a cadre of naive do-gooders who try to relieve the sufferings of a Government yard refugee camp with catchphrases from a Marxist handbook, suggests an even more poignant futility.

The Mona Campus as a creator of anti-heroes, as a context for futility, as an artificial place, is extensively explored in N.D. Williams's *Ikael Torass*,[26] whose locus is substantially the campus, and whose purpose is the exploration of the relationship, or chasm, between the benumbed consciousness of the anti-heroic narrator, a student on campus, and the violent urgencies of the lumpen-proletarian world in which the campus is dislocated. Brathwaite's letter to the campus community, then, is part of what seems to be, in the terms of the 1986 Conference of English Departments, an "emerging tradition in West Indian Literature".

III: With a Dash

Michael Dash's review of *Jah Music* and *The Visibility Trigger* is a response by a member of the Mona Campus community to the hurt that Brathwaite's letter undoubtedly caused people, who had thought themselves humanely concerned with the poet in his grief. Its approach is oblique; as through the quotation taken from Beckett's *Waiting for Godot* which it employs as epigraph.

> Vladimir: What do they say
> Estragon: They talk about their lives
> Vladimir: To have lived is not enough for them
> Estragon: They have to talk about it

This is interpreted by Dash as Beckett's dramatisation of "the human need to resist oblivion through incessant speech." By analogy, Brathwaite's stream of publications and republications falls into the category of "incessant speech". It becomes part of a futile effort to vindicate self through language and "to protect himself against the void", that Brathwaite makes along with an existentialist writer such as Beckett. This line of approach ought to have led Dash towards a genuine examination of Brathwaite as a late twentieth century poet, contributing to a modernist European aesthetic. Since *Jah Music* contains many poems that Brathwaite has termed jazz poems, a review of that collection might also fruitfully have discussed Brathwaite's notion of a jazz aesthetic, to see if he is really related to existentialist or *ecole de desespoir* writing.

Brathwaite, in "Jazz and the West Indian Novel", presents jazz as a music that is simultaneously "folk" and "modern"; rooted and avant gardist; capable of expressing both the tension of the alienated individual and the shout and song of the collective voice. One needs to relate the jazz poems to Brathwaite's description of a jazz aesthetic, and to see how successfully the poems have resolved the tension between rootedness and alienation, between the solitude of the individual talent and the sense of communion. Dash, unfortunately, does not do this. Like Brathwaite's listener/critic's, his wide-angled ears and new-fangled equipment produce only dissonance and noise, or, as Dash himself terms it, "acoustic excess and unrestrained audibility." According to him:

> Brathwaite's experiments in sound are no longer a matter of harnessing the energies of the spoken word. This has yielded to an interest in the sounds of musical instruments as the poet attempts to imitate or, perhaps,

compete with the saxophone, the trumpet or percussion instruments of the Jazz musician. Such experiments always fall short of success. The original instrument or performance defies verbal transcription. This reaching beyond language for pure sound is an admission of the inadequacy of words. However, poetry must be an attempt to transcend the failure of language, not succumb to it. These poems work best as a reflective response to the disturbing or startling moods created by Parker, Miles or Basie.[28]

The jazz poems, some of which I've analysed in *Pathfinder*,[29] are not about language seeking to become pure sound and failing to become the music that it is imitating. They are rather about music and the lives of particular musicians evoking moods and feelings which the poet translates into both aural and visual imagery, so that the reader / listener apprehends the visual and conceptual shape of sound. Thus Bird's riffs suggest circles and spirals. "Notes fell like figure-forming pebbles/ in a pond." Melba Liston's trombone suggests a different sort of circle: the pool, the blue lagoon. And in the process of making the link between sound and image, Brathwaite names an old song (blue lagoon), and associates Liston, who worked and taught in Jamaica, with the soul of the island, as well as with her own down-home Alabama rootedness. Thus the poet tells Liston that her music "curls like (her) hair around its Alabama root." A simple, honest praise poem.

"Birds", for Marjorie Whylie, and "Flutes" for Pam Mordecai are both beautiful impressionistic poems, the first based on visual impressions, the second on sound impressions. Impressionism is not about language reaching desperately beyond itself. It is, rather, about eye or ear linking streams of images or strands of sound. It is less concerned with the sharp edges that separate images one from the other, than with the stream within which they move together. Images tend to grow out of each other in this type of writing. Thus in "Birds", the drummer's hands seen in rapid motion become a flight of sparrows to the poet's eye – an image which is then projected on to the violinist with his /her "twittering" fingers rapidly moving. The "twitters" of the violin are a sound-image, which also conveys the visual impression of rapidly scurrying movement, or fluttering wings. The staccato sounds of the piano suggest blackbirds hopping. Then the linkages are made through sound: dynamite for the explosive power of the drums, rustling grass and tinkling bottles for the tambourines, the sharpness of needles and the swiftness of lightning for the piccolo. The poem ends with the impression of the trumpeter, whose strength and fervour transform him from the "crab cracked" – that is inured, enduring, earthy, grounded, surviving – peasant that he is – into a heraldic figure: Gabriel of the coming Apocalypse, and the golden eagle, as well as the "burning spear" of African liberation, which is probably what the music is about.

In "Flutes", the first images concern the making of the flute from the clipped, dry bamboo twig, burnished yellow in the sun. This warmth will glow in its released music "as the wind learns the shape of its fire", and the fingers explore its stops (here described as holes drilled by termites). The music thus released by breath and skill of fingers is a triumph over the termite of time, and shatters the silence. Both ideas have occurred before in *The Arrivants*. As in "The Making of the Drum", the poet is talking about his own craft. The "wrestle and groan" of the bamboo clump in the wind is the ordeal of primary gross experience. The burning of the twig to a yellow glow is a process of purification equivalent to the heating of the sticks, or the drying and stretching of the skin in "The Making of the Drum".

The reward for having endured is voice, sound, the discovery of shape and fiery form, a Blakean, Romantic ideal, part of "the aesthetic of energy" that was defined in "The Problem of the Problem of Form".[30] Having given breath to the medium, the poet moves further inward – symbolised by the closing of his eyes.

> my eyes close
>
> all along the wall . all along the branches . all along the world
>
> and that that creak and spirits walking these graves of sunlight
>
> spiders over the water . cobwebs crawling in whispers over the stampen green
>
> find
>
> from a distance so cool it is a hill in haze
> it is a fish of shadow along the sandy bottom
>
> that the wind is following my footsteps
> all along the rustle all along the echoes all along the world
>
> and that that stutter i had heard in some dark summer freedom
>
> startles and slips from fingertip to fingerstop
> into the float of the morning into the throat of its sound

He lets the music enter and begins to travel in consciousness beyond the barrier or wall that separates conscious from unconscious perception, until he arrives at the tree. The tree in Brathwaite is an ancestral symbol. Here it is also the *poteau-mitan* of the hounfort, a point of intersection between the "normal" world of concrete material objects, and the world of *les invisibles*, the spirit world of ancestors.

These spirits then arrive across the gulf of the Middle Passage. There is no possession here, but a powerful awareness of their presence. They reside in the harmattan's haze, and watch him from Jamaica's blue hills. Long before it was commonly accepted, Brathwaite had identified the haze in Caribbean skies during dry season, as dust from the Sahara. This dust became a powerful metaphor of the evanescent but real presence of Africa in the Caribbean, and occasioned a number of "harmattan poems" ("Sun Song", "Suman", "Kite"). The image of the fish at the bottom of a clear pool is an even more assured image of the calm apprehension of the ancestors. Hence the last two lines of the first section convey the poet's sense of being blest by the fostering wind of inspiration as he walks the pathway of his vocation, "all along the rustle all along the echoes all along the world." The repetition of "all along" conveys the total, all-embracing nature of his fulfilment, and his perfect assurance "that the wind is following my footsteps."

"Flutes", then, is about anointment, and the movement from "that stutter i had heard in some dark summer freedom" to the full-throated music of elated freedom sound: "into the float of the morning into the throat of its sound." The poem has so far been woven around three ideas: breath, bamboo flute, and sound. The images cluster around these ideas. Wind is related to breath, harmattan haze; flute to tree, branches, web of ancestors; sound to groan, rustle, echoes, tone, silence, creak, shatters, whispers, throat of sound.

The final section of the poem is an elated description of the discovered flute-voice.

>   it is a baby mouth but softer than the suck it makes
>   it is a hammock sleeping in the woodland
>   it is a hammer shining in the shade
>
>   it is the kite ascending chord and croon and screamers
>   it is the cloud that curls to hide the eagle
>   it is the ripple of the stream from bamboo
>
>   it is the ripple of the stream from blue
>   it is the gurgle pigeon dream the ground dove coo

It is innocent, primal and new-born (gurgle of baby); pastoral and dreaming (hammock sleeping in woodland); it is also forceful and powerful (hence the reference to Ogun's hammer); it is transcendent, rising in elation over "screamers", what Yeats termed "the fury and the mire of human veins"; it insulates, however briefly, from the vision of rapacity, the eagle/vulture of empire that pervades *X-Self*; it is the gentle peace song of dove and pigeon, traditionally holy birds; it is the poet's (sun) sense of having attained the zenith of his power, now that his own distinctive sound has been born.

>   it is the sun approaching midday listening its splendour
>   it is your voice alight with echo . with the birth of sound.

The poem, then, is about birth and life and a coming into voice. Dash, however, wearing the blinkers of Beckettian absurdity, sees desperation, a frantic and linguistically incoherent attempt to reach beyond language, which is itself a struggle to stave off death and oblivion. This notion may have been inspired by the jazz poem dedicated to Miles Davis. Davis becomes in the lonely strangled flight of his riff, Daedalus/ Icarus and Lucifer, all mythic overreachers, hurled down by Jah or Zeus for flying too near the sun, or for wanting to be the sun. The jazz soloist as overreacher – Miles trying to follow Dizzy Gillespie and growing "dizzy with altitude" – is doubtless a persona for the poet as overreacher. But all real poetry seeks to expand language by moving beyond the strictures of the medium, and may indeed fail to do so in the same way that the stricken yard bird who seeks to be an eagle may find himself and his voice plummeting "through the sunlight like a shining stone."[31] This, however, is not an admission of the inadequacy of words, but an acknowledgement by one artist in his medium of words, of the courage and daring which was displayed by another artist in his medium of pure sound as he explored new and forbidden space.

The other point in Dash's critique is that Brathwaite writes morbid poems dedicated to the "fallen members of a spiritual avant garde" – Rodney, Nkrumah, Mikey Smith. Poems such as "The Visibility Trigger", "Poem for Walter Rodney" and "Stone", dedicated to Nkrumah, Rodney and Smith respectively, are cited as examples of "dismaying verse in the service of worthy causes." Like Césaire, Guillen and Depestre, according to Dash, Brathwaite fails as an elegiac poet. He also masochistically identifies with the suffering of each martyr, which is little more than a mirror for his own fearful insecurity. Only one faintly positive comment is made of the two anthologies:

> In both collections, lavish verbal monuments to musical achievement or human sacrifice do contain arresting moments when imagery acquires a powerful suggestiveness. For instance, there is something explosively Césairean in the multi-layered image of the tree and the ship spiralling heavenwards in the poem "The Visibility Trigger".[32]

This singular "arresting moment" stands out in a generally unsuccessful elegiac poem where "the sermon-like monologue prevails over the enigmatic fable." Beginning with a rejection of both form and content, monologue and fable, Dash explores neither, and the poem remains for him an enigma.

"The Visibility Trigger" explores the moment of collision between Europe and Africa. This moment is first dreamed by the sleeper of the tribe, the poet/shaman/seer; a figure who appears first in Harris's *The Sleepers of Roraima*[33], then in Michael Gilkes's *Couvade*.[34] The sleeper of the tribe is also keeper of its creative imagination, and channel of the collective Muse and spirit of creativity resident in a people. According to Gilkes, whose play *Couvade* premiered at Carifesta 1972 in Guyana, and was viewed by Brathwaite there, once the dreamer remains asleep and is allowed to dream, then there is harmony between humanity and the Cosmos. But when the dream is shattered and the dreamer awakens to the brutal world and game of the stone, then chaos enters the Cosmos.

This is what happens in "The Visibility Trigger", which first appeared one year after *Couvade*. The dreamer dreams a dream in which he foresees the death of the tribe. He dreams that he offers a stranger the token of peace and welcome, the kola nut, but this is answered by murderous gunfire. He intuits the ferocity of what is about to be released in the images of the fiercely hissing cauldron and the maggot of disease draining the vitality of the warrior.

Disaster is also divined in what the dreamer hears.

> I could hear salt leaking out of the black hole of kaneshie
> i could hear grass growing around the edges of the green lake
> i could hear stalactites ringing in my cave of vision

The draining out of the salt lake is the drying up of a valuable commodity, salt being in those days of early encounter, a highly prized substance. The silting up of the lake is a similarly negative omen. In each case, the dreamer "hears" geological process. Since one cannot literally hear grass grow or salt leak out, what the images suggest is the immense and ominous interior silence; a stillness so absolute that the dreamer becomes aware of the frozenness and congealment of time and nature.

Stalactites also belong to geological time, frozen time. They take centuries to form. But these stalactites have begun to grow in his "cave of vision", and he now hears them ringing. The stalactites represent an accumulation of vision, the slow, almost timeless growth of traditional African wisdom. They suggest the total integration of the primal mind with the earth and the processes of nature. The primal vision seeks to merge itself with natural process; to become one with, rather than manipulate the universe. At this moment of encounter between the primal vision and the pragmatic materialism of Europe, the primal consciousness of the dreamer becomes aware of self as other. So profound a gap then opens between self and cosmos, that the stalactites of vision begin to vibrate with sound. Such seismic vibration indicates profound and abnormal unsettlement; cosmic error; disturbance within the mental cosmos.

The image of the "cave of vision" naturally leads to the image of bats which normally inhabit caves. The bats within the cave of vision are blind and represent the muse on the verge of being violated. The normal image of the Muse or spirit of creative imagination, is the bird. Brathwaite employs birds and butterflies several times in *The Arrivants* as images of the muse. The bat, then, is a counter-image; a reversal of the bird image. It is the muse gone blind, the vision gone haywire, helter-skelter flight in a world of darkness. The bat also presages death; hence its resemblance to the owl as jumbie bird, harbinger of howl and death.

The sleeper of the tribe remains asleep as the dream comes true with the interloper penetrating the "silence" of his village. Penetration is presented in terms of the contrast of "missile" images (oar, prong, roads, rods, straight objects) with the spherical or circular icons of the tribe (bowl; calabash).[35] The "silence" that the interloper penetrates is a property of the primal ethos; something vast like time, or space or eternity. It exists equally in forest and in the Sahara, which in *Masks* swallows up, contains and negates human activity and meaning. The true conquistador finds a way of ignoring this silence by reducing meaning to the single-minded simplicity of his purpose. Hence the brutally purposive violence of "hack" and "tramp": butchery and militarism.

At the core of the poem, the sleeper of the tribe ("and unprepared and venerable i was dreaming") describes the collision of two systems of being, doing and seeing. The African system is governed by a sense of cycle. Time, work, agriculture, the stages of life such as birth, initiation and death ("birth, child, warrior/and the breath which is no more") are all part of the cycle. Death, indeed, simply represents another phase of cyclic process, since it leads to rebirth and the repetition of the entire cycle. Time, too, is a cyclic process: "time wheeled around our memories like stars." Time is circular movement around a central hub or axis of memory or tradition; movement whose resemblance to the orbitting of constellations around the sun, suggests the balanced harmony and interrelatedness of things. Since the axis of memory – accumulated and time-honoured custom, ritual, ways of doing and being – is stable, Time's movement doesn't affect its balance. It rather affirms the fitness of things.

The conqueror's concept of time is as a straight line. This concept becomes a missile, shattering the cyclic universe of the African and imposing on him confusing notions of process, and relationship to Cosmos. Birth ceases to be natural ("birth was not breath/ but gaping wound.") The sacred, magical bond between hunter and animal is severed, when hunter learns to kill animal for market sale rather than for his need. The natural order of things is reversed. Warrior becomes child, where before one moved from child to hunter to warrior. And the child, Okonkwo, to whom the warrior has been reduced, dies as life moves backwards along the no longer familiar cycle.

It is at this point that we arrive at Dash's "arresting moment" of "Césairean" "multi-layered image of the tree and ship." The sleeper of the tribe no longer prophesies or intuits disaster; he describes it; for it is no longer a mere foreday-morning nightmare, but a lived and living reality.

> and i beheld the cotton tree
> guardian of graves rise upward from its monument of grass crying
>
> aloud in its vertical hull calling
> for crashes of branches vibrations of leaves

This pronouncement is the climax to the rhetorical sweep of the rest of the poem, what Dash terms its "sermon-like monologue". The "and i beheld" is biblical, prophetic and apocalyptic, and is as rhetorically formulaic as Isaiah's authoritative: "Thus saith the Lord". There is the alliterative force of "guardian of graves," and the rumble of "monument" as the great ceiba, home of ancestral duppies, is riven. The placement of "crying / aloud" is absolutely correct.

Insofar as imagery – as distinct from rhetorical movement and sound – is concerned, the passage is a perfect example of how Brathwaite fuses two or more ideas or states of consciousness, which is a constant tendency in his work since *Islands*. In this case, the two states are the old coherence of the primal mind, and the new dispensation that will decimate the tribe and shatter its psychic cosmos. The ceiba tree, described two lines later as "the great grandfather", is great grandfather because it is the home of ancestors, and thus the repository of the history, memory and centred consciousness of the tribe. Even in the Caribbean it continued to be associated with the dead as living, fostering forces and voices, and featured in divination and initiation rituals.[36] Brathwaite transforms the ceiba, home of ancestors, into the hull of the slave ship bearing its burden of shattered souls, in an image that fuses both the tribal and the enslaved states of the African.

The poem then enters its final silence, this time a "lull of silver". This is perhaps the lull during which the people of Africa were being sold for silver, the silence of betrayal. This lull precedes the final shattering, when the ceiba splits with a sound of thunder and a cry of violation and murder. The idea of violation links up with the earlier description of the elders as foolish virgins. The poem's final lines are addressed to the violators.

> and our great odoum
> triggered at last by the ancestors into your visibility
>
> crashed
>
> into history

Here, the rather strange suggestion is that the fatal collision between Africa and Europe was willed and catalysed (triggered) by the ancestors, who explosively propelled Africa into the visibility of Europe. This runs counter to the poem's main argument that Europe aggressively sought out colonies for material exploitation. It is perhaps the rationalisation which the sleeper of the tribe places on a catastrophe too large for comprehension. Africa, which some Europeans used to say had no "history" before the arrival of Europeans in Africa, has now entered "history" via catastrophe.

IV: Of Brown

> and my mother rains upon the island with her loud voices
>
> with her grey hairs
> with her green love (*Mother Poem*)

Beverly Brown's "Mansong and Matrix: A Radical Experiment" [37] contrives to prove Brathwaite a promoter of exclusively male myths of origin, process and being. Woman in Brathwaite is, according to this essay, reduced to voiceless, passive, inert landscape. This contrasts with Zee Edgell's *Beka Lamb* and Jean Rhys's *Voyage in the Dark*, where women are doers, at the centre of their lives and worlds, and fictions. Brown's case is based on Maureen Warner-Lewis's "Odomankoma Kyerema Se" where, according to her, it is shown that "Brathwaite allows for androcentric birthing, so that even foetal blood may be credited to a male figure and the sea is the recipient of Father-Ancestor rivers."[38] Her case is also based on Gordon Rohlehr's review of *Sun Poem*,[39] from which she extracts a number of quotations to prove that Brathwaite's poetry employs "male /patriarchal-based creation myths", that counterpoint "a male-centred memory of the history" of creolization. One piece of "evidence" adduced in favour of her argument is Rohlehr's observation that:

> The mention of 'sunsum' (personality/experience) alerts us that this poem will be about spirit and essence transmitted, as the Akan believe, through the father, and becoming part of the bloodline of family and nation.[40]

Although the passage quoted speaks of "**part** of the bloodline" being male, Brown takes the statement to represent the whole of Akan thinking on the subject of procreation and, by extension, a substantial portion of Brathwaite's supposedly male-centred ideology as well. Akan philosophy, however, includes notions of both masculinity and femininity, as well as of their inter-relationship within the psyche. Danquah, an expert cited by Brown, tells us that

> The Akan maintain that each individual is made up of three constituent factors: (i) blood (mogya), derived from his mother; (ii) an individual personality – the 'personality-soul' (sunsum) derived from his father, and (iii) a 'life-soul' (kra), a divine spark which is associated with the life principle identified with blood, derived from the moon, or later, one of the planets.[41]

According to this statement, personhood is the result of a balanced interrelationship between the masculine, the feminine and the "divine", which is itself substantially feminine, the "life-principle" being associated with "blood" which is female and lunar. Brathwaite is concerned with this balanced wholeness, and laments its severe disruption in "Springblade" which contains images of castrated sons, violated daughters and the desecration of kra in contemporary Jamaica.[42] "Springblade" is an outcry against the upsurge of rape in Kingston during the early seventies. The poem condemns rape as violent male aggression, and advances through metaphor the theory of psychic disruption, directly based on Akan philosophy. Like "Kingston in the Kingdom of this World", "Springblade" explores the result of the impact of "missile" on "circle" which is described in "The Visibility Trigger". Even in *Sun Poem,* a work in which Brathwaite deliberately constructs a framework of solar mythology within which to locate Caribbean masculinity, there is no notion of a self-sufficient, self-impregnating, self-regenerating maleness. The sun-ship renews itself by means of an impregnation of the sea, out of whose womb he divinely emerges each day. Isis, the female sun deity and sister/consort of Osiris, precedes gen/isis, the birth of man, genesis. The mother is always there, not to be passively "man/ipulated" by even her son, but as an active and eternally shaping force in both the son's genesis and his growth.

Mother Poem and *Sun Poem* both unite autobiography and myth, and stand in a familial and dialectical relationship to each other. They are both authentic responses to Barbados and to the voices and persons who inhabit that fertile rock-seed. If *Sun Poem* seems to deal mainly with boyhood, male growth, male conflicts, problems and processes, *Mother Poem*, which comes first, as Isis precedes genesis, places women and the female voice at the centre. One of the tragic perceptions of these two poems, indeed, is how male and female voices are both imprisoned in their separate monologues, even on issues where mutual dialogue and compassion might have liberated them both. Thus the silent father of *Mother Poem*, bitterly confesses his frustration and withering, and his sense of having been supplanted by his son in his wife's affection; while the mother confesses her frustration and disappointment in both her husband and the emasculating system, to an unanswering parish priest, while she saves only "mouthing" for her man.

Brown is certainly wrong when she writes that Edgell's Beka and Rhys's Anna "as subjects, can and do speak 'otherwise', making audible what suffers silently in the holes of Brathwaite's discourse."[43] Though they do indeed suffer, "silent" is precisely what Brathwaite's women are not: from the village women in "The Dust", whose conversation is steeped in the memory of past apocalypse and contains omens of the one to come; to their older versions in "Cane", who have redefined their options and their selves, and are on the verge of burning in a fire that is simultaneously internal and external, to the mothers in *Mother Poem* whose voices present us with perhaps the most varied kaleidoscope of female experience that yet exists in West Indian Literature. The women's voices define, complain, confess, accuse, pray, prophesy, denounce and curse. In "Hex", the old haig or witch is imaginatively and sympathetically seen as seer, prophet, calling down retribution on the heads of those sons who have abused her through their neglect. She is later identified by the poet as "Black Sycorax, my mother", a subversive rebel woman who occurs at four distinct points of the poem ("Hex" pp. 45-49; "Nametracks" pp. 56-64; "Dais and Nights" pp. 67-76; "Cherries" pp. 77-81). Twenty-five pages, the very core of the poem, are involved with the active rebellion of the woman, whose emergence from invisibility parallels that of Tom, who in *The Arrivants* journeys from hat-in-hand acquiescence towards the rediscovery of the Ogun within himself: "lost pain, lost iron/emerging wood-work image of his anger."

As Sycorax, the mother becomes the voice of selfhood as mystery and magic on the one hand, and as " mud", ground, the earth itself and its fertility ("man-/ure"); my mother who fathered me; sustainer from birth to the "eve-/ing" when the cycle closes, and earth enwombs her children once more. She is also the voice of Africa in Caliban's head, and teaches him to connect "man" with "mandingo"; that is, to root himself in the alter/ native consciousness. As Africa, she is Eve, the ancestress of the human race.

Brathwaite stresses not only the particularity of Black colonial experience, but the distinctive roles played by the Black man and the Black woman in the post-Emancipation system of plantation production. The father's confrontation with Prospero in warehouse or on plantation is direct and humiliating. Just to enter the warehouse of the "thin-skinned" merchant is to re-enact the trauma of childhood neurosis of schoolboy confronting capricious headmaster. Initially, his wife is protected from this directness of confrontation through her very domesticity as woman-in-the-home who "sits and calls on Jesus" whose help she'll need sooner than she imagines. She waits for her man's return

> with her gold rings of love
> with her miner's trove that binds her to his world.

Behind this innocent portrait of the contented young wife lies the shadow of history. The reader is meant to connect this passage to an earlier allusion to Columbus and Raleigh, whose quests for gold led in the first case to madness and genocide, and in the second to disastrous failure and execution. A word like "trove" shifts the level of allusion from history to myth and legend, in which treasure troves are inevitably guarded by dragons or booby-traps. The gold rings of marriage, so highly prized as the reward of a woman's quest, will prove insidious, revealing too late the danger that has always surrounded their attainment. They bind the woman to the man's world – a bondage which she now accepts, but which will, in Prospero's good time, prove unattractive.

The bond between husband and housewife is economic. The value of the wife's labour depends on the value placed by Prospero on her husband's. If he is reduced to a slave, she will be reduced to the slave of a slave.

We see her contemplating this truth in the epiphanic "Twine" (pp. 6-9) where she begins by describing how the warehouse has destroyed her man, but soon shifts to noting that all her work, as ideal wife and nurturer of a no longer big or strong man, has been negated. In other words, though the husband is apparently at the centre of her consciousness, she is really involved in the process of reassessing herself, her work, her position and her story. In more ways than one, her husband has ceased to occupy the centre of her being. She'll try to fill the vacancy left by his absence with Jesus, the Anglican parson, the revivalist pastor, and with a Sisyphean promotion of her son.

Meditating on the plantation to which her husband has had to return after the collapse of his lungs in the dusty warehouse, the mother, with her expanded awareness, describes endless cycles of loveless toil in her enumeration of Prospero's backbreaking estates: "buckley, vaucluse, mount all, fair field, bissix, clifton hall, small;"

> de cane green, de cane ripe, de cane cut, de fields hot
> cutlass sweet, cutlass sweat, cutlass singing

The sound of work permeates her monologue as she comes face to face with Prospero's system: "trash, windmill, crack, bubble o vat in de factry." The sense of cycle is captured in the image of the windmill, "spinnin, spinnin, spinnin". This image, in fact, explains why the monologue is entitled "Twine". It is about a web of fate being spun, and Sycorax's growing recognition of history as a net of twine spun by the endless revolutions of the sugar mill, Barbados's version of the spinning-wheel of the Parcae. History is about vat, cauldron, the bitches' brew of blood and sweat bubbling to crystal, and the possibility of the "blood o de fields" leading to the "flood o de ages", an ultimate apocalyptic uprising of the oppressed. This vision, alive since "Cane" resides at the bottom of the woman's rebel mind, but will be raised to the surface as the poem proceeds.

Mother Poem also recognises that women's experience in the Caribbean had its own peculiar plantation hinterland, in the historically documentable fierceness of encounter between enslaved woman and slave mistress. In "Dais" and "Nights" Brathwaite presents this encounter as the origin of a disruption, via race and class, of the common line of female experience. Believing that the experience of Black women requires to be articulated by Black women, Brathwaite has filled his poems with Black female presences and voices. Shakespeare's Sycorax is a "blue-eyed hag"; Brathwaite's is "Black Sycorax my mother," an altogether different woman in terms of social and historical experience and notions of struggle and coping. The Greek Amazon is replaced by her double, Yaa Asantewa, warrior-queen and keeper of the Asante nation, captured and humiliated by the British in the 1900 war for the Golden Stool, sometimes known as the Yaa Asantewa war.

There was nothing silent or passive about that Yaa woman. Aphrodite, recognised as "your gentile Venus" in "Glass"[44] is replaced by the diva, Aretha, identified as a sun goddess, an Isis in *Sun Poem* ("Sun, who has clothed Arethas voice in dark gospel"). Aphrodite is also replaced by Angela Davis, another version of Yaa Asantewa, and one who is very clear about the dimensions of race and class in the feminist revolution.

Brathwaite has shifted to centre Billie and Bessie and Melba Liston, and the still unnamed and perhaps unnamable voice of "Cherries", who now directs her violence against the Black man, denying him progeny, future or regeneration. This rebel woman has existed before in the Caribbean and fought Prospero that way in the days of direct encounter on the plantation. Her method was abortion, which she did consistently as her act of rebellion, denying Prospero any further sacrifice.[45] Now, unleashing her rebellion of the womb against the Black man, she becomes the collective will and voice of all the "submerged mothers" of *Mother Poem;* the neutered soul of the raped idiot girl, who is the only silent woman in *Mother Poem*; the now militant voice of Donna, the schoolgirl-whore-mother in *X-Self* (pp. 70-72), who knows that she's only an ego-trip for her bourgeois male escapist lover; the more dreadful voice of the mother driven mad in "Hex" and of the mother in "Springblade" who gleams from the ghettos and whose fingers already grasp and cannot unhook from the missiles that she will one day hurl at the world. Clearly, any assessment of Brathwaite's presentation of woman, must take into account the militant voice of "Cherries" as she denounces and detaches her self from "manimal". Brown does not even acknowledge her presence in her crit.

Brown's ignorance of content is appropriately matched by her ignorance of style, image and situation in Brathwaite. Contrasting (so she imagines) Rhys with Brathwaite, Brown declares:

> See /seascaping is internal, unlike the sea which is externally determined by the sun-god in *Sun Poem*. Manscape is replaced by "the room; female archetype" a different sort of spacing altogether. Anna spends a great deal of her time between abortive love affairs with men, "remembering all the rooms of her life."[46]

Brown goes on to quote Helen Nebeker's statement that Anna's memories revolve around "creole culture, female individuality and sexuality" and that remembering is juxtaposed with the "smell of the sea (female archetype of life, the unconscious); [and] the rotting smell of the earth and water." Brown states that "In Brathwaite the sea is associated with masculine action. In Edgell and Rhys it is associated with female personality."[47]

First the question of "rooms" as against "manscape". *Mother Poem* takes place largely in rooms: from the first room where the newly married woman indulges in a sentimental dream as she awaits her husband-and-still-lover with her gold rings and her green love; to the shop where Miss

Own dreams of Meroe water, while retrieving saltfish from the murky pickled womb of the barrel; to the tiny parlour where the mother confesses to or accuses priest and confronts schoolmaster; right down to the musty room of "Moth Air", which is a pun on "Mother" indicating what her life, dreams and work have become in a far too early middle age.

Brathwaite's rooms are obviously different from Rhys's, as are his women who are, as we saw earlier, recognisably Black lower-class women, as against Rhys's basic white and off-white colonial women, who have lost, in a patently anti-feminist and racist England, the special status that whiteness, and its concomitant of automatic privilege, gave them in the West Indies. Antoinette Cosway is an exception, in that she loses what little status she's inherited, when her property is signed away by her stepfather and step-brother, who are, one guesses, Rhys's reversal of the wicked stepmother stereotype. Rhys's women, deprived of a context which they would have had only if they could have retained that special and superficial identity which race and property alone reinforced in the Caribbean, are, ironically, far less active in their rooms than are Brathwaite's women who, precisely because they are Christophene's sisters rather than Antoinette's or Anna Morgan's, are always doing things.

Poverty, oppression, their men's infidelity, misunderstanding, press in on them from every quarter, so that their rooms become battlefields where they confront the agents of Prospero: parson, debt-collector, hen-pecked schoolmaster. Challenging Chalkstick the teacher, the Black mother, by sheer force of her authority as a Black mother, browbeats him into admitting her son to the college "downhill" (dunghill). In that scene she is fiercely ironing clothes with an old-time hot flat-iron. In other words, she is an Ogun/Shango figure; and the galvanise sheets on her have-nothing cottage go "tic tic, tic", objectifying the time-bomb of her rage which, though suppressed now, will, like Tom's in *The Arrivants* be given terrible apocalyptic voice as she grows in self-awareness and visibility.

Deprived of context, Rhys's women mope; richly reminisce as they piece together their stories and their shattered psyches, in rituals of alienated self-healing. They display an amazing disjuncture between an active interior life and a passive exterior one, both of which lives coalesce in the uniform greyness and utter nullity that England and Europe are for both woman and man, once they are sun-begotten and sea-begotten. Their rooms match their state of mind and general irrelevance to Prospero's neuter and neutralising ethos. One may compare Naipaul's Kripalsingh in *The Mimic Men*, actively reincarnating his dead life into the fiction of history, but in reality, terrified of the fearful flow of present life, from which he neurotically retreats to seek refuge in his room.

Brathwaite's working-class women's housewifery is early defined as unpaid labour ("Twine" pp. 6-7). They have little time to mope. Some also work as peasants at croptime. Some are fishwives. Others sell in the city and village shops to "keep body and soul-seam together." The only one who does mope is Christie, victim of rape, whose mother regards her inability to function with sad resignation:

> christie still bout here turnin foolish
> > she us : ed to help me to sew
> > an mek up de cloze pun de singer
>
> sewin machine : but she fingers gone dead
> > and she int got eyes in she head.
> > then one two tree wutless men come up in here
>
> an impose a pregnant pun she..
> > one tek
> > but de other two both foetus dead.
>
> now she sittin up dere wid she hann in she lapp in de corner
> > rockin sheself in a chair by de window
> > and as far as i know, she too cud be dead.
> > > ("Angel/Engine" pp. 97-98)

How does one gauge the voice here? The speaker herself has been the victim of sexual abuse at the hands of her "copperskin cousin", for whom she eventually bears two children, a scholarship-winning boy, who goes downhill to the college, and Christie. There seems to be more resignation than indignation at the "wutless", "advantageous" men. This is clearly a repetition of her own response to being "jumped" upon by her cousin. Her greatest problem seems to be the fact that Christie has become an additional economic burden, where before she had been able to contribute to the survivalist economy of the household. Yet, there is something deep and sorrowful in her benumbed voice that suggests that the mother has internalised the additional pain of the daughter's experience as a cyclic repetition of her own. This is confirmed by the fact that this portrait of Christie is the prelude to the mother's joining of the Zion revivalist church. The meetings of this church take place in another "room" in the carpenter's shop. "Angel/Engine" demonstrates the difference between Brathwaite's women and Rhys's. Alienated, Rhys's women are self-healing, self-anointing. Antoinette may long to embrace Tia, her Black sister and double across the gulf of years and space. Anna may dream of her island, her servants, and the Black lower-class festivals of her girlhood. But in reality both women are locked in within themselves, and must find both liberation and healing by an act of memory and extraordinary imagination, which will, however, not change the external conditions of oppression in which they are imprisoned. Antoinette intuits this, and dreams that she has set fire to Prospero's fine castle, and then awakens to carry out her dream.

Benumbed and almost distracted, Brathwaite's woman seeks communal healing in the rootical church. Her dreams are almost all concerned with the therapy that only the communion of the group can give. "Fever", which recounts her dream of a Spiritual Baptist initiatory "mourning ground" experience, also becomes a metaphor of the poet's personal awakening to a vocation of exploring "the old water courses", the memories, and dreams and inner history that are collected deep in the core of the island and its people. Later, in "Moth Air", she meditates on the loveless menage of her life, symbolised by the semi-darkness of the room, the absence of children and husband, and the dust and soot in her kitchen. Moths, which chew clothes, are an apt image of decayed domesticity. Like Anna, the woman here reviews her life and is flatly frank. She remains with her unfaithful husband out of routine and the fact that she has accommodated herself too thoroughly to the trap.

> but uh cahn laff
> it off   :   uh cahn leff
>
> e : we custom each udder
> too much : too much cloze
>
> to menn, too much pot
> to scrub , too much ash
>
> to clean out under me finger
> tips, too much red
>
> in me wailin eye   :   too
> much cobweb to clear
>
> from de window   :   too much rock
> stone to brek   :   too much black
>
> to push up de hill.
> ("Moth Air" pp. 90-91)

To leave would be to admit the waste of effort and tears; to stay is to continue to bear an intolerable burden. Her attitude is heroic. It accepts the idea that the burdens are "too much" as a challenge to be up and doing. Her domestic routine moves from the conventional housewifery of mending clothes to the convict-like ordeal of breaking stones, to the mythological punishment of pushing blocks (blacks) uphill. But it is the fidelity with which she faces these tasks that distinguishes her from Rhys's collapsed white bourgeois protagonists. She will wake up from her reverie to take care of a grandchild and light a fire, which in the poet's eyes is an omen of fires to come that will burn both the plantation and the world.

> spark eye
> crackle o' bone-

juice an de whole sing-
in forest on fire : whisp-

erin whips on de shiv-
erin stone o de kitch-

en where she turns
alone to the o-

ven burn-
in burn-

in world
without

world with-
out world

without
end

amen   (p. 93)

Earlier in "Twine" we had seen the same transition from the interior monologue of a protagonist to the poet as omniscient narrator and sympathetic participant in the lives that he describes. If in "Twine" his intervention signalled that he had entered into and subsumed the grandfather's experience ("my ghost in your footstep, my eyes red in the hunger of your eyes"), here he identifies with the grandmother's silent heroism, recognising in her courage the omen of apocalyptic possibility.

What happens next is the woman's entry into the African-based Zion Church, "whose worship is based upon motion, kinesis, energy, communal celebration."[48] The meeting takes place in what Brathwaite describes as "a carpenter's shop owned by my own great uncle", where he observed a woman being possessed after the fashion enacted in "Angel/ Engine". According to Brathwaite, the woman was being possessed by Shango, who in New World transformations of African godhead is frequently represented by the locomotive. Both the woman and the congregation become the engine. Apart from Shango, there is Damballah, whose icon is the snake, and who is represented in the poem by the hissing sound that the woman makes in the process of her transition from saying "Praise be to God" to saying "Praise be to Shang." Brathwaite notes that she loses the ability to say "God", but never quite fully pronounces "Shango". He does however feel that she has come very close to her African origins. She has journeyed far from the assumptions of Prospero's Church, where the parson is distant and cold.

The process of her healing is totally different from that of Rhys's women, who lack support systems of any kind, and are as frequently betrayed by women as they are by men. Clearly, then, the difference between Brathwaite and Rhys does not lie in the notion that Rhys as a woman employs the room as context and symbol for women's activities, and state of mind, while Brathwaite as a man concentrates on sun, sea and "manscape". The difference exists in the race and class of the women presented by these two writers, and in what consequently takes place in the rooms that both present.

As to the question of how Brathwaite presents the sea: whether it is a male or female archetype; whether it is associated with masculine action or feminine personality, the answer is clearly, both. In *Mother Poem*, which Brown claims to have considered, the sea is the voice and the rhythm of female consciousness. In *Sun Poem* it is the medium of male activity, and the waves sing with the lilt and rhythm of Dylan Thomas's "Fern Hill", celebrating boyhood. In *Mother Poem*, the sea is capable of overwhelming surge and swell. Sycorax's grieving over her hard-hearted sons in "Hex" is caught in the haunting sound of the sea at night in Barbados.

> but she weepeth long into the night
> white trail of salt is there upon her cheek (p. 45)

The despoliation of the land in "Woo Dove" evokes the blue desolate anger of the sea/mother who is significantly glimpsed through brambles and cactus.

> there is blue between cactus and claws
> of the ocean: sea-island cotton cracks out of her cinder and shell
> the rocks on the hill have been tuned to black harps by the long
>
> seaswell ("Woo/Dove" p. 42)

Here the land offers cactus, desert; the sea claws, sharpness, raggedness; the sky blues. Yet there is a strange exaltation and dark music (rocks tuned to black harps) in that last unending surge. It is the intense surge of feeling that leaps from under the poem's narrative, surprising us from around the curves of conversation, the broken coral roads of the plot.

The surge of the sea becomes more pronounced in "Driftword" as the mother dies, and in dying becomes part of the cosmos. Consider this passage:

> as she touches again the salt and wet of his kisses
>
> she is his secret limestone cavern
> mothered from hiss and cobalt
> and his breath is leaves
>
> her own lips tingle with sea-grape
> the yellow curl of cashew
> and the leathery red of the fat-pork that burn on the cattlewash
>   dunes
> she has become the pools of his island: conch   lobster   flying fish
> scales

> closing her eyes he can hear the breakers breaking in her bleak
> of bone
>
> blue surge, white leap of blood, soft crackle of pebble
> and the small dead cells of the sea shells crying under that watery
> rule
>
> holding her now, she is the bright beast of bathsheba:
> dark rock unceasingly martyr'd:
>
> nemrack of reefs lamentations arising out of   the distantest
>   pool
>
> ("Driftword" pp. 115-116)

Brathwaite's evocation of the sea here, which is sensuously alive with the smell, taste and tang of salt and sea grape, the sound of wave on shingle, water on rock, achieves the sheerest magnificence. What the poem says and how it is said become so inseparably fused that one almost shies away from analysis. There is the sibilance of the first four lines. That is the sound of the foam as wave breaks against rock, hollowing out the limestone caves of Barbados, viewed here as sea-engendered, and endowed by Brathwaite with a special protective quality of home, mother, womb.

There is the use of sound echo: "cashew" "cattlewash". Here the sea-sounds are muted as the hush and wash of water pay homage to the dead mother. There is also a unity of the senses. Sight and taste suggest sound. The "curl of cashew" echoes the curl of wave, the "tingle" of sea-grapes while it expresses a quality of taste, is also the sound of wave on shingle. The long lamenting line noted earlier becomes more insistent: "closing her eyes, he can hear the breakers breaking in her bleak of bone." The four closely repeated plosives suggest the insistent beating of the waves on the black rock of the Cattlewash coast. These plosives will later be repeated in "bright beast of bathsheba". The mother is becoming part of the cosmos, the skeleton and bedrock of the island. "Bleak" points us, not only to the rugged eastern coastline, but also to the feeling of emptiness and desolation as the poet closes the eyes of the mother and at the same time ends the poem's cycle.

The landscape into which the mother sinks and which she becomes, contains its history of colonisation, penetration both sexual and otherwise, and the muted pain, yet survival of the conquered.

> blue surge, white leap of blood, soft crackle of pebble

Here the sea is "male" and the land that it penetrates "female". The landscape contains its grief and laments the souls of those who perished in passage, "dead cells of the sea shells", husks washed up on the eastern shore facing Africa, still crying under Britannia's watery rule. "Dark rock unceasingly martyr'd " points us even here to Brathwaite's awareness that he's writing about a specific place and people and race, and their long history of martyrdom. Here, on the coast facing Africa, he remembers that distant ancestral "Mother" and "those 50 million Africans, torn out of tongue, torn out of mother, torn out of soil and soul."[49] Thus the lament for the dead grandmother opens out, as the poem has constantly dilated, into a brief seasong for the martyrs of the middle passage, *les morts guinés*.

The last line is a tremendous, disconsolate surge of grief: "nemwrack of reefs lamentations arising out of the distantest pool." "Nemwrack" is a Brathwaite neologism, suggesting torture and wreckage of name or "nam". Literally it says that the reef's lament for all those lost souls is echoed within the caves far inland at the island's deep core. The mother contains that history in both her guises: sea and land. One notes the central placement of "lamentations" in the line to enable movement to the poem's crest of sound; and the diminuendo effect of the receding sea in the last five words.

Brathwaite ends the poem with a slow stately movement of acceptance, organised around the concept of woman as landscape. Hence, where sound was the predominant element in the seasong, sight, the eye following the outline of terraced steps of the island's plateaux is the most arresting element of the final movement. The movement of the eye is from the hills, down each terraced step to the seashore. It guides the voice in its tonal journey downward and outwards to the final affirmative resurgence "towards the breaking of her flesh with foam." It is the movement that the rainwater makes on its way down to cave and sea, and returns us to "Alpha" and the poet's shared dream with the mother in "Fever":

> the ancient water courses
>
> trickling slowly into the coral
> travelling inwards under the limestone
>
> widening outwards into the sunlight
> towards the breaking of her flesh with foam

Here, sea, sun, soil, stream, cave, coral and humanising flesh are together in an intense celebration of impregnation and rebirth. Interiority and exteriority are perfectly balanced.

In face of the poetry itself, then, Brown's claim for a special interiority in Rhys's use of sea imagery in contrast to Brathwaite's gender-determined focus on a male sun god controlling the female sea, is untenable. In *Mother Poem*, the sea and water images do possess an interiority, and are often perceived less as external spectacle than as voice, something heard and felt: groundswell, lamentation or trickle. "The sunken voice of glitter" ("Alpha") is one of the first indices of Brathwaite's apprehension of the internality of the woman's consciousness. Conceptually, it unites both sight and sound, exteriority ("glitter") with interiority ("sunken voice").

It is in *Sun Poem*, with its emphasis on the visual, that light penetrates water to produce spectrum, the rainbow whose colours frame the poem. In Brathwaite, it is common for the meaning of a phenomenon to shift as the perceiving eye changes its perspective. His sea is of itself neither male nor female, but can become in the eye of the poet whatever the poet chooses to make it. The sun, too, is variously associated with life, doom, oppression, all-seeing vision and energy. Beyond the question of gender and perspective exists the notion of the arbitrariness of how the consciousness interprets what it apprehends. The poet, therefore, not only interprets the world in terms of established mythologies, but also manipulates these mythological frames whichever way the experience directs. The poet, in addition, creates new idiosyncratic myths and image patterns.

Since this is how Brathwaite's poetry functions, any attempt to impose on it fixed and preconceived models, is bound to be frustrated by a discovery of the work's ambiguity, multi-facetedness and arbitrariness. Both Dash and Brown have sought to impose on the work theories that the work does not support. If Dash has misinterpreted such of the poetry as he has read, Brown in what must be an even more "radical experiment" than she imagines, has managed to theorise about poetry that she has not even bothered to read. Both critics, then, have stopped halfway on the road to doing the poet justice, and have consequently produced only crit...

BOIS!

(*Paper presented* at *the Conference of English Departments UWI, Mona, Jamaica, May 1988*)

References

1. Brathwaite, E., "Six Poems", *Kyk-Over-Al*, Vol. 9, No. 27 (Dec. 1960), pp. 83-86.
2. Ibid., p. 86.
3. *Sunday Gleaner*, 28 Jun., 1964; 12 Jul.; 2 Aug.; 30 Aug; 11 Oct.; 8 Nov.; 6 Dec., 1964; 7 Feb. 1965.
4. Brathwaite, E., "Jazz Portraits" in Brown, S., ed. *Now* 2, 1973, pp. 39-45.
5. E.g. "Blues" in *Other Exiles* (London: OUP, 1975) retains five of the original six Jazz Poems of 1960, but excludes "The Listener" for which "So Long Charlie Parker" is substituted.
6. Dash, M., Review of *The Visibility Trigger* and *Jah Music* in *Journal of West Indian Literature*, Vol. 1, No. 2 (June 1987) pp. 87-90.
7. Brown, B., "Mansong and Matrix: A Radical Experiment", in Peterson, K. & Rutherford, A., eds, *A Double Colonization: Colonial and Post-Colonial*

Women's Writing (Denmark: Dangaroo Press, 1986), pp. 68-79.
8. Brathwaite, E., Letter of Nov., 22. 1986.
9. Risden, W., Review of *Masks* in *Caribbean Quarterly*, Vol. 14, Nos. 1 & 2, (Mar-Jun 1968) pp. 145-147.
10. Rohlehr, G., *Pathfinder: Black Awakening in **The Arrivants** of Edward Kamau Brathwaite (*Port of Spain: 1981), Ch. 4.
11. Carter, M., "I Come from the Nigger-Yard" in *Poems of Succession* (London: New Beacon, Books Ltd., 1977), p. 38.
12. Brathwaite, E., "Arrival" in *Other Exiles* (London: OUP, 1975), p. 6.
13. "Clock", ibid., pp. 21-22.
14. Brathwaite, E., "Clock" for Albert Ayler, in *Jah Music* (Kingston: Savacou, 1986) pp. 19-21.
15. Brathwaite, E., "Caribbean Culture: Two Paradigms", in Martini, J., ed. *Missile & Capsule* (University of Bremen, 1980), pp. 9-54.
16. Brathwaite, E., "Clock" for Albert Ayler, op. cit.
17. Berendt, J., *The Jazz Book* (London, Toronto, Sydney, New York: Paladin Granada Publishing, 1976 (reprinted 1979)), p. 233.
18. Brathwaite,E., "Jazz and the West Indian Novel", in *Roots* (Havana: Casa de las Americas, 1986), p. 57 (originally published in *Bim,* Nos 44, 45 & 46, 1967-68).
19. Dash, M., op. cit. p. 87.
20. ibid., p. 88.
21. Brathwaite, E., "Timehri," in Coombs,O., ed. *Is Massa Day Dead?*(New York: Doubleday/Anchor, 1974), pp. 29-44 (quotes taken from p. 33).
22. Brathwaite, E., Letter, Nov. 22 1986.
23. ibid.
24. Walcott, D., "The Star-Apple Kingdom" in *The Star-Apple Kingdom and Other Poems* (NewYork: Farrar Strauss &Giroux, 1979), p. 49.
25. Walcott, D., "Gib Hall Revisited", in *The Gulf & Other Poems* (London: Jonathan Cape, 1969).
26. Williams, N.D. *Ilkael Torass* (Havana: Casa de las Americas, 1976).
27. Brathwaite, E., "Jazz & the West Indian Novel", *Roots,* p. 57.
28. Dash, M., op. cit., pp. 88-89.
29. Rohlehr, G., *Pathfinder,* Ch. 3.
30. Rohlehr, G., "The Problem of the Problem of Form: The Idea of an Aesthetic Continuum and Aesthetic Code-Switching in West Indian Literature", Paper read at English Dept. Conference, UWI, St. Augustine, May 18-23 1983.
31. Brathwaite, E., "And miles & miles & miles &" for Miles Davis, *Jah Music*, pp. 16-17.
32. Dash, M., op. cit., p. 89.
33. Harris, W., *The Sleepers of Roraima* (London: Faber, 1970).
34. Gilkes, M., *Couvade* (London: Longman, 1974).
35. Brathwaite, E., "Caribbean Culture: Two Paradigms", see ref #15.
36. Warner-Lewis, M., "The Nkuyu: Spirit Messengers of the Kumina", Savacou, No. 13, 1977, pp 57-78. Also Brathwaite, E., "Kumina: The Spirit of African Survival in Jamaica," *Jamaica Journal,* #42, 1978 (pp 44-63).

37. Brown, B., "Mansong and Matrix: A Radical Experiment". See Ref. #7
38. Ibid., p. 70.
39. Rohlehr, G., "Megalleons of Light: Edward Brathwaite's *Sun Poem*", *Jamaica Journal,* Vol. 16, No. 2 (May 1983), pp. 81-87.
40. Ibid., p. 70.
41. Danquah, Cited in Sawyerr, H., *God: Ancestor or Creator?* (London: Longman, 1970, p. 19).
42. Rohlehr, G., "Songs of the Skeleton Part II: A Poetry of Dread", *Trinidad & Tobago Review,* Vol. 4, No. 5 (New Year 1981 & vol. 4, No. 6 (Croptime: Mar-Apr 1981).
43. Brown, B., op. cit., p. 77.
44. Brathwaite, E., "Glass" in *Black + Blues* (Havana: Casa de las Americas, 1976), pp. 24-25.
45. Reddock, R., *Women, Labour and Struggle in Twentieth Century Trinidad & Tobago* 1898-1960, Ch. 2, esp. pp. 105-109.
46. Brown, B., op. cit., p. 76.
47. Ibid., p. 75.
48. Brathwaite, E., Edward Kamau Brathwaite's *Mother Poem*: Reading and analysis by the poet, London, ATCAL, 1980.
49. Brathwaite, E., "Metaphors of Underdevelopment: A Proem for Hernan Cortez", in *Africa-Europe* (Leuvense Schrijvrsaktie, 1984), pp. 35-57.

THE REHUMANISATION OF HISTORY
Regeneration of Spirit: Apocalypse and Revolution in Brathwaite's *The Arrivants* and *X/Self*

1: The Dehumanisation of History

The Arrivants, particularly its central movement, *Masks,* is about process where history is absorbed in time's neuter and neutralising continuum. Poems such as "Chad" and "Timbuctu" make this point with their respective focus on pre- and post-historic times, within the timeless context of the Sahara. Contemplating the ruins of the once great centre of learning and trade, Timbuctu, Brathwaite wonders what after all is the meaning of history, the accumulated bequest of human activity, in the face of Marvellian "deserts of vast eternity".

Yet Brathwaite is centrally concerned with a history that he presents as dense, multi-layered, multi-dimensioned and meaningful. He focuses both on its particularities and on the vast wide frame of human movement and making, within which particular moments of history are located. Human creative spirit saturates and energises history, recalling and redeeming it from time's neutralising void. The constant impulse to make and move beyond, enables humankind to break a cyclic process of creation, destruction and reconstruction which could otherwise be seen as both implacable and pointless. *The Arrivants* and *X/Self* both explore the human impulse to make and move beyond, as well as to destroy and reconstruct.

If time neutralises human effort, thus existentially "dehumanising" history, humans in quite another sense are prime contributors to the dehumanisation of their own activity. Brathwaite's focus on history as particular and willed human activity has resulted in the prominence in his writing of a concern with the question of human responsibility for the shape that history assumes. Thus, the central thrust of his writing has been less towards an illumination of time as neutralizing agent, and more towards an appreciation of people as both the dehumanisers and rehumanisers of history.

This has involved exploration of the complementary aspects of the human spirit: its destructive and creative impulses, and their strange interplay in the generation of history and civilisation. In *The Arrivants*, Brathwaite's focus is on the interplay of African, Afro-American, Caribbean and Euro-American histories. There is, however, a widening of concern with Native American and Mesoamerican histories in *X/Self* which is about empire, its consequences and probable future from Rome to the present time. *X/Self* makes it now possible to view *The Arrivants* as a major stage in the unfolding development of an idea concerning the unimmaculate conception of the New World.

Brathwaite locates the seed of origin in the disintegration of Rome and the outward encircling movement of the vulture of empire and conquest.

> rome burns
> and our slavery begins
>
> vultures wheel over kiev over kybir over ayub khan
> vultures wheel over the ganger over the crossed swords of shiva
> over the dead garden of mahatma gandhi
>
> vultures wheel over the styx over maggoire over the ice
> brick blocks of the alphs
>
> over the frozen body of el cid, of lidless legba l'ouverture
> . . . .
> . . . .
> they wheel high over the desert over tripoli and tunis over
>
> the head waters of the nile over
>
> chad over timbuctu over lagos over ile ife over ibadan and the
>
> fat markets of abomey[1]

The outward movement of the vulture, that is, of the destructive aspect of Spirit, touches the entire world. African slavery is simply one manifestation of the vulture, but it is one of the worst because slavery, the conversion of human being into capital, is a prime act in humanity's ceaseless dehumanisation of history, lacerating both flesh and spirit. Slavery served as a catalyst in the propulsion of the material avarice of capitalism into societies which soon became enmeshed in systems of production and marketing they could not, and still cannot dream to control. Brathwaite describes the growth of capitalism in terms which suggest that once unleashed, it developed into an almost autonomous machine that even its inventors could not control. The poems in *X/Self* entitled "Mount Blanc" and "Nuum"[2] describe the emergence of this machine, the development of its technology, and its devastating impact on the rest of the world.

Brathwaite is even more explicit in a lecture entitled "Metaphors of Underdevelopment: Proem for Hernan Cortez",[3] where he claims that Europe, still feeling disequilibrium after the collapse of the Roman Empire, stabilised itself by the evolution of a new world order, centred not on the medieval union of Church and State machines, but on money.

> And then money (MAMMON) became the centre of this shattered universe: markets, bourgs, bourse, traders, banks, bourgeoisie, taxes, tax-collectors,

regulations, fines, prisons, leviathan, navigation, war, commerce, merchants, mercantilism; travel to new lands, explore, exploit, control; the shift of power outwards: spire, spear, arrow, bullet, cannonshot, ship, sail, horse, the charge of the light brigade; print, bible, heaven; the conquest of sky by sun-jet angel missile. No prayer, but purse, no custom anymore but customhouse and curse. Marco Polo overland to China; the Portuguese by stepping stone to Africa; Columbus to San Salvador; looking for power, for powder, gun/powder; converting the grain to gain, unholy grail.

Therefore: Montezuma collapsed; Chitzen Itza defeated; Geronimo doomed; saschatewa, mohica, esquimaux and whale worshippers are marked with the hex; Timbuctu, Kumasi, Ile-Ife, Benin working its bronze, Zimbabwe... hearing the future of the avalanche... disorder, horror of unburial, dischordant skeletones... Caribs moving towards heroin and syphilis, Cherokees moving towards the horse, the wesson rifle and the wagon chain: Ibo and Mago to barracoon and charnel ship; Zulus towards Soweto and the locomotive tank; Masai beyond the elephant to the jumbo jet; Caliban to New York, Paris, London town.

Here then, is a comprehensive vision of the collision of Old and New World histories as dehumanisation to the point of recurrent genocide; a vision indeed, which presents many of the icons of progress in a negative light, as it grieves at the tragic interplay of human energy and the impulse to dominate, consume and destroy. It is in the face of this vision that Brathwaite measures the capacity of the human Spirit to rehumanise what it has dehumanised. In the process, he repeatedly explores inter-related concepts of Spirit, Apocalypse and Revolution.

II: Spirit

Brathwaite's idea of Spirit has been shaped from several sources: Christian, Hegelian, Akan and Dogon. Commenting on the imagery of *X/Self* for example, he writes that: "Mt. Blanc is a symbol of materialism; while Kilimanjaro, its opposite, is a symbol of the spirit."[4] Thus the materialism of expansionist Europe undermines first European, then African and New World spirituality. Here the vision is simple and dualistic: Materialism/Europe/Mt. Blanc versus Spirit/Africa/Kilimanjaro.

On the other hand, Brathwaite's "Hegelianism" leads him to a more complex and more optimistic vision of Spirit as being continuously and progressively emergent from the dialectical dance of opposites in history. Thus, far from being simply the opposite of matter, Spirit is dialectically related to matter, which it confronts and vitalises. This sense of Spirit as active, rather than inertly passive under the assault of matter, is just as pervasive in Brathwaite's poetry as the simple opposition of triumphant materialism and helplessly inert spirituality.

The African notion of Spirit as immanent all-pervasive and perhaps more real than matter, leads Brathwaite to the concept of "Nam". "Nam" is described thus:

DISGUISE OF MAN IS NAM: MAN BACKWARDS. Etymologically it is a root word (African and Oceanic and Amerindian and Indo-European) meaning root or core or spirit... seed if you like or soul: dry and reduced and irreducible and green: the utter inner self.[5]

"Nam" a term like many others recently of Brathwaite's own coinage, is generically related to "Onyame", the Akan Creator God, "yam", sustaining staple food on both sides of the Atlantic; "name" and Dogon "Nummo" the original creative Word. "Nam" is firstness of Spirit and a kernel-seed of being which might be obscured or imprisoned but is, like Newtonian matter, susceptible to neither creation nor destruction. "Nam" is the primal life-impulse, the Word of God, whose activation in the universe is described in Ogotemelli's discourses with Marcel Griaule. "Nam" is also the essential personhood inherent in every human being which, surviving man's direst efforts at its mutilation, is perpetually rediscoverable.

When, however, the human Spirit has been historically brutalised:

broken by time, by neglect, the tough boots
of Columbus, of pirate, the red boots of flame;
cracked soles of Africa, broken by whip.[6]

the process of recovering "Nam" becomes arduous. Several of Brathwaite's poems deal with the shattering of primal vision and Spirit. "The Visibility Trigger", a poem that comes close to the centre of *X/Self*, describes this shattering in terms of images of the broken circle and the riven despoliated tree. Circle is wholeness of psyche, integrity of aboriginal world-view; cyclic sense of time and work; sensibility in harmony with the rhythms of the land and the cosmos. With the intrusion of the European, circle becomes target to be shattered by missile. Custom, courtesy, communion, symbolised by the kola nut which the elders offer the interloper, are answered by gunfire as Brathwaite imaginatively reenters the moment of the "fall", of the murdering of Spirit.

Desecration and diminishment of Spirit are taken a stage further as Europe and Africa together participate in the slave trade. Brathwaite re-enters this moment both through the directly descriptive chorus of the newly enslaved which ends the "New World A-Comin" sequence in *Rights of Passage* and indirectly in "Noom" the central sequence of *Sun Poem*, through fabricated myth. "Noom" tells a story of the imprisonment and reduction of the Nummo. The word "noom" is a neologism which combines "noon" with "doom," and thus suggests its meaning: the negation of "Nam", name and Nummo, and the consequent darkening of the sun.

"Noom" describes the arrival of the Loa – that is African Spirit: God as energy, life-force – on the rugged Eastern coast of Barbados, a moment that signals their separation from Dogon and Dahomey. This arrival is re-counted in terms of Good Friday imagery – darkness at noon, the despairing cry of the dying god – which links the Nummo with Christ and suggests that both of these sun gods and sons of God lost their shining charisma in the process of slavery and enchainment which degraded their arrival in the New World.

"Noom", however, is not only about the fatal separation of the life-Spirit from its ancestral source, but also about the shape which this same Spirit imposes on the new landscape as it endures a harsh process of indigenisation. "Noom" is a creation myth which purports to explain why the Atlantic coast of Barbados, the coast which faces Africa, is in its ruggedness so uncharacteristic of the island's topography. The shape that the imprisoned Spirit imposes on the landscape is informed by pain, rage and protest, a quality of both desperation and revolt. Since in both *Mother Poem* and *Sun Poem* landscape is closely related to hidden dimensions of Spirit, Brathwaite is suggesting the subterranean existence of an African presence in an island that one normally regards as the most anglicised of the Caribbean.

Another image of the reduction of Spirit appears in "Kingston in the Kingdom of this World"[8] originally also entitled, "Good Friday 1975". If "Noom" explores the moment of arrival in the New World, "Kingston in the Kingdom of This World" explores the contemporary moment: the state of Spirit after centuries of enchainment. The protagonist of this poem is Voice, Word, the Word in prison. Insofar as he is in Kingston, we can safely conclude that he is Black and "conscious". But, as the title of the poem suggests, Kingston is a microcosm of the kingdom of this world: the oppressive nature of Kingston is, as in several of the sequences of *X/Self*, part of the universal enchainment of Spirit. The Voice in the poem is thus that of "Nam", firstness of Spirit, now burdened down by the imprisoning structures of the kingdom of this world; now raging and reduced. The voice is also that of Christ soliloquising in prison, abandoned by his disciples and awaiting trial and the death-sentence. He recalls the Sermon on the Mount, one of the cardinal social statements of his ministry, which included both beatitude and denunciation and was crowned by the feeding of multitudes who abandoned him when he failed to leave them guidelines as to how they, without either toiling or spinning, might emerge arrayed better than Solomon in all his glory.

Now in prison. Christ remembers his career as activist for the Spirit, the great fisherman of souls.

> The fish swim in their shoals of silence
> our flung nets are high wet clouds, drifting

He and his disciples had hauled in souls under the high clouds with their promise of rain; netting them with a doctrine that devalued the power structure, placed natural freedom of Spirit above material production, and gave a sense of worth to the ordinary and essential: the salt of the earth.

But there are extra dimensions to Brathwaite's "Voice" that are not to be explained by reference to Christ's Sermon on the Mount. The Voice, for example, declares:

> with this reed i make music
> with this pen i remember the word
> with these lips i can remember the beginning of the world

These declarations associate the imprisoned Voice first with a Pan-like natural music, then with the poet as representative of all makers with the word, and finally with the "Word" of St. John's gospel, which existed in the beginning, was with God and was God.

"Kingston in the Kingdom of This World" is constructed on a series of contrasts between what the Voice, "Nam", represents, and what prison, either as Blakean "mind-forg'd manacles" or physical lock-up means. These contrasting states of being are presented in terms of contrasting rhythms and flows of energy which affect length of line. The idea of the reduction of Spirit is conveyed in truncated lines that contrast with the mighty energy-filled lines in which the Voice proclaims its true identity as Spirit, Word of God.

> gospel was a great wind freedom of savannas
> gospel was a great mouth telling thunder of heroes
> gospel was a cool touch warm with the sunlight like
>
>   water in claypots, healing

The descriptions of gospel have as much to do with the verbal powers of the shaman, as with the conventional Christ figure. Thunder – a reference to Shango – great wind, freedom, savannas, contrast with the gentler qualities of soothing, healing and spiritual restoration. The Voice associates itself with flowers, water, flutes and language, in contrast with withered beauty, ecological pollution, attenuated grace and debased language. The core of the poem comes when the Voice contrasts the "Authority" that he was trying to establish in, or restore to, the world, with the debased authority of his captors.

> my authority was sunlight: the man who arose from
>   the dead called me saviour
> his eyes had known moons older than jupiters

The man who arose from the dead is Lazarus, so at this point the Voice is that of "Christ", affirming his life-giving restorative function. But the next line: "his eyes had known moons older than jupiters" suggests the Dogon, with their phenomenal knowledge of astronomy, much of which informs their philosophy and world-view. This parallel between the Christ-figure and the Nummo is constant in this poem, and will later inform *Sun Poem* ("Noom") and *X/ Self* ("Xango"). It exists because of the interlocking cross-cultural contexts out of which Brathwaite's work generally grows.

Often, though, various cultural contexts are presented in opposition to each other. This may be seen in "Kingston in the Kingdom of this World" in the contrast between the primal authority of the Nummo/Christ and that of the kingdom of this world.

> ...the white eye of interrogator's terror
> siren price fix the law of undarkness
> the dreadness of the avalanches of unjudgement

"Undarkness" is a Brathwaite coinage by which Europe is seen through African eyes as "undark" in much the same way that the Eurocentric vision often speaks of the "non-white" world. "Undarkness" also denies light or vision to the bearers of the "word" into the heart of darkness. The "law of undarkness" is the negation of the "law of darkness"; that is African legal, political, social, economic and philosophical structures. The "avalanches of unjudgement" are what Europe – here associated with the engulfing and death-bringing snows of Mount Blanc – unleashes on all those conquered peoples. *X/Self* shows how Europe transplanted its medieval systems of tort and torture, its renaissance traditions of inquisition and witchhunt, and its modern inventions of state terrorism and concentration camp.

Part of the pain of the Spirit's imprisonment is that the disciples have either misunderstood or forgotten or rejected the non-materialistic gospel of the Sermon on the Mount, and accommodated themselves to the material interests of the kingdom of this world. This cry will be heard again in "Shaman" (*X/Self*) and "Hex" (*Mother Poem*).

> i would call out but my lost
> children cannot unshackle their
>
> shadows of silver

The chains are no longer of iron, but of silver, the metal of betrayal. It is as much the disciples' indifference to what the Spirit represents – word, gospel, freedom, the authority of sunlight and imagination – as the perverted authority of the system – imprisonment, torture, exploitation, atrocity – that condemns the Spirit to indefinite detention, and this strangled soliloquy, which has not yet become public outcry.

III: Apocalypse

Spirit may be imprisoned or beaten, but in Brathwaite it is never totally defeated or killed. It is always capable of regeneration; and part of Brathwaite's value as both historian and poet has been his stress on the human capacity for renewal through the coming into consciousness of the subjugated mind. Slaves, he notes,[9] remained "invisible" faceless unpersons until they revolted. Revolt results from implosions within the psyche of the reduced person, triggered by a growing historic consciousness of the reasons for subjugation. "Kingston in the Kingdom of this World" dramatises the awakening of this historic consciousness; and though the voice in that poem has not yet called out to either the system's commissars or the lost children, such consciousness illuminates the necessity for action as, inevitably, the interior brooding of the subjugated Spirit becomes public and political.

At this point, implosion exteriorises itself in social upheaval and may, under extreme circumstances, become revolution. The process by which the reawakened Spirit attempts to transform the withholding structures of a dehumanising history is what is meant in this essay by "Apocalypse". Apocalypse as a social and political idea has always involved two acts or processes: the violent destruction of an old world and the coming into being of a new one. Implied in these processes have been the ideas of reversal, judgement, rectification and purgation, and the emergence of a new and just authority. In reality, neither process occurs in the manner anticipated. The old order never quite disappears, nor does a truly a new order emerge. Vestiges of the old order permeate the new, to mock the dreams of idealists who may have sacrificed everything for change.

Nevertheless, the idea of Apocalypse pervades modern, and particularly New World literatures, and has been employed to describe the iconoclastic urge in "modernist" art forms, which are constantly seeking the new and strange. Douglas Robinson in his *American Apocalypses* describes the apocalyptic idea as:

> definitively seeking to explore the unveiling of the future in the present, the encroachment of a radically new order into a historical situation that has disintegrated into chaos,[10]

Inserted between the present and the future, the apocalyptic moment illuminates, as Hiroshima has illuminated, both the world as it is and the world as it might be.

West Indian literature, too, is saturated with the spirit of Apocalypse in the sense that it perceives itself as dealing with the end of Old World structures and the inchoate emergence of New World ones. The idea of a reordering, a transcension or even the abolition of history is common to several West Indian writers – Harris, Walcott, Lamming, Denis Williams, Brathwaite, Césaire, Carpentier and Glissant. In each case, it involves the subversion of traditional structures, be they aesthetic, mental or political; though in each case, foreknowledge of the likelihood of the persistence of old worlds in new has bred misgiving, tragic irony or desperate hope.

Derek Walcott, for instance, is simultaneously attracted to and repelled by the political aspect of the apocalyptic idea. In *Dream on Monkey Mountain*,

Makak after agonies of self-discovery and self-renunciation, both of which centre on the explosive emergence of his smothered dreams of justice and revenge, reluctantly beheads the White Goddess – who may be muse or demon – and retreats to "the green beginnings of the world." These "green beginnings" seem to be an idealised region of the mind that is free from both the dehumanization of the past and the burden which the present bears of rehumanising history through violent encounter. The "green beginnings" are a womb-like state of "amnesia" beyond or before history, an "adamic" state in a New World of the mind.

Walcott's pastoral retreat from a solution within history is the result of a fear, similar to D. H. Lawrence's dread of the proletarian dream of an apocalyptic reversal of the social order. Lawrence notes the attractiveness to the nonconformist poor all over the world of the denunciations in "Revelation" of the great, the rich and the powerful.

> Down among the uneducated people you will still find Revelation rampant ... the huge denunciation of Kings and Rulers, and of the whore that sitteth upon the waters, is entirely sympathetic to a Tuesday evening congregation of colliers' wives, on a black winter night, in the great barn-like Pentecost chapel. And the capital letters of the name: MYSTERY, BABYLON THE GREAT, THE MOTHER OF HARLOTS AND ABOMINATIONS OF THE EARTH thrill the old colliers today as they thrilled the Scotch Puritan peasants and the more ferocious of the early Christians.[11]

"Revelation" is welcomed by "the never truly humble poor" as:

> a grandiose scheme for wiping out and annihilating everybody who wasn't of the elect, the chosen people, in short, and of climbing up himself right to the throne of God.

Lawrence views with horror the desire of the poor to control and restructure their own destiny, and in an otherwise fascinating study, comes close to granting moral legitimacy to the powerful simply because they are powerful, and of dreading democracy simply because it is a doctrine espoused by the "weak" and "pseudo-humble".

In the case of Walcott, the fear is the traditional neurosis of the old plantocracy: that popular revolt in the Caribbean will rapidly degenerate into racist revenge.[12] Walcott saw this tendency in the Black Power movement of the late sixties and early seventies, and expressed his fear of Black people in the Caribbean coming into historical consciousness. This fear is translated into sardonic dismissal of "Black consciousness" in *Another Life* and "What the Twilight Says: an Overture", and grotesque comedy in the "Trial Scene" from *Dream on Monkey Mountain* where Lestrade's attempt to place the white world on trial is presented as absurd.

Walcott's misgivings are, in fact, shared by other writers, though there are differences in how each writer signals a caution about revolutionary vision, process and change, as well as varying degrees of scepticism and hope. Brathwaite, for example, recognises the ambiguity of the apocalyptic moment: its simultaneously death-bearing and life-enhancing quality. Like Walcott, he recognises that revolutions conducted by the terminally ill in Spirit degenerate, as in "Springblade", where thwarted and emasculated Jamaican youth transfer aggression from the "system" to the "sisters". Brathwaite's vision of Black youth in Harlem or Brooklyn in the post Black Power period, is even more hopeless.

> i see my brothers high and nodding
> shadow boxing to the tune of needles
> angels of the fix
> bartering their sanity for trips
> around the skeleton
>
> i hear them screaming
> REVOLUTION
> as the world revolves around
>
> marcus malcolm mississippi memphis
> but there ain't no vein
> of revolution
> only the blues
> and coltrane's gospel pain[13]

These youth, like those of "Springblade", are terminal people. They represent the dead-end of normal social relationships and sanctions. They are seen as

> victim(s) 'of the cities' victory
> victim(s) of the cities' skin and trinkets
> wilderness of wind and shellac[14]

Marginalised to a point where they are almost outside of historical process, they are oblivious to past struggle. Brathwaite asserts that before one can make the leap from this terminal situation towards the generation of renewed personhood, one must first achieve the very thing that Walcott seems to fear: historical consciousness. Where some thinkers expect spiritual transformation to be a result of revolution, Brathwaite believes that personal epiphany must precede communal epiphany.

Brathwaite is particularly concerned with the paradoxes and difficulties that attend the advent of revolutionary awareness; not the least of which is whether "time's long attack" on the psyches of the subjugated has not been too devastating for any revolution of the mutilated to reverse. As the *omowale* recognises in *Masks*:

> the termites' dark teeth, three
>
> hundred years working,
> have patiently ruined my art[15]

This is the central issue of both *The Arrivants* and *X/Self*: how to move from subjugation to rebellion; then, having rebelled, how to keep pure the ideals for which one rebelled. Like D.H. Lawrence, Brathwaite recognises that the flame of rebellion is alive in even the most apparently humble folk. Unlike Lawrence, he accepts this rebellion as necessary, and in both *The Arrivants* and *X/Self* envisages the eventual emergence of an Ogun/Shango persona; a spirit of fire, energy and iron resolve in the breasts of the subjugated. Even Tom, that embodiment of the reduced Spirit, who has learnt to perceive history as nullification, also nurtures a dream of Noah's rainbow with its promise of apocalyptic fire in some remote "next-time".[16] Though as a necessary survival mechanism he keeps his "hate smothered down/ to the bone/ to suit the part/ [he's] playing,"[17] his urge to negate the nullifying process of his history never dies. It, however, takes a long time and doesn't clearly happen until "Negus".[18]

Part of the irony of Tom's situation lies in his sons' transferral of their inherited revolutionary impulse from the dehumanising system to Tom himself, whose gestures of protest have been too weak and too broodingly introverted to be sympathetically understood as such. Doubly ironic is the fact that they have also inherited, and will later display, mechanisms of role-playing more damaging than their father's. Tom knows himself even though he evades open rebellion. Tom's sons attempt open rebellion but evade self-knowledge. *The Arrivants* works towards a reconciliation of the two: self-knowledge and rebellion, without whose coincidence any revolution is meaningless.

Tom's dream of a resurrection, a rising up or uprising of his people, steadily surfaces from the depths where he has, through his mechanism of self-censorship, confined it. By "Wings of a Dove" it has begun to burn very close to the surface of consciousness. Here the protagonist is Brother Man, the finished product of urban waste, whose very being seems invaded by the parasitism through which his labour has been the sustenance of bourg and metropole. Though Brother Man may appear to resemble the derelict youth of "Glass", he becomes, as the poem proceeds, the transformed reborn voice and bearer of omen. He moves from the pacifist ethic of old-time Rastafarianism to becoming the mouthpiece for apocalyptic upheaval. The particular nature of his awakening – through possession by voices of Biblical prophets – reflects an aspect of proletarian experience that involves an immersion in the apocalyptic texts as a theology of liberation, or at least retribution.

Brathwaite's Rastafarians resemble Lawrence's puritanical colliers in this respect though, as we have noted, his attitude towards the proletariat entering their voice is quite different from Lawrence's anti-democratic disdain. Brathwaite makes Brother Man, at this nexus of self-affirmation and political definition, the history-filled and prophetic voice of a wider proletariat. His mistrust of white men, con men, brown men and white-black men is not irrational xenophobia, but accurate appraisal of an emerging class of new rulers, that is simultaneously aggressive in its greed of gain and defensive in its cultural rootlessness. This class is viewed by Brother Man as having only an aborted future, and as being an omen of disembodied possibility.

>   na
> feet feel firm
>
> pun de firm stones; na
> good pickney born
> from de flesh
> o' dem bones[19]

The release of Spirit, the journey towards Nam begun in "Wings of a Dove" is the central theme of *Islands* which may be viewed as deepening phases of a descent into submerged areas of the Collective Unconscious, each of which is preceded and catalysed by a different ritual of possession. Thus the persona enters the vestibule of the inferno of History and Self through the gateway of jazz.[20] He begins the movement out of limbo with the pukkumina vibrations of "Shepherd"[21] immediately after which he begins to prophesy in the many and strangely-blended tongues of Jeremiah, Sartre and Ferlinghetti.[22] Secondary manifestations of loa become fairly frequent from now on, as, for example, in "Limbo"[23] and "Rites"[24] with its brief intimation of Ogun-Shango. Voices of prophecy pervasively inform the poem's sound as, for example, in "Wake"[26] where we shift in an accommodation of ancestors, from West African to Haitian prayers, psalms, the invocation to Legba, echoes of the Gospels and Jeremiah's pessimistic tones as the society rejects or simply ignores its prophets.

The apparently calm voices of the women in "Cane" soon give way to the loa of fire and passionate resolve,[26] preparing the reader for "Ogun" which, in its movement from the flat surfaces of everyday activity towards possession, is in fact a summary of the movement of the entire trilogy from tough weather-beaten surface shell to the kernel-core of Nam, the tree's green original centre of Being. Ogun is timid Tom and crippled Legba in the process of discovering their own submerged Spirit. He is carving a block of wood partially eaten away by termites into an image of himself, his "Nam". The inert "block of wood" conveys metaphorical connotations of "stupidity", "apathy", "dullness" and "doltishness", and represents the process of reification which Tom has endured; his past deformity of image and benumbed beaten Spirit.

The act of creation involves a rediscovery and release of Spirit, which precedes the movement towards the "lost iron" of revolutionary consciousness. Rebirth of Spirit is clearly signalled in the beautiful lines:

> until his hands could feel
>
> how it had swelled and shivered breathing air
> its weathered green burning to rings of time
>
> its contoured grain still tuned to roots and water[27]

"Spirit" is literally, or generically, breath. Thus its possession of, or reemergence within the weather-beaten but enduring heart of matter, is portrayed as a deep inhalation of breath by the medium. This is in itself a point of interest, since normally we think of the Creator breathing life into inert matter. Here, however, it is the apparently inert medium that inhales the breath of Spirit; which is another way of saying that Tom has ceased to smother the Spirit which has always been imprisoned within him. Liberated, Spirit does not forego matter, but energises, rehumanises it and inspires it for the tasks of resurrecting the terminal person and transforming human institutions in the natural world of history.

Such transformation involves the destruction of the corrupt aspects of the old order. But what is the process by which the refiner's fire of Spirit liberated moves beyond its mission of destruction to become an agent of regeneration? In "Leopard"[28] Brathwaite underlines the urgency of this question for Caribbean and New World peoples transfixed in this apocalyptic moment between the proven morbidity of the old order and the unknown and at times unimaginable future, by drawing attention via metaphor to the patterns of violence, rapine and conquest in the pre-diasporan history of Africa. Employing the image of the caged leopard as a metaphor of the situation of the exploited and explosive so-called developing countries, he makes a plea for humane liberation:

> Give him a tree to leap from,
> liberator; in pity let him
> once more move with his soft
>
> spotted and untroubled splendour
> among the thrills and whispers
> of his glinting kingdom;
> or unlock him and now let him
>
> from his triggered branch
> and guillotining vantage
> in one fine final falling
>
> fall upon the quick fear-
>
> footed deer or peer-
> less antelope whose beauty,
> ravaged with his sharp brutality
> propitiates the ancient guilt

> each feels toward the other:
> the victim's wish to hurt,
> the hunter's not to;
> and by this sacrifice
>
> of strong to helpless Other,
> healed and aneled;
> both hurt and hunter
> by this fatal lunge made whole.

The leopard is Spirit as a potentially free and fearsome energy which resides within the "liberator" – that is, the person about to free himself through violent effort. Yet Brathwaite allows the liberator two alternatives. The first is to relocate the leopard in its original and primal kingdom, a world conceived of as one of light and wonder. There, Spirit or "Nam" is triumphant, free and at home, in full harmony with the environment. Such restitution of primal Spirit would require on the part of the liberator, revolutionary man on the verge of releasing this caged and fearful aspect of himself, a quality of compassion. Compassion is necessary if the pure naked premoral energy of Spirit is to be contained for creativity; just as Energy in William Blake becomes anarchic without its outward circumference of Reason. Compassion, or "pity" as it is termed in "Leopard", is the restraining circumference which Brathwaite suggests to a Caribbean and Third World in which revolutionary upheaval is a perennial possibility, and in some countries almost an annual reality.

Brathwaite, however, as if he recognises the unlikelihood of anyone choosing the first option in a world where the old order that the liberator seeks to transform is manifestly uncompassionate, spends much more time articulating the second. Here, Energy/Spirit is not relocated in its natural habitat – there's no returning to the ancestral kingdom – but is unleashed for its final encounter with the enemy. This final encounter is both political and psycho-sexual, and is envisioned through an image which works simultaneously on these two planes. Hence the released leopard stalking and killing its prey suggests an army of sansculottes, triggering and guillotining their way towards liberty and the cemetery, as well as a rapist/murderer violently possessing his victim, in the delusion that he is, through sexual revenge, healing himself of past hurt.

It is, curiously, the psycho-sexual aspect of the image that is developed; so much so that the original leopard image becomes subsidiary to the idea of rape, and rape is the image through which the retributive revenge of the oppressed is commented upon. The uncompassionate liberator may become, like the rapist, an unleashed wild-cat fulfilling a feral need for blood, rather than an apostle of new consciousness. While he may envisage a "peerless beauty" at the end of revolt, he destroys it in the act of violent possession.

Yet, ironically, he never achieves full conquest of his prey, since beneath her forced submission lies "the victim's wish to hurt;" that strange link which makes victim and assailant, masochist and sadist and, the poem implies, liberator and oppressor monstrous doubles of each other. Awakening, or rather, bringing to the surface "the victim's wish to hurt", he's simply created another victim who will in time reenact, as he is now doing, the vengeful psychology of the victim. The victim, in the act of destroying the violator and eradicating the stain of violation, will create new victims. "Nam", reacting to violation, can choose only this negative method for its self-defence.

Nor has he satisfied the latent desire which lies at the root of his attack. That love, suggested in his latent wish not to hurt, is the creative and redeemable aspect of Spirit which, since Spirit is indestructible kernel seed of being, dwells even in the most violent of men. But love can in such circumstances manifest itself only negatively, by effecting a crumbling of the all-conquering ego while the ego is in the very act of a revenge through which it had hoped to fulfil itself. This is possibly, the meaning of the lines

> and by this sacrifice
> of strong to helpless other
> healed and aneled;
> both hurt and hunter
> by this fatal lunge made whole.

where the assailant's strength collapses and the helpless victim conquers in a reversal of roles. The "wholeness" which the ego gains in an epiphany of such terror is totally an illusion. The reality is one of mutual destruction, the annihilation of both self and other, both victor and victim. The word "aneled", which means anointed for burial, makes this clear. The ultimate revolutionary choice is between compassion and catastrophe.

This remarkable poem deals simultaneously with the bitter climax of three parallel confrontations: that of coloniser and colonised, male and female, and the one that has always been taking place within the human psyche between Eros and Thanatos, the creative and destructive aspects of Spirit. It is amazing that Brathwaite should, as early as 1961 when "Leopard" first appeared, have equated these three levels of confrontation – the political, gender and psycho-sexual levels – and seen their joint resolution as the ultimate task of civilisation, as it wavers between the options of terminality and the rehumanisation of history.

IV: Dreadful New World Genesis: *X/Self*

If "Leopard" foretells the tragic failure of any uncompassionate revolution, it also views as unlikely the prospect of a compassionate one. As it moved from the hopeful renaissance years of the sixties with their "exploding dimensions of song" and political activity, Brathwaite's poetry had to come to terms with the assassination of the Black Power and Civil Rights movements in their Christian, Islamic and urban guerrilla phases. This brought him face to face with what he'd always known: the problem of even imagining the possibility of a successful rebellion of the weak, the underdeveloped and the divided. How was one to maintain hope in the face of so much failure among Africans at home and abroad? What prospects existed for a just reordering of History? Could this happen without recrimination and revenge? Can the products of a dehumanised process, history, transcend that process? How does one encounter and transform a structure of power on terms other than those predicated by that structure of power?

These questions, latent in *The Arrivants* resurface in *X/Self,* a more complex exploration of the theme of Empire than *The Arrivants* which is also concerned about the cyclic establishment and disintegration of Empires – the Egyptian, Sudanese & West African as well as the British Empires. The first half of *X/Self* deals with the everchanging proportions of "Rome" after eight centuries of Christianity. The poem suggests the validity of the Pirenne thesis, that the vast movement of Germanic peoples into the Roman Empire caused not the disintegration, but the consolidation of structures based on the intermeshing of Church and State. *X/Self* is about this consolidation of "Rome" as structure, law, ideology, cosmology, long after "Rome" has ceased to exist as the administrative centre of an empire. "Rome" emerges as a metaphor, a paradigm of the convergence of forces into a massive and dominant polity; so that today, "Rome" is America.

Since the consolidation of "Rome" is based on the reduction of her colonies, *X/Self* explores patterns of equilibrium and disequilibrium; growth and degeneration. It is particularly concerned with the forced transplantation of these patterns in the New World, and moves beyond the predominantly African/Afro-American/Afro-Caribbean parameters of *The Arrivants*. The range of voices is wider in *X/Self*. More Europeans are allowed to speak. Meso-America is accorded a central place. Strange juxtapositions of voices and historical personages occur, as Charlemagne addresses his "brother" Henri Christophe; Caesar and Nixon reveal resemblances; Othello, Tennyson, Cortez and a host of other historical and fictional characters appear in strange contexts.

The New World sensibility, a product of widely contradictory and at times bizarre forces, becomes "X/Self" – the unknown undiscovered self. This unknown self exists in a context of overwhelming demoralisation, whose main elements have been the direct results of Empire. Driven by his experience of the Caribbean city – Kingston in the kingdom of this world – Brathwaite throughout the second half of *X/Self* provides a sustained vision of hunger, violence, emaciation, waste and defeat.

Yet the New World sensibility is potentially rich, precisely because of the strange mixture of elements – the magic of both Prospero and Sycorax – that has gone into its making. *X/Self* is among other things a journey into a mind that has been formed through a wide experience of literature and history. This mind is poised, sophisticated and intelligent in its understanding of various worlds. It has range and depth; and is as intense in its lamentation as its satirical laughter. *X/Self* is Brathwaite's most eloquent testimony that a relentless vision of ruin can reside in close proximity to a spirit of hope and affirmation.

Our main concern with *X/Self* is with what it tells us about the idea of a rehumanisation of history through the activation of regenerated Spirit in a process involving destruction and renewal. The poem is a prolonged exploration of the apocalyptic idea. It is about systems of imperial organisation constantly coming into and going out of existence. Its eventual focus is on the terrible birth of the New World at the price of the annihilation of the great civilisations of Aztec, Inca, Maya and Ashanti. It recognises the apocalyptic principle as central to both the foundation and the continued transformation and renewal of New World civilisations.

"Dies Irie" which occurs after we have completed one-third of the journey through *X/Self* is a deliberate invocation of the apocalyptic moment. It follows a contemplation of how the Europe of industrialism, ecological waste and economic and cultural imperialism has penetrated polluted and destroyed Asia and Africa. Linking the Bhopal disaster with Nazi gas chambers, Nagasaki with Viet Nam and Auchwitz, *X/Self* is a passionate outcry against the miners, militia and bankers of Imperialism,

> they burn
> they eat the land
>
> they vomit it up
> they leave lakes of desolation
>
> ochre choler water
>
> that returns no benediction
> plantations of dead plankton[29]

Empire, as presented in *X/Self*, has always operated without moral sanction. Contemporary imperialism is however, more devastating because it is more advanced technologically, and more ruthlessly oriented towards the accumulation of Capital. It pollutes, devours and kills for profit, converting Ashanti to ashanty towns – ("ashanty towns arise and rust within their oxides.") Benin, famous for its bronzes, becomes a catafalque – a tomb. The "ikons" of desecration left by the miners of empire are ash, starvation, bewilderment. It is in the face of this reality that X/Self, the name Brathwaite suggests for that ageless Tiresian Voice who narrates the poem, invokes the Dies Irae which, employing Dread talk, he converts to "Dies Irie", a much desired, highly gratifying day.

Brathwaite, having achieved his first objective, that of locating contemporary structures and practices of Empire in their historical context, now suggests the future – the apocalyptic downfall of Empire; the day of the resurgence of suppressed Spirit. "Dies Irie" is a parody of the Roman Catholic "Dies Irae" which is a solemn evocation of the ideas of Doomsday and Judgement. It is a moment that Verdi and Mozart have celebrated in their respective requiems. Brathwaite, however, nativises the concept of the Dies Irae and in two versions of this poem (i.e. in *Third World Poems* and *X/Self*) the music is played by Satchmo and Nyabinghi respectively. "Dies Irie", like *Revelation* on which it is based, is dream, "prophesay" an intense fantasy of retribution, shared by all suppressed peoples. It first identifies the idea of Apocalypse as a profoundly religious – indeed both Christian and 'pagan' – one. It is one of the things that Christianity (both Catholic and Calvinist) shares with 'paganism'.

> Day of sulphur dreadful day
> when the world shall pass away
> so the priests and shamans say.[30]

Apocalypse is also a political idea and will result from the international upsurgence of hitherto suppressed peoples, who will force Mount Blanc (Europe/America/Empire) to recognise its atrocities. The Apocalypse is conceived as a sort of universal assizes in which the whole of history and time will be judged, particularly that dehumanised aspect of history and civilisation which has glorified war and trade, and forged the link between the military and the industrial, annexing science, technology and even the arts and religion to economically strategic war-mongering.

The poem identifies the prosecutors against Mount Blanc: Ho Chi Minh, Martí, Makandal, Fedon, Fatah, Sun Yat Sen, Nyabingeh, Che Guevara, Nanny, Mahdi, the Maroons, Rodney, Robeson, Ras Makonnen, the Sandinistas, Cuba, the Zulu, Sioux and Seminole, Shaka. The list is long and multinational. A few of the crimes of Mount Blanc are identified: My Lai, Sharpeville, Wounded Knee, the doctrines of herrenvolk and fascism, Soweto massacre, Harlem... The heroes of Mount Blanc are named Verwoerd, Voster, Pik van Botha and Malan of South Africa, and the merchants and statesmen of Mount Blanc who support them.

The cry in the poem is for justice and vengeance; its point being that justice in history has always been the justice of the powerful, who have generally kept from the centre of their assessment of self and civilisation their woeful record of atrocity and genocide. The resurrection and judgement of the dead in "Dies Irie" is a dreadful epiphany: a revelation of the hidden areas of history; a reconceptualisation of words such as history, civilisation, power and justice. (It is incidentally, this same dream of historic justice that is mocked by Walcott in the trial scene of *Dream on Monkey Mountain*, where Lestrade, the mulatto who has just discovered his blackness, attempts to place the entire white world on trial).[31]

Brathwaite is, of course, fully aware of the improbability of any just reordering of history ever occurring, but clings to a notion that one day judgement will be pronounced. It is this wavering between a sense of improbability and a hope for justice, that informs his revision of the earlier version of "Dies Irae" (*Third World Poems*). Louis Armstrong is replaced by Nyabingeh as the angel of the last trumpet. Armstrong represents the improbability of the dream of Apocalypse, Nyabingeh the "hope" for judgement. Something is gained in the sense that Nyabingeh are associated with "dread" and the message: "Death to black and white oppressors." They are therefore more appropriate dark angels of the Apocalypse than Louis Armstrong, whose weapons against oppression were joy, elation, affirmation and a deliberate wearing of the masks of "coon" entertainer and "Uncle Tom" – what is termed in *Rights of Passage* his "boot black smile", his "warm humility".

On the other hand, one rather likes the idea, as improbable and absurd as it may seem, of confronting all the dreadful death-dealing machinery of Mount Blanc with the supremely affirmative elation of a Satchmo riff. One also favours the prospect of world leaders and warmongers past and present, chipping towards the mercy seat of the "mighty and majestic godhead" to the joyful strains of "When the Saints Go Marching In", to receive their "sentences of righteous rage."

One also regrets the omission from *X/Self* of the line "saviour of the broken herd" – a line of deep sad bitterness. For the broken herd keep yearning for a saviour, but seem doomed, even to the very end of *X/Self*, to remain broken. By definition, the "broken herd" can have no saviour for if they had a saviour, they would hardly be broken. As helpless, leaderless and heroless as they have been described in *Rights of Passage*, the broken herd have been broken because their saviour himself has been broken too; that is their religions, philosophies, selves and souls have been historically devastated. *X/Self* is largely about this devastation. Brathwaite replaces "saviour of the broken herd" by "herder of the lost herero" which, while it hopefully suggests a patriarchal Maasai presence capable of bringing together all the scattered and lost tribes, is not as true emotionally as "saviour of the broken herd", a line that contains the bitter ambiguity of the apocalyptic dream; which is that it is dreamt only by the most devastated, those least likely ever to be able to fulfil it.

Brathwaite's problem of envisioning an apocalyptic reversal in the New World is compounded by his contemplation of the Haitian Revolution in "Cap", a poem of the early 70s based on his response to a mural in Port-au-Prince depicting the country's history "as a single, unfolding episode in montage."³² The poem begins by identifying the Arawak presence at the very crest of the cape where Christophe's fortress/monument is built. Since the Arawaks are a supposedly vanquished and virtually exterminated people, their presence here in this time can only mean that the true original ancestral Spirit of the land has not died; and awaits its time to defeat the conquistador. This is part of the general argument of *X/Self* – that the Spirit of the past is never quite vanquished. Thus "Rome" persists in spirit, and is reincarnated in a new time and place, as are "Africa" and Aztec/Arawak/Maya. Mt. Blanc and Kilimanjaro have their equivalent in the New World in any of the great Central American volcanic mountains: Popocatepetl, Illimani, Coropuna, Cotopaxi, all of which are invoked as residences of the sleeping Spirit of fire, secreted in the land and people.³³

The Spirit of the Caribbean past, as presented in "Cap," whether it manifested itself in Carib, Arawak or African – Lamming's "Tribe Boys" – was a spirit of resistance. This Spirit manifested itself in several moments; the suicidal martyrdom of the Caribs at Sauteurs: the Africans who jumped overboard while crossing the middle passage; the suicide of the defeated Maroons in Brazil in 1696; the courage with which Toussaint's barefooted battalions confronted French cannon during the Haitian Revolution. It is that Spirit which awaits anyone who thinks of ascending the peak of Cap Haitien, where, we are told, "toussaint is a zemi". Toussaint is a zemi only because he represented, while alive, the purest spirit of revolution. Affirming the same value as the Arawaks, Toussaint becomes a zemi or a loa, an ancestral spirit. One notes that the Petro cult in Haiti combines native Caribbean (i.e. Arawak, Carib etc) and African (Dahomean, Yoruba etc) religions. Dead in body, Toussaint becomes in spirit the embodiment of this mergence of ancestral energies. Like Anansi in *Islands*, "he stares from the flesh of the stone". That is, he is a frozen, inert, but potentially active presence. Frozen in stone, he achieves, like the static lovers in Keats's Grecian urn, a kind of eternal potentiality, which can be reincarnated in the flesh of the living.

Toussaint also represents a timeless condemnation of all who have betrayed the spirit of the land, and these may include Henri Christophe who, simultaneously seeking magnificence and fearing extinction, virtually re-enslaved his people in order to build his monument on the Cape. Yet Toussaint may also represent the pure but frozen and unattainable ideals of Revolution. Revolution itself is a never-ending, paradoxical process:

the steel of the machete
the knife of the god
thongs of the whips

drink water like trees
africaines from the slave ships
dance out of the riflemen's loins

become dessalines dessalines

The first four lines here suggest that the implements of war, revolt, forced labour and castigation have, through the revolution, become part of a process of redemption. The words "drink water like trees" are a token of hope that all this bitter history may be rehumanised to produce grace, growth and graciousness. On the other hand, the next three lines provide a rapid succession of images which begin with "africaines from the slave ships". This reminds us of the high proportion of African-born slaves in Haiti's pre-revolutionary years, and suggests that the capacity for revolt existed because African Spirit had not been successfully quenched. These enslaved Africans "dance out of the riflemen's loins" to "become dessalines dessalines". These dancers are free spirits, born out of revolt, conceived in war ("riflemen's loins").

Dessalines becomes the incarnation of their spirit of inflexible, and total revolt. The repetition of "dessalines dessalines" sounds like the chant of popular acclaim. But Dessalines, who after the Revolution proclaimed himself Emperor, began a campaign to exterminate all whites, and was himself assassinated in 1806. As part of the passing tableau of history, Dessalines raises the question of whether revolutionaries are doomed to become the dictators and reproduce the repressive structures against which they once revolted. Brathwaite, who poses this question in *The Arrivants*, suggests as we saw in our analysis of "Leopard", that limits need to be placed on the spirit of revolt; that an excessive spirit of recrimination can lead to vengeful blood bath, which defeats and negates the spirit of liberty in whose name revolt originally took place. Dessalines was the tragic result of this excessive spirit of recrimination, and left Haiti a heritage of

> the spangle of death from the hot
> of the trees

He named no successor, and his assassination plunged Haiti into further internecine violence, out of which emerged Henri Christophe, another of the great military leaders of the Revolution.

We thus see Christophe next on the mural. But he's called "christophe columbus," that is, he's associated with the European discoverer, intruder, conquistador presence, whose paradoxical journey towards conquest and genocide and the dark epiphany of a terrifying self-knowledge, is explored in "Titan".[34] Christophe's Journey up the mountain is, like Cortez's invasion of the pyramid-temple of Akbal, the Aztec death-god, a degraded *via dolorosa,* revealing only the Shadow, the dark double.

> and christophe columbus climbs up to his mountain top
> with the face of his horse in the faith of his shadow
>
> he stumbles on priest on an ivory slave on a spaniard
> the places of pain become pig
> snouts the black becomes white becomes black becomes rain

> falling to plunder
> the roof of the world.[35]

It is Christophe's mountain because it is the place where he built his monument, his citadel. The mountain/citadel is a concretisation of his ego. Autocracy always seeks to overpower the average citizen's mind by monstrously immense architecture: pyramids, basilicae, colosseums, palaces of sane and mad Sun Kings, Louis or Ludwig; great walls of China or Zimbabwe or Macchu Picchu, citadels.

Christophe climbs the mountain "with the face of his horse in the faith of his shadow" because he's proceeding resolutely towards a gloomy unknown; perhaps towards death. There's also the psychological dimension of shadow; that is, the id, the hidden and frightening other side of one's nature. Christophe's epiphany is a discovering of this hidden other not only within his own nature, but within the revolution itself. Winning power after the civil strife that followed Dessalines's assassination, Christophe hastily remade himself in the image of the oppressor – fortress, emperor, forced labour on the citadel, a return to monarchical ideals which the revolution had been fought to destroy. This rapid transformation of Christophe into his opposite and double and other, becomes a paradigm of the process of change/unchange that has been Haiti's history since the revolution: "the black becomes white becomes black..." The faces change, but the pattern and process remain the same.

The irony of the idea of rain plundering the roof of the citadel, to which Christophe's megalomaniacal notion of "the world" has shrunken, is that Christophe has constructed his fortress so well and so inaccessibly that he needs fear only the rain; only what is natural, God-given and redemptive. Christophe's nemesis is not the feared uprising of a suppressed people; not the feared attack from the defeated European nations – France, Spain and England – but the spirit of Toussaint, who is now a zemi.

> he stares from the stone, from the eye
> lids of flame
> at his fate

Toussaint's tragic fate is not to have died in the frozen European fastness of the Jura mountain, a literal prisoner of Mt. Blanc; but to have fought and died to produce the travesty that Christophe has become. He becomes Christophe's judge, the cloud of doom which, like the Aztecs, Christophe has sought to escape by means of his monument, and Dessalines, by means of the sacrificial wastage of lives.

This contradictory sense of the necessity for revolution and the constant betrayal of revolution permeates Brathwaite's two trilogies and *Black + Blues*. It is there in many of the post-1970 poems, inspired by a contemplation of the city of Kingston, Jamaica. We earlier mentioned "Springblade" as an example of this ambivalent vision. *X/Self* is actually structured on such ambivalence. The poem is based on the dualities of Africa/Europe, Black/ White, Caliban/Prospero, Slave/Free, Colonised/ Coloniser, New World/ Old World, Kilimanjaro/ Mt. Blanc, Spirituality/ Materialism, the primal/ the technological, pastoral innocence/ urban degradation, the adamic landscape/ the ecological wasteland, "the opulence of poverty"/"the poverty of opulence." But more important than these dualities is the fact that they are presented not as Manichean opposites, but as the yin and yang of intermeshing states and processes. Rome burns, but "Rome" persists as both structure and process. Caliban replaces Prospero and reproduces Prospero's system. The Old World penetrates the New and perpetuates itself, until plastic and cellophane become almost everyone's future. Old and New World protagonists, Charlemagne and Christophe, Cortez and Moctezuma become *semblables*, doubles.

In the face of not only the duality but the dialectic of forces alive in the making of New World history, Brathwaite's presentation of the ideas of apocalyptic destruction and rebirth becomes almost like a never-ending debate, where the issue remains unresolved almost to the very end of *X/ Self*. "History", as presented in *X/Self*, reveals that although moments of apocalyptic upheaval do occur in which entire empires go out of existence or come into being, the patterns of Empire and conquest and validation seldom change. Charlemagne, the Frankish conqueror of Rome and much of Western Europe, far from promoting his own Germanic civilisation and culture, accepted the deeply engrained doctrine of Graeco-Roman superiority, and proceeded to renew the Latin/Xtian civilisation of the Holy Roman Empire at the expense of his supposedly "inferior" and "heathen" Germanic one, whose shamans were prevented on pain of death from practising the old religion.[36]

In the New World, the Aztecs adopted and extended the hierarchical structures of the older Toltec civilisations they had conquered, and in time were able to pervert history in order to claim a legitimate line of succession from the founders of the old Toltec Empire. Henri Christophe, as mesmerised by the idea of France's superiority as "Charlemagnia" was by Rome's, helped establish Euro-centred values and tastes as post-Revolutionary norms, and was partly responsible for the destruction, perversion or stagnation of Afro-Haitian civilisation in the Caribbean. His failure is presented as the paradigm of the later failures of Afro-Saxon regimes in the Twentieth century Caribbean.[37]

Neo-colonial politicians, white, brown or black, speak in the accents of an autocracy and cultural imperialism learned from Europe. A South African "aparthate" voice justifying the destruction of African nations and customs reveals a startling affinity with a neo-colonial Black elitist voice. Both have a vested interest in maintaining structures based on economic privilege for a small ruling oligarchy, and the dehumanisation of labour. Thus the South African voice declaring:

> soon i will be asked to ask them to forget forgive
> their savage homelands their dark & dung & kraal & bantustans
> and
> call me bucky massy   yes   yes good   yes god   yes gold
>
> therefore no mud hut villages wearing those pygmy straw
>   hats you will see within the pages of the phantomb
>
> no afro hair dos in our schools no dialect around the holy house
>   and on these
>   premises

fades smoothly into the neo-colonialist voice justifying its betrayal of democratic ideals and maintenance of "the status crow."

> in fact, in order to avoid drop-face and rising cost of expec-
> tations
>   there will be no more promises before election time
>   in fact there will no longer be election time[38]

Such abrupt reversals are common in New World politics with its proliferation of dictatorships, military governments, and failed radical regimes.

Post-independence Caribbean politicians have had only small success in altering the fundamental structures of plantation society: great house and shanty, citadel and dungle, town house and wilderness. Political cynicism and exaggerated authoritarianism are, indeed, little more than masks to cover a failure that is reflected in the rigid dualities of class:

> without a future
> all houses will be condominiums   buses towns
> landscraped plantations planned like towns
>
> chapel courthouses main guards & supermarket prison empty
> church
> yards ring a round with roses of barb wire...

That is one version of urban Jamaica. This is the other:

> beyond that there is rab & wilderness & terrorists & cultural
> gorillas
>
> caliban

The ruling-class Jamaican voice echoes that of the white South African or North American:

> we don't want catch no niggers out here no way neither nor any
> rasta man nor hippie[39]

because in each case the gap between the ruling elite and the scarecrow poor is filled with dread that can and does result in murder from either party.

The phrase "landscraped plantations" tells us that the city as a wasteland of condominium clusters is the contemporary version of the old plantation, with the top soil scraped away to produce an ecological desert, that is both a metaphor and an illustration of the true wilderness: the spiritual desert that it contains. The fakedness, fragility and utter deadness of this world are portrayed in "Twoom" (room + womb + tomb), where a bourgeois art show featuring a display of white plaster-of-paris cats is contrasted with the brutal images of life and death outside the art gallery. The neo-colonial city offers one a choice of morgues, both of which are under the eternal surveillance of the vultures of Empire.[40]

The youth, who should possess the energy to attempt a transformation of this dead manscape are either indifferent or cynical, having listened in the past to too many futile or dishonest politicians ("Mai Village").[41] The rebels among them fail to create revolution: "the people's liberation army surrendering to sodom & gomorrah in their bvd's."[42] The image – taken from the collapse of the Grenada Revolution – is the nadir of *X/Self*, the poem's Naipaulian moment of utter hopelessness and pathetic absurdity.

V: The Awakening of the Voice: Maroonage: Revolution: Xango
It is, however, also the turning point, and is followed by Section IV of *X/Self*, where the options of maroonage, and full-fledged rebellion are repeatedly explored, as the poem attempts to outline an alternative to "Sodom and Gomorrah". One such alternative that actually precedes "Twoom" is examined in "Nam". First entitled "Soweto", "Nam" is about rebirth of Spirit (Nam); and though the landscape of rebirth is South Africa, the name "Nam" may also be Viet Nam, where the vulture suffered its most significant defeat in contemporary times. Since Brathwaite first wrote "Soweto" in 1979, the reactions of sympathy, particularly from radical youth world-wide, have been simply astounding. They suggest that it may still be possible to modify, if not transform, political process; to humanise the vulture.

The first seven lines of the poem refer to the changing cinematic image of the African from the savage demonic hordes of Tarzan films or horror stories; from the "rolling mothball eyes" made popular by minstrelsy and maintained by Satchmo; to the images of resistance and rebellion which have grown since Soweto school children, bypassing their beaten elders, began the Azanian Revolution. This awakening is described in the image of a mighty dust storm: "oceans rolling over the dry sand of the savanna" – and it brings new hope to the poet who as "shaman" changes his lamentation at the people's indifference to his warning,[43] to a magical naming of the tribes, as if to evoke from their very names energy, power and resolution:

> and we know somewhere there is real fire
> kasuto mokhathi namibia azania shaka the zulu kenyatta the
> shatt
> erer the maasai wandering into the everlasting shadow of jah44

The revolution will be "hell and halleluia," retributive fire and a welcome song of praise that the passive youth of "Mai Village" have finally come off the fence and entered into their voice.

> bellowing against bullhorn and kleghorn
> bellowing against bargwart and the searchlights of dogs
> bellowing against crick and the kick in the stomach

Now there is constant outcry, where before in "Kingston in the Kingdom of This World" the protagonist had not yet given vent to his urge to cry out. The poem remarks at the suddenness with which Soweto became the world's most massive issue since Nazism and Viet Nam. The poem makes the linkage by alluding to the genocide perpetrated by Germans in Namibia, decades before Hitler.

Soweto awakens in the protagonist hope for the rebirth of Ogun Shango, and evokes a sense of the holy, expressed in his dream of a land whose myths, symbols, shrines and gods have been restored. Soweto signals the beginning of the apocalyptic moment through its recovery of voice.

> soon
>
> soon
>
> soweto
>
> we have waited so long for this signal
>   this howl of your silence
> this heat of herero this hero[45]

The millenarian faith of the poem is suggested in the passage adapted from *Revelation* proclaiming the fulfilment of prophecy.

> *and i beheld the great beast strangled howling in its own chains*
>   *led by the fetlocks*
> *and the opulence useless*
> *and the guns shattered and silent*[46]

This "and i beheld" not only enhances the shamanistic element of the poem, but reverses the omen with which "The Visibility Trigger" ends.

> and i beheld the cotton tree
> guardian of graves rise upward from its monument of grass crying
> aloud in its vertical hull calling
> for crashes of branches vibrations of leaves.[47]

Whereas in "The Visibility Trigger" the shaman or sleeper of the tribe is recalling a dream turned nightmare of the shattering of the tribe, in "Nam" the shamanistic voice appropriates the prophecy of St. John the Divine to declare the arrival of the Apocalypse.

This is the same moment that Brother Man dreamed of in "Wings of a Dove". In *X/Self*, it assumes visible shape in a poem/icon that is part volcano, part mushroom cloud. Sound is added to icon and image in this statement of hope:

>   and we rise
>   mushroom
>   mau
>   kilimanjaro
>   silvers of eagles
>   tears
>   savannas
>   nzingas of rivers
>   umkaklabulus of mountains
>   and the unutterable metal of the volcano
>   rising
>   rising
>   rising
>   burning[48]

Human effort, as suggested by the allusions to the Mau Mau and the Congolese Warrior Queen Nzinga, is combined with the detonations of earth and sky. The presence of Ogun Shango is heard and felt in the thunder-claps of "umklaklubulus" – a beautifully onomatopoeic Zulu word – and in the rumbling line: "the unutterable metal of the volcano."

Rebirth of Spirit requires prayer, invocation, incantation: shamanistic approaches to Word and Voice. Entering one's voice and giving voice are therefore important functions in Brathwaite's poetry. *Rights of Passage*, indeed, begins with a statement of the major functions of the voice when it proclaims the poet's aim of exploring the

> ...taut
> surfaces of things
> I sing
> I shout
> I groan
> I dream
> about [49]

The deepest and most necessary of these functions of the voice, is that of becoming the channel for internal and suppressed or censored energies. This is how spirit and will become renewed for the herculean task of transforming a history of "wreck/age." After "Nam", the major thrust in *X/Self* is towards the awakening of the voice. The poem becomes more incantatory, more shamanistic; even though the poet as shaman has clearly recognised himself as a Cassandra figure or a sad Jeremiah, ignored or rejected by an indifferent world.[50] Invocation, requiring a mixture of faith in prayer and magic, and a belief in the possibility of recalling "lost pain lost iron" lost energies, does not however blind the poet's eye to the odds against which such energies will have to be deployed.

"Stone", for example, offers maroonage, the original guerrilla warfare of the Caribbean, as an historical phenomenon that may guide future struggles against Mount Blanc.[51] Maroonage here has an extended meaning in that it involves a turning inwards on self: a deliberate disentanglement from Mount Blanc's economy of imposed detritus of word, food and toxic waste or blandishments of "dangerous... generosities wrapped up in cellophane and xmas paper."[52] Maroonage is suggested in spite of the poet's awareness that the great Maroon communities of the past have been defeated, or have had to compromise with the enemy. He is also aware of the virtual impossibility of disentangling from America's cultural and economic web; the allurement of metropolitan taste, style, fad and fashion; the driven need to find even the most menial employment abroad in a context of real starvation at home.

In spite of such awareness he advocates maroonage as an absolute necessity, and invokes the spirit of Nanny Nanahemmaa – Jamaican Maroon Queen Mother – who, like Toussaint in "Cap", has become a loa or zemi, because of the quality of her historic resistance to the plantation's militia.[53] Nanny is invoked as a Muse of fertility and the natural life and as a talisman against drought and dry rot of Spirit. Similarly, the spirit of the "runagate" (runaway and renegade) is invoked as counter to the city's devastation.

> runagate
> runagate
> runagate
>
> look how our villages are grown up tall
> into this strangled city
>
> tales of another leader lost
> solares bolivare palanquin
>
> washed away with the frogs and the river and the mud &
> accompong
>
> runagate

> runagate
> runagate[54]

There is always this great sense of "in spite of" informing the courage of the poem's affirmations. Here it is the rebellion of the Maroon, in spite of the disappearance of tribe and village, the emergence of "strangled city". The "strangled city" reference is to Martin Carter's poem of the fifties, "Not Hands like Mine", which tells of the gradual extermination of the Caribs, and the urban ordeal of the post-Emancipation African. Maroonage is advocated in spite of these realities, and in face of the deaths of resistance leaders and the erosion of the Cockpit Country fastness.

"Ice/Nya" is a recapitulation of the main idea of *X/Self:* that is that the unchecked expansion of Mount Blanc will mean the ultimate reduction of Kilimanjaro. A future of void, desert and regression is predicted for those peoples who remain passive and silent while they are being destroyed. Foreseeing the possibility of such a future, the poet again assumes the role of warner, prophet and shaman of the Apocalypse – "Sun Song", "Citadel" and "Xango" all seeking to define the relationship between the creative Spirit and the apocalyptic moment.

"Sun Song", one of the original "Harmattan Poems" of 1970-71, begins with a beautiful evocation of the Caribbean dry season, which contains a paradox of flowering in the midst of desolation. Drought in this poem is a state of expectancy, rather than the despair and defeat of Brathwaite's urban poems. In "Sun Song" the harmattan is forerunner of the hurricane, an Ogun Shango loa. The poem, therefore, ends with a passionate invocation of the spirit of flame, as a refiner's fire necessary for the world's cleansing. The apocalyptic idea is accepted and the apocalyptic moment summoned as the only means of vindicating past affirmations and ensuring future rebirth.

The second section of "Citadel" parallels the "Vèvè" section of *Islands* beginning "so on this ground write." The poem of the Apocalypse will contain the qualities of Ogun Shango: iron and fire: firmness of Spirit, energy and will. It will demand its libation of blood; that is, passion, sacrifice and pain, before it becomes "iron/metal speaking freely of the fire." To speak "freely of the fire" is to give full voice to the idea of revolt; to uncensor the inhibited loa of revolution within oneself. The poem of the Apocalypse is music played by the blacksmith/warrior loa Ogun Shango: "the fire/harp blaze howling hot and long lambent in the grip of god."[55] Such music contains the sound of hell fire and recrimination ("howling hot"); yet it is also the opposite: "long and lambent". The dictionary definition of "lambent" is "playing lightly on a surface without burning it", or "shining with a soft clear light without fierce heat." The poem then, must embody the two sides of Apocalypse: destructive/recriminatory and creative/ renascent.

The poem is also healing, magic, obeah, alchemical spell against maljo, the baleful eye of Mount Blanc with its immense genius in parasitism and experience at creating and projecting distorted stereotypes.

> so we make pots
> potients against the sound of lamentations
> against the maljo blowing from the devil's ridge

The image of the pot, insofar as it relates to Haitian religion, projects the poem as a vessel, govi, container and home for the secret inner self – the *"gros-bon-ange"*.[56] As a container of Spirit, the poem protects Nam from Prospero's reductive magic. As "potient" (potent potion), it protects against lamentations and the cold death-wind of Mt. Blanc.

The poem is finally Ananse's fragile web, spun not in the Great House but in the tenement yard, out of which has grown the truly indigenous aesthetic of the Caribbean:

> and from this tennament, this sipple spider space we hold
> we make this narrow thread of silver spin the long time of sand

The thread from which the poem is woven is time itself, Marvell's and Eliot's vast desert stretching before and after, which in Brathwaite's work permeates the structures of history.

The final poem of *X/Self* is "Xango". In Xango, the loa of thunder who is associated with Ogun, X/Self finally discovers his Nam. This discovery, hinted through omens earlier in the poem, is similar to Tom's recovery of his Ogun personality in *Islands*. Both of Brathwaite's trilogies move towards the emergence of the Ogun/Shango family of loa. "Xango" invokes the entire family: Erzulie, wife or consort of Ogun, Damballah and Agwe, and Shango. The *Black + Blues* version of the poem carries an epigraph: "The god Shango was conceived in love and rises to destroy the world." Shango, then, is the movement from love towards Apocalypse, paralleling Christ whose mission of love, healing and redemption is followed by his second coming as judge, with a mission mainly of condemnation and destruction.

The poem begins with a welcoming of renewed Spirit: "Hail/ there is new breath here." The first member of the Ogun/Shango family to appear is Erzulie; "erzulie with green wings/feathers sheen of sperm". Muse not only of beauty, but of fertility, Erzulie is the "new breath" of Spirit, the freshness of journeying that Brathwaite feels in producing his first poems since *The Arrivants* ("Xango" belongs to the first wave of poetry after *Islands*). Hence Erzulie is first welcomed as consort of Agwe, loa of the ocean and all journeying across water.

> there is a west wind
> sails open eyes the conch shell sings hallelujahs

She is also the Muse of Africa manifesting herself in new ways in his poetry. Hence:

> i take you love at last my love
> my night my dream my horse my gold/en horn my Africa

The Muse of Africa here is a combination of desire, dream, imagination and music. Joyful possession of this Muse creates vision, language and "riddim".

> we word with salt this moisture vision
> we make from vision
> black and bone and riddim

The reference here is to the Dogon creation myths described by Griaule in his *Conversations with Ogotemmeli* in which the Nummo, creator-spirits in the form of serpents, infuse matter with life-force, which assumes the form of water and the Word.

> The life-force of the earth is water. God moulded the earth with water. Blood too he made out of water. Even in a stone there is this force, for there is moisture in everything.[57]

The poet who is giving words and savour to a vision perceived as moisture, is a type of Nummo; a vessel for and conveyor of the creative word. In "Citadel", he speaks of "the cup of my word", an image which portrays language as a vessel containing moisture.

The "huh", "hah", "hah" are explosions of breath connected not only with the primal sounds of the loa's lovemaking, but also with the early stages of divine language.

> the earth had a language, the first language of this world and the most primitive of all time. Its syntax was elementary, its verbs few, and its vocabulary without elegance. The words were breathed sounds scarcely differentiated from one another, but nevertheless vehicles. Such as it was, this ill-defined speech sufficed for the great works of the beginning of all things.[58]

"Xango", then, is a creation myth in which is described both the conception of Xango and his emergence as the muse of *X/Self*. The boy Xango is distinguished by a number of icons: a gourd tree, "knotted snakes and coffle wires", "water courses, valleys, clotted blood", bamboo clumps, the rainbow and bougainvillea petals. These icons identify him as an Afro-Caribbean Muse. The gourd tree which also appears in "The Making of the Drum" bears the calabash whose dry rattling sound, by supplementing the detonations of the drum, is crucial to sustaining the energy and fervour of time's dancers.[59] Herskovits notes that Erzulie, Xango's mother in this poem, is wife of Petro deity Simbi d'l'eau who "inhabits the mango and calabash trees."[60] Griaule writes that among the Dogon the calabash "is a symbol of the woman and of the sun, who is female."[61] The gourd icon, then, associates Xango with energy.

rhythm and fervour, fertility and creativity, the female principle.

It also locates him within the Damballah/Ogun/Erzulie family of loa. Simbi d'l'eau is, like Damballah, symbolised as a snake, and is patron of fresh water and springs.[62] Xango's association with snakes confirms his relationship to Damballah or Simbi d'l'eau as a loa of fertility. The rainbow and river images also suggest Damballah. It should, however, be noted that Xango, like the Ogun of *The Arrivants*, bears the marks of New World plantation slavery: the chains of the slave coffles, and the clotted blood which in Brathwaite is a recurrent image of withered heritage, the dried-up or drying bloodline.

The impact of his emergence as Muse in Brathwaite's work is one of vitalisation.

> these tendrils knitted to the cold
> >   un
> > pearl and wail
>
> the earth on which he steps breaks furl
> >   in rain
> >   bow
> >   tears[63]

The image of tendrils is suggested by earlier images of snakes and water courses. "Unpearl" is really "unpurl", unravel, and follows from both "knotted" and "knitted". The word is related to the various images of uncurling and unfurling which one saw in *The Arrivants* and like them, suggests awakening, unwinding, a "freeing up" of the poetry. "Pearl" is connected in earlier Brathwaite with images of crystal, jewels. It suggests processes of slow concentrated hardening and relates to the poetry of "hardness" and "imagism" which Brathwaite recognises as the polar opposite of the shamanistic poetry of the Voice that he'd begun to write during the sixties. The "unpearling" of the line, then, is its disintegration, its relaxation, its "deconcentration", its opening up under the impact of the Voice. "Wail" may suggest "lament", though here it refers to the characteristic singing style of both Afro-American and Afro-Caribbean religious groups, and by analogy to the whole aesthetic of the Voice. Thus, taken as a whole, the passage celebrates the poet's entry into his Voice ("wail") and into the life and warmth of his African heritage after years of intricate entanglement ("tendrils") with the frigid death of Europe ("knitted to the cold").

The rainbow, apart from associating Xango with Damballah, is also the track along which Nummo travelled from the sky to earth, and is termed "the Nummo's track" by the Dogon.[64] It is connected with the life-force, the constant interplay between heaven and earth, sun and water,

> The rays of light and heat draw the water up, and also cause it to descend again in the form of rain. That is all to the good. The movement created

by this coming and going is a good thing. By means of the rays the Nummo draws out, and gives back the life force. This movement indeed makes life.⁶⁵

Apart from this, the rainbow in the Old Testament mythology signifies the Covenant between God and Noah that the world will never again be destroyed by water, only by fire. It is this Covenant, appropriated by Afro-Americans in one of their gospel songs, that James Baldwin recalls in his illuminating collection of essay/testimonies, *The Fire Next Time*. Brathwaite's Uncle Tom prays earnestly to "see the rainbow/of Heaven/ God's curved/mourning/calling."⁶⁶

The rainbow, then, is a perfect icon for Xango, signifying both his lifebearing and his destructive capacities. It spans the space between two Apocalypses – the past destruction by water in which the ancestral survivor was Noah, mythological father of Blacks and Whites, Ham, Shem and Japhet, and the future promised annihilation by fire. The rainbow is also the central symbol of *Sun Poem* whose changes are linked with the colours of the spectrum.

Xango is also associated with bamboo clumps and flowers; natural vegetable life and "the tiger clue", an incongruous mixture of icons. The bamboo clumps connect him with Haitian loa of the Ogun family – Ogun Banandjo, Ogun Badagri and Ogun Batala – loa associated with travel, prophecy, connaissance, esoteric knowledge and healing. These loa live in bamboo clumps.⁶⁷ Xango, as loa of all that is natural and rooted, manifests himself in a correspondingly vital language when he possesses the poet as houngan or shaman.

> his syllables
> taste of wood of cedar lignum vitae phlox
> these gutterals
> are his mon général mon frère

"Lignum vitae", wood or tree of life indicates Xango's identity as a loa of beginning, while "gutterals" (gutter + gutturals), the primal elementary sounds of the Nummo, are associated with the poor Black people of the diaspora who have maintained ecstatic Orisha reverence in the Caribbean and Americas. Brathwaite's poetry is an attempt to employ the philosophy of these people as the basis of new and complex metaphors. Such complexity arises naturally out of the liminal nature of the New World experience, which is by force of history, transcultural and many-veined.

Xango's association with the tiger icon could imply two things. The tiger may be a Blakean symbol of form transfused by fierce and fiery divine energy. Blake's poem "Tyger" employs images of the forge, flame, anvil and blacksmith, which, translated into a Yoruba or Dahomean context would all apply to Ogun Shango who is, among other things, a blacksmith. The tiger may also be an Aztec telluric force, connected with the disappearance of a "sun", or order of time and history, and "the appearance of a new sun or tiger."[68] *X/Self* is very much concerned with the re-emergence of the Spirit of Mesoamerican civilisations, and the Xango archetype embraces that rebirth as well. The association of Erzulie with the hummingbird was the first signal in the poem of the return of Quetzalcoatl.

As Xango grows to manhood, he is revealed as an apocalyptic force and hailed by the poet as the militant energy that he bears within himself. The salutation *"mon général mon frère" is* an obvious echo of Baudelaire's *"mon semblable mon frère"*, or T.S. Eliot's adaptation of Baudelaire's line in The Waste Land. Brathwaite perceives Xango as double ("semblable"), that often fearsome other that is a hidden or censored part of self. Emerging from the tomb of his past, the boulder of a burdensome and distorted history rolled away, Xango is a bell-ringer for liberty, announcing loudly to the awakening people the message of their freedom.

> his childhood of a stone
> is rolled away he rings from rebells of the bone his liberated day

The phrase "rebells of the bone" suggests both the bone-deep engrainment of rebellion in the Caribbean person, and the fact that such rebellion grows out of the very skeletonisation of peoples by Mount Blanc.

The rest of the poem imagines the impact of reborn Xango on the present order. As the awakened force of "native" America he reverses the advance of conquistador and capitalist, restoring herds of stampeding bison and stopping the flow of Coca Cola. This is, perhaps, more pre-historic than post-historic Xango.

> the bison plunge into the thunders river
> hammering the red trail blazing west to chattanooga
> [...]
> jp morgan is dead
> coca cola is drowned
>
> the statue of liberty's never been born

But history *has* happened, and the Statue of Liberty is as much a reality as the genocide commited against Native Americans in Liberty's name. *X/Self,* indeed, has argued that the elevation of the former is intimately related to the extermination of the Native. Mt. Blanc grows at the expense of Kilimanjaro; the technological feeds on the primal; the factory and mine replace the forest; lake becomes desert. Central to Mt. Blanc's process, *X/Self* has argued, has been a genocide so pervasive that it has become normal, and is treated as peripheral in Mt. Blanc's histories and efforts at self-assessment.

The dream of a reversion to "the green beginning of this world"[69] is as Brathwaite is fully aware, an impossible one. His focus, therefore, is on the present condition of the New World person who, if he has in his music retained a vibrant oral tradition, may in his life be equally the product of a whoral one. He has embraced and absorbed so many contradictory influences: "book and bribe/bomb/blast and the wrecked village", "computer conjur man", abortion, pollution, police brutality and jazz, that he's become X/Self, an unknown quality. A blend of ancestral and ultra-modern elements, computer and conjury, places him a little outside of the predictions of Prospero's arithmetic. The quality of his hurt, the strength of his survival, the enduring vitality of his creative force as seen in his ever-vibrant music, make him a time bomb.

Brathwaite views whatever explosions may come as both necessary and justifiable preludes to renewal.

> for there is green at the root of his bullet
> michaelangelo working at the roof of his murderous rocket.

Michaelangelo's heroic feat in painting the ceiling of the Sistine Chapel (1508-1512) was one of the great moments of the Italian Renaissance. Working for four years while lying on his back, Michaelangelo painted the story of the Creation of the World, the Creation of Adam and Eve, the Fall, and the Deluge – the full Judeo-Christian creation myth. At first glance it seems outrageous to compare this fact with that of a contemporary Xango-like freedom fighter creating his "murderous rocket" of liberation. Brathwaite, however, has argued in *X/Self* and some of his later essays that the magnificent achievements of Rome have been won at the price of great destruction in Europe and beyond. The Renaissance was happening at the same time as witch hunts and the Inquisition; the Church, with its history of bloody Crusades and intolerance, has been founded on the abbatoir.

Michaelangelo, then, embodies the central paradox of History: that of phenomenal creativity growing out of equally phenomenal destructiveness, grace juxtaposed to or issuing from the heart of atrocity. Xango, who seeks to bring into being a new world-order, is equally a renaissance presence, and will embody the same paradox. It is also possible that Brathwaite has in mind not only Michaelangelo's depiction of Creation, but his rendering of The Last Judgement including the "Dies Irae" in the same Sistine Chapel, twenty-three years later. Together, these two great themes distinguish Michaelangelo as an artist concerned with the beginning and ending of time, and an appropriate Old World person to remember at the end of *X/Self*, a work that has explored the relationship between creation and destruction in the evolution of both a New World Order and a new world-order.

Yet he is, ultimately, more concerned with the life-enhancing than the death-bringing qualities of Xango.

>   greet
>   him
>   he speaks near
>
>   you
>
>   hear
>   him
>   he teaches
>
>   face
>   and youth
>   and how to use your seed and soul and lissom
>
>   touch
>   him
>   he will heal
>
>   you
>
>   word
>   and balm
>   and water
>
>   flow
>
>   embrace
>   him
>
>   he will shatter outwards to your light and calm and history
>   your thunder has come home[70]

Xango here is endowed with the healing properties of both Ogun Batala and Christ, while the association of "word" with "water" reaffirms his affinity with the Nummo. The poem, it may be noticed, assumes the shape of a pictogram, which is both Haitian vèvè and a combination of crosses, symbolising the Afro-Caribbean folk resolution of Mount Blanc and Kilimanjaro.

The apocalyptic aspect of Xango is, however, not forgotten. Xango explodes when he is embraced. His explosion will have a profoundly disturbing effect on vision ("light") composure and history. The Apocalypse will make necessary the revisioning of concepts, values and human civilisation itself. The last line, "your thunder has come home" tones down the original line "your terror has come home",[71] but still manages to convey the idea of karmic retribution falling on the head of the historically guilty. Such retribution, however, is not presented as an end in itself, but as the prelude to the reordering and rehumanisation of history.

Xango, who is both the dead-end of a history of brutalisation and the green beginning of a new order, is an omen of what could happen if all the devastated peoples of the world were to revolt and return to its monstrous source all the terror which has historically been visited upon them. His emergence is a warning to Mount Blanc about the urgent need to transform the frozen structures and processes of empire in a world where more and more "developing" nations have begun "speaking freely of the fire". His emergence also signals Brathwaite's belief in humanity's capacity to resist the inhuman conquistador principle, which in *X/Self* has been symbolised by the vulture or condor perpetually on the wing. Xango is a resurrection symbol, man's retrieval and recreation of his sense of the sacred and humane, if even at the price of violence.

The faith to believe that such rebirth remains perennially possible, has been difficult to sustain in *X/Self*, where at one point the poet/ shaman declares

> i just can't get/up stand /up stand/up for i rights bob
> marley in this ya ghetto too much live i now in this wild evil
> world of axles wrecked gear boxes scatter/pillar levers
>
> the huge red silent pain of dead. fish dead. car screams
> their lobster sponges dried out breathe
>
> ing rasp & rust and rasspan angles banggalang & booming babylon[72]

It does, however, endure this world in which it is beleaguered and beaten down by rusting machinery, the city's cacophony and overwhelming discord and dereliction. Against the archetype of reduced scarecrow man, cripple and mimic man, Brathwaite places that of Xango, the unshackled human Spirit and emancipated divinity of man, whose resurrection he views as the poet's eternal responsibility.

Wilson Harris, in his seminal essay, "The Question of Form and Realism in the West Indian Artist",[73] observes that although artists may begin with a vision of the reduced person, they must:

> move that diminished creature through (their) work in a manner that is disturbing, so disturbing that vitality and power are realised as a very strong possibility.

Brathwaite, despite his consistent focus on images of human dereliction, shares in this aesthetics of hope, vitality and redemption, which may turn out to be the most valuable gift that the New World can offer the Old.

(Unpublished essay – November 1985, July 1986, 1988. The first three sections were presented as an Inaugural Professorial Lecture, University of the West Indies, St. Augustine, 10 December, 1986)

References
1. Brathwaite, E., "Salt", *X/Self* (London: OUP, 1987), pp. 8-9.
2. ibid., pp. 31-36.

3. Brathwaite, E., "Metaphors of Undevelopment: Proem for Hernan Cortez", in Eugene van Iterbeck (ed) *Africa/Europe*, Sixth European Poetry Festival, (Belgium, Leuvense Schrijvrsaktie), 1984.
4. ibid., p. 49.
5. Brathwaite, E.. "Caribbean Culture: Two Paradigms," in Jurgen Martini (ed.) *Missile and Capsule* (Bremen, 1983), pp. 36-37.
6. Brathwaite, E., "Coral", *The Arrivants* (London: OUP., 1973), p. 233.
7. Brathwaite, E., "The Visibility Trigger", *X/Self*, pp. 48-50.
8. Brathwaite, E., "Kingston in the Kingdom of this World", in *Third World Poems* (Essex: Longman, 1983), pp. 53-56.
9. Brathwaite, E., *The Development of Creole Society* (Oxford: Clarendon Press, 1971).
10. Robinson, D., *American Apocalypses* (Baltimore & London: The John Hopkins University Press 1985), p. xii.
11. Lawrence, D.H., *Apocalypse and the Writing on Revelation* (Cambridge: Cambridge University Press, 1980), p. 62. (ed. Mara Kalnis).
12. Walcott, D., "What *the Twilight Says*" in *Dream on Monkey Mountain & Other Plays* (New York: Farrar Straus & Giroux, 1970), pp. 2-40; "The Muse of History" in Coombs, O., (ed) *Is Massa Day Dead?* (New York: Doubleday Anchor, 1974), pp. 1-27.
13. Brathwaite, E., "Glass", in *Black + Blues* (Havana: Casas de las Americas, 1976), p. 25.
14. Brathwaite, E., "Caliban", *Black + Blues*, pp. 30-31.
15. Brathwaite, E., "Sunsum", *The Arrivants*, p. 150.
16. Brathwaite, E., "Tom", *The Arrivants*, p. 150.
17. Brathwaite, E., "Didn't He Ramble", *The Arrivants*, p. 22.
18. Brathwaite, E., *The Arrivants*, pp. 222-224.
19. Brathwaite, E., "Wings of a Dove", *The Arrivants*, p. 44.
20. Brathwaite, E., "Jah", *The Arrivants*, p. 162.
21. Brathwaite, E., "Shepherd", *The Arrivants*, p. 185.
22. Brathwaite, E., "Caliban", *The Arrivants*, p. 19.
23. Brathwaite, E., "Limbo", *The Arrivants*, pp 193-195.
24. Brathwaite, E., "Rites", *The Arrivants*, p. 200.
25 Brathwaite, E., "Wake", *The Arrivants*, pp. 210-213.
26. Brathwaite, E., "Cane", *The Arrivants*, pp. 228-229.
27. Brathwaite, E., "Ogun", *The Arrivants*, p. 248.
28. Brathwaite, E., "Leopard", *The Arrivants*, pp. 244-247.
29. Brathwaite, E., "Nuum", *X/Self*, pp. 34-35.
30. Brathwaite, E., "Dies Irie", *X/Self*, p. 37.
31. Walcott, D., *Dream on Monkey Mountain & Other Plays* (New York: Farrar, Straus and Giroux, 1970), pp. 310-320.
32. Brathwaite, E., *X/Self*, p. 122.
33. Ibid., p.105.
34. Brathwaite, E., "Titan", *X/Self*, pp. 61-63.
35. Brathwaite, E., "Cap", *X/Self*, pp. 53-54.
36. Southern, R.W., *Western Society and the Church in the Middle Ages* (London: Penguin Books, 1970), p. 174.

37. Brathwaite, E., *X/Self*, pp. 55-60.
38. Ibid., p. 58.
39. Ibid., p. 59.
40. Brathwaite, E., "Twoom", *X/Self*, p. 69.
41. Brathwaite, E., "Mai Village", *X/Self*, p. 69.
42. Brathwaite, E., "Twoom", *X/Self*, p. 90.
43. Brathwaite, E., "Shaman", *X/Self*, pp. 65-68.
44. "Nam", *X/Self*, p. 73.
45. Ibid., p. 78.
46. Ibid., p. 78.
47. Brathwaite, E., "The Visibility Trigger", *X/Self*, p. 49.
48. Brathwaite, E., "Nam", *X/Self*, p. 79.
49. Brathwaite, E., *The Arrivants*, p. 4.
50. Brathwaite, E., "Shaman", *X/Self*, pp. 65-68.
51. Brathwaite, E., "Stone", *X/Self*, pp. 93-95.
52. Brathwaite, E., "Shaman", *X/ Self*, p. 67.
53. Brathwaite, E., *Wars of Respect,* (Kingston: Agency for Public Information (API), 1977).
54. Brathwaite, E., "Stone", *X/Self*, p. 95.
55. Brathwaite, E., "Citadel", *X/Self*, p. 101.
56. Deren, M., *Divine Horsemen: Voodoo Gods of Haiti* (London: Thames & Hudson Ltd., 1970), p. 30 (first published 1953).
57. Griaule, M., *Conversations with Ogotemmeli: An Introduction to Dogon Religious Ideas* (London: OUP, 1965).
58. Ibid., p. 20.
59. Brathwaite, E., *The Arrivants*, p. 97.
60. Herkovits, M., *Life in a Haitian Valley* (New York: Doubleday/Anchor, 1971), p. 320.
61. Griaule, M., *Conversations with Ogotemmeli*, p. 105.
62. Courlander, H., *The Drum and the Hoe: Life and Lore of the Haitian People* (Berkeley, Los Angeles, London: University of California Press, 1960), p. 327.
63. Brathwaite, E., "Xango", *X/Self*, p. 108.
64. Griaule, M., op. cit., p. 108.
65. Griaule, M., op. cit., p. 107.
66. Brathwaite, E., *The Arrivants*, p. 14.
67. Herkovits, *Life in a Haitian Valley*, p. 321.
68. Harris, W., "Guyana Prize Address" in *Kyk-Over-Al* 30 June 1988, p. 29.
69. Walcott, D., *Dream on Monkey Mountain and Other Plays* (New York: Farrar Straus & Giroux 1970), p. 326.
70. Brathwaite, E., "Xango", *X/Self*, p. 111.
71. Brathwaite, E., "Shango", *Massachusetts Review*, 1974.
72. Brathwaite, E., "Shaman", *X/Self*, p. 67.
73. Harris, W., "The Question of Form and Realism in the West Indian Artist", *Tradition The Writer & Society* (London: New Beacon Publication, 1967), p. 15.

GUYANA PRIZE FEATURE ADDRESS
"TROPHY AND CATASTROPHE"

Mr. Chairman, Your Excellency the President, Ministers of Government, members of the Diplomatic Corps, friends and fellow-travellers in this vale of tears and laughter:

I would like first of all to say my sincere thanks for the honour which you have conferred on me by inviting me to address such a gathering on such an occasion. The establishment of the Guyana Prize for Literature in such hard times as these is an act of peculiar grace, equalled only by that first memorable Carifesta of 1972, which was also a Guyanese initiative. It isn't often – with all due respects to the Commonwealth Prize, the Booker Award or the W.H. Smith Award – that the Caribbean writer finds a serious sponsor.

Even in the area of research, it is generally easier to find a sponsor for research into our chaotic politics or our foundering economies, than into our remarkably vibrant literature. Thus, both creative writer and academic suffer in a situation where it is not unusual for publication to lag behind creation for ten years or more.

During the 1950s and 1960s, Caribbean writing attracted the British publishing houses. It was new and passionate and signalled the eruption into visibility of the colonial person who, if he had never quite accepted his servitude, had at the same time never quite articulated his deepest and most burning necessity in a fiction and language that was unmistakably his own. Part of the interest of the British publisher no doubt lay in the fact that a relatively easy market existed for writing that was new and strange. There was, also, a curious pride and proprietorship; for this new writing was seen as demonstrating the flexibility of the English language. Despite the astringent satire which it directed at colonial education, the new literature was taken as proof of the virtues of that education which, against all odds, had taught inarticulate Caliban to speak.

One has only to read those inane reviews that used to appear in the *West India Circular,* the journal of the old sugar interest, to realise that our literature was being promoted as a quaint curiosity, or as a marketable commodity whose meaning did not, and could not possibly matter. At a 1971 conference, I heard more than one of our writers remark that it was only with the advent of West Indian critics and reviewers such as Edward

Kamau Brathwaite, who wrote long essays in *Bim* since 1957, that they gained a sense of what their work meant to the community for whom it was intended.

After the novelty of the 1950 to 1965 period had worn off, and Reid, Mittelholzer, Lamming, Selvon, Naipaul, Salkey, Hearne, Harris and Walcott had been established as our most important voices, the willing sponsorship of British publishing houses was, it seems to me, tacitly reduced. One waited for a second wave of writers to follow in the wake of the first. But this did not happen for several reasons. First of all, the writers of the fifties had said most of what it was possible to say about the folk life, politics and landscape of small impoverished societies. Secondly, the early elation had begun to encounter the hard realities of self-government and independence, and an already serious vision had darkened considerably by the mid-sixties. Thirdly, and most important: new writers were finding it increasingly more difficult to get published, the publishers being more concerned with the easier task of promoting already established voices, than with risking money and energy on the encouragement of fresh talent.

If we think of the writers who emerged between 1965 and 1970, we'd find that Jean Rhys was a survivor from nearly four decades earlier, Edward Kamau Brathwaite had been publishing poems in *Bim* since 1948 and was, like Walcott, only three years younger than Lamming; Michael Anthony and Earl Lovelace were among the few to be given exposure and encouragement in the immediate post-Independence period; while poets such as Dennis Scott and Mervyn Morris, who had developed their own styles, would have to await the emergence of those brave little West Indian publishing houses, New Beacon and Bogle L'Ouverture, which in the post-1970 period have borne the brunt of the new publishing. I must have at least one hundred poets in slim collections, which have been either self-published or are the results of the efforts of Savacou, Bim, Karia Press, The New Voices, or the Extra-Mural Department of UWI.

While the presence of local and foreign-based Caribbean publishers is a sign of independence, there is a limit to the exposure which the small publisher can give to a writer. Sometimes an entire genre suffered from an inadequacy of promotion, as was the case with drama, which after the series of one-act plays published by the UWI Extra-Mural Department from the late fifties to the mid-sixties, went into a slump until the seventies, when the Walcott plays began to appear. Walcott's main publisher now is not British, but American.

Relief of a sort came with the short-lived Allison and Busby, who republished Lamming and C.L.R. James, and promoted the novels of Roy Heath. Relief of a sort has also come from Casa de las Americas, the Cuban publishing house, which in 1978 extended their annual literary competition to include writers from the Anglophone Caribbean. Guyanese writers such as N.D. Williams, Angus Richmond, Harry Narain and John Agard have won the Casa prize. Kamau Brathwaite has won it twice, once for *Black + Blues*, a collection of poems, and in 1986 for *Roots*, a collection of essays.

Very recently, through the agency mainly of West Indian publishers, we've seen the healthy and exciting emergence of several women writers such as Merle Collins, Grace Nichols, Erna Brodber, Velma Pollard, Olive Senior, Lorna Goodison, Christine Craig, Pamela Mordecai, Jean Goulbourne, Jean Binta Breeze and Opal Palmer. I think, indeed, that it is safe to predict that our most significant voices for the next two decades will be female. There are several reasons for this. First: the time demands it. All over the world women have been coming into visibility, and redefining in ways as significant as their male counterparts, the fundamental reality of human existence. Caribbean women are part of this universal redefinition, this transformation of reality. Second: the emergence of women writers in the Caribbean indicates that the other half of the Caribbean sensibility is seeking fulfilment through self-expression. If the male writers sought their liberation of spirit in the face of rigid colonial structures, the female writers seek theirs in the face of equally rigid patriarchal ones.

The third reason why our next wave of writers may well be women lies in the contempt for things of sensibility which our societies have unconsciously bred in the minds of young men. Young men have absorbed a notion of development based on the idea of science and technology, to the exclusion of the Arts. It is quite normal in a class of, say, sixty literature students at UWI, to find only three males. While there is no necessary or inevitable correspondence between studying literature as an academic discipline and becoming a creative writer, it is still true to conclude that over the last fifteen years far more women have been exposed to a wider range of literature than their male counterparts. Given this exposure and the already described need for self-definition, the women will be carrying the major burden of our writing in the near future.

Popular artistic forms such as the calypso, reggae and the emerging "dub" poetry, are still largely dominated by young men. The calypso, contrary to some opinions, is neither dying nor deteriorating. If there are fewer narrative calypsos, there are more celebratory ones. The calypso today also contains a range of political recall as well as an analytic grasp of the political moment that is equal to, if not greater than, what obtained in the age of Attila. It provides us with an index of popular attitudes to an increasingly bewildering social experience, and has had to wrestle with the growing problems of madness (Terror's "Madness", c. 1978), drug addiction (Duke, Sparrow, Explainer, Singing Francine among others have all sung on this theme), unemployment, corruption and vagrancy.

The darkening social experience since Independence has changed the nature of calypso laughter which, in the process of adjusting to bewildering paradox, has become a very complex thing. Chalkdust's "Learn to Laugh" advocates bitter mirth. It disturbs precisely because it unmasks the source of laughter, revealing it as chaos, bitterness and helplessness; as well as its function: masking, evasion and dereliction of the intolerable responsibility for setting the situation right. The language of some calypsos has returned to the singalong simplicity of the old-time kalinda chants, while that of those singers who have accepted a burden of self-definition has become more metaphorical, more dense, and more capable of expressing a wider range of feeling.

But calypsonians, like most other creative artists, face extreme problems when it comes to having their records produced. The young singer, like the young writer, may find that there is no one who is prepared to invest in an unknown voice. Or an investor may not offer fair terms. Tales of the exploitation of singers can fill a book. Plagiarism for commercial gain has been a major concern. Subtle or overt political censorship has existed in some Caribbean territories. Such censorship places an additional pressure on the singer, whose revenues are inevitably affected when his songs aren't played on the radio. A paradoxical situation is often created, where one sector of the community blames singers for composing trivial party songs, while another sector damns them for telling too much depressing political truth.

It should be clear, then, that all categories of artists need help of some sort. There is pressing need not only for awards such as the Guyana Prize for Literature, but also for a CARICOM Publishing House, which should belong equally to the public and private sectors in the Caribbean, and which, utilising the infrastructure that already exists in abundance throughout these territories, should publish school books, literary, academic and historical texts, as well as the burgeoning music of the region. There is no reason why, equipped with skilled panels of editorial advisers in each discipline, panels drawn, as CXC panels are, from all over the region, such a CARICOM Publishing House should not be able to select work that has merit and quality; work that is vital to our perception of self and possibility; work, too, that is informed by that critical intelligence which will be necessary for our self-knowledge and our location of the Caribbean self in the world and in the cosmos.

Such a CARICOM Publishing House can become a means whereby we may ingather our wandering wits, or, to use Martin Carter's arresting image: collect our scattered skeleton. No regional cultural policy will emerge without something like it. We need institutions that are more permanent than Carifesta, which, indeed, will give us something to celebrate whenever Carifesta comes around. A CARICOM Publishing House should also serve to stem the annual outflow from the region of millions of dollars, which is what we as a region pay foreign publishing houses, by presenting them with our captive primary and high school markets.

The act of writing poetry, prose or drama is, now that we know the extent to which science and technology are controlled by the metropole, one of the most crucial necessities and possible frontiers for development in the Caribbean. We cannot control the price of oil; we cannot control, try as we may, the price of bauxite; nor can we control the American quota for sugar. But we can control our exploration and presentation of ourselves. The Arts are probably the only area in which sovereignty is possible; though even here the burden of autonomous statement is exacting as frightening a toll as the region-wide collapse of our economies. This is so not only because of the difficulties artists experience in getting their work published, but also because of the difficult conditions in which the average citizens of these territories have been existing for some time.

At times these conditions objectify themselves, crystallise themselves, as it were, into moments of terrible atrocity, that have wrung from the poet and novelist and playwright outcry after outcry. Since Independence, we've had in the Caribbean guerillas and gundowns, the Malik affair in Trinidad with its gruesome lettuce-patch murders of the Trinidadian Skerritt and the Englishwoman, Gail Ann Benson. Guyana became unwittingly involved in that drama when Malik, who was married to a Guyanese, chose this landscape as the stage for his final act of folly: an attempt to walk from Berbice to Brazil. We all know the literature that grew out of that catastrophe: Vidia Naipaul's lucid essay, "The Killings in Trinidad", and his stark best-selling novel, *Guerillas,* which became very popular in North America, a country so much engaged in the conversion of fact into fiction, that many people there can no longer distinguish between the two. Trinidad, which is very similar to America in this respect, converted the Malik affair into the Carnival Ole Mas Band, BENSON UNDER HEDGES.

Jamaica has since Independence been conducting its fixed dialectic of gunmen. This unending, fratricidal conflict has concretised itself in acts such as that of gunmen feeding children and mothers to the flames in Orange Lane; old ladies burned to death in Eventide; and, worst of all, the sacrificial waste of the 1980 elections when well over five hundred people were killed. This scenario is being re-enacted in far more gruesome terms in Haiti, to whose assistance Jamaica, pre-schooled in similar atrocity, has self-righteously rushed.

The Jamaica tragedy has given rise to several poems. One has only to read Brathwaite's Kingston poems such as "Springblade", "Starvation", "Dread", "Wings of a Dove", "Sun Song" and "Kingston in the Kingdom of this World" to see how this tragedy has affected the expression of one of the region's leading writers. The Orange Lane fire is directly alluded to in his "Poem for Walter Rodney" where he makes the connection between two atrocities, twinning the cities of Kingston and Georgetown. Recognising in contemporary Jamaica patterns and structures of mind as old as the slave plantation, Brathwaite has shown in some detail how what he calls "the return of the status crow" has produced "the resurrection of the dread." The poems of Dennis Scott, Brian Meeks or Kendel Hippolyte, Scott's play, *Dog,* the reggae songs of Marley and the recently murdered Peter Tosh, the dub poetry of Linton Kwesi Johnson, Mutabaruka, Jean Binta Breeze and Mikey Smith, who couldn't believe that children were being deliberately thrown into the Orange Lane fire, but was himself soon to be stoned to death by people who disagreed with his political views – all provide us with a range of artistic responses to Jamaican atrocity, and define the bleak spiritual landscape out of which many Caribbean writers operate.

One of the duties of the Caribbean state should be to provide the citizen and artist with the necessary space within which he can operate, even when the citizen and artist see through and beyond the structures and devices of the state. Where such space does not exist, literature creates it through protest, or through the imaginative territory which it liberates in quest of living-room for the spirit. The creative voice in the Caribbean has always challenged the political reality or unreality, fostered by ideologues for or against the prevailing political order. When this happens, the creative voice may find itself confronted by the ignorant machinery of an oppression which, when it is not fostered directly by the state, may be tacitly permitted to happen because of the indifference or neglect of the state. The word may then find itself in chains.

Kamau Brathwaite's "Kingston in the Kingdom of this World" dramatises the outcry of the voice against such imprisonment. The poem's voice is simultaneously that of a Christ figure awaiting trial and crucifixion; that of the artist, whose authority of sunlight, vision, music, dance and the illuminating power of the imagination is pitted against the incarceration of the state; and that of the Dogon Nummo, the primal creative word and voice and spirit of Africa, rotting in a Jamaican jail. I'll read this poem now for Mikey Smith, for Walter Rodney, for Martin Carter and for George Lamming, allowing, as you may have noticed, the living and the dead proportional representation.

Kingston in the Kingdom of this World

The wind blows on the hillside
and i suffer the little children
i remember the lilies of the field
the fish swim in their shoals of silence
our flung nets are high wet clouds, drifting

with this reed i make music
with this pen i remember the word
with these lips i can remember the beginning of the world

between these bars is this sudden lock-up
where there is only the darkness of dog-bark
where i cannot make windmills of my hands
where i cannot run down the hill-path of faith
where i cannot suffer the little children

a man may have marched with armies
he may have crossed the jordan and the red sea
he may have stoned down the walls of jericho

here where the frogs creak where there is only the
    croak of starlight

he is reduced
he is reduced
he is reduced
    to a bundle of rags
        a broken stick
            that will never whistle through
            fingerstops into the music of flutes
            that will never fling nets white sails
            crossing

gospel was a great wind freedom of savannas
gospel was a great mouth telling thunder of heroes
gospel was a cool touch warm with the sunlight like
water in claypots, healing

    this reduction wilts the flower
        weakens the water
        coarsens the lips
    fists at the bars, shake rattle and hammers at the
        locks

    suffer the little children
    suffer the rose gardens
    suffer the dark clouds howling for bread
    suffer the dead fish poisoned in the lake

my authority was sunlight: the man who arose from
    the dead called me saviour
    his eyes had known moons older than jupiters
my authority was windmills: choirs singing of the
    flowers of rivers

your authority is these chains that strangle my wrists
your authority is the red whip that circles my head
your authority is the white eye of interrogator's terror:

    siren price fix the law of undarkness

the dreadness of the avalanches of unjudgement

it is you who roll down boulders when i say word
it is you who cry wolf when i offer the peace of wood-
    doves

it is you who offer up the silence of dead leaves

i would call out but the guards do not listen
i would call out but the dew out there on the grass
    cannot glisten
i would call out but my lost children cannot unshackle
    their shadows of silver

    here i am reduced to this hole of my head
    where i cannot cut wood where i cannot eat
        bread
    where i cannot break fish with the multitudes

my authority was foot stamp upon the ground
    the curves the palms the dancers
my authority was nyambura: inching closer
    embroideries of fingers silver earrings:
        balancers
            and
                i am reduced
                i am reduced
                i am reduced
                to these black eyes
                this beaten face
                these bleaching lips blearing obscenities

                i am reduced
                i am reduced
                i am reduced
                to this damp
                to this dark
                to this driven rag

                awaiting the water of sunlight
                awaiting the lilies to spring up out of the iron
                awaiting your eyes o my little children

                awaiting

    Guyana has matched the rest of the Caribbean in atrocity. We had the mind-blowing Jim Jones Affair being enacted in the Guyana forest of the night, involving a handful of white masters of the religious word and nine hundred black slaves to it. This atrocity has produced about a dozen prose accounts, including one from Shiva Naipaul who, imitating his elder brother, as he usually did, also squeezed a novel out of the catastrophe. There were also two or three American movies, one of which was significantly entitled not an American, but *The Guyana Tragedy*. Popular response in Guyana was provided by two songs, one by Nicky Porter and the other by the Trade Winds, who summarised the Jim Jones catastrophe with the couplet:

He tell them to think and they thinking
So he tell them to drink and they drinking

What the Caribbean mind can't comprehend, it converts into a macabre carnival of humour, behind which still lurks the cadaver of evaded catastrophe. Here the Trade Winds are, perhaps unconsciously, establishing the link between centralised propaganda, mind-control and self-destruction, and suggesting a lesson pertinent not only to the Jim Jones commune, who were in any case no longer capable of learning it, but to the Guyanese nation as a whole.

Guyana can also boast of the death of Walter Rodney which, like the Grenada fiasco three years later – Grenada is already an American movie – was a devastating body blow to an entire generation; the literal reduction to ashes of passion, energy, commitment, courage, laughter and intelligence. That death has evoked an entire anthology of poems, as well as collections of papers from conferences and seminars on the meaning of the life's work of an outstanding historian, Caribbean and international personality, who could not find a job at the University of Guyana, even when the History Department there was being headed by an American alcoholic, of whom the kindest thing that one can say is that he was colourless and nondescript. That this could happen under a regime which, four years earlier, had had the generosity, scope and vision to inaugurate Carifesta, is perhaps the most astounding paradox to have been produced in a country of astounding paradoxes.

Moving as all these elegies to Rodney undoubtedly are, I'd have preferred other poems and Rodney alive. I'd even have preferred him to have rejected what Linton Kwesi Johnson termed "History's weight", and obeyed the advice which Wordsworth McAndrew offered him in a 1976 poem, written in reaction to his being denied the job at U.G. McAndrew at that time had already intuited a sort of doom, and advised Rodney to leave a country which could or would not find use for either his academic excellence or political commitment.

McAndrew himself, by far Guyana's best and most active folklorist, who almost single-handedly provided a forum for scores of new Guyanese short stories, unearthed the customs, sayings and practices of Guyanese from all corners of the land, took his own advice and left Guyana. The warehouse manager, where he first sought work in New Jersey, gave him a simple arithmetic test which he clearly expected him to fail. When Mac returned after a few minutes, the manager exclaimed in that mixture of amazement and contempt with which Prospero is sometimes grudgingly forced to acknowledge Caliban as a being capable of intelligence: "Gee! He got them all right!" Our national talent has been to make the real man into a small man. As the voice in "Kingston in the Kingdom of this World" laments: he is reduced. He is reduced.

Tonight, we are celebrating the sponsoring of literature by state and school. It is worth reminding both state and school of the strain under which writers exist, particularly when they are politically critical of the state. In Trinidad, five poets were among the 1970 detainees, and Jack Kelshall, whom Guyanese of the early sixties might well remember, became a poet after he was wrongfully imprisoned in the 1970s. Martin Carter had, of course, experienced this under the British nearly two decades earlier.

Under such stasis, such unchange, some writers have chosen the amnesia of alcohol. Others, like Mittelholzer, Leroy Calliste, Eric Roach, the painter and folklorist Harold Simmons, and the poet and teacher Neville Robinson committed suicide by rope, poison, the knife or fire. It is a dangerous thing, often a fatal thing, to even possess sensibility in such an age, where there are so many ways that a person can be destroyed. We live in societies in the Caribbean where the price of a certain type of clarity is sudden death; where the price of a certain type of commitment is certain arrest; of a certain quality of feeling is possible self-immolation.

The grimness of the age has affected the styles and modes of functioning of both the state and the individual. If many individual sensibilities have succumbed to despair or become fixed in automatic attitudes of protest and resistance, the state has tended to ossify into rigid authoritarian attitudes, which are really the mask of a fundamental impotence.

Surveying West Indian societies since independence, one is forced to conclude that we remain colonial in how authority reacts to critical challenge; that certain aspects of our consciousness have become paralysed in ancient attitudes of crippledom; that, sadly, it has proven easier to mummify entire nations than the individual corpse.

Our neo-colonial situation of simultaneous freedom and mental enchainment is one of deep and perplexing paradox. In Trinidad last year it was possible for black policemen to unleash an unprovoked attack on black people demonstrating against the anti-black racism of South Africa's apartheid State. The same Trinidad moved a vote in the United Nations to enforce sanctions against South Africa. Faced with such inconsistency, deeply rooted in our colonial past and blossoming daily in our neo-colonial present, the mind of artist and critic alike seeks naturally to express and explore paradox.

I have, consequently, named this address "Trophy and Catastrophe". If the catastrophe refers to these societies in which we now live and breathe and have what remains of our being, the trophy refers to the Guyana Prize for Literature which, Your Excellency, you have with such imagination and generosity inaugurated. I am proud to be identified with this effort and this occasion, and to congratulate the winners in each category. I hope the prize is only the beginning of a new dispensation for writers, and that the graciousness which inspired its inauguration will also inform the political future of the Guyanese people.

(Address delivered at the Inauguration of the Guyana Prize for Literature, National Cultural Centre, Georgetown, Guyana, on December 8th, 1987. Published in *Kyk-Over-Al* 38 (June 1988), pp. 13-22.)

APOCALYPSO AND THE SOCA FIRES OF 1990

I: Apocalypso: Digging Horrors and the Blues

The idea of the Apocalypse has been a constant one in post-Independence Caribbean music. One grew accustomed, since the late sixties, to Jamaica's politics being discussed in the music in terms of a deathless confrontation between the cohorts of Zion and those of Babylon, as well as to the imagery of blood and fire, the recurrent prophecy about the burning city and hope for some ultimate judgement that would, in Jah Rastafari's good time, be visited on the workers of iniquity.[1]

In Trinidad, the apocalyptic vision existed in political poetry after 1970,[2] glowing a sombre dull red in those whose hopes for the black revolution had become shattered by the defeat of Black Power. It is significant that Rastafarianism, its music and imagery, began to gain ground in Trinidad and Tobago soon after 1970. By the mid-1970s an apocalyptic sound had entered the language of some calypsos. There was the threat, promise or prophecy of a coming time of fire and revolution.[3] The number of apocalyptic calypsos grew steadily after 1975 as calypsonians changed from predicting explosion to describing disintegration.

Many people began to recognise that the Apocalypse was taking place, not as a single comprehensive moment of explosion, but in slow motion. Its indices were the human and material dereliction in the city, the demoralisation and rotting edges of the town which V.S. Naipaul, returned in 1971 to write an investigative report on the Malik atrocity, described as sitting "like lead on my spirit." Naipaul's *Guerillas,* the fiction which grew out of this encounter is an apocalyptic text, filled with nauseating descriptions of a burning inferno-like rubbish dump at the edge of the city, the dirt, disorder and rot at its centre, and the moral degeneration of all the important personages in the novel's sad and savage drama of decay.

Not long after this, the Mighty Sparrow in "Ah Digging Horrors" (1975) itemised the things which created in him a feeling of "horrors" and "blues".

> Cost of living strangling everybody
> No food in yuh house to feed yuh family
> It's a free-for-all here, I'm afraid
> I believe we need psychiatric aid
> Unscrupulous employers and unscrupulous workers
>   couldn't care less
> This place in a mess.

Chorus
Ah digging horrors
Ah digging the blues
Anytime ah choose to peruse the daily news
Ah digging horrors, because
All ah reading 'bout is guerillas more laws, and wars.

Looting, shooting rioting and raping
Nurses aiding mad people in escaping
Lord, with all this resentment and hate
Mih blood pressure in a terrible state
Unions creating confusion
Police spreading brutality in the land
Mih heart in mih hand...

Somewhat in the documentary mode which Chalkdust had resuscitated in the late sixties, Sparrow's "Ah Digging Horrors" suggests that the national mind is unable to keep pace with the vortex of disintegration. As the seventies proceeded there was an intensification of each area of "horror" identified by Sparrow. The cost-of-living grew more burdensome as land, building and food prices escalated. The sense deepened of national life being a "free-for-all", that is, a mad, anarchic scramble characterised by an absence of scruple or moral sanction at all levels of social and economic existence. Sparrow's recognition of the nation's mental and spiritual illness – ("I believe we need psychiatric aid") – would be reflected in several other calypsos of the late seventies and the eighties, such as Terror's "Madness" or Chalkdust's "Port of Spain Gone Insane".

Beyond the perception of horrors and the blues lay the prophecy of revolution. Valentino, surveying in "Dis Place Nice" (1975) the people's passive acceptance of their grim lot, predicted "revolution" and "fire". Similarly, Stalin, surveying in "Nothing Ain't Strange" (1975) the seasonal extermination of "guerillas", and feeling the steady cheapening of life, affirmed the citizen's right not only to dissent, but to reclaim an heritage of ingrained resistance and revolt, centuries old and perpetually renewable. Two lines of perception, one of which led to the simple cataloguing of "horrors" and the other of which sought to illuminate possibilities for escape or revolt, existed side by side in the calypsos of the seventies and eighties. Between these two lines of perception lay the notion of an elaborate operation of concealment being in existence. Chalkdust's "Nixon's Mistake" (1975) chided impeached President Richard Nixon for not studying the politicians of Trinidad, who could teach him, so sang Chalkdust, to break-and-enter, steal and "cover-up."

So emerged Delamo, foremost of the apocalyptic singers, with his trilogy of "doom-burdened" songs – "Apocalypse" (1980/81); "Sodom and Gomorrah" (1981/82) and "Armageddon" (1985) all of which catalogued the horrors of the last days of Eric Williams and the Chambers interregnum, with deepening gloom. Delamo's declaration in "Armageddon" that "There'll be no solution/ Until the last days of Armageddon" placed salvation beyond historic time or human capacity. According to this vision, not only Trinidad, but the whole of humankind was doomed unless, as seemed patently unlikely to happen, human nature underwent a total spiritual rebirth. On the other hand, Delamo in "Ah Want a Wuk, Georgie" communicated the smouldering rage and potential violence of the growing cohort of the unemployed. The spiritual Armageddon involving principalities and powers would, it seemed, have its forerunner in the bitter confrontation due to take place in the kingdom of this earth, between the dispossessed and their rulers.

Sparrow in this era produced a quartet of dread calypsos: "We Like It So" (1982), "Capitalism Gone Mad" (1983), "Prophets of Doom and Gloom" (1983) and "Sam P" (1984). The first one was both a defence of his defection from the PNM after Dr. Williams's death and an attack on the PNM faithful who had remained loyal to their party even in the face of the general degeneration of economic and social life. The second is a lament against the now outrageously high cost of living. The third was his answer to the President's bland dismissal of "prophets of doom and gloom." In it, he provided even more reasons than he had done a decade before in "Ah Digging Horrors", why citizens should be pessimistic about their future under a supine political regime.

It is worth asking, as an exasperated Sparrow does in "We Like It So (or "Steelbeam") why the rage which always seems to be smouldering in the breasts of the dispossessed, was not released against the old PNM long before the 1986 elections. Part of the answer seems to lie in the emergence during the latter half of the 1970s of a lucrative grassroots huckstering movement. This was celebrated by Chalkdust in "Thanks Geddes" (1980) as a triumph of Black Power activism and scathingly denounced by Delamo as a new type of "black-versus-black exploitation" ("Sodom and Gomorrah"). Whatever its character, such street-trading, when added to the poor relief panacea of "Special Works" and "DEWD", sustained the turbulent children of the Black Power era, whose loyalty was given not to Geddes Granger / Makandal Daaga of the NJAC, but to the PNM, and has remained intact despite the eternity of overflowing pit latrines, craterous roads, poor hospital facilities and malnutrition described by Sparrow in "Ah Digging Horrors" (1975) and "We Like It So" (1982), or Shorty in "Money Is No Problem" (1979).

The calypsos which chronicled these and other areas of collapse increased in volume during the early years of the eighties. Short Pants, for example, composed over a score of them between 1975 and 1984, which he published in his Kaiso Souvenir entitled *Things Goin' Thru Mih Mind* (1984). This collection of calypso lyrics, which also includes a handful of compositions by Unknown and Commentor, deserves special study, for its relentless cataloguing of social, moral and economic collapse. Yet, despite the grimness of the vision in social and political calypsos, the bulk of both performed and recorded music was given over to celebration. The strategies for escape became more elaborate as the sense of doom spread. Apocalyptic calypsos and "party" songs, doom-saying and celebration developed side by side. At times, as in Sparrow's "The Bomb" (1978), a party song might employ metaphors of destruction. But the ticking of the time-bomb turns out to be no more than the music of carnival about to explode into life, not death. Not yet.

Each type of calypso found its advocate. Chalkdust, for example, time and again affirmed his vocation of social commentator, political satirist, chronicler of the non-achievements of the state and investigative reporter on secret corruption, such as the maturing O'Halloran scandal. This he viewed as the true role of the calypsonian.[4] Short Pants shared Chalkdust's opinion. Kitchener, however, declared in 1976, a year when the CDC was offering a special prize for the best political calypso that:

> "People do not go to the Dimanche Gras competition to hear the political opinion of the calypsonians... They want to be entertained. They should confine their political songs to the tent and not bore the audience to death on Carnival Sunday night when they are getting in the mood for Jour Ouvert."
>
> The CDC, Kitchener said, must stop the prize "for a political calypso immediately, because it had no place in the Dimanche Gras show." All that the CDC had done, he added, was give calypsonians an opportunity to attack the Government and turn the show into a dreary one.[5]

There was more to Kitchener's objection than was immediately apparent. Not only was he affirming his chosen vocation as celebrant of Jour Ouvert, high-priest of Panorama and King of the Road, but also defending his role as a loyal supporter of the ruling PNM. After such magnificent political calypsos as "Black Power" (1971) "No Freedom" (1973) and "Jericho" (1974) all of which, in spite of their celebratory rhythm, documented developments such as the Black Power marches, the tightening of national security through harsh Sedition Laws, and the police annihilation of "guerillas", Kitchener studiously avoided Chalkdust's turf, whose very ingredients were the horrors and the blues. He would in 1977 celebrate the PNM 1976 victory over the newborn ULF.

> We will beat them, next elections
> It is not as easy as they say
> It will take a stronger Opposition
> To beat the PNM party today
> The Doctor say PNM
> We here to stay – PNM etc.

The real implication of his objection to the presence of political calypsos in the Dimanche Gras competition, was that he wanted to protect a PNM, badly shaken by the resignations of its secondary leadership between 1970 and 1976, from the kind of scathing commentary that Chalkdust ("Ah Put on Mih Guns Again") and Blakie ("Twenty Years is too Long") had been making in 1976.

Kitchener also celebrated George Chambers's 1981 victory, with a mocking attack on his arch-rival Sparrow, who had supported the badly defeated ONR.

> Not a damn seat for dem
> Sparrow, that's ingratitude
> Not a damn seat for dem
> You bite the finger that give you food
> Not a damn seat for dem
> Look how you hug up Doctor Willie
> Not a damn seat for dem
> People fraid you in this country
> ("Not a Damn Seat" (1982))

Supporting the six-times-victorious PNM went hand in hand with turning away from the burgeoning corruption and atrocity. When the Sam P. Wallace scandal broke in 1982, and the extent of O'Halloran's fraud in that business alone – a matter of some 250 millions – registered on the nation's consciousness, Kitchener composed "Soca Corruption" (1983) in which he simultaneously dealt with and evaded the dreadful implications of corruption.

> If I have a few million
> And they want to link it with corruption
> Is mih damn business
> If is true how they describe
> Ah get mih money by taking bribe
> Is mih damn business
> If they say ah gone abroad
> To get away from the charge of fraud
> Is mih damn business
> If they say it is a fact
> Ah have no intention of coming back
> Is mih damn business
>
> All o' we does thief but is the one that they does hold become the guilty man
>
> *Chorus*
> Soca – Corruption
> Soca – Confusion
> Soca – Destruction
> Soca – Invasion
> Soca – Inflation

> Soca – Recession
> Soca – in winin
> Soca – in grin'in
> Soca – in thiefing
> Soca – in wukking
> Soca – in rocking
> Soca – in ducking

This calypso alludes covertly to four parallel scandals including the Sam P. Wallace, D.C. 9 and CDC scandals. The voice of the protagonist changes from stanza to stanza, but all of them are flippant and brass-faced as many people have been then and are now with respect to the issue of corruption, the extent of their involvement in it and the question of taking responsibility for their tainted stewardship. The voice here proclaims the ethic of the white-collar crook: corruption exists only when one has been caught and legally convicted. All else is "business" in every sense of the word.

At one level this is biting, sophisticated satire. At another it is evasion of the horrors and the blues. Corruption is reduced to "Soca corruption", the horrors and the blues to the gaiety of the party scene. Kitchener has composed numerous calypsos bearing the name "Soca" – for example "Soca Jean", "Soca Millicent", "Soca Evelyn". "Soca Corruption" suggests that 'Corruption' is simply another desirable female in a harem of Soca women. Beneath the mask of flippancy in which the song and dance of corruption is equated with carnival bacchanalia, Kitchener is aware of the triple reality of corruption, confusion and destruction. If existence is "wining" and "grinding", it is also "thiefing", and the thieves are joyously triumphant and as gaily amoral as any carnival winer or grinder. No great moralist, Kitchener perhaps still does feel a twinge of sadness at the moral collapse of a system he had supported so fervently just the year before. One notes that the first voice declares "All o'we does thief." This sentiment would be echoed by a PNM politician in the 1986 elections campaign when, taken out of context, it would evoke, at last, a howl of indignation from the electorate, who refused to be equated with the O'Hallorans of society.

Sparrow, meanwhile, viewed the Sam P. Wallace/O'Halloran affair with vengeful joy, as justification for his abandonment of the PNM and support for the ONR. First in "Prophet of Doom" he made the calypsonian's perennial claim to affirm the citizen's right to know and state the full depressing truth about social and economic reality.

> If you happen to see and know
> When politics going wrong
> With facts and figures prepared to show
> It's better to bite your tongue
> Them political boss
> Consider you a cross

> An obstacle to be removed at any cost
> A social conscience is really very dangerous to your health
> The awesome strength of the powers that be
> Most certainly will be felt
> To tell them that their priorities and their performance is under par
> They will then proceed to describe to you what you are
>
> *Chorus*
> A megalomaniac
> A power seeker
> A crazy or cracked
> Trouble maker
> If you tell them that the economy is no longer in full bloom
> Then you become a prophet of gloom and doom.

Sparrow's complaint here is similar to Chalkdust's in 1968-69 and throughout the seventies; or to Blakie's in 1977 after he was pressured by the CDC for singing "Twenty Years Is Too Long", or to Sugar Aloes's in 1990 and 1991 ("The Judge" and "My Decision") or to Relator's in 1981 ("China Syndrome") or Short Pants's (1975) "The Law Is An Ass". All of these singers have complained that the "system" via calypso judges, radio station managers or even more direct methods, brings pressure to bear on the truly independent critic. Stalin had complained in 1975 ("Nothing Ain't Strange") that:

> Because you won't let people talk for you
> Or do the things that they want you to
> Your life ain't safe whether night or day
> Because any number can play

Similarly, in 1983, Sparrow protested against the atmosphere of covert threat and open insult by which the citizen who criticised the system often found himself afflicted. True to the tradition of protest calypsos, Sparrow counters threat with aggressiveness and turns insult back on itself. His final stanzas are a catalogue of the horrors current in 1983.

> Questionable deals made in haste
> Continue to grow and grow
> Blatant refusals have replaced
> The people's right to know
> Predictions are made daily
> To rule for a next century
> And all indications are that it may well be
>
> Retrenchment and redundancy
> Beginning to strangle we
> Inflation and low productivity
> Done take over already
> The Integrity Commission plan
> Is a next project also ran
> The only thing man concern with is re-election

> In this land of steady power failures
> People houses in darkness
> But on every tree round the Savannah
> Displays luciferous politics
> You have to ask yourself what is worse
> Between a schizophrenic baboon
> A megalomaniac and a prophet of doom and gloom

Insults are turned back on their source. Is it better or worse to be "a prophet of doom and gloom" – that is, himself, the calypsonian as honest chronicler of decay and as warner-man – than to be what he implies his main critic is: "a schizophrenic baboon" and a "megalomaniac?" The extremity of both insults is a hint of the viciousness that was already entering discourse, and would dominate the tone of the next decade in the full frontal crudity of a Watchman or a Sugar Aloes.

The next year (1984) Sparrow was even more trenchant in his attack; for if "Prophet of Doom" is an open display of anger and a descent into direct insult, "Sam P" is poised, humorous and more scathing in its bitter mockery.

> They bring down Sam and force him to drink
> Now is time to urinate, they can't take the stink
> All them big heroes in their fancy suits
> Covering their nose, quaking in their boots
> Who make the contract
> Who get the kickback
> Nobody ain't want to answer that!
>
> *Chorus*
> Now ah hear the president – fraid
> The whole ah parliament – fraid
> Permanent secretary – fraid
> Business and industry – fraid
> Corruption in high society
> Have them trembling with anxiety
> Everybody fraid, Sam P.
>
> Opposition with basin and po'
> Man they form a ring round Sam for the pee to flow
> But not a trickle
> O' evidence come down
> Try every angle
> Sam P back too strong
> Government made fun
> Of the Opposition
> Till Sam P confess in Old San Juan
>
> *Chorus*
> Ah hear the Foreign Exchange Board – fraid
> The Treasury overlord – fraid
> The Army Commandant – fraid

> The whole o Central Bank – fraid
> The Opposition's enquiry
> Stumbled on a conspiracy
> Everybody fraid – Sam P.

Taken at a rollicking, joyous pace "Sam P" (1984) was Sparrow's perfect counter to Kitchener's "Not a Damn Seat for Dem" (1982) and his ambiguous "Soca Corruption" (1983). Its central metaphor is that of the stench of corruption; hence the scatological image in which a character named "Sam", brought down to construct a racing complex, drinks too much liquor and ends up urinating on his frightened and mortified hosts. Like Kitchener's "Soca Corruption", "Sam P" makes effective use of the call and response technique, though while Kitchener has two refrains, "Is mih damn business" in the stanzas and "Soca" in the chorus, Sparrow confines the refrain to the chorus, where the single repeated word "fraid" captures the atmosphere of panic that has overtaken every corner of the political, economic and administrative life of the old regime. This panic replaces their boldfaced mockery of opposition efforts to unearth hard evidence of a corruption that everyone could smell.

"Sam P", for all its brash gaiety is every bit as corrosive and apocalyptic as say Chalkdust's dark and violently comic "Bring the Ayatollah" (1980), whose mode of vicious recrimination would be resurrected in the calypsos of Watchman. Its central metaphor of stench suggests a decaying society and explains the growing gloom in a morally conscious singer such as Delamo and the near despair of "Armageddon" (1985) which was sung in the year after Sparrow's "Sam P". For at the centre of "Armageddon" is a total disillusion with political process and the notion of human self-development through the transforming power of education; a disillusion that is with the ruling oligarchy that had come into being with the PNM, extended educational opportunity and the consequent growth of a new meritocracy. What the corruption issue of the eighties had shown and what calypsonians had begun to divine, was that any ruling oligarchy would rule primarily in its own self-interest, manipulating the economy, the law and the systems of information and validating discourse in order to sustain its hegemony from here to eternity. Some of the verses in Kitchener's "Soca Corruption" indicate the cynicism with which this ruling bureaucratic elite justified its tenacious stranglehold on power and privilege:

> Little do they know whichever man replaces me
>   Is the same affair
> Once he have the privilege to handle the money
>   He hand ain't have hair

Such an argument had been current in the streets for nearly two decades. Grassroots defendants of the status quo accepted this line of reasoning and intended, corruption or no corruption, to vote the PNM back into office and keep them entrenched there as long as possible. Sparrow complained in "Prophets of Doom" that

> Predictions are made daily
> To rule for a next century
> And all indications are that it may well be

He also recognised that the State had maintained control of the major electronic media, and had effectively manipulated information towards the reinforcement of its own hegemony.

One is therefore forced to conclude, that it was not disillusionment at the corruption of the *ancien régime* that led to the defeat of the PNM in 1986. It was neither the ONR's "politics of conscience" nor the NAR's slogan of "One Love"; the nation was too far gone in decadence, had acquiesced too often and too long in every species of corruption, to experience any genuine moral awakening. It was, rather, the concrete reality of recession, the foundering businesses, lost jobs, capital flight and Mr. Chambers's fifty per cent (50 %) devaluation of the once proud Trini dollar that undermined confidence in the *ancien régime*. Moneys stolen from the late sixties to the early eighties, when viewed in the stark light of recession, began at last to be seen as moneys that might have been employed towards national development. The unfortunate Mr. Chambers tried too late to institute the sort of fiscal austerity that the age seemed to demand.

Celebrated at the start of his term of office in Explainer's calypso ("Georgie, if you true we will follow you"), Mr. Chambers soon enough became the scapegoat for an economic situation he had inherited from his predecessor, the "Corporation Sole", Dr. Williams. He also inherited the atmosphere of moral collapse, and would soon have to outstare the basilisk of corruption as the Sam P. Wallace/O'Halloran issue broke wind towards the middle of his 1981-1986 term of office. Seeking to project an image of diligence and efficiency, he adopted the slogan, "Fete over, back to work", implying in the process that the days of wine and roses under Dr. Williams – days described well by Stalin in his apocalyptic "Breakdown Party" (1980) – had been days of carnivalesque frivolity and waste.

"Productivity" became Chambers's great watchword, one that was soon drained of its meaning by Tobago Crusoe, who in his calypso "Productivity" (1984) merrily named dozens of things, most of them deplorable, that Trinidad had "produced". Black Stalin, too, in his much neglected "Make Them All Right" (1984), asked what was the point of working hard to produce for an uncaring, unappreciative system during one's youth, when one's fate in old age might well be to become a derelict or vagrant. He cited the case of Uriah Butler who had been hauled before the courts as a squatter on state lands some years before Eric Williams found it politically expedient to elevate him to the dubious status of "national hero".

Mr. Chambers's "Productivity Drive" produced as little productivity as

Mr. Manning's more recent "Unemployment Consultation" (1992) has generated employment. The situation continued to decline. Desperately seeking to place as much distance as possible between himself and Dr. Williams, Chambers attempted via the now forgotten Ballah Committee (1982) to document the economic disasters which certain of the Government-to-Government projects undertaken by the Corporation Sole and Father of the Nation, had turned out to be. But Mr. Chambers was in a double bind since, lacking a distinctive image of his own, something that was necessary for leadership in a flamboyant country such as Trinidad, he was forced to promote that of his powerful, undead predecessor.

Thus Mr. Chambers's approach to self-validation was characterised by a curious though unavoidable ambivalence: on the one hand, a subtle erosion of Williams's image through the reversal or scaling down of the latter's policies; on the other hand, a need to promote Williams's "Father-of-the-Nation" image by naming after Dr. Williams the two most massive and debt-creating – that is with the exception of ISCOTT, another Williams white elephant – monuments of the 1970s: the Mount Hope Medical Complex and the Financial Complex. Such naming was in direct contravention of Dr. Williams's pronouncement that his name should adorn no monument whatsoever, that no statue should be erected in his honour and that no crowds should view his body or gawk at his dead face.

Because he could neither resurrect nor become Dr. Williams, whose stony-faced reticence he had copied, Mr. Chambers was made the butt of a barrage of jokes, one of which eventually found its way into Plainclothes's 1984 calypso "Chambers Done See". There, under the guise of commending Mr. Chambers for his foresight, the calypso was in fact proclaiming his suddenly acquired reputation for being "duncy". The truth of the matter was that Chambers was now feeling the nuclear fallout from the oil-boom decade, and bearing the accusations that it was such waste that had caused the recession to destroy the good life in Trinidad. Valentino's "Recession" (1983) was a good example of what many people had begun to argue.

> Ah smelling something
> Them big fellas have something burning
> All you eh smellin?
> Dem big fellas have something burning
> After they done occupy their space
> They bring a bankruptcy in the place
> After they done get high on their million
> They creating world recession
>
> The men in business, for their own interests
> And the political exploitists
> Is who have this place in this kinda jam crisis
> Although recession killing the country
> Max Senhouse still needs the money

Is he who bringing on this recession on we

I am up to date
With my people I love to relate
So I keep in tune
With what's going on from June to next June
Soon there will be no more DEWD
The situation with oil getting crude
There will be strikes and more retrenchment
Oh Jah! Save the innocent

Them people that spend and spree so much money
They had no problems with currency
Until the death of Dr. Willie
He too lend out so much money
And indebting up this country
So is he who brought all this recession on we

Recession is blamed on both external factors – the economic situation in the world, the England-Argentina War – and on internal ones such as corruption in high places at home; the marketing initiatives of local businessmen which had encouraged consumerism during the oil-boom; the fiscal policies of Dr. Eric Williams, which placed too few restrictions on foreign exchange; and the bad loans made by Dr. Williams to mendicant Caricom neighbours. The calypso also notes the leniency of the law towards a big businessman caught smuggling a large sum of money out of the country, and contrasts the situation of the unemployed, the DEWD worker, the worker on the brink of retrenchment in a contracting economy. Valentino predicts a future of strikes and retrenchment and in stanza four concludes that the working-class are the innocent victims of a genocide plot.

This conclusion is of great importance if we are to arrive at a logical explanation of what happened to the regime that succeeded Chambers's six years as Prime Minister. By 1984 the so-called "Peoples' Calypsonian" had arrived at the strange crossroads between logical analysis and mystification. Logical analysis enabled him to assign responsibility for the worsening economic situation to a variety of definable forces and sources, some of which were imposed from outside, while others were rooted in the society itself. Mystification, however, pointed the seeker towards cosmic sources of his plight, or towards the "wickedness of mankind," a deep, inscrutable evil permeating the scheme of things; or perhaps, a quite identifiable enemy, whose goal was the genocide of Black people.

Significantly, Johnny King's "Nature' Plan" (1983/84)[6] was, at nearly the same time as Valentino's "Recession" advancing an outmoded Social Darwinian explanation of why Black people were at the bottom of society in places such as South Africa. "Nature", said King, in terms Tennyson or Hardy might have understood, had decreed the destruction of the weak, the humble and the meek. Since Black people were all of these, Nature had enslaved them and made their lives miserable from the cradle to the grave. In sweet, beautiful and, utterly sincere tones, Johnny King proclaimed the cosmic victimhood of African peoples, at a point in time when Trinidadians had again begun to view themselves as victims of "the wickedness of mankind."

But King's cosmic philosophy also included the notion of a Black Apocalypse. One day, it runs, without notice or clear reason, "Nature" will suddenly turn around like the Medieval wheel of fortune, and as capriciously as he/she/ it has for all these centuries victimised Black peoples, Nature will now destroy their enemies. One's aim when weak and Black should be to "hold on," to endure until the time of the great turnaround.

If Johnny King chose South Africa as the venue for current Black victimisation, Chalkdust would the following year (1985) give the "enemy of Black people" a local face. First of all, he rejected the argument of "Nature's Plan", declaring in "White Man's Plan" (1985) that there were clear historical reasons why Africans had been enslaved and exploited none of which had anything to do with an abstract force termed "Nature". Secondly, in "Grandfather's Backpay" he argues that Black people's work has not only never been appreciated, but has, indeed, seldom been acknowledged as work. Exploited and perennially underpaid, the Black worker has helped establish the economic basis for the superiority of a superordinate class, which has passed down its wealth and its attitude of arrogance to succeeding generations of exploiters. This ruling class is given a local face and a name – it is "them French Creoles!" The family names that Chalkdust lists as French Creole are both well-known French Creole names and names of English and Scottish Protestants. French Creole in "Grandfather's Backpay" includes cocoa and citrus farmers, merchants and proprietors, all united by an instinct to exploit the faithful but landless Black worker-victim.

The protagonist demands his grandfather's backpay, that is, the tangible recognition of his years of labour and the respect he deserved but never received. He also ends with a war cry after three stanzas of warning "them French Creoles":

> I want mih grandfather backpay
> War! War! War declare today!

It is the same gratuitously apocalyptic voice that Johnny King associates with the sudden reversal of Nature's plan in some unimaginable and obscure future. The difference is that Chalkdust is not prepared to wait for either Valentino's "Jah" to "save the innocent", or for Johnny King's Nature to turn around, "bringing death to the wild play" of oppressors. He invokes and declares war himself, in the process of so doing, he becomes the harbinger of the new era, one that has been fraught with the identification and slaughter of scapegoats.

Such victimisation began to happen towards the middle of the Chambers era. For there was something ritualistic about the flaying of Chambers by means of contemptuous laughter. Such laughter was a means of striking back at one who had introduced tough budgetary measures that reduced state expenditure on social programmes and public works. All the name-calling and viciously reductive picong signalled a nation apprehensive of the death of Dr. Williams's welfare state; and the deep panic of a class in arrested formation; the chronic insecurity of a fragile petite bourgeoisie, built not on any original creativity; not on ownership of industrial resources; not on solid and saleable artisanship; but on the dispensation of patronage often for work not done, and on a consumerism that the country could no longer afford. Mr. Chambers was ready for the calypsonian's knife of wit.

Gypsy provided it in "The Sinking Ship" (1986) whose opening tells less than the truth when it says that "The Trinidad, a luxury liner" had been sailing smoothly under Dr. Eric Williams, an old captain whose demise resulted in the incompetent captaincy of Mr. Chambers. Immediately, just so, with no previous warning, the ship hits rough waters, founders and begins to sink. The rest of the calypso provides witty and accurate analysis, by means of metaphor, of why the ship has foundered: a decline in oil revenues ("the oil pressure reading low"), graft, corruption among the officers who steal from the ship's safe. The point is that the image of Mr. Chambers as the incompetent captain who has blindly sailed the cruise ship into a hurricane, is established *before* the deeper and more accurate assessment of disintegration during the Williams era is even suggested. The calypso ends with the captain desperately signalling an SOS to the IMF from a lifeboat somewhere.

"The Sinking Ship", great kaiso that it undoubtedly is, yet illustrates a most curious feature of Trinidad's political culture: that even when people have before them all the facts necessary for arriving at balanced judgements, they may prefer to live by fictions of their own manufacture and closer to the heart's fantasies. Calypsonians had, as we have shown, explored the decline of Dr. Williams's PNM while Williams was alive. Mr. Chambers had inherited an already sinking ship. But the myth of Mr. Chambers's stupidity, taking shape around the same time as his 50% currency devaluation, had become a necessary complement to the canonisation of Dr. Williams. Having died on the job, as Relator in "Take a Rest" (1980) and Delamo in "Apocalypse" (1980)[7] had predicted he might, his ashes floating on the Gulf of Paria into which he had once told those who voted against the PNM to jump, Dr. Williams had undergone "a sea-change into something rich and strange."[8]

He was now a combination of saint, martyr and scornfully retributive spirit, thumbing his nose at Trinidadians, on whose uselessness he had often expatiated, and sneering with calypsonian Penguin at their discomfiture:

> Betty goatie
> Betty goatie
> I doing well
> Is **dem** in hell

Dead, Dr. Williams is depicted as having escaped for good the hell of being Prime Minister of Trinidad. Free at last, free at last, he is beyond scapegoating; beyond, too, the absurd burden described since 1958 by the Mighty Striker of patching Anabella's stockings, holding up Johnson's trousers or providing the unfortunate Dorothy with a new man. It is now his turn to mock at all who had lived off his energy, taken for granted his dedication and finally done him to death with the teachers' and nurses' agitation of 1980.

Penguin employs the device of the voice from the grave to explore the bitter, resentful consciousness of the leader after the process of scapegoating has been completed. Beneath its tone of sardonic triumph, the voice seeks desperately to vindicate itself, to heal the bruised ego, to put on record all its years of effort in service of the nation. There has been no similar calypso that has sought imaginatively to explore what the still living Mr. Chambers might be feeling in his self-imposed exile of silence and invisibility. One has had, instead, the very opposite: Cardinal's "Jump In" (1988) in which the former Prime Minister is among those being hilariously rounded up at gun point and herded into a waiting police van to answer various charges of misdemeanour, and a calypso by Dr. Soca, a singing gynaecologist, entitled "The Blonde", which ridiculed the ex-Prime Minister for his alleged but unsubstantiated involvement in one of the ancillary scandals in the Great O'Halloran Affair.

II: Change: Enter the Dragon

By the time that the NAR assumed power, then, public consciousness had gone through several dimensions of disillusionment, beneath which lay an unarticulated rage that needed only to define its object. Penguin's "The Devil" (1980) had established that a diabolical capacity resided within human consciousness, informing social and political life and controlling how important institutions functioned. Devils exist in business, halls of justice and police uniforms; they are child abusers, and top members of the political directorate. ("Some like to deck in suit whole day / And round their neck a balisier"). Stalin's "Vampires" (1981) employs a different image with much the same purpose in mind: that of identifying a diabolical element within political process. It would require little imagination to make the shift from metaphor to actuality; from a notion of the diabolical to the literal belief in politics as spiritual warfare between angels of light and the demons of darkness; between "messengers of God" and the dragons of hell; between the redeemed, the born-again and the unregenerate.

Johnny King's "Nature's Plan" (1984), Chalkdust's "White Man's Plan" (1985) and "Grandfather's Backpay" (1985), then Stalin's "Bun Dem" (1987) all provided indices as to how the "enemy" was being defined; what face he was being given. Taken together, these calypsos offered an array of enemies for the gratification of public revenge: Nature, the white race, History, "dem French Creoles" and in the case of Stalin's "Bun Dem" a long list of the historic enemies of Africans at home and abroad.

"Bun Dem", like Shadow's "Judgement Day" or indeed Kamau Brathwaite's "Dies Irie" in *X/Self*, employs as its central metaphor the very Christian notion of the Day of Judgement. Such a day, in Black Stalin's estimation, can make sense only if it involves a reappraisal and a deconstruction of all the symbols of oppressive history. Judgement Day is the climax of the Apocalypse in which Columbus, Queen Victoria, Botha, Mussolini, Hitler, Margaret Thatcher, the Ku Klux Klan, along with a few contemporary Caribbean political leaders who are seen as maintaining or supporting structures of oppression, are all accused, arraigned, condemned and consigned to eternal hellfire. All of these greater or lesser figures or figureheads of history parade before the gate of heaven, whose keepers are Saint Peter and Black Stalin who functions as a sort of junior prosecutor, plaintiff and judge rolled into one; one who has the special knowledge of atrocities perpetrated against the non-white races that, presumably, St. Peter lacks in his own voluminous cosmic computer. All are joyously cast into the fire.

One can find this dream of judgement, condemnation and retribution running through all Black literatures – whether that of the African American Church whose sermons re-enact it each week, or in its poetry and drama. It is there in the movement towards Apocalypse in Brathwaite's *The Arrivants* and *X/Self*, it is satirised in Walcott's *Dream on Monkey Mountain* but reappears in "The Schooner *Flight*" with Shabine's declaration that he holds the fate of these countries and their governments in his hands. Even the act of satire in *Dream on Monkey Mountain* acknowledges the presence and potency of the apocalyptic dream. This dream is sometimes enacted in the actual burning and looting of cities, which are the oppressive Babylon of many a reggae song.

If during the *ancien régime* of the PNM the idea of a constant cataloguing of slow disintegration had become a doleful habit of seeing into the death of things, under the NAR it would also involve the dream of fire, the notion of retribution, the identification, preparation and slaughter of the scapegoat. The passive apprehension of apocalypse under the degenerate PNM became transformed in the twinkling of an eye into the active cry for political Armageddon after the accession of the NAR. The reasons for this are more complex than our analysts have so far suggested.

Even before the 1986 Elections the NAR, particularly its ONR element, had been associated with big business interests. These interests had flowered under the PNM whose achievement had not been to erode old money, but to midwife the emergence of a new class of professionals, businessmen and public servants even as they created a huge state sector that wielded greater economic power than the old elite. Williams never forgot that the old money was alive, and as late as the late seventies he was still talking about the P.O.P.P.G as being a threat to what the PNM stood for, though the P.O.P.P.G. as a formal unit had disintegrated in the fifties, and the conglomeration of business, class and ethnic interests represented by that party had long formed other and more complex alignments in independent Trinidad and Tobago.

Yet Chalkdust would in "Trinidad Ent Change" (1992) state that the old P.O.P.P.G. was now the NAR. Having already identified "dem French Creoles" as the inveterate enemies of Black people, Chalkdust must be viewed as a major reinforcer of the Eric Williams engendered notion that PNM as a party of Black people were still being threatened by the P.O.P.P.G. – a party of French Creoles, big businessmen, the old mulatto and off-white upper middle class, whose apparent return to power, authority and visibility under the NAR was most bitterly resented by the new Black Yuppie professionals who had grown to savour the taste of power and patronage under the PNM. When the NAR assumed power under the banner of "One Love", many of their core supporters had already been identified as old P.O.P.P.G. / "French Creole" / big business off-white / mulatto types.

There was a deep terror of change felt even by those who had voted for it. Crusoe Kid's "Change" of the previous decade had signalled this fear of change. The question "Who we go put?" had been asked over and over again by calypsonians such as Pretender who in "Black Power" (1971) sang "I aint holding no brief for Dr. Willie /But who we go put if we move he?" Fearing change, the electorate returned the PNM in 1976 and 1981 with increased majorities, and would demand of the NAR when it replaced the PNM in 1986, instant, total and painless change.

Protector's "We Talking Change" (1989) is typical of how people felt. Protector, like Luta in 1986, called for a change in attitude on the part of the people. While, however, Luta's calypso was clearly directed to the nation, whose collective responsibility it was to transform national sensibility, Protector's real message seems to be that a new government has not produced change in the national attitude. "We Talking Change" juxtaposes disillusionment at such long standing ills as reckless driving, venereal diseases, rip-off vendors and big businessmen, the uncouth behaviour of males towards females, racial prejudice and street crime. When all of these abuses have been corrected (he doesn't say by whom, people or Government or both) he will then hold his hand in the air and shout "One Love", the NAR slogan.

It sounded plausible, but it also sounded self-righteous, and it was unfair to expect that total social transformation, which had only been fitfully demanded of the *ancien régime*, would even begin to be achieved by the NAR in two or three years and without the concerted effort of the nation as a whole. Between 1987 and 1992, calypsos chronicled the trauma of political succession occasioned by the end of thirty unbroken years of PNM rule. Shocked, terrified at its own temerity in destroying the only political establishment that two generations of Trinidadians and Tobagonians had known, the nation, via the mass media, calypsonians and that tangled grapevine of malicious gossip and genuine social horror which sustains its cathartic weekly Press, placed the new NAR regime under severe, incessant, microscopic and at times malign scrutiny. Its every twitch was observed, analysed and commented on with a scepticism that flowered into scorn as the NAR not only did not magically transform the society into Protector's desired utopia, but instituted harsh budgets in an attempt to service the enormous debts they had inherited.

Consisting of elements of the traditional government and the whole of the traditional opposition, the NAR was a collection of misunderstandings, a confusion of political styles which ranged from stiff dignified authoritarianism to the rowdy histrionic populism that had characterised the ULF in opposition. The party split along the stress-lines of its contradictions and could not develop the flexibility of spirit or courtesy of discourse to strengthen the weak coalition that it was, into something that could transcend the traditional perspectives and move beyond the contours of a frozen, paralysed and fragmentary political tribalism. The NAR never quite legitimised itself and after its fragmentation never regained the confidence of a public that had to begin with been frightened of change. It had also made itself vulnerable to the bitter criticism of its enemies.

Response to the NAR was generally partisan and often hysterical. The government's achievements were few in the first two bruising years, which they claimed were spent assessing the dimensions of the chasm into which the country had fallen, and seeking, outside the tentacles of the IMF, loans for a holding operation. Their considerable achievements began to manifest themselves from midterm: many primary schools built or repaired within the budget; San Fernando elevated to city status with a rebuilt and improved Naparima Bowl as its much-needed cultural centre; the St. Paul's Multipurpose Complex constructed, giving an immediate lift to sport and creative activity in South East Port of Spain; the Mount Hope

Hospital opened as the UWI Faculty of Medicine and School of Dentistry in Trinidad; the Rudranath Capildeo Learning Resource Centre constructed in Couva; bus terminus stations converted into clean, airy, aesthetically pleasing structures, with space for vending; administrative centres for the proposed counties built; many self-help schemes successfully carried out, some bringing running water and electricity to areas of the country which had never enjoyed these privileges; industrial cottages, youth training programmes, farmland; the crucial revitalisation of Trinidad's relationship with her CARICOM neighbours, after the long years of Eric Williams's contemptuous disdain for a region that owed Trinidad money; vigorous, honourable and responsible foreign policy; a serious stand against corruption; the Tobago runway lengthened to accommodate jumbo jets, and the Tobago Deep Water Harbour constructed and accommodating the largest cruise ships. These achievements were generally ignored and even ridiculed as "elections gimmicks", and the nation was encouraged constantly to contemplate how badly off it was in comparison with former years. It is interesting to note, however, that every foreign popular concert was selling over 15,000 and 20,000 tickets; very few entertainment events were not fully patronised and almost all holiday flights to North America were and still are fully booked. The fact is that NAR learned to counterbalance wage cuts with drastic reductions in the marginal rates of taxation.

Calypsonians echoed popular sentiment and became more than ever the unofficial opposition to the Government that Valentino had in the seventies defined them as being. Afraid, like the rest of the society, and lacking the special courage that was required if the various interest groups and ethnoses were to move outside of the accustomed contours, the frozen configurations of the past, calypsonians returned with a vengeance to the old habit of cataloguing decay, the old perspectives of disintegration. The challenge was to accept the idea of change, to define a programme of work and to work stoically for change in face of whatever pressures circumstances might generate. Denyse Plummer with "A Nation Forges On" (1988), Stalin with "We Can Make It if We Try" (1987) and "Look on the Brighter Side" (1991), Tambu Herbert with "The Journey Now Start" (1989) and David Rudder who in the "Power and the Glory" (1988) felt "a new spirit" rising, provided the strong, healing, courageous songs which the nation needed in what was a wholly original and tremendous setting forth.

But on the whole, most social/political calypsos between 1987 and 1992 were documentaries of disintegration. Their themes were the same as during the time of the *ancien régime*, the PNM years: hunger, unemployment, social decay, crumbling institutions and racial animosity. They also dealt quite directly with issues such as the NAR's tax measures, stressing of course, the wage cuts but omitting the compensatory tax-cuts at the marginal rates. They celebrated the leadership crisis and the party schism (e.g. Cro Cro "Three Bo' Rats", 1988; Watchman "Attack with Full Force", 1991)

The nurses' strike was mentioned as one of the reasons for the 1990 insurrection in several 1991 calypsos. The fear of censorship, strong in Chalkdust's "Who Next" (1972) Stalin's "Nothing Ain't Strange" (1975) Sparrow's "Sedition" (1972) and "Prophet of Doom" (1983), was revived in Black Stalin's "Nah Ease Up" (1990) Sugar Aloes's "The Judge" (1990), "My Decision" (1991), and mentioned scornfully in Watchman's "Attack with Full Force" (1991) and Pink Panther's "For the Good Times" (1991). Suggestions by the Prime Minister after the insurrection that singers should compose more "nation-building" calypsos were interpreted to be a threat of censorship, while Sugar Aloes assumed that his demotion by carnival judges from second to fifth place, after a recounting of their score sheets, had to be due to direct interference by "Robbie", who had the year before expressed his disagreement with the judges' high placing of that singer in the Dimanche Gras Competition.

The issue of divestment of state-owned assets, one of the hot debates of 1990, was well treated in De Fosto's "Trinidad for Sale" (1991). A devoted worshipper of Dr. Williams whose doleful eulogy he had composed in 1981, De Fosto was a willing mouthpiece for *ancien régime* sentimentality, which held it sacrilege for Trinidad to sell any of its state-owned enterprises, regardless of whether these enterprises were recording profits or, as in the case of ISCOTT, daily and phenomenal losses.

During the five years of the NAR government, calypsonians, following the cue of journalists, opinion pollsters, fundamentalist cult leaders and embattled trade unionists, functioned mainly as the delegitimisers of the NAR who, as we said, had lost public confidence because of terrible dissension and ultimate disintegration. It may be argued, then, that calypsonians did not so much delegitimise the NAR as highlight the fact that the party had on its own lost the brief legitimacy it had enjoyed as the first truly "national" and broadly multi-ethnic party in Trinidad and Tobago. Yet, when one considers the tone of the most successful calypsos, the partisan positions openly adopted by some singers, and the biased content of many calypsos, one must conclude that the majority of political calypsos between 1987 and 1991 did not just describe, but actively contributed to the process by which the NAR was delegitimising itself.

The contribution of calypsonians to the delegitimisation of NAR assumed three interlocking phases: excoriation, disembowelment and finally interment. The first sign of excoriation, the flaying of the skin off the regime, occurred in 1987, a few weeks after the government assumed office, when the retributive venom of Black Stalin's "Bun Dem" was channelled away from a cadre of international figures – Hitler, Mussolini, Columbus, Drake, Raleigh, Queen Victoria, Ian Smith, Botha, Margaret

Thatcher, Eugenia Charles – towards the political directorate in Trinidad and Tobago. Within a month, the NAR with its first budget, which suspended public servants' cost of living allowance, had become fuel for the righteous hell-fires of the Apocalypse. Supporters of the defeated PNM, meanwhile, assuaged their bitterness by narrowing down the dimension of Merchant's "Pain" from its general expression of world-sorrow to their own localised self-pity at having lost the elections.

Part of the bitterness against the NAR lay in the fact that it sought to improve infrastructure in Tobago to facilitate the growth of tourism there. Projects to extend the Crown Point runway and deepen the harbour at Scarborough, which PNM administrations had been promising to do for over two decades, and the NAR had set about doing, were viewed with envy and meanness by some Trinidadians as Robinson's attempt to improve his home-base, Tobago, at Trinidad's expense, even though it was pointed out that far less than ten percent of the budget had been assigned to Tobago's development. The rivalry between the sister-islands was dramatised in Sugar Aloes's "The Argument" (1988) and Tobago Crusoe's "Get on with the Job" (1988), the latter of which suggested that a Tobago point of view was that Trinidadians had rejected Robinson because he was a Tobagonian, one who had been defeating the PNM in Tobago since 1976. Crusoe advised Robinson to quit Trinidad if that island continued to scorn his efforts, and return home to Tobago where he would be welcome.

Flaying continued with calypsos such as Cro Cro's "Three Bo' Rats" (1988) which caricatured and ridiculed the leadership rivalry within the NAR; Watchman's "Positive Vibrations" (1990) which suggested assassination as a modest proposal to terminate the NAR regime, and Chalkdust's witty "Chaffeur Wanted" (1989) which compared the Prime Minister to an incompetent unlicensed chauffeur, and the members of parliament to unruly and at times drunken passengers, some of whom were trying to tug at the steering-wheel while the maxi-taxi was in motion. In the entire scenario, one factor was constant: the narrowing down of "the Enemy" from history, the white man, the ruling class and the French Creoles to "Robbie", who apparently had come to represent all these agencies in his person. Arrogance and vindictiveness were changes successfully laid at Mr. Robinson's door, from which he could find no refuge. The charges of "arrogance" related to what was termed his "leadership style". The charges of "vindictiveness" related to his reading in Parliament of the Drug Report and calling of names of former PNM ministers in relation to the Drug Report, as well as his successful pursuit of the O'Halloran Affair and exposure, at the Opposition's persistent request, of those who were allegedly involved in it. Robinson became metamorphosed from what Valentino in "No Revolution" (1971) had termed "a man with love and feeling for his people", into an object of hate.

His party was accused of heartlessness and bitterly blamed for events such as the termination of the school-feeding programme, which had in fact happened in mid-1986 towards to the end of the Chambers regime. Although that programme was resumed and expanded by the NAR in their midterm, many calypsonians in 1990 and 1991 still blamed them for its stoppage. Between 1989 and 1990 some calypsonians learned to add a special "Robbie" stanza to their tent performances in order to gain automatic applause. The Prime Minister was accused by Sugar Aloes in "Public Advice" (1989) of having signed a "pact" with presumably evil forces and having replaced a weathercock atop the Red House with a "dragon". This dragon had been directly responsible for the drowning of five children from a Laventille family one afternoon at Carenage and for the explosion of corroded dynamite at Camp Omega in which six soldiers had died. A fundamentalist preacher wrote a number of articles concerning the dreadful implications of having a dragon-serpent presiding over one's national affairs.

Robinson replied to Sugar Aloes that *he* had never replaced the weathercock by a dragon. The dragon was a PNM installation for which he was being wrongly blamed. He also felt that Sugar Aloes had been placed too high in the Calypso King Finals of 1989; that he was " the property of the PNM" and should not have been in the finals in the first place. This naturally led to the outcry coming from Sugar Aloes, Watchman and Chalkdust that limits were being imposed on the calypsonian's freedom of expression; that the art form was being censored. Sugar Aloes proudly proclaimed his loyalty to the PNM. "As an adult," he said, "I reaped all the benefits I have today and for my fourteen (14) children from the PNM. I am not an ungrateful person." (*The Sun*, Weekend, March 3-5, 1989. p. 3). He continued to sing to undermine the NAR, focusing with even greater severity on the Prime Minister in his 1990 composition, "The Judge" and in his 1991 offering, "My Decision".

Discussion on the dragon issue disclosed that both Sugar Aloes and Mr. Robinson were wrong about its origin. Gerry Besson, local historian and publisher, dated it as being more than eighty years old. Ardent PNM supporters, however, swore that they had once seen a weathercock atop the Red House. Ironically, one piece of visual evidence which at least proves that the dragon predated the NAR regime, was a photograph of the Red House printed in the 1981 PNM Manifesto on page 118, which displays the tiny but quite distinctive shape of the dragon on the weathervane. The silly issue died, only to be resurrected after the 1990 insurrection when it helped reinforce a popular notion that the insurrection and the fires which accompanied it were the work of the dragon and fitting retribution for a mythologically "evil" regime. Between 1989 and 1990 it was customary to read words such as "evil", "wicked" or "diabolical" in articles or letters referring to the Prime Minister and his economic measures. The "conditionalities" imposed by the IMF were also referred to as "draconian" and the phrase, "the IMF dragon" became quite common in the discourse of this period of demonisation. Commentor in 1990 sang a calypso entitled "Dragonslayer". On the jacket of the album in which this song is recorded is depicted a dragon of huge proportions squatting on the Twin Towers, and being pulled down by a determined group of workers and common folk.

Constructed with some intelligence, "Dragonslayer" is one of those calypsos like "The Sinking Ship", "Vampires", "Chauffeur Wanted" or "Apocalypse" that builds its argument around a single central image or conceit which is extended throughout the calypso. Here it is that figure of the traditional carnival, the dragon, and his band of imps, symbolising the IMF and members of the Government of Trinidad and Tobago. The argument of the calypso is a simple, orthodox one: that whenever a country accepts an IMF loan, it increases its burden of debt, sacrifices its economic independence, and puts its people under such pressure that social upheaval becomes inevitable. After having observed the effects of the IMF in Brazil, Jamaica and Nicaragua, Trinidad and Tobago should have avoided the IMF dragon.

The effect of "Dragon Slayer", however, has to do not so much with this fairly trite, if partially true argument, but with Commentor's successful blending of the folklore of both the popular "Science Fantasy" novels and the folklore of the traditional Trinidad Carnival, in presenting the case against the IMF. It has to do with the fictional presentation of the rather grim struggle by which Trinidad, like the rest of the Caribbean basin and the other "developing" nations, was now beset, as she reluctantly adjusted to economic recession.

> They playing mas with poor people future
> Boasting how they ain't fraid powder
> The band sponsor from the USA
> "Imps and Dragon" he tell them play
> The imps in the House of Power
> Squeezing the poor endlessly
> Cause the Dragon there on the tower
> We blood can't satisfy he
>
> They cut way half o we salary
> Pum pum pum they feeding the Dragon
> [...]
> Dragon up dey – Pull the Dragon down
> Cutting we tail – Pull the Dragon down
> We cyan see the way – Pull the Dragon down
> Dragon up dey – Pull the Dragon down

The "Dragon" becomes the *cause* of the nation's indebtedness, rather than the agency to which the Government reluctantly went after facing a bankrupt treasury and trying to avoid going to the IMF for two years. Their critics in the PNM opposition, indeed, chided them for not having gone to the IMF sooner. Commentor condemns them from the opposite end, for going at all and thus dishonouring their elections' promise.

> Election time they say have no fear
> The Dragon will never come down here
> The first time the imps get a chance
> You know they bring the Dragon to dance
> He samba on top o' Brazil
> He skank down in Jamaica
> He doing a Debt-Trap boogie
> To wipe out Nicaragua
>
> Mass retrenchment and more lock out
> Pum, pum, pum, they feeding the Dragon
> To push we more in the Dragon mouth
> Pum, pum, pum, they feeding the Dragon

The calypso does not go far enough in its analysis. It suggests no way of avoiding the debt-trap. It evades the fact that "mass retrenchment" and "lockouts" were the order of the day between 1985 and 1986 and actually slowed down somewhat between 1987 and 1989, while inflation was controlled by the NAR midterm. It also omits the adjustments in the tax structure which tended to soften the effect of the wage cuts here exaggeratedly listed as "half o we salary". In fact, "Dragonslayer" is yet another illustration of the kind of biased analysis that has been typical of the majority of our commentators over the past six years. For while it is true to represent the IMF as an instrument in the hands of metropolitan economic imperialism and to view its designs on the Caribbean as part of a wider hemispheric strategy of control, it is not true that the IMF caused Trinidad to wander into the Valley of Debt. For that error, Trinidad, particularly Trinidad of the 1974 to 1984 decade, has only itself to blame.

So "Dragonslayer" is both naive and specious when it attributes the failure of financial and other institutions in Trinidad to the Dragon's insatiable appetite for peoples' organisations.

> Aliens land holding the Dragon back
> He tell the imps go and change the act
> He eat up Workers Bank and Telco
> [...]
> Into the Valley of Debt (Death?)
> He eyeing we bank NCB
> He goh nyam we whole alphabet

The Workers' Bank foundered because it had overextended its credit during the wildcat decade from the mid-seventies to the mid-eighties. The more careful NCB was also faced by a spate of bad debts. The PTSC had for decades been running at a loss and was now in an era when the state, itself bankrupt through the delirious investment practices of the last five years of the Eric Williams regime, could no longer afford to subsidise the Corporation. TELCO, whose long and miserable record had been wickedly satirised since the late seventies when they were at their worst, by Penguin in "TELCO Poops" (1979), could not be accurately viewed as a victim of the IMF. During the wildcat boom period the nation had pumped millions of dollars into TELCO for lines not laid, for phones that never worked, and to get which involved a long and shamefully humiliating ordeal of waiting, sometimes for five or six or even ten years.

Thus, while the dire consequences of going to the IMF certainly deserved rigorous analysis in calypsos and elsewhere, "Dragonslayer" does not upon close examination display the mixture of subtlety and balance to do what it is trying to do: provide the nation with advice and insight that could either show them a way out of the impasse, or imbue them with a positive spirit to endure the hard times. Like all the others it appeals to the gut response in a time of crisis. It also helped reinforce – perhaps without meaning to – the more atavistic interpretation of the "dragon" image, in which the real woes of the country became attributable to a fetish object, to evil sorcery, devil-dealing, the satanic pact of the obeahman from Castara. Margaret Hector, a NAR minister, who happened to be a Spiritual Baptist leader, said in an interview that people used to refer to her as "Robinson's Minister of Obeah" (*Sunday Express* May 5, 1991, p. 13).

The PNM exploited popular superstition during the 1991 elections campaign by attributing fires that destroyed houses and businesses in Port of Spain to work of the "Dragon". The carved walking-stick which an admirer presented the wounded Prime Minister after his Red House ordeal was rumoured to be a "mounted" magician's wand.[9] His state visit to Africa in 1991 became, according to local folklore, a trip made for the purposes of acquiring obeah. The first and still the most ridiculous public act of the newly elected PNM would be a midnight exorcism in which the "evil" sea-serpent/dragon/weather vane was removed and an indiscriminate winged-object, decreed by a respected zoology professor to be a mixture of dove and vulture, bearing another indiscriminate object, a mixture of olive branch and crown of thorns, installed in its stead. Calypsonian Frisco, who in 1991 sang "Wizard: Take Down the Dragon" would claim credit for the removal of the serpent. Protector, disappointed at NAR's failure to produce Utopia, sang "Satan", another calypso of 1991 whose aim was to demonise the political regime.

The scapegoating of Mr. Robinson has been a most remarkable aspect of political process in contemporary Trinidad. It has involved the awakening and channelling of folk superstition; the replacement of empirical historical analysis by gut-response and hysteria; the encouragement of a constant rhetoric of diabolization, such as the one employed by Errol

McLeod of the OWTU in his Divali messages, in which the Government and the employer class were characterised as "Rawan", the Hindu black, skinned demon-god,[10] whom the working class would, by the holy light of their rhetoric, overcome some day.

An atavistic situation was created in which the sacrifice of the scapegoat, and his replacement by a reputedly born-again Christian would somehow lead to the redemption of the nation. After nearly a year, the millennium has still not arrived, The vortex of the NAR years has simply become the void of the PNM renaissance; but the void lies at the centre of a now unacknowledged hurricane, that seems merely to be biding its time before it howls again.

III: The Soca Fires of 1990

If real corruption could have been presented as "Soca Corruption" by Grandmaster Kitchener as he experienced the silent, slow Apocalypse in 1983, real fire just as easily became "soca fire" in the aftermath of the 1990 holocaust. 1990 could truthfully be termed the climax of both the "Soca" – that is the desire for cathartic escape from reality through hard-pounding frenzy – and the dream of a refining or avenging fire that had haunted calypso for two decades since the Black Power apotheosis of 1970. Calypsonians given to shamanistic prophecy claimed, truthfully to have predicted the events. Black Stalin, for example, one month after the insurrection declared

> In times like these, when you have a crisis, it is when the art form and creativity blossoms. We should see a healthy Carnival. If the truth is really to be told, it is up to us, the calypsonians to tell it, *for we are the true prophets of this nation.*
>
> To prove this, the calypsonian prophesied what happened here recently a long time ago in song. In "Nah Ease Up", I listed a total of sixteen ills that the man in the street and the voters were fed up with. Nobody in authority paid heed to it. You can't blame any one person for what happened. We must all share the blame.
>
> When I sang in this year's semifinal, only my performance was not shown on television, due to 'technical difficulties'. Yet, when the Imam took over, one of the first things shown was that performance, although it was not supposed to have been taped. There are people in high places who continue to play games with the art and the artist.[11]

Stalin was correct. Calypsonians, as this study has sought to illustrate, had for decades, been providing a continuous chronicle on developments in social and political life. The sixteen abuses that Stalin had listed in "Nah Ease Up" (1990) were little different from all the things that Protector wanted to see instantaneously changed in "We Talking Change" (1989). Stalin's basic peeve was the same as Sugar Aloes's, Watchman's, Cro Cro's and Chalkdust's, in whose ranks as people's voices, "serving every constituency," he located himself. NAR politicians, he claimed, had threatened censorship and sent "warnings" to the more aggressive political calypsonians. Stalin reclaimed the calypsonian's freedom to sing whatever he felt about whom he pleased, without observing any limits on this freedom of speech. There should be no limits placed on the articulation of the people's needs or complaints. Stalin, like Chalkdust and Watchman sought not merely to preserve, but also to extend the freedom and immunity won by calypsonians over the years. One of the developments since the 1970s has been the steady extension by the calypsonian of the tent's privileged space into areas of normal civic life. This has posed as many problems for the eighties as it did for the thirties and forties because, though the calypsonian has increasingly included the methodologies of the investigative journalist, and the analysis of the academic expert, he remains what he always was, a creator of fictions, whose raw material includes rumours, gossip, commesse, hunch, half-truths, the rawness of the average gut response. Such raw materials have led the calypsonian both to accurate conclusions about politicians and social processes, and to character assassination.

In a society where journalists often do not verify the facts of the stories they present, calypsonians, operating in a medium that feeds on constant mixtures of fact and fiction, see little reason why they should present balanced or factually accurate accounts of social and political experience. As with all other satirists, they affirm the freedom to arrive at general truths via distortion and caricature. Beginning with this quest for an extension of the privileged space of the tent, the calypsonian of the eighties has assumed the right to a one-sided monopoly of discourse, which is every bit as authoritarian as the power-structure he attacks. He doesn't want or permit the people he attacks to reply. In other words, what the contemporary calypsonian seeks is a people's monologue which ultimately becomes the monologue of his own individual voice, that he attunes to the shifting currents of public opinion. What he seeks is the same power and authority as the politician, who is as careful in the masking of his deficiencies as the calypsonian is relentless in unmasking them.

Stalin in "Nah Ease Up" recognizes this almost natural opposition of interests between the calypsonian and the political directorate. The political directorate, he says, embraces the calypsonian only when he sings in praise of the regime, but wants to prevent him from singing unpleasant truths about the regime's performance. Sparrow, a major legitimizer of the early PNM in the fifties, had arrived at the same conclusion as he parted company with that party in the eighties. "Prophets of Doom" (1983) begins with the same complaint as Stalin's "Nah Ease Up" seven years later, or, indeed, his "Nothing Ain't Strange" of 1975. Little has changed on the frontier of masking and unmasking, defence and attack where political directors and the people's spokespersons confront each other.

But Stalin was defending much more than just his right to sing the unpalatable truth. He was also defending his standing in the world of calypsonians, his image, powerful since Black Power days, of being one of the fearless critics of the *ancien régime*. There had been signs since 1985 with "Sing for the Land" and later "We Can Make It If We Try" (1988) that Stalin had mellowed into a patriotic moralist, a transformation that the current political regime under constant attack on all fronts, would have welcomed in more calypsonians. Stalin's patriotism was regarded by his fellow-flagellants as a sign that he was softening towards the system. Some saw in his beautiful anthem "We Can Make It If We Try" (1985), sure signs of his having sold out to the regime, as they had accused Gypsy, whose "Sinking Ship" (1986) had been played on NAR platforms during the 1986 elections campaign, and Chris Tambu Herbert, whose "The Journey Now Start" (1989) had been adopted by the Ministry of Sport and Culture as the theme-song for the T & T football team before it stumbled "on the road to Italy".

Stalin's new severity of tone in "Nah Ease Up" was meant to be a reminder to excoriating and disembowelling calypsonians of a slightly younger generation that the veteran singer was still capable of inflicting serious blows on the system; that he was still part of the brotherhood, and despite his earlier call for courage, patience and sustained effort at self-redemption, self-liberation, he was on the side of the people, and not of their leaders. "Nah Ease Up" complains about the ten percent wage cut, but does not mention the thirty-five percent reduction from a maximum marginal rate of taxation of 70% to 35% or the abolition of the Unemployment Levy. Other complaints involved the question of racial disharmony, a hardy perennial in Trinidad's politics,[12] which had abated somewhat after the NAR coalition of the major ethnic constituencies, then flared up anew when the party split asunder between 1987 and 1988. The perception was that the NAR leadership had failed the electorate, though it was equally true that the electorate itself lacked the energy or depth of desire to convert the rhetoric of racial unity into a lasting reality.

Stalin does not attempt to explore the extent to which some calypsonians' unbridled freedom in articulating their own racial positions and preferences may have contributed to the increase in "racial talk" he complains about in "Nah Ease Up". Ironically, his own "Caribbean Unity" (or "The Caribbean Man", 1979) had generated a lengthy debate on whether an Afrocentric view of Caribbean reality should not be equated with racism.[13] The next calypso to evoke such extreme debate on the race issue was Cro Cro's "Corruption in Common Entrance" (1988). The question to be asked, then, was whether in a country predisposed to racial discourse it was fair to lay so much blame on the political directorate and omit all the other types of commentator who had added to racial discourse in the eighties.

"Nah Ease Up" also accused the Government of forgetting the electorate, not consulting the people, going to the IMF and spreading heartbreak and sorrow. These accusations recur in most of the political calypsos of the period. The general perception seems to have been that NAR deliberately chose the worst of a number of options that were open to them. What the other softer options were was unfortunately not made clear by the many political and economic geniuses who pervaded the print and electronic media in those days. Calypsonians, too, were at a loss for viable alternatives in a situation where options were few and uniformly painful, and choice limited to what Conrad in *Heart of Darkness* termed, "a choice between nightmares". On reflection, Stalin's call for patience and long-suffering in "We Can Make It If We Try" (1988), Sparrow's plea to the society to avoid racial confrontation in "We Can Make It Easy if We Try" (1991), were more realistic attitudes to adopt under the circumstances, than one of embattled futility which in the end changed little, solved nothing and destroyed much.

Thus while it is true to say that many calypsonians had "prophesied" the events of 1990, it is also true to say that few of them had been able to see beneath the " taut surfaces of things."[14] The most popular of them were satisfied to provoke, feed on and remain at gut responses. There was a remarkable absence of candour, balance or fairness in our national sensibility, and calypsonians trading on the gut response did little to create such qualifies. Absence of balance, an inevitable prerequisite for, as well as product of the ritualistic frenzy necessary for scapegoating, ultimately took the form of the 1990 insurrection, the looting and gutting of the city, the totally unnecessary deaths of the twenty-four victims, and the shallowness of many of the responses to such a catastrophe.

The range of response in calypsos and non-calypso songs to the events of July 1990, was extremely wide, though most songs carefully avoided the depths of the catastrophe. Many indeed viewed the occasion only as the ultimate illustration of what the "wickedness" of a "heartless" government had produced. Some of the calypsos of this category were Cro Cro's "Say a Prayer for Abu Bakr", Kenny J's "Say a Prayer for T & T", Pink Panther's "For the Good Times", Stalin's "Revolution Time", Iwer George's "Rough Neck", Rikki Jai's "Another Bakr Will Come", Mastertone's "2001", Trini's "Animal Farm", Cardinal's "Abu Coup" and Sugar Aloes's "My Decision". Such calypsos employed a wide variety of musical structures and verbal strategies, but often had similar content. Most saw the insurrection not as something that had been planned years earlier and the arms for which purchased and smuggled in several months before. They rather focused on the social disaffection to which they saw the insurrection as a justifiable reaction.

Apart from the COLA, 10% and VAT issues, the nurses' strike and the price of school books, calypsonians highlighted the charge of the Prime

Minister's "arrogance", which Sugar Aloes and Pink Panther among others illustrated with the untruth that he left his society in crisis to watch the World Cup Finals in Italy. The NAR who reintroduced school-feeding on a wider scale in 1988, were blamed for the PNM's stoppage of it in mid-1986. Some called for sympathy not for the victims of the insurrection but for the insurrectionists. A few expressed disappointment that the Prime Minister had not been murdered. "If Abu had shot and wiped out the whole Cabinet," sings Iwer George in "Rough Neck", a rare variation from his usual "bam-bam" and "juck-waist" theme, "he would have been here tonight." Sugar Aloes complains in "My Decision" (1991):

> We all wanted the system changed
> But we had a better way
> Not for someone to start something
> Then do the job half way.

His regret is that the wrong people were killed.

> When I see so much innocent people
> Lost their lives in vain
> While the real culprits still alive
> To give poor people more strain

Bakr emerges from these calypsos as people's hero. Iwer George comments on the necessity for the common man to be a "rough neck" to survive "under Robbie now". Dr. P.K., Patrick Watson, a singing economist from UWI, St. Augustine in "Support the Amnesty", viewed Bakr as a revolutionary hero and called on the state to release the Muslimeen without testing the amnesty's validity in court. Cardinal in "Nation Building" also viewed it as pointless to spend so much money on the Muslimeen trial instead of on a worthier project such as the proposed Arima hospital. On the other hand, Happy, a much underrated Tobago calypsonian, contemplating the genesis of a new world-consciousness in the destruction of the Berlin Wall, obliquely criticises the coup attempt in "Make Love Not War", as an example of obsolete political thought and action.

> Who want to champion the poor
> Who want amnesty for breaking law
> Make love instead of war

Not so Cro Cro, who argues that Bakr, like Christ, "did it for all of us" and blames "Trinidadians" for having psyched him up, then left him in the lurch.

A number of calypsos sought to capture the drama of the time. These limited themselves to description and generally avoided moral assessment of the events. Such calypsos include Shadow's "Tempo", Brown Boy's "Looters in the City", Sparrow's "Abu Bakr Take Over" and Organiser's "Who Is Your Leader". "Looters in the City" lists the often incongruous items stolen without passing judgement on the looters who, according to this calypso, included members of the police service. If anything, this calypso celebrates the redistribution of material goods on the part of Port of Spain's sans-culottes.

> The people on the Beetham was smiling
> Because they furnish their house from Huggins
> This ain't no skylark
> Shanty Town was looking like Ellerslie Park.

There is comic focus on characters such as "big bottom Nicole" who steals "a posie and toilet-bowl" and malicious reference to the Muslimeen "looting" (i.e. shooting) "a bullet in Robbie r—s." In one line, this calypso calls for a prayer for the Muslimeen.

The police raids on looters' homes, or havens such as the Vendors' Mall in Port of Spain, are presented as comic retribution in which crooks have been caught red-handed by other crooks wearing the uniforms of the state. Named among those caught are prominent members of Kitchener's tent, where the calypso was being sung. Looting, then, is presented as comic melodrama crowned by good natured picong. The response studiously excludes anguish which, if it exists at all, is carefully concealed in five stanzas of reportage. Highlighted instead is the pragmatism of the looters who equipped themselves with clothes, schoolbooks and household items, for which the women among them received high praise from a minor political party which likes to regard itself as the conscience of the nation. One prominent clergyman claimed to "understand" why people who are hungry would loot food, but could not "understand" why they would steal "material" items such as computers, microwaves and stereo sets. A weekly columnist justified the looting as a simple reversal of the "looting" practised by the business community on the nation at large.

Looting, when viewed through the eyes of a Syrian businessman, calypsonian Anthony Salloum, Mastertone, evoked a quite different response. The calypso "2001" is doleful, not humorous. Salloum had lost his business in the soca fires of 1990. His calypso seeks to revisit the year 1990 from the vantage point, of future time, the year 2001, and through such detachment in time and mental space, to view the events of 1990 in sad perspective. The calypso "2001" evades asking the real question that is embedded and implied in it: which is, "Why do the *Black* – i.e. the Afro-Trinidadian – urban masses hate the Syrian business community with the sort of ferocity that was manifested in disproportionately large number of Syrian businesses gutted in 1990?"

Avoiding such a specific question, the real question on Salloum's mind, "2001" provides the same explanations as a score of other 1991 calypsos: harsh fiscal measures by the state placing unbearable strain on the suffering poor; the gap between the haves (among whom he is careful not to number the merchants) and the have-nots. Omitted from "2001" was the "explanation" offered by pro-Muslimeen spokespersons and accepted by Cro Cro in "Say a Prayer for Abu Bakr" that "Syrian" merchants were believed to be in control of the drug traffic. There would be greater indignation expressed in 1992 calypsos[15] over the Mansoor Affair, in which a Syrian businessman used letters written by important legal officials and vouching for the good character of his family, to lighten the prison sentence that a USA court had imposed on his dope-running son, than at the revelation in Parliament of the O'Halloran Affair, in which hundreds of millions of dollars had been gained by fraud at the expense of the people of Trinidad and Tobago.

Perhaps the best of the narrative and descriptive calypsos on the insurrection was Organizer's "Who Is Your Leader". Catchy, sweet and delivered in Organizer's clear-voiced style, this calypso describes impressions that its narrator felt on viewing the remarkable video-tape of the invasion of Parliament. It chooses as its title and point of departure the question Joseph Toney was asking of Trevor Sudama and the "Club 88" opposition faction at the moment of invasion, " Who is your leader?" It then focuses on one of the Muslimeen who, hooded strangely against the fierce desert sands of El Socorro and Barataria, was captured for a few significant seconds on candid camera taking the lead in the kicking and gun-butting of members of the House. This figure, dubbed Santa Claus in the calypso, becomes the bizarre hero of the soca invasion of Parliament.

"Who Is Your Leader" captures the drama of the event from doubly safe vantage points in time and place. The film of the invasion was first broadcast several days after the event; while the protagonist views the event from the safe vantage point of his sofa, that blessed distance from which, nightly, atrocity becomes entertainment.

> Well, my dear
> Ah siddung on mih sofa digging the scene
> I must declare
> Ah thought was war on the T.V. screen
> Ah see a fella resembling Santa
> Armed with an automatic repeater
> Indicating he ain't no joker
> He hit Toney in head
> Everybody say he dead

There are several points of significance here. First of all there was the presence of the camera in Parliament, candidly capturing all the boisterous nonsense that had been going on in there for years (c.f. e.g., Explainer's "Kicksing in Parliament", 1981). This novelty, introduced during the NAR regime, brought the light farce of parliamentary debate into the living room to such an extent that politics became more and more like the theatre it is sometimes considered to be. Lady B, indeed, in "Move the Camera" (1990) compared parliamentary behaviour under the camera's eye to a self-indulgent soap opera. Now, in 1990, the camera was capturing a bizarre drama of the Wild Western Main Road. Politics and theatre had indeed become one, and the media which had for years blithely blended fact and fiction to produce the human melodrama which our political discourse has largely been, was now presenting politics as theatre, marrying illusion and reality.

The initial reaction of many people to the appearance of the Muslimeen on the screen was that "Play of the Month" was being advertised and though it soon became clear that these actors were in deadly earnest, it was certainly difficult to shake the impression that one was participating in a weird fantasy, a grand national suspension of reality – Peter Minshall's *Rat Race*, *Danse Macabre* or *Santimanitay* transposed from their locus in the annual Carnival, and transmitted into the blind delirium of foolish flesh. The fact that the Shell Football finals were being played at the Stadium and transmitted on the radio amidst snippets of news about the insurrection, while Carnival Steelband Panorama music was being transmitted by the Muslimeen-controlled television station, simply heightened the sense of macabre farce and absurdity that emanated from the whole mindless, ghastly affair.

From the safe domestic complacency of his living-room sofa, Organizer's protagonist relaxes "digging the scene", relishing the theatre of the thing; the imagined "dance" of Ministers to blows and bullets; the rumoured sexual humiliation and emasculation. His hero is the bizarrely red-riding-hooded "Santa Claus", a costumed clown as weird as the invasion itself, and an apt symbol of the quixotic delusion that partially underlay the insurrection. Caught in the camera's fixed one-eyed stare, a line of vision as narrow as the calypsonian allows his own to become, Santa Claus deserves the dubious immortality that the calypsonian bestows on him.

The final stanza of "Who Is Your Leader" discloses, as Brown Boy's "Looters in the City" also disclosed, that beneath the carefully adopted mask of distance and objective observation, this calypso is deeply partisan and expresses the resentment of the urban underclass at the NAR, first for defeating the *ancien régime* of the PNM and then for exposing to full public view the diseased innards of the O'Halloran Affair.

> On that day
> Parliament pack with politician
> Needn't say
> All of them come with one mission
> The past regime they came there to slaughter
> With mamaguism, bad talk and laughter
> But they didn't quite get their desire
> Up came the almighty man

Who upset their evil plan

Pow! pow!pow!pow!pow!pow!
They got the answer
Ah hear prrrrrrrrrrrrrrrrrrrrrrr
Who is the leader?
Ah hear pow!pow!pow!pow!pow!pow!
No more fancy speech
Ah hear prrrrrrrrrrrrrrrrrrrrrrr
The true leader reach

What is illustrated here is the depth psychology of the scapegoating process, in which it is a repeated pattern that the person who uncovers hidden ancestral guilt is himself summarily put to death. René Girard in his extensive discourses on the phenomena of sacrifice, martyrdom and ritual murder notes that Saint Stephen had only to cry out to the Jewish Sandhedrin that their ancestors had always killed the prophets, and that they too had killed Christ, for them to stone him to death. Girard concludes that:

> The words that throw the violence back upon those who are really guilty are so intolerable that it is necessary to shut once and for all the mouth of the one who speaks them. So as not to hear him while he remains capable of speaking, the audience 'stop their ears'. How can we miss the point that they kill in order to cast off an intolerable knowledge and that this knowledge is, strangely enough, the knowledge of the murder itself?[16]

In Trinidad, the true cause of many people's cynical and bitter mockery of the humiliated parliamentarians lay in the NAR's mission – a mission particularly dear to Robinson and Richardson – to unearth matters that the *ancien régime* had worked so hard to bury. For in so doing, Robinson and Richardson were unmasking not only the PNM, but an entire culture that had grown out of its thirty years of office; a society, too, whose social and cultural mechanisms are all attuned to the task of evading moral responsibility, sidestepping moral commitment and, when these strategies fail to dispel the fact and the magnitude of corruption, outstaring guilt. The spontaneity and intensity with which so many calypsonians sang figuratively to mangle and disembowel the already physically battered NAR parliamentarians[17] clinches my contention that the nation had become caught up in a ritual of classical scapegoating at its most archetypal. In such scapegoating, guilt is transferred to the accuser, who then becomes the monstrous double of the very people he is accusing.[18] He is then run out of town and beaten or stoned to death in a frenzy of communal rage.

The calypsos of 1991 functioned largely as the cudgels and stones of our contemporary Trinidad version of the ancient mass ritual of scapegoating. Its weapons were the very ones Organizer says the NAR parliamentarians had intended to use against the *ancien régime* during the "Corruption Debate" of July 27, 1990; "mamaguism, bad talk and laughter." Mamaguism, badtalk and laughter are the staple qualities of verbal and theatrical performance in Trinidad. Powerful as weapons of reduction and flagellation, they became between 1987 and 1992 the chief means by which calypsonians helped delegitimise the NAR and reinstate the PNM. Watchman's "Attack with Full Force" was the most successful 1991 calypso of this type. Its main argument was that there was a leadership crisis in all the major parties, which had manifested itself in the NAR in terms of an attempted coup within the attempted coup. It provided no verifiable evidence to support this thesis which was the most extreme form that scapegoating and blame-shifting assumed between 1990 and 1991.

The insurrection also gave birth to less direct and more metaphorical calypsos than the ones we have been so far examining. Among these were Bally's "Calypso Coup", Lady B's "Hostages", Crazy's "Fools", Chalkdust's "You the Jury" and Rudder's "Hoosay". In these, there is a more deliberate adoption of masks. Bally for example deals with the insurrection through the mask of music itself. Lady B compares the real hostage situations in the Red House and TTT with an array of real life situations in which people are figurative hostages: the poor and hungry held "hostage" by an economic system; the householder held "hostage" by mortgage payments, the battered woman held "hostage" by the brutality of her man. Her aim, under such a transparent mask, is no different from the more direct calypsos. It is to transfer sympathy from the hostages in parliament to the citizenry at large, who are portrayed as being perpetual victims of society, politics and an inescapable network of systems and institutions.

Crazy's "Fools" invites the listener to revise his definitions of what is foolish, to include people such as the inventors of bombs, warmongers, rapists, "a Prime Minister who is a liar", whoever took away COLA and those " who divide and rule". Local political folly is juxtaposed to the macrocosmic foolishness of international politics, while the calypsonian, like the sweet-and-bitter fool in Shakespeare's *King Lear*, seeks through his own mask of wise foolishness or foolish wisdom, to goad both the local and international powers-that-be into humanity, sanity and perhaps understanding. In "You the Jury", Chalkdust presents the issue behind the metaphor of a court-hearing in which, calypso-drama style, cases are presented by prosecution and defence counsels for both the Muslimeen and the state who are both on trial. The calypso leaves judgement to the public. Such deliberate ambivalence, although soundly rooted in calypso drama tradition, is viewed by a more tendentious singer such as Watchman as Chalkdust's "two-tonguedness" (see "Leader of the Opposition", 1992) and rejected for a more direct bludgeoning of the state.

"Calypso Coup", in which occurs the idea of Soca fire from which this essay derives it name, deserves special treatment. Like Kitchener's "Soca Corruption", in which corruption becomes a national song and dance act, Bally's "Calypso Coup" illustrates the problem of reconciling a vision of horrors and blues with the mood of celebration and escapism typical of carnivals throughout the years. In 1991 this difficulty could be seen in Duke's "Get On Radical" which sought in a celebratory uptempo rhythm that masks the seriousness of its message, to censure both the insurrectionists and the masses, the shooters and the looters for having given in to anarchy. The tempo and the spirit of celebration put such an emotional distance between the singer and the perceived horror that in his tent performances of "Get on Radical", Duke would invite women in the front row to "show me how you can get on radical," thus further emptying the word "radical" of whatever little political meaning it may have had, and stressing the fete, bacchanal and sexual licence aspects of the party calypso, rather than the explicit moral admonition of his descriptive political ballad.

Superblue's "Get Something and Wave" reveals no such ambivalence in its wholehearted dismissal of horrors and blues and celebration of the carnivalesque spirit of freedom. The protagonist of this calypso is Mother Muriel, a Spiritual Baptist Leader, who locating herself outside of political or economic process, admonishes the Police Commissioner, Abu Bakr and the Prime Minister for instituting a curfew and controlling her time. She claims her freedom to "break away", that is lose and find herself in utter abandon, declaring that "the economy will build," presumably of its own accord, but certainly without her stir.

Mother Muriel spoke and sounded her bell for those scores of revellers who partied all night at special "curfew fetes" in nightclubs and bars around Port of Spain, in delirious defiance of whatever the insurrection or curfew might have implied. What was being defended was a cliche: the idea of the "free" hedonistic Trinidadian, Saga Boy and Tan Tan, the carnival man and the bacchanal woman. "Get Something and Wave" proclaimed celebration in face of a dereliction that was simply ignored. Similarly, Christopher Tambu Herbert's "Rant, Rave and Misbehave" celebrated the wild freedom of the masses, transformed from their recent orgy of looting into revellers whose cry was "We own this town", though after the soca fires, there was considerably less of the town left for anyone to own.

In converting real fire into Soca fire, Bally's "Calypso Coup" drew on the imagery of a score of earlier calypsos that had employed metaphors of explosion and conflagration to describe the power of their music. There have been musical explosions of all sorts. Music has been habitually described as "hotter than fire", as "hot, hot, hot", as "fiery", as "hotter than a *chula*." As we noted earlier, Sparrow in 1978 sang "There is a bomb to blow up the city; hear it ticking' ("The Bomb"). The bomb in question turned out to be one not of gelignite, but music, which would figuratively demolish the city on Carnival Day. Since carnival is that neutral time when in the masquerader's imagination, civic, moral and psychic structures are temporarily demolished, and since it is the melody and rhythm of calypso music that release these forces of demolition, it is appropriate and comes naturally to the calypsonian to liken his music to dynamite.

But alongside such imaginary demolition of my strangled city through the music's marvellous earthquake of sound, lay the real bombings and fires that did occasionally demolish areas of the city, and the bomb scares which often interrupted school and office work throughout the seventies and eighties. In 1979, for instance, Kitchener in "Town Burning Down" (with its chorus "Oh gosh/What's wrong/Downtown/Port of Spain burning down") graphically described one of these great fires.

The use of music to signal intensity, frenzy, violence and even chaos became quite frequent in David Rudder's and Tambu Herbert's compositions, as both of these Charlie's Roots band-singers entered the calypso tent with the even deeper chaos of African-American popular music in their Caribbean belly. One thinks of Rudder's "Outta Hand" with its opening cry, "Is everybody ready to get outta hand?" as well as the crowd's assertion that they are "jamming [...]because the world got so much pain." The crowd also declares, "Is better we bus down the blinken door/ Dis is war." Similar ideas appear in Rudder's "Permission to Mash up the Place", where music and dance are connected with the reversal of normal order, and rhythm is viewed as the "door" in a "journey to the other side."

Perhaps the most memorable use of music as metaphor for social disintegration is Rudder's "Madness". There the fete becomes a natural / national metaphor. Rudder himself explains the metaphor and paradox of this song in which a driving uptempo and apparently "happy" rhythm actually masks a vision of distress, confusion and sadness:

> **D.R.** The sound seems to be a happy sound, but it's really a very sad song. It's a sound that rejects Trinidad society. The fete is actually the society that is Trinidad and Tobago. The fact is that we have squandered about 50 billion dollars in ten years and everybody has come down to earth now. After the artificial standard of living that they have put themselves on, they now have to come down to a realistic level.
> **J.L.R.** That's why you talk about the budget in the song.
> **D.R.** Right. It's like everyone's punishing themselves by going mad, It's triggered off by the budget "the man in Whitehall" read – when he says this is end of it. All the money's gone. So in the song, every single individual in the song is unemployed: the woman who lost her Texaco work, the ex-DEWD man, the ex-union man who lost his job, the French Creole businessman who lost his businessplace. They all in the end come together to fight the promoter. They tell the promoter the fete can't be over, here. We have confrontation here. In the end, the whole society actually came out against the government and marched – businessmen everyone. That's why I keep telling everyone, this is not a fete. I'm not

singing about a fete. I'm talking about madness, a society that's gone mad.[19]

The actual conversation of which this statement by Rudder is part of the transcript, took place in the U.K. at the National Sound Archive on Thursday, October 8th 1987, "Madness" was one of the calypsos sung by Rudder during the 1987 Carnival season, that is, one month after the NAR December 16, 1986 victory. It would, therefore, have been composed and mixed sometime in the middle of the previous year, *before* the change of the *ancien régime*. "Madness", then, is both a reaction to the state of the nation towards the end of the 30 year PNM regime, and a prediction of the chaos that would confront the new incumbents after December 1986, and which surrounded and inhibited their every effort for the duration of their sojourn in powerlessness.

Central to this chaos was people's refusal to believe that the fete was indeed over. It is this refusal that characterised the above mentioned "curfew fetes" of late July and early August 1990, whose patrons, like participants in some medieval or Minshallesque *danse macabre,* tried to reject the reality of the coup, of death, stench and the devastated city. The charismatic and euphoric mood that surrounded the NAR 1986 campaign, was really the same frenzy of despair manifesting itself as its opposite, blind faith and born-again affirmation. It did not prepare the public for the hard, bruising fact of the nation's bankruptcy or for the sacrifice that would be necessary if we were to survive. Many people's faith was based on a false notion that the "fete" of the oil-boom days would, somehow, continue.

Bally's "Party Time", perhaps the greatest political statement for 1987, likened the entire 1986 elections campaign of 1986 to one grand fete. Like Fighter's "Indian Party" (1958) Swallow's "Don't Stop the Party" (1979)[20] or Stalin's "Breakdown Party" (1980), "Party Time" explores the ambiguity created by the two meanings of "party" – i.e. political party and an occasion for merrymaking.

> Jump high, jump down low
> And wave your manifesto
> Ramajay! Come leh we ramajay!
>
> The five years nearly done
> Is time to have some fun
> So ramajay! Come leh we ramajay
> Was a Carnival
> If you see ram goat
> Join the bacchanal
> Just to tief your vote
> R.A.N, N.P.M.
> Begging you fete with them
> Cause its party time

So in 1987, there was Rudder's "Madness", a calypso precisely poised at the moment of transition between the different lunacies of two regimes and Bally's "Party Time", a dismissal of the politics of promise and euphoria with which NAR began its reign. Bally, like Rudder, fully extends and explores the fete/party metaphor. Politicians become D-Js, the electorate a manipulable dancehall crowd. The spirit of carnival reversal is captured in the reversal of the letters in the names of the two major parties of 1986. The dual meanings of the word "party" make Bally's point about the farce of politics and the superficial levels at which political campaigning is generally pitched. Advertisement, self-projection, image-manipulation are natural aspects of the Mas' of politics, or the politics of masking. The D-Js control the fete – and this quite literally in 1986, where Gypsy's "The Sinking Ship" and Deple's "Vote Them Out" were NAR theme songs, while the PNM, caught without a song, sought to resuscitate Kitchener's 1977 and 1982 efforts: "The Doctor say/We here to stay" and "Not a damn seat for dem." The masses were expected to move simply and mindlessly to the rhythm.

Two years before "Calypso Coup", Rudder, in "One More Mr. Officer", (1989) explored the idea of music being the only thing that lay between the people's frustration and anarchy in "the kind of time when the economy died." In that calypso, where the desperation has past the point it had reached in "Madness", the party crowd command the DJ to run the music

> Or we will come out and burn this town
> To stop the music you've got to be mad.

And in 1990, Rudder would sing not only the prophetic "1990", but an entire album of calypso of resistance, dedicated it is true, to the South African struggle, but containing sentiments that were easily transferrable to any Black urban ghetto situation. "Fire in the Laager" communicated quite directly with ghetto Port of Spain, and "Victory Is Certain" was a slogan for their blind hope in struggle. Chris 'Tambu' Herbert, too, would in the video of his 1990 Road March "No No We Ain't Going Home" feature women in army fatigues storming a fete. The language of that calypso speaks of capturing, burning down and blowing up the city. Wayne Brown perceptively commented[21] on the unusual level of violence in the calypso's imagery, recognising that it forebode no good. Such violence was at least a decade old, and dated from the time when the sense of Apocalypse as slow inevitable disintegration changed imperceptibly into helpless rage at imminent collapse, then into the recurrent dream of fire. All that was necessary after that was to locate the victim, to find someone to burn. Significantly, Tambu in "The Question" (1990) was asking, "Do you want fire and brimstone?"

By 1991, then, the party/fete mask, like the musical explosion/ fire/bomb mask had been employed many times in calypso imagery. It took a special talent such as Bally's to breathe new life into such old imagery, as he does in "Calypso Coup".

> They break down the Mecca
> Forget bout Bakr
> Oh what a pity
> So I [...]
> Calypsonians planning to
> Rule the city
> Night and day with pencil and paper
> We siddung planning
> For J'Ouvert morning
> Who can't fête better run for cover
> When we take the town
> Will be one big explosion
>
> Fire! We coming to take over
> Fire! We goin' burn dem with Soca
> We winin, we grindin, we jump up,
>   we tumble down
> Ah seh, Fire! oh-oh! Fire! oh-oh!
> Fire! Fire! all over town.
> Fire! Fire! oh-oh! Fire! Fire! oh-oh!
> Soca fire all over town

"Calypso Coup" begins with a reference to the bulldozing of the Mecca Calypso Tent, a stone's throw away from the equally disputed lands on which the Muslimeen had built their headquarters, and invites us to compare the two issues. In both cases the process by which the land had been occupied was debatable. In both cases the occupants' property had been bulldozed into rubble, the Jamaat's after and in direct retaliation for the insurrection they had engineered.

"Calypso Coup", then, is saying that calypsonians, too, had sufficient grouse to do what the Jamaat did. It uses the metaphor of music to talk about the coup, but it also views the situation of the artist through the metaphor of the coup. "Calypso Coup" declares "We go control the radio/ The T.V. also /Is only Soca", alluding not only to the occupation of Radio Trinidad and TTT by the' Muslimeen, but to the aforementioned fact that the insurrectionists played three or four hours of protest calypsos on TTT during the first night of the insurrection. Bally alludes to this fact to underline the artist's perennial complaint about local electronic media having become mere vehicles for American cultural hegemony. A coup staged by calypsonians, then, would seek immediately to locate local cultural expression at the centre of any agenda of electronic transmission. The calypsonians' revolutionary objective is to set the media ablaze with "sweet sweet soca", from which they will grant absolutely no "amnesty" to the dancing public under their musical control.

Bally seasons "Calypso Coup" with puns, two of which "Jam – at/

Jamaat" and "Bakr-nal/Bacchanal" cement the link between the proposed calypso coup and the real events of July 1990; between, that is, the enraged calypsonians evicted from the fortuitously named "Mecca" Tent and the Jamaat whose occupation of their headquarters had been before the courts for some time. "Calypso Coup", like Organizer's "Who Is Your Leader", Watchman's "Attack with Full Force" and other calypsos, refers with relish to the rumoured sexual humiliation of male politicians. Although there is no reference to this in the various affidavits submitted with respect to the Muslimeen trial, the public savoured the idea of the emasculation of the hated leader, some people regretting only that humiliation had not been crowned by a death which they seemed to believe could make a difference to their own impoverished or degraded state.

"Calypso Coup" was the best of those calypsos that sought to extract laughter from the events – including torture and murder – of the coup. In stanza three, it celebrates the fact that a number of leading calypsonians (Watchman, Tambu, Johnny King and Kenny J) belong to the police service. There is also effective play on the names of other singers such as Protector, Bomber and Luta (Looter) all of whom are accorded key roles in either the protection, demolition or despoliation of the city.

> Watchman and Kenny
> Will commandeer the city
> With Protector
> The Charlotte Street area
> Will be controlled by Bomber
>   Dem and Luta
> Port of Spain by now will be smoking
> With sweet sweet soca
> Hot like pepper
> Tourists now will come for sight seeing
> From America
> They coming down from Libya...

Behind the use of the names of these calypsonians is an accurate sketch of the stages in which the attempted coup became an anarchy of conflagration and looting on the streets. There is also an allusion to the invasion of Trinidad by foreign media. The various crews from CNN and BBC, all accustomed to the transmission of anguish as a spectacle, are equated with an influx of carnival tourists filming the greatest show on earth. Along with these "tourists" from America are those from Libya – a country with whom the Muslimeen had connections. The calypso's point seems to be that Trinidad had become a theatre for antagonistic international forces, neither of which is more than superficially concerned with the fate of Trinidadians. The foreign crisis media hastened out of Trinidad as soon as the Iraqi invasion upstaged the sad local brouhaha. Some of them had expressed anger that official government information sources in Trinidad had provided so little information.

The insurrection gave rise to a number of reflective songs. Some like Ebony's "Pack Up" and Eastlyn Orr's "People Where You Goin" were defiant, and advised people who were thinking of running away from Trinidad to stay and struggle to rebuild their country. Orr pointed out that the situation at the margins of America was even worse than it was in Trinidad. She was put under pressure from the management of Kitchener's Tent and quitted the tent early in the 1991 season. Interestingly enough, only a few calypsonians, Short Pants and Commentor, one recalls – recognized this treatment of Eastlyn Orr as a case of the censorship of calypso, in a year when the mere suggestion by the Prime Minister that calypsonians should adopt nation-building themes, had been viewed and bitterly attacked as an implied threat of censorship. Just as arrogance coming from the gun-toting heroes of the street, or the calypsonians themselves was not recognised or criticised as such, censorship coming from within the calypso tent headed by the great Grandmaster himself, was met with indifference.

Other reflective songs were nostalgic. Richard "Nappy" Mayers "Bring Back the Old Time Days" expresses sweet sad nostalgia for an age of good neighbourliness and warm folksiness. "Let the Flowers Bloom Again", a non-calypso launched by the business community via Mr and Mrs Rick Hernandes/F.C.B. Advertising on Republic Day 1990, and promoted through a continuous series of T.V. video ads, evokes an atmosphere of sweet, childlike innocence and racial harmony, all of which are imaged by the colours of three different hybrid anthurium lilies – dark red, white and bright red. These colours fade into those of the national flag against the background of Denyse Plummer's voice and the voices of a children's choir. Meant to be a song of healing, "Let the Flowers Bloom Again" draws on the sentimental rainbow image as it invites the nation to

> sing rainbows in the mountains
> sing laughter in the rain
> sing power to be and do

Such pastoral sweetness, particularly when promoted by big business, was immediately associated with an attempt to restore via nostalgia, the charismatic illusion of December 1986. Yet not all commentators were sceptical. One referred to "Let the Flowers Bloom Again" as "a glorious tune", "a local tune worthy of international marketing and assured of international success"; an event "which does us justly proud and helps alleviate the current state of local gloom."[22]

Another commentator, however, criticised the video commercial for using "mainly white and light-brown children in attempting to set a tone of hopefulness", contrasting it with a current Servol video about the failure of dialogue or courteous exchange within the black family, which ends with the voice of one angry young adult threatening, "Ah go kill yuh." This commentator found both commercials offensive and felt that they reinforced ethnic and colour stereotypes, and illustrated that, "Tragically, the society has not yet purged itself of both the false and negative views of black-skinned people."[23] So "Let the Flowers Bloom Again" brought healing to some and chagrin to others. When the revived PNM in 1991 adopted the slogan, "The Balisier Is Blooming Again," it was in direct and triumphant mockery of what they considered to be a NAR song.

Denyse Plummer, a singer whose roots lay not in calypso but in sentimental ballads, had over a six year period grown to be accepted in the calypso world as a hard-working tough professional. She had won the Calypso Queen title on two occasions, was joint winner of the Young Kings competition in 1991 and had graduated from singing songs written by professional songwriters, to writing a few of her own. Her 1991 composition,

> "Don't Cry La Trinite" was written in a hotel room in Toronto during the July 27 crisis. Denyse had to fly out to perform in Caribana. Arlene [her sister and manager] stayed behind. "It was one of the few times we weren't together. She'd call us and cry on the phone. We talked about the song," Arlene recalled.[24]

"Don't Cry La Trinite" is at one level simply a song of comfort in which the people of Trinidad are told to regard the insurrection and the fires as a test of faith and spiritual strength, and are reassured that they are still beautiful.

> No longer may I seem to be
> A paradise of glory
> Or a river of pleasure running out to the sea
> But I take my refuge in a higher power, you see,
> My body will be restored,
> And my heritage is still beautiful to me.
>
> Don't cry for me my children
> For all the fire that falls upon me
> Don't cry for me my children
> It was given to me to test me
> But I will not be shaken
> I am La Trinity
> And there is no destruction
> If you look you'll still see
> There is the sea and sand
> Child, I am your rock
> I am your island.

The mystic power of the Trinity Mountains and by implication, the Holy Trinity after which the island had been renamed by Columbus, is invoked by Plummer to reinforce the courage of Trinidad's children at a moment of deep national crisis. Since this crisis was catalysed by an Islamic group, it may not be far-fetched to say that Plummer's "Don't Cry La Trinity" has presented the nation's struggle as spiritual warfare in which La Trinite, the country, transmutes into the spiritual forces of Christianity implied, or contained in the name that Christopher, bearer of Christ, had given the island. The powerful founding hegemony of Christianity is stated and magically invoked in the face of "Islamic" threat.

This mood of defiance is maintained in another television advertisement, performed by Plummer, the Mighty Trini (businessman Robert Elias) and calypsonian Gypsy, in which the singers articulate the confidence and determination of the Port of Spain business community:

> Well we here to stay
> We ain't going no way
> We in this thing together
> We goh build back town
> We will turn around
> We will come back good as ever
> We will come back good as ever.

Canadian-based calypsonian Jayson, with "Soldiers We Are All", injected a note of sober reflection as he encouraged the nation to assume communal responsibility for the rebuilding and protection of the city. Melanie Hudson, a young singer of the same vintage as Machel Montano, sang the David Rudder composed, "I Will always Be There for You", a sentimental "calypsong" in which "Mother Trinidad" reassures her children of her bountiful forgiveness and support to the very last, regardless of what the children might do. Such simplistic self-forgiveness, similar in many respects to the mood of Plummer's "Don't Cry La Trinite", is finally counterbalanced by Mother Trinidad's demanding from her children a responsibility which some of their elders, to her shame, have not displayed.

Melanie Hudson also sang "Cry My Beloved Country", a lament very much in the spirit of those pre-1986 calypsos which focused on the social problems such as drug addiction, prostitution and crime. Part of the blame for this situation of general collapse is attributed to the fact that "leader fighting leader while the people lose their mind/ Once we had a vision, but now we seem so blind." This song has two messages. One is that the patriot must acknowledge the true state of things and shed "tears for the country, tears for the land." The other is that the nation must fight against the demoralisation into which it has sunken.

This latter sentiment kept being repeated in the calypsos sung at the Independence Calypso Monarch Finals of 1991, where several singers expressed a general disillusionment with politicians and their pre-elections promises and proclaimed their own dedication to ideals of national unity, popular participation and communal responsibility for the solving of problems. Examples of this trend were Bally's "Bally, Who You Voting

For"; De Fosto's "Then and Now"; G.B.'s "Is You" and Axeback's "Reflections". It was not easy, however, for some calypsonians to arrive at this position. Consider the following lines from De Fosto's "Then and Now":

> We should never point fingers at anybody
> We should share the blame equally
> So let us build back our country now, you and me.
> On the journey that would set us free.

One might be fooled into believing that De Fosto has truly accepted the notion of communal blame for social ills and communal responsibility for national reconstruction, when in fact he is seeking exoneration for those who ravaged the city and made their own situation worse. Thus, another stanza of the calypso reads:

> Now today some children drinking sugar water
> Their mothers lose their jobs, their fathers too
> So they all on the streets looking for a dollar
> In despair, without hope; what more can they do?
> You see, times hard so people doing anything
> And like no one coming to their rescue
> So they loot and shoot and some on drugs and all
> So don't blame the youths at all.

People are presented here as victims of social circumstance, without even the choice of saying "No" to crime, violence or drug addiction. De Fosto is not really trying to spread blame equally across the ranks of society. That is merely his mask of fairness, behind which he, like the majority of his colleagues, blames only the Government.

> So don't blame Mr. Robinson
> If he want to build a monument
> Do not blame Pantin for crying, I say.
> Do not blame the Government
> If our COLAS were taken away
> Do not blame the people for protesting, I say
> Because we shall rise again one day.

The looters and shooters are again exonerated since it is the Government that is to blame for creating the economic and social situation to which the urban poor simply reacted. "Then and Now", consequently, ends up with evasion of responsibility for lives and property mindlessly destroyed, and leaves it unclear how this blameless and innocently self-destructive people is going to "rise again one day."

De Fosto's faith, like that of Superblue's Mother Muriel, is blind. A few weeks after the insurrection he had expressed the same faith in "My Trinity", a song described as a "Gospel-and-Baptist influenced spiritual" and meant to be a healing song for his guiltless nation.

Ah feeling yuh pain
Ah feeling yuh tension
We shall be strong again
Just you wait and see
Let us move on
To a brighter destiny
Oh my Trinity.²⁵

Axeback in "Reflections", taking his cue from both Funny's "How You Feel" of the twenty-fifth Anniversary Independence Calypso Monarch competition of four years previously, and Luta's "Think Again" (1991), asks the nation and its political leaders alike to consider whether they have not contributed to their own economic woes through a failure to promote self-sufficiency, the frittering away of opportunities, the failure to transform old colonial society, to put nation before self, to create genuine equality of opportunity, and to develop and maintain a healthy work ethic. Axeback suggests that the attitudes of many citizens have contributed only to "Gross National Downfall". A Tobago-based calypsonian, Axeback was more balanced in his according of blame than many of the Trinidad singers. He focuses in "Advice to Politicians" (1991) on the NAR's failure to fulfil its pre-election promises. Politics has for generations been only "old talk" and this had not changed with the NAR. The people are looking for leaders who can help them, and will withdraw their love from any leader who cannot or does not.

G.B., (Gregory Ballantyne) is concerned in "Is You" (1991), not with the question of blame, but with that of responsibility for creating a new society. In lines reminiscent of Luta's 1986 calypso, "Change Your Attitude", he warns the electorate on the eve of another election that the people have to depend on themselves, not on charismatic leaders, foreign lending agencies, borrowed technologies, or the imported theologies of deliverance via telescreen or shortwave radio. G.B. warns:

... what we have here is a tendency
That a saviour go come for we
And it make no sense
You give up your personal independence.

No politician can do what you can do for you
Trinidad, is you have to do
No political clan can wave no magic wand
Is you must come with a plan
We must need politics it is true
But is just an avenue
Cause is you have to do
Political destiny: is you control the keys
Trinbago, use dem nah, please,

"Is You", like Rajah's "Is We" or Maestro's "The Poor Man" of the seventies, marks a shift from the tendency to sentimentalise "the people", "the masses", "the poor", "the black", "the marginalised", "the alienated", "the disadvantaged". It thus belongs to a tiny family of post-1990 calypsos which insisted that the insurrection be placed in a wide historical context. The best of these was Luta's "Think Again" which begins by taking the nation back to the eighties, when calypsonians were derided by people in authority for their gloomy prognostications.

> In the days of plenty
> Calypsonians warn this country
> The way we moving we will end up in disaster after the oil boom
> People take orange skin and pelt we
> They make kooyah mouth behind we
> While the administration simply called us prophets of doom
> But these are the days that we predicted
> Yes, this is the time we say would come
> When the poor, hardworking, homeless and afflicted
> Would not be sure 'bout where the next meal is coming from.

Luta then proceeds to show that the situation NAR inherited could not be remedied overnight or without effort and changed attitudes on the part of the people.

> Well if you think you could face that overnight
> And you think NAR had the country blight
> Ah say, think again
> You think you could run by Uncle Sam
> Siddung and get free ham and jam
> Think again
> The ship sinking and the IMF hit we hard like a hurricane
> And if you think that's not the price of freeness
> I beg you to think again.

The politics of confrontation, growing racial tension as the society splits along its stress line, the refugee situation, partisan politics are all adduced as evidence of a society that was not thinking too deeply; a society that had refused to make the necessary sacrifices to redeem the wasted time and money of the boom years.

> You think government should rearrange
> But your old attitudes must be unchanged
> Think again
> Double standards in society
> Is enough to drive one insane
> And if you think the youths are the ones to blame
> Think again

His focus is, consequently, next on the youth and here his attack is on the education system, its failure both to eradicate illiteracy and to provide young people with serious moral exemplars that might enable them to survive in an essentially hypocritical society. The question had arisen during 1990 of why the urban youth were turning to caudillo-type leadership such as Abu Bakr and choosing gunman-heroes and the ethic of violence. Luta's answer is to analyse the education system of which, as a teacher, he has inside knowledge. Education is education for alienation.

> The education system
> Mass-producing dotish children
> They graduate at secondary but their standard is elementary
> Seventy-three per cent cannot read
> Exams: a handful succeed
> Yet we beat our chests and boast about high literacy
> School girls and their principals are lovers
> Drugs, sex and violence in schools running neck and neck
> The youths have no respect for their elders
> Because the elders themselves show them no respect

Luta discloses that the child learns how to survive in a world where nobody seems to care, by not caring himself. It is, according to Luta, not just a question of an uncaring government, but of an uncaring society which has made little attempt to live by its proclaimed values and ideals. He concludes his stanza on education by alluding ironically to Eric Williams's famous statement that the nation's future lies in the book bags of its school children:

> And if you think the future is in the schoolbag
>   of the children of Port of Spain
> When the schoolbag pack up with gun, knife and chain
> Ah beg you to think again

His final focus is on the July insurrection, which can now be located in the context described in the first three stanzas. As viewed here, 1990 was the logical product of what we earlier called the slow Apocalypse: the breakdown of values and institutions. Luta dismisses idle suggestions, rife in the society at the time, that Mr. Robinson and the NAR were "blighted". The forces pitted against the Government were political, not metaphysical, and came together in the Summit of People's Organisations, SOPO, a loosely-structured body of protesting groups which, in a manner reminiscent of the early 1969 NJAC, sought to pool, magnify and channel resentment against the state. The Muslimeen had joined SOPO whose rhetorical revolutionary bluff they called, when they invaded Parliament. This aspect of 1990 remains unscrutinised in Watchman's "Attack with Full Force", but it is highlighted by Luta as the most significant aspect of that year, and the crowning evidence of his society's moral degeneracy.

> You claim to be kind and loving
> God-fearing and law abiding

> But then you lend support to a violent revolution
> Properties looted and destroyed
> Poor people were made unemployed
> Others maimed and killed while their relatives mourned in frustration
> Big men you regard as respectable
> The way they behave you and all can't believe is them
> How frightening to see a **priest** among other people
> Refuse to condemn the actions of vicious, wicked men.

Here Luta forces the people to face the tragedy of 1990 without the "soca" mask of escapism. He also illustrates his point about the maddening double standards in his society with his example of the priest who refused to condemn the perpetrators of the coup. That priest became, like Bakr, hero of those who sympathised with the insurrectionists and their agenda to remove the government by any means possible. Luta also questions Bakr's stated motives for staging the insurrection by suggesting that he may have had a hidden agenda. That is, he advocates scepticism in just that area that naive commentators such as Cro Cro advocate blind sentimental faith in Abu Bakr.

> If you think Mr. Bakr did his thing
> On behalf of the poor and suffering
> Ah say think again!
> You think if Bakr is in command
> You could call him duncy or mad man
> Think again

Strangely, Watchman in an interview had also acknowledged that the Bakr type of leader would not tolerate satire, laughter, or calypso picong, as did Chambers, Williams and indeed, Robinson.[26] Luta recognised a deeper arrogance and a worse authoritarianism in Bakr than in the three prime ministers, each of whose stewardship, he implies, had its flaws and would bring its particular retribution in time.

> And if Williams, Georgie or Robinson
> Cause my country to suffer pain
> And you think that they ain't gon pay some day
> Ah beg you think again.

Luta here makes the necessary concession to mandatory Robinson-bashing, but he also invites his audience to recognise that Robinson as leader was not responsible for more or less suffering than either of his predecessors. There would be mild protest at Luta's exclusion from the Calypso Monarch finals of 1991, some of it coming from Mrs Jennifer Johnson, the Minister for Youth, Sport, Culture and the Creative Arts; some from Sparrow, some from correspondents to the daily press. But "Think Again" would not get the recognition it deserved until 1992 with the Sunshine Awards in New York; though it demanded greater courage for the calypsonian in 1991 to go against the grain of popular feeling and force the public to reflect on its own face.

IV: Rudder's "Hoosay": Moon-Dance of the Doomed

Socially conscious calypsonians, then, seem to have been faced with a number of dilemmas in 1991; how to reconcile the grim events of July 1990 with the spirit of celebration that is supposed to imbue any Carnival season; how, that is, to convert real fire into "Soca fire"; how to rationalise rapacity and evade guilt, shame or responsibility; how to present an obviously futile gesture of tragic waste as a triumph of the urban masses; how to promote a theory of retribution in order to explain away the scapegoating of the leader, while at the same time avoiding asking the crucial question of whether the people's suffering was also retribution, and if so, for what sins of commission or omission?

Many singers as we have seen simply ignored the dark side of 1990 and dealt with the insurrection and the looting and arson which followed in its wake as if they were aspects of theatre. Disaster was thus rendered as tragicomic spectacle. Real fire became "soca fire" as the destruction of the city, annually predicted in calypsos for two decades, and now finally achieved, was presented as reason for celebration. Only a handful of the calypsos escaped such mindlessness. We have commented on a few of these. Now we will close this overview with an examination of Rudder's "Hoosay", the best of 1991 calypsos and the least known. It was, indeed, not till 1992 that "Hoosay" gained true recognition at the Sunshine Awards. This is strange, for "Hoosay" was performed in the tent during 1991 and appeared on the *Rough 'N Ready* album. In the spirit of Rudder's much acclaimed "1990" which it resembles in melody and tonality and transcends in poetic beauty, "Hoosay" fell victim to the spirit of escapism which characterised the months after the insurrection. It was mentioned by Keith Smith as:

> a troubling song, much more so to me than last year's "1990" because while "1990" dealt with themes universal, "Dance the Moon" [an early name for "Hoosay"] is about us and Rudder does not provide the escape which Blues does. Rather he shoves Bakr in our face, noting that he is the darker side of us and that this Edenic Trinidad of dancing, singing souls, is no longer true if, indeed, it ever was.[27]

Beyond this, it gained little mention.

In this calypso Rudder is at his most metaphorical, his most oblique; yet he clearly wanted his audience to decipher the metaphors. Alongside the lyrics of the calypso printed on the dust jacket of his 1991 album, he has provided brief notes which explain the title of the calypso, "Hoosay". In these notes Rudder briefly draws attention to the fact that the Muslimeen uprising took place on the Friday immediately preceding the Hosein festival, which commemorates the battle of Kerbala, a fratricidal struggle in which Hussain and Hassan, the grandsons of the prophet Mohammed, were killed. The images in the calypso are drawn from the general iconography of Islam, with the star, the crescent moon and the tassa drums featuring prominently in the poem's refrain.

One recurrent idea in the calypso is that of the defiled sacrifice, the polluted symbol, the broken or degenerated ritual. This idea is suggested from the very start of the calypso.

> Wear something red was the popular cry
> And like the pavement and streets were filled with envy
> Because by morning light they were covered with our blood
> I tell you not one soul here escaped the frenzy

This is an allusion to "Red Day", November 17, 1989, when a substantial segment of the nation rallied around the national football team by wearing the national colour, red. Rudder now contemplates how a moment of seemingly supreme togetherness and joy could have been converted into the mass frenzy of looting and anarchy; how the implications of the image could have been so totally reversed; or even more startlingly than this: how two moments, on the face of things so different from each other, contained beneath their surfaces the colour of an identical frenzy.

In the next few lines, Rudder suggests the political ethos within which the insurrection occurred.

> Sometimes you're gambling for king
> And wild is the joker
> And sometimes the sight of the moon
> Just riles up the lost, the, hungry, the mad
> These are the troubled times that we have down in Trinidad

The King and The Fool/Clown/Joker are doubles of each other; tragedy's other side is absurdity; King Lear and his Fool share one soul. So society, caught up in an agonising and hazardous quest for genuine leadership – "gambling for king" – discovers Bakr, a wild joker whose improbable and theatrical intervention into the card-game creates additional chaos.

The ideas of the reversal of symbols and the pollution of ritual are sustained in the first reference to the moon. For the sighting of the new moon is a signal that the time of fasting and abstinence is over; that an ordeal has been endured and a ritual of purification has been fulfilled. It is a moment of joyful accomplishment. Here, however, the "moon" suggests the unattainable, desired, material ideal – beauty, wealth, the good life. The hungry and the mad whose "lunacy" is awakened by the sighting of the moon, become the exploitable victims of their king, the wild joker. Protest politics in Trinidad has for the better part of this century amounted to little more than the organisation, exploitation and channelling of lumpenproletarian rage against all of the stereotyped agencies of oppression: the police, the political directorate, the business class, the owners of property. Bakr's outfit fed on urban distress, and presented itself as an agency which, though it neither toiled nor spun, had miraculously attained the means – Arab money – to alleviate it.

Here was an appeal even more beguiling than the doctrine of Black Power in 1970: instant deliverance, justice, revenge, the righteous rage of Stalin's "Bun Dem" or Rudder's own 1990 composition "Fire in the Laager", directed at last towards its true object – a three-year-old government that had created centuries of poverty, the worldwide recession, the massive national debt, the shortage of nurses, the falling oil prices, the rising unemployment and the shameful decades of corruption. Most of the political analysis and all of the agitation between 1986 and 1990 pointed to one end – the refusal of an entire nation to recognise its face and to assume responsibility for its condition.

"Hoosay", like Luta's "Think Again", forces the nation to assume this burden of responsibility. Thus Rudder's chorus presents the aftermath of looting which the insurrection inspired, not as comic spectacle or justifiable retribution against an "iniquitous" regime and its "diabolical" leader, but as the degeneration of thousands into "strange dogs," a subhuman state of anarchy and avarice.

> Because under the crescent moon
> And above the bloody asphalt
> Strange dogs were barking
> Deep in the night
> Under the crescent moon
> I say the drums were silent
> But somehow the rhythm continued
> Oh what a sight.

The crescent moon above signals the Muslimeen ambition of ascendancy, the dream of the wild joker-king. The bloody asphalt below indicates the price of useless human sacrifice at which such ascendancy will be achieved. The silenced drums are the tassa drums of the normal Hosein festival, interrupted and abolished by the Muslimeen revolt. But these "Hoosay" drums, really, commemorate bloodshed, sacrificial waste. Religious symbolism attains real flesh and blood, a lived actuality. The Hosein festival, for years little more than an empty symbol which many Trinidad Muslims reject because of what they see as its carnivalesque nature, has become suddenly real, with real fighting, real deaths, real fratricidal gore, as at Kerbala. Thus, although the drums are silent the rhythm continues.

Inflicting this ancient frenzy on Trinidad, Bakr has not only made "history", he has disinterred it, invoking it from its tomb of deepest darkness.

> On the night of the day

> It was the night of the day
> The night when they say
> That the martyrs died

The chorus stresses a depth of night ("deep in the night", the twice stated "night of the day" followed by "The night") punctuated by the baying of "strange dogs" at the moon. Here again our attention is drawn to the idea of a polluted ritual, the debasement of concept. Here it is the idea of martyrdom, clearly believed in by the Muslimeen that, juxtaposed to the frenzied barking of the dogs, is devalued. Sacrifice has its double, its other side, in sacrificial waste, useless, thoughtless worship of the idea of victimhood. ("Dogs" was also the name given by Grenadians to the automatic rifles of the People's Revolutionary Army. Originating in the USA, some of these weapons resurfaced in Trinidad during the Muslimeen Uprising of 1990 and were still being unearthed years later.)

In Stanza Two. Rudder pinpoints the theatrical element of the whole affair.

> Fame
> Yes, we're famous as hell
> Don't you know we're a star
> At long last we've made it.

Not only Bakr but the nation itself, the collective "we", has finally achieved stardom and fulfilled its theatrical nature – Trinidad on CNN who clearly felt that the whole event ought to have been staged for their benefit; Trinidad on B.B.C.; Bakr's eagerness to send his messages of self-justification and blessed assurance to the world.

But the word "star" like the word "moon" suggests opposite things or states. On the one hand it suggests the illusory silver screen with its powerful connotations of role-playing. On the other hand it illuminates and returns us to the founding murder, the original sacrifice.

> Star
> Like the star in the moon
> Shining over the tomb
> Dance the moon you can't fraid it

Bakr may have relished the stardom of an easily gained political prominence, but his star is the one that illuminates a tomb. "Dance the moon you can't fraid it" is a direct address to Bakr, his followers and his eulogisers, who are being sardonically told to continue the dance of death, the celebration of sacrifice that they have begun, by playing their role to its mythologically foreordained end, which is death.

> Come on dance brother dance
> But death is your drummer

> Prance sister prance
> The future is at stake
> So jump high, jump low
> And this Hoosay will take the cake

A deadly detachment separates the poet here from all those caught up in the dance of death. These people include those who looted; those who partied all night at clubs during the early days of the Emergency; those whose response to catastrophe remained flippant and shallow; those for whom "star" means celluloid fame rather than the cold clear vision of tragic waste. The commands "Dance!" "Prance" "jump high, jump low" directed at his "brothers" and "sisters" are, of course, the standard commands of the party calypso. "Brothers" and "sisters" are the now empty signifiers of grassroots camaraderie, barely surviving from the Black Power era of two decades ago.

Rudder instructs his bretheren to continue their masquerade; though he warns them darkly, with Minshall-like pessimism, that their dance is the *dance macabre* and their drummer death. Yet this dark vision does not entirely destroy the calypsonian's role as warner/prophet. He retains sufficient social responsibility to remind his masquerading brothers and sisters that "the future is at stake"; a sentiment which is less "closed off", less absolute than "death is your drummer." For if, as in the medieval *danse macabre*, death is beating the bass drum, there can be no future.

The phrase "take the cake" goes back to a Southern U.S.A. and Haitian custom of awarding a cake or a lemon meringue pie as the prize for winning a dance competition. Hence the names "cakewalk" and "meringue" which both refer to dances. The former indeed, refers to a minstrel dance. So the last two lines of stanza two mean: If you keep on with your *danse macabre*, this Hoosay will be the greatest festival of death that you've ever celebrated.

Rudder begins stanza three with a sorrowful allusion to his own 1989 song "The Power and the Glory":

> The power and the glory
> Is so close at hand
> But the beast he was lurking
> For he too sits in the wings

The imagery here is Christian. The phrase "the power and the glory" derives from a doxology attached to the Lord's Prayer, as well as from *Revelation,* where "Blessing and honour, glory and power" are praise words offered in adoration of the Godhead. Rudder in his calypso "The Power and the Glory" sang of "a new spirit rising." Significantly, his music was that year (1989) employed by Minshall in his production of *Santimanitay* at Jean Pierre Complex. At the end of that mas' about human atrocity and viciousness (one recalls the jagged teeth of the masks), Minshall sought somehow to invoke a new spirit of life and light. Unfortunately, neither Minshall's magic nor Rudder's could move the society beyond its suicidal instinct for self-destruction or its unleashed ferocity of tooth and fang. Self-destructiveness was evident in the way that even positive social measures were negated and undermined; self-laceration could be seen in the viciousness of social and political commentary where lies, abusiveness, skewed analysis and character assassination had become cherished national norms. Such norms were then adopted by calypsonians as ideals and applauded by the public as insight.

Returned to all of its contexts, the phrase "the power and the glory" is Rudder's way of describing a vision of a new heaven and a new earth, that is, a new order of human spirit and community beyond what currently exists: the state of apocalyptic collapse, the decline and fall of virtually everything. Deriving his symbolism from the Biblical version of the end of things and from the Carnival tradition of the Dante-inspired Devil Mas', Rudder sees a new order as possible only after the Beast of the Apocalypse has been defeated.

If this makes him appear to resemble our current demonologists who invested with evil powers the serpent/dragon weather-vane which until recently used to perch atop of the Red House, it should be pointed out that Rudder locates the Beast within each person. As a nation, we have not displayed the necessary awareness of the presence of the Beast within ourselves and have thus reduced ourselves to an essential bestiality.

> So when we searched for the moon
> All we saw were the vultures
> But then a chosen people
> Never worry 'bout these things

Blissfully unaware, of the Beast within, secure in the fable of being "a chosen people", complacently assured of our destiny, we have as a people suffered a tragic distortion of vision. The "moon" thus dies as either a romantic or a religious symbol and is replaced in our vision by the vultures which circled both Laventille where unrefrigerated, looted supermarket meats rotted in the days after July 27, 1990, and Parliament, where human bodies decomposed.

Music, which had for some time become a metaphor for violence, no longer suggests, but literally *becomes* violence. The symbols re-enter the original act of murder through which they derived their genesis; the founding murder.

> So the roll of the tassa
> Became the rhythm of bullets
> And the thundering boom bass
> That was a bomb
> In this Muslim time
> When the Hoosay is number one.

The moment becomes "this Muslim time" where, unfortunately, through the desecration of festival and sign, an entire religion has come to typify blind rage, presided over by and leading to the Hoosay's mask of elaborately crafted bamboo and papier-mache tombs.

In the final stanza, Rudder bitterly re-examines those myths of innocence, gaiety and irresponsibility through which the nation has interpreted its residence on earth.

> Not in this house
> Not in this garden of Eden
> Oh how we danced
> To the beat of this lovely lie
> Until a man opened a door
> And showed us our other side
> And all our meccared illusions
> Walked right on by

The events of 1990 are here perceived as an unmasking: a stripping away of the illusion that Trinidad is a Paradise, a "mecca"; "this wonderland of calypso, this wonderland of steelband" according to Baker (1967); "the mecca of the Steelband" according to Mudada (1987); the place where no wars occurred because of the safety valve of carnival, according to Chalkdust (1988); the country that, despite all its lunacies is, according to Cro Cro (1991), "still the best".

All such cliches are discarded as Bakr, a strange Legba-figure, opens the door to our darker side by removing the barrier between our lived fantasy and the subterranean reality of chaos which fantasy keeps at bay. So,

> Now Trinis know
> What is UZI diplomacy
> Now Trinis know
> What is SLR love
> In these troubled times
> Under the stars above.

"Uzi diplomacy" – the dull monologue of the Libyan-financed, Israeli-made, American-supplied gun – replaces discourse, negotiation, verbal exchange. "SLR love" is a similarly Orwellian perversity of contradiction. Rudder's vision has achieved an international dimension with his concern over the last four years for the Caribbean and its ancestral linkages; for Haiti, Panama, Beijing, the dance of the Eagle and the Bear, the changes taking place in Eastern Europe and South Africa. In his notes to "Hoosay" he locates the Muslimeen uprising in Trinidad in its international context observing that:

> ... militant Muslims in Trinidad stormed the parliament in an attempt to overthrow the government and demand immediate elections... Six days later, Iraqi leader Saddam Hussein invaded Kuwait.

"Uzi diplomacy" and "SLR love" characterized both situations, which could both be used to illustrate what happens when the currency of diplomatic verbal exchange becomes devalued and language itself rots and crumbles. At such times, symbols collapse, meanings merge into their opposites and the barrier between civilised activity and barbarity, thin at the best of times, completely disappears. Then, what is left is the murderous immediacy of the automatic rifle, or whatever killing-machine best suits the fancy of a world that Orwell had accurately predicted; a world whose brutish sensibilities have been nurtured on daily scenes of carnage, fed to them as either fact or fiction on the tele-screens of a monolithic and frozen power-structure.

If in stanza two Rudder focuses on the cinematic, perversely theatrical nature of the July 27, 1990 happening, by the end of the song he has entered that sinister, dark space behind, beneath and within Abu's and the nation's theatre of the Absurd. Bakr becomes Legba, the crippled doorkeeper between the theatre and its Double, the one who "opened a door and showed us our other side." And in another, healthier sense, Rudder too, in "Hoosay" assumes the role and responsibility of Legba. He becomes muse and guide, mediating between the superficial flippant, escapist and cynical responses to catastrophe typical of the majority of 1991 calypsos, and the anguish of acknowledging our darker selves along with the pain of assuming the burden of responsibility for our situation.

Hail the man! Mighty poet of a shallow people in a savage time.

(Hitherto unpublished essay, with the exception of the "Hoosay" segment which was published as "Mighty Poet of a Shallow People in a Savage Time", in *Trinidad & Tobago Review*, March 1992, pp. 17-19.)

References

1. See Rohlehr, G., My *Strangled* City *and Other Essays*, pp. 85-141.
2. Rohlehr, G.. ibid. pp. 169-269.
3. E.g. Valentino's "Dis Place Nice", 1975.
4. Chalkdust, "Juba Doobai" (1972); "Calypso vs Soca"; "Quacks and Invalids" (1987).
5. "Kitch Hits Out at Prize for Political Calypso", *Sunday Guardian*, (March 7, 1976).
6. "Nature's Plan" was recorded in 1984, but released in 1985.
7. See Rohlehr, G., "Man Talking to Man: Calypso and Social Confrontation in Trinidad 1970 to 1984", in *My Strangled City and Other Essays*, pp. 324-341.
8. Ariel's song from Shakespeare's *The Tempest*, Act 1. Sc II, lines 398-399.
9. Blood, Peter, "PM Joins the Stick Men", *Sunday Express*, September 16, 1990, p. 21.

10. See McLeod, E., "Divali Message", *Sunday Express*, Oct 29, 1981, p. 38.
11. Blood, Peter, "The Shape of Carnival to Come: a Survey", *Sunday Express* Section Two, August 26, 1990, p. 8.
12. See Ryan, S., *Race and Nationalism in Trinidad and Tobago* (Toronto: University of Toronto Press, 1972).
13. Deosaran, R., "The Psychology of Racial Conflict with a Calypso Beat", in *Social Psychology in the Caribbean* (Port of Spain: Longman Trinidad, 1992), pp. 317-370.
14. Brathwaite, E.K., "Prelude" to *Rights of Passage* in *The Arrivants* (London: OUP, 1973), p. 4.
15. See e.g. Watchman's "Leader of the Opposition" and Sugar Aloes's "Unnamed Calypso" of 1992.
16. Girard, Rene, *Things Hidden Since the Foundation of the World* (Stanford California: Stanford University Press, 1987), pp. 171-172 (Translated by Stephen Bann & Michael Metteer).
17. See e.g. Watchman's "Attack with Full Force", 1991.
18. See the Richardson and the Mansoor letter.
19. Rudder. D., *Kaiso Calypso Music: David Rudder in Conversation with John La Rose* (London, Port of Spain: New Beacon Books, 1990), pp. 29-30. (my emphasis)
20. Swallow's "Don't Stop the Party" was appropriated by St. Vincentians and used during political campaigns there. Similarly Tambu's "This Party Is It" would be used by Basdeo Panday in Trinidad during one of his rare moments of affirming the NAR.
21. Brown, W., See *Express*, Wed Feb 13, 1991. Brown had first made this observation in early 1990.
22. Perot, Dr. Ivan, "Glorious Song to Do Us Proud", *Express,* Section Two (June 300, 1991) p. 38.
23. Kambon, Asha. "Subtle Messages", *Sunday Express*, Section Two (June 30, 1991) p. 36.
24. Waterman, Kathy, "Total Woman Power Behind Denyse (sic) Throne", *Sunday Express,* (February 10, 1991) p. 16.
25. Grant, Lennox, "De Fosto Sings to Heal the Trini Soul", *Express,* Mon. Oct. 22, 1990, p. 22.
26. This intolerance was illustrated in 1992, when Baker, a Tobagonian calypsonian, was threatened by Bakr supporters who objected to his calypso "From Baker to Bakr".
27. Smith, Keith, *Express*, Sat. Feb 2, 1991, p. 9.

ABOUT THE AUTHOR

Gordon Rohlehr is Emeritus Professor at the University of the West Indies at St Augustine. Unquestionably one of the Caribbean's finest critics and thinkers, his territory covers both literature and popular culture, particularly calypso. His publications include: *Pathfinder: Black Awakening in "The Arrivants" of Edward Kamau Brathwaite* (Tunapuna: College Press, 1981); *Cultural Resistance and the Guyana State* (Casa de las Américas, 1984); *Calypso and Society in Pre-Independence Trinidad* (Port of Spain, 1990); *My Strangled City and Other Essays* (Longman Trinidad, 1992); *The Shape of That Hurt and Other Essays* (Longman Trinidad, 1992); *A Scuffling of Islands: Essays on Calypso* (Lexicon Trinidad Ltd, 2004); *Transgression, Transition, Transformation: Essays in Caribbean Culture* (Lexicon, 2007); and *Ancestories: Readings of Kamau Brathwaite's "Ancestors"* (Trinidad: Lexicon, 2010); *My Whole Life is Calypso: Essays on Sparrow* (2015); *Perfected Fables Now: A Bookman Signs off on Seven Decades* (Peepal Tree 2019) and *Muses, Mazes, Muses, Margins* (Peepal Tree 2020).

ALSO AVAILABLE

My Strangled City and Other Essays
ISBN: 9781845234379; pp. 309; pub. 2019; £19.99; Caribbean Modern Classics

Gordon Rohlehr's critical work is outstanding in the balance it achieves between its particularity and its breadth – from the detailed unpacking of a poem's inner workings, to locating Caribbean writing in the sweep of political and cultural history – and the equal respect he pays to literary and to popular cultural forms. His "Articulating A Caribbean Aesthetic" remains a stunningly pertinent and concise account of the historical formation of the cultural shifts that framed Caribbean writing as a distinctive body of work. Indeed, along with Kamau Brathwaite and Kenneth Ramchand, no critic has done more to establish the subject of Caribbean writing and its distinctive aesthetics.

These essays, written between 1969 to 1986, first published in radical campaigning newspapers such as *Tapia* and *Moko*, and first collected in 1992, were the work of a young academic who was both changing the university curriculum, and deeply engaged with the less privileged world outside the campus. Rohlehr catches Caribbean writing at the point when it leaves behind its nationalist hopes and begins to challenge the complexities of the post-independence phase. Few critics have written as clearly about how deeply the colonial has remained embedded in the postcolonial.

What shines in Rohlehr's work is not merely its depth, acuity and humanity, but its courage. He writes when his subject is still emergent, without waiting for the credibility of metropolitan endorsements as a guide to the canon. "My Strangled City", a record of how Trinidad's poets responded to the upsurge of revolutionary hopes, radical shams, repressions and disappointed dreams of 1964-1975 is an indispensable account of those times and the diversity of literary response that continues to speak to the present. And if in these essays Trinidad is Rohlehr's primary focus, his perspective is genuinely regional. His native Guyana is always present in his thoughts and several essays show his deep interest in the cultural productions of a "dread" Jamaica, and in making insightful comparisons between, for instance, reggae and calypso.

Perfected Fables Now: A Bookman Signs off on Seven Decades
ISBN: 9781845234508; pp. 288; pub. 2019; £19.99

Since the mid-1960s, Gordon Rohlehr has been an incomparable recorder and analyser of Caribbean literature and culture and their intersection with history and politics. His work on the emergence of Caribbean writing from its colonial shell and his analysis of calypso as the voice of Trinidadian consciousness establishes him as essential to our time as William Hazlitt was to the early 19th century in documenting and characterising the turbulent spirit of his age. Radical, but never willing to compromise his sense of what was fraudulent or power-seeking amongst his fellow travellers, Rohlehr is the best touchstone we have for both what the Caribbean has achieved and of its struggling, neo-colonial fragility in the face of the new imperialism of economic and cultural globalism.

Now – though who knows? – in putting together what he says is his last book, Gordon Rohlehr doffs the costume of the carnival figure of the "Bookman", the recording Satan of the devil band, who walks with his book in which he writes down the names of the damned. And here we have the clue to the fact that along with the serious analysis of calypso, his summing up of what is essential in the work of Derek Walcott, Earl Lovelace and V.S. Naipaul, and the essays of remembrance for those like Walcott, Lloyd Best, Pat Bishop, Tony Martin and others who have made their earthly exits, there is a devilish humour at work. This comes out particularly in an essay that joyfully demolishes an attempt to characterise the Caribbean in any other than its own terms – as a new Mediterranean, for instance – and the subservience of Trinidad's rulers to the neo-colonialisms of tourism, visiting American ships and the U.S. embassy. What is often salutary, if uncomfortable, is to be reminded by the long span of Rohlehr's observations that problems seen as contemporary were being identified by the nation's calypsonians sixty years ago.

Rohlehr's voice is always distinctively personal, though the Bookman has rarely revealed much of himself, but in one of the concluding essays he writes about his Guyanese upbringing from the 1940s to the 1960s in a way that is both very funny and sad and gives an understanding of what has shaped his vision.

Muses, Mazes, Musings, Margins
ISN: 9781845234652; pp. 184; pub. 2020; £13.99

There is nothing quite like Gordon Rohlehr's *Musings, Mazes, Muses, Margins* in Caribbean writing; probably its nearest neighbours are Kamau Brathwaite's *The Zea Mexican Diary* and *Trenchtown Rock*. Over a period of more than forty years, Rohlehr, supreme public critic of the post-colonial Caribbean, its creative writing and the historian and deep analyser of calypso, has been paying quiet attention to his inner consciousness, a fictive journeying that has much to say about outer personal and wider Caribbean realities. It is a book that ranges over a variety of forms – diary, recorded dreams, poems, a kind of flash fiction, polemics, prophecies, and philosophical reflections – all enriched by a lifetime of reading, thinking and articulate writing. As befits the slippery connections between inner and outer worlds, Rohlehr's writing is distinguished by an infectious humour and a delight in puns.

In the act of questioning what the years of "wuk" have achieved, Rohlehr asks himself and us the most profound questions – not the unanswerable metaphysics of "What are we here for?" but the material, ethical question of "To what end do we exist?" In the context of a Caribbean of disappointed post-colonial hopes, Rohlehr both confronts an existential void and records the increments of creativity and achievement that offer future hope.

The book begins with the Guyanese child, born with a caul over his face, gifted with a prophetic vision deeply immersed in the African being that is part of his inheritance. He records how he was told – beyond his memory – how family members "steamed" his eyes to destroy something embarrassing to a colonial, lower-middle class family. The visions and intuitive knowledge disappeared, but if the family elders believed that they were cauterising something to destruction, they failed utterly to kill the visionary dreamer, the Daniel Lyonnes-Denne, who is one part of the triumvirate that also includes the public Gordon and the reticent Frederick.

In his previous books, Gordon Rohlehr confronted the Caribbean world head-on. Here, he approaches from the margins, and who is to say his dream-work doesn't tell just as powerful truths about Caribbean reality?

All the above and around 450 other titles published over the past 35 years can be bought from www.peepaltreepress.com, ordered over the phone at +44 (0)113 245 1703, or by mail to Peepal Tree Press, 17 Kings Avenue, Leeds LS6 1QS, UK.

INDEX

Abrahams, Roger, 162
Abyssinians, "Satta Amasa Gana", 55
Achebe, Chinua, 115, 124 n. 18
ACLALS 1971, 17, 64
Africa and attitudes to Africa in Caribbean Writing, 13, 19, 24, 71, 102, 104, 122, 159, 160, 180, 182, 187-188, 189-193, 202, 206, 208, 209, 210-211, 214, 220, 222, 227, 229-231, 233, 238, 242, 246-247, 251, 256-257
Africa in Caribbean culture, 17, 25, 26, 31, 71-72, 79, 138, 148
Africa, descent through memory into, 17, 19, 70
African American writing, see Baldwin, Ellison, Morrison, Reed, Toomer
African revivalism in Black Power movement, 39, 45
African-Indian rivalry in Trinidad and Guyana, 117, 118
Agard, John, *Man to Pan*, 38, 66 n. 48, 176, 177, 268
Akan culture and philosophy, 31, 157, 188, 189, 193, 212, 213, 229, 230
Amerindians, 68, 246
Amin, Idi, 48, 184
Ancestors, dialogues between the living and the dead (see also Lamming, *Season of Adventure*), 25, 68, 78, 157, 191, 192, 206, 207, 211, 238
Anglican church, 30, 31, 160, 161, 166, 215
"Apocalypse Dub", (Scott), 34, 53, 54, 59
Apocalypse, trope of, 11, 34, 38, 53, 54, 59, 122, 175, 189, 191,192, 205, 213, 229, 233-234, 244, 245, 253, 255-256, 259, 262, 277-278, 289, 290, 292, 297, 299, 302, 315, 324, 331; dream of reversal of social order, 235, 244
"Apocalypse" (Delamo), 38, 175, 278, 290
Armstrong (Sachmo) Louis, 245
Artaud, Antonin, 45
Asante nation, 215
Atilla the Hun (Raymond Quevado), 166, "Graf Zeppelin", 174
Autobiographal texts, 11; in Kamau Brathwaite's work: 180, 181-182, 188, 189, 196, 198, 201, 213
Axeback (Rawle Titus), "Reflections", 321, 322,
Ayler, Albert, 199, 200, 201, 202
Baker, "From Baker to Bakr", 324
Bakr, Abu, 305, 306, 308, 312, 316, 317, 324, 325, 326, 327, 328, 329, 332, 333, 334 n. 26
Baldwin, James: *Go Tell it on a Mountain*, 18, 28, 30, 68; *The Fire Next Time*, 259
Bally (Errol Ballantyne), "Calypso Coup", 311, 312, **316-317**; "Party Time", 314, 315; "Bally, Who You Voting For", 320
Barrett, Lindsay, *Song for Mumu*, 169
Baudelaire, Charles, 260
Baxter, Ivy, 162
Beckett, Samuel, 21, 45, 61, 103, 107, 109, 207; *Malone Dies*, 103, 124; *Waiting for Godot*, 204
Bennett, Louise, 35, 157, 158, 161, 162; "Me Bredda", 177; "street poems", 158
Berry, James, 170
Besson, Gerry, 298
Black Power, 39, 107, 117, 118, 147, 235, 236, 242, 277, 279, 280, 293, 302, 304, 328, 330
Black Stalin (Leroy Calliste), 174, 302, 303; "Repainting the Portrait of Trinidad", 37, 175; "Vampires", 38, 291; "Money", 59; "Make Them All Right", 175, 286; "Nothing Ain't Strange", 278, 283, 296; "Breakdown Party", 37, 286, 314; "Bun Dem", 292, 296, 328; "We Can Make It If We Try", 295, 304, 305; "Nah Ease Up", 296, 302, **303-304**; "Sing for the Land", 304; "Caribbean Man", 304; "Revolution Time", 305
Blake, William and Blakean energy, 16, 130, 131, 206, 232, 240; "Tyger", analogies with Shango, 16, 259
Blakie (Carlton Joseph), "Twenty Years too Long", 281, 283
Bomber (Clifton Ryan), 317, "Bomber's Dream", 40-41, 48; relationship to "Spoiler's Return" (Walcott), 46
Bongo Jerry, "Sooner or Later",

"Mabrak", 61, 62
Brathwaite, Kamau, 8, 9, 11, 13, 16, 17, 69, 97, 124 n. 23, 129, 153, 166, 177, 181, 202-203, 225, 267, 268, 270, 271; *Rights of Passage:* 253; "New World A-Comin", 230, "Shepherd", 238; "Limbo", Rights", 238; "Wake", 238, "Cane", 238; "Leopard", 239-240, 241, 247; *Islands,* 38, 66, 188, 201; *The Arrivants,* 11, 12, 14, 18, 68, 157, 180, 201, **227-228**, 258; "Wings of a Dove", 237, 238; "Stone Sermon", "Negus" 18, 30, 237; *Masks,* **227**, 236: "Chad", "Timbuctu", 227; "The Making of the Drum", 206; *Other Exiles,* "Arrival", 197-198, "Clock", 198-200, 201-202; "Glass", 186, 226;, "Dread", 270; "Harmattan Poems": "Sun Song", 255; *Sun Poem,* 11, **180-194,** 212: "Noom", 230, 232; *Mother Poem,* 11, 30, 58, 67, 192, 196, 201, 213; "Peace Fire", 58; "Dais and Nights", 214, 216, 221; "Hex", 232, 233; *X-Self,* **241-264**; transhistorical juxtapositions in *X-Self,* 242-251; annihilation of great civilisations in birth of New World, 201, 207, 216, 228, 243; "Mount Blanc" as symbol of white, imperial Europe, 245, 254-255, 256, 260, 263; "Nuum", 228; "Metaphors of Underdevelopment", 228-229; "Visibility Trigger", 195, 204, 208-209, 213, 230, 252, 253; "Voice", 232; "Xango", 232, 255, 256, 257; "Shaman", 233; "Dies Irie" and the critique of imperialism and cry for justice, 243-244, 292; "Cap", 245, 254; "Titan", 247-248, "Nam", 241, 251, 253, 254; "Stone", 254-255; "Ice/Nya", 255; "Citadel", 255-256, 257; *Black + Blues,* 22, 34, 180, 190, 191, 248, 256, 268; *Jah Music,* 195, 196, 198, 200, 204, "Birds", "Flutes", 205-206; *Visibility Trigger,* 195, poems of elegy for Rodney, Nkrumah & Mikey Smith, 208; "Poem for Walter Rodney", 208 270-271; "Nametracks", 177, 214; Criticism: "Caribbean Man in Space and Time", 11 n. 4 ; "Caribbean Culture: Two Paradigms", 11, 200, 225 n. 15, 230; *Contradictory Omens,* 177 n. 3; *The Love Axe/l,* 64 n. 5; "Timehri", 201-202; "Jazz and the West Indian Novel", 204, 225 n. 18; KB on Martin Carter, 138, 143, n. 12; "Springblade", 24, 34, 169, 190, 202, 212-213, 216, 236, 248, 270; "Kingston in the Kingdom of This World", 30, 34, 68, 213, 231, 232, 233, 234, 252, 270-271, 274; "Ogun", 18, 31, 53, 238; Ogun in Brathwaite's work, 18, 31-32, 187; "Starvation", 34, 202, 270; "Octet"/ "Jazz Portraits", 195; Wilson Harris on KB, 25; Frank Collymore on KB's novella, 181; the concept of Nam, 50, 240; the "status crow", 59, 63, 250, 271; on black self-dispossession by slavery and colonialism, 187-188; on Dogon mythology in KB's work, 188, 190, 191, 193, 229, 230, 232, 257, 258, 265, 271; concept of sunsum in, 192; jazz aesthetic in Brathwaite's work, 195-196, 204-205, 238. Critical views of KB's work: Michael Dash's criticism of KB's work in context of grief and campus politics, 195, 196, 201, 202, 204, 207, 208, 210, 211 224; review of *Jah Music,* 203-204; Beverley Brown, feminism and misreading of KB's work, 195, 212-224; women and gender equality in Brathwaite's work, 196, 212-213, 215-216, 221-224; compared to Jean Rhys, 217, 221-223; themes of communal vs private and individual in KB's work, 218-219; Brathwaite's Black mothers' as activist fighters, 217: in "The Dust", 32, 212, "Hex", 213-214, Donna in *X-Self,* 216, "Cherries", 216, "Angel/Engine", 218, 220, "Moth Air", 183, 217, 219; "Twine", 184, 215, 217-218, 220; "Woo Dove", 221; "Driftword", 221-223; "Alpha", 223; letter to campus community on absence of community after death of his wife, 196-197, 202-203, 224; public persona and private face, 197; place of an-

cestors and history in Brathwaite's work, **227-263**: interplay of African, Afro-American and Euro-American histories, 227; the concept and disintegration of Rome in *X-Self*, 228, 242; capitalism and the machine, a world based on money, in *X/Self*, 228-229; the idea of spirit in Brathwaite's work, as a dialectical dance of opposites, 229-230, 236-240; the concept of Nam in Brathwaite's work, 229-230; missile and circle, 60, 192, 200, 210, 213, 229-230; the enslaved person, 233; apocalypse as death/life bringing, 236; persons outside the historical process, 236; on the necessity of rebellion in the Ogun/Shango persona, 237, 292, and fear of revolution's betrayal from within, 248; *X/Self* as a collection based on dualities, 249-250; rainbow as symbol, 259
Brecht, Bertolt, 39, 40, 42, 48
Breeze, Jean Binta, "Riddym Ravings", 170
Brodber, Erna, 268; *Jane and Louisa Will Soon Come Home*, 14, 169, 203
Brother Mudada (Alan Fortune), 332
Brother Resistance (Roy Lewis), 38, 176
Brown Boy (Knolly Brown), "Looters in the City", 306, 307, 309
Brown, Beverly, "Mansong and Matrix: A Radical Experiment", 212, 225; critique of Brathwaite's alleged androcentricity, 196, **212-224**; ignorance of content and style in Brathwaite's work, 216
Brown, Stewart, 195
Brown, Wayne, 163, 166, 315
Byles, Junior, "Beat Down Babylon", 55
Calliste, Leroy, 275; "Valley Trumpeter", 38; suicide, 165
Calypso, 11, 15, 33, 34, **35-38**, 59, 156, 157, 161, 162, 164, 166, 168, 170, 172, **174-177**, 268-269; Walcott on, **39-49**; calypsos and apocalypse, **277-333**: arguments between social commentary and entertainment, 280; pro and anti-PNM calypsonians, 280-281; racial ideology in 1980s calypso, 288-289; reparations and the French creoles, 289-290; the flaying of George Chambers, 290-291; reflecting on the Eric Williams legacy, 290-291; the NAR and politics as Manichean spiritual conflict, 292; racial apocalypse, 292; calypso as delegitimising the NAR, 296-297; Trinidad and Tobago conflicts, 297; responses to the Muslimeen attempted coup, 296, **302**, 305-307; A.N.R. Robinson as target of calypsos, 297-298; charges of threatened censorship, 298, 303; the IMF "bail-out and failing state industries, 299-300; fiction and commentary, satire and distortion, 303-304; support for Abu Bakr, 305-306; calypsos of record, 306-307; looting as comic melodrama, 307-308; the Syrians, Mansoor affair and racial revenge, 307-308; the coup as entertainment, 309; ritualised scapegoating, 309-311; calypsonians as re-instators of the PNM, 311-312; critics of anarchy, 312-313; madness or party time, 313-315; sentimentality and calls for unity and reconstruction, 317-321; support for looters, 321; pleas for self-dependence, 322
Camus, Albert, 45, 98, 106; Clamence in *The Fall*, 33, 107, 142
Cardinal (Elon Bagoo), "Jump in", 291; "Abu Coup", 305; "Nation Building", 306
Caricom Publishing House, a proposal for, 269-270
Carlyle, Thomas, 110, 114, 187
Carpentier, Alejo, 45, 234
Carter, Martin, 10, 64, 269; "I Come from the Nigger Yard", 9, 32; "I am No Soldier", "After One Year", "Death of a Comrade", 137; "University of Hunger", 139; "Not hands like mine", 139; "Poems of Shape and Motion", 15-16; "Proem", *Poems of Succession*, 21; *Poems of Affinity*, **126-143**; symbolic beasts in, crab, 128,

131-132; owl, 134; cayman, 134; "After One Year", 34; "Bastille Day-Georgetown", 126, 133-134;"Our Time", 128, 134;"Playing Militia",129-130, 137; "I am No Soldier", 32; "Our Voice Betrays", 129; "Let Every Child Run Wild", 130-131, 137; "Some kind of fury", 131; "Paying Fares", 131, 132, 133; "Black Friday", 131-132; "In a Certain Time", 134; "I Still Stare", 134-135; "Pattern", "Being Always", 135; "As New and as Old", 135-136; "With that Loan", 135, 137-138, 140; "Rice", 138-139; "Beans of God", 139; "Our Number", 140; "Bent", 139-141; "Ground Doves", 141-142; Prose articles: "Open Letter to the People of Guyana", on degradation of nation, 126-127, 129, 132;"Location of the Artist", on artist's responsibility,127-128; on the move from rhetoric to reticence", 15; metaphors of combustion, 16; riddles, 35, 137, 138; Brathwaite on Carter, 138

Casa de las Americas, publishing house and prize, 267

Censorship, 269

Ceremony of souls, as key trope in Lamming's work, 18, 19, 24, 36, 70, 76, 78, 83, 87, 89, 90, 92

Chalkdust (Hollis Liverpool), 174, 280, 332; "Why Smut", "Juba Dubai", 175; "Learn to Laugh", 269; "Port of Spain Gone Insane", 278; "Nixon's Mistake", 278; "Thanks Geddes", 279; "Ah Put on Mih Guns Again", 281; "Bring the Ayatollah", 285; "White Man's Plan", 289, 291; "Grandfather's Backpay", 289-290; "Trinidad ent Change", 293; "Who Next", 296; "Chauffeur Wanted", 297; "You the Jury", 311

Chambers, George (PM), 278, 281, 286, 287, 288, 290, 291, 298, 325; white elephant projects, 287; butt of calypsonian ridicule, 287-288

Chomsky, Noam (and Edward Herman), *The Washington Connection and Third World Fascism* and *After the Holocaust*, 60

Christophe, Henri, 186, 242, 246, 247, **248-249**,

Clarke, LeRoy, *Douens*, 14

Cliff, Jimmy, 51, 56

Code-switching in Caribbean aesthetics, 13-15, 34, 44, 46, 49, 156

Coleridge, Samuel Taylor, "The Ancient Mariner", 54

Collymore, Frank, "Hymn to the Sea", 177

Coltrane, John, ('Trane'), 16, 26, 236; *A Love Supreme*,18 ; *Sun Ship*, 18; *Kula Se Mama*, 18

Commentor (Brian Honore), 318; "Dragonslayer", 299

Connor, Edric, 162

Conrad, Joseph, 104, 105, 106, 109, 113, 305; *Heart of Darkness*, 60, 73, 74, 101, 102, 114, 115; *Nostromo*, 101, 104; *The Secret Agent*, 102, 105; *Almayer's Folly*, 102; *An Outcast of the Islands*, 102; comparison with V.S. Naipaul, 102-104; comparison with George Lamming, 113-114; Achebe on Conrad, 115-116

Corsbie, Ken, 35

Count Ossie, 50

Crazy (Edwin Ayoung), "Fools", 311

Creighton, Al, 45

Crichlow, Kenwyn, 8

Criticism in Caribbean, tendency to judge by metropolitan standards; cultural diversity and tendency to judge ethnocentrically, 40, 116, 156

Cro Cro (Weston Rawlins), 332; "Three Bo' Rats", 296, 297, 325; "Corruption in Common Entrance", 304; "Say a Prayer for Abu Bakr", 305, 306, 308

Crowley, Daniel, 35, 66, 119, 124 n. 25, 162

Crusoe Kid, "Change", 293; "Get on with the Job", 297

Cuba, 52, 53, 165, 244; revolution as icon in Anglophone Caribbean, 53

Cudjoe, Selwyn (as interviewer), 94-124

Damballah, 52, 220, 256, 257, 258

Dance, 15, 17, 25, 26, 29, 30, 36-37, 40, 42, 43, 50-51, 55, 56, 66, 73, 75,

120, 158-159, 169, 181, 271, 313, 330; colonial prohibition of African dance, 71
Danquah, J.B., 212, 226 n. 41
Darke, Fr Bernard, 126, 132
Dash, Michael, 195, 196, 201, 202, 204, 207, 208, 210, 211, 224
Davis, Angela, 216
Davis, Miles, 208, 225, "Miles Beyond", 178
Davis, Wayne, 165; "Prison Blues", 178
De Fosto (Winston Scarborough), "Trinidad for Sale", 296; "Then and Now", 321
Delamo (Franz Lambkin), "Apocalypse", 38, 176, 279, 291; "Armageddon", 175, 278, 279, 285; "I Want a Wuk, Georgie", 279; "Sodom and Gomorrah", 175, 278, 279
Deple (Tyrone Hernandez), "Vote then Out", 315
Deren, Maya, *Divine Horsemen*, 72, 73, 93, 265 n. 56
Dessalines, Jacques, 247, 248
Divided personalities, 21-22, 72, 83
Dogon mythology, 188, 189, 191, 193, 229, 230, 232, 257, 258, 265, 271
Donne, John, 47, 75, 194, 199
Doubles, see also self and other, doppelganger, 46, 53, 75, 80, 81, 200, 202, 203, 215, 218, 241, 247, 248, 260, 329
Dr P.K. (Patrick Watson), "Support the Amnesty", 306
Dr. Soca, "The Blonde", 291
Dragon and weathercock saga, 298-299; superstitions exploited, 301
Drumming and linkage to Africa and revolt, 15, 17, 25, 27, 29, 35, 50, 55, 58, 71, 72, 73, 76, 78, 89, 157, 158, 159, 160, 163, 189, 205, 206, 257, 265, 327, 328
Drummond, Don, 38, 50, 165, 171
Du Bois, W.E.B., 94
Duke (Kelvin Pope), "Get on Radical", 312
Ebony (Fitzroy Joseph), "Pack Up", 318
Ecclesiastes, 138
Edgell, Zee, *Beka Lamb*, 212, 213, 216
Elder, Jacob, 162
Eliot, T.S., 20, 40, 109, 189, 256; *The Four Quartets*, 41, 48; "The Dry Salvages", 136, 138, 143; *The Waste Land*, 99, 260
Ellison, Ralph, *Invisible Man*, 18, 30, 107, 108, 109, 124, 150
Erzulie, 256, 257, 260
Ethiopians, "Selah", 55
Existentialism, 20, 22, 24, 32, 61, 98, 106, 107, 109, 110, 128, 135, 136, 196, 204
Explainer (Winston Henry), 268; "Georgie if you true", 286; "Kicksing in Parliament", 308
Ferlinghetti, Lawrence, 238
Folk, in literature, 10, 11, 15, 19, 26, 40, 42, 44, 73, 157, 161, **162-163**, 166, 190, 204, 267
Folk-tales, songs, folklore 35, 57, 66, 112, 119, 120, 121, 138, 156, 157, 160, 162, 163, 165-166, 167, 173, 182, 274, 299, 301
Form in poetry: 13-67; oral and scribal, 15, 17-18, 25-29; rhetorical forms, 30-34; secular forms, 35; calypso and reggae, 36-40, 49-51; the theatrical, 41-46; classic, 47-49; modernist influences, 20-25; crystal and chrysalis, 51-55; jazz and drum, 55-57; countercultural influences, 57-61; Rastafarian influence, 61-63
Franklin, Aretha, *Amazing Grace*, 18
Freire, Paolo, 133
Frisco, "Wizard, Take Down the Dragon", 301
Froude, J.A., 110, 111, 114, 187
Funny (Dondrick Williamson), "How You Feel", 322
G.B. (Gregory Ballantyne), "Is You", 321, 322
Genet, Jean, 45,
Gibbons, Rawle, 45
Gilkes, Michael, 13, 14; *Couvade*, 14, 208, 225
Gillespie, Dizzy, 206
Ginsberg, Allen, 58
Girard, Rene, 17, 309, 333
Gobineau, Arthur de, *The Inequality of Human Races*, 159, 187
Goode, Coleridge, 158
Goodison, Lorna, "Mulatta", 177
Goveia, Elsa, *Study on the Historiography*

of the British West Indies, 110, 124
Granger, Geddes aka Makandal Daaga, 279
Greene, Graham, 102, 103, 104, 105; *The Comedians*, 115; *Journey Without Maps*, 102; comparison with V.S. Naipaul, 103, 104
Grenada, 161, 184; revolution, implosion of, 251, 274
Griaule, Marcel, *Conversations with Ogotemeli*, 194, 230, 257, 265
Grotowski, Jerzy, 45
Growling Tiger, "Yoruba Shango", "Workers' Appeal", "Money is King", The Gold", 161, 174; "Let the White People Fight", "What is the Shouter", 161
Guevara, Che, 52, 244
Guyana Prize, 266, 275
Gypsy (Winston Peters), "The Sinking Ship", 290, 304; "Well We Are Here to Stay", 320
Haiti/ Haitian, 10, 18, 19, 36, 71, 72-73, 89, 93, 115, 184, 238, 245, 246, 247, 248, 249, 256, 259, 262, 265, 270, 330
Happy, "Make Love Not War", 306
Harriott, Joe, 158, 178
Harris, Wilson, 9, 16, 45, 86, 94, 95, 96-97, 106, 114, 177, 190, 234, 267; concern with the diversity of the Caribbean person, 95; *Palace of the Peacock,* 14, 61, 68; *The Whole Armour*, 83; *The Sleepers of Roraima*, 208, 225; *Tradition, the Writer and Society*, 16; *Eternity to Season*, 37: "The Fabulous Well", 140, 143; History, *Fable and Myth in the Caribbean and the Guyanas*, 65; "The Question of Form and Realism in the West Indian Artist", 263; concept of implosion, 16; on Brathwaite, 25
Hearne, John, 267, Mark Latimer in *Voices Under the Window*, 19
Hector, Margaret, 302
Herbert, Christopher "Tambu", "The Journey Now Start", 295, 304; "Rant, Rave, Misbehave", 312; "No No We Ain't Going Home", 315; "The Question", 315
Herskovits, Melville and Frances, 162, 257

Hill, Errol, quarrel with Walcott, 42, 43, 44, ; *The Trinidad Carnival*, 42, 66; *Man Better Man*, 43, 46
Hippolyte, Kendel, **55-63**, 271; *Island in the Sun – Side 2*, 22; "The Last Waltz", 56-57; "bed-time story W.I.", "Your Main Street Ends in Soweto", 57; "systematomic hegemony", 57-58; "Per Capita", 60-61, 63; "Orange Lane, the Fire's Light", "Suburban Footnote", 61, 62; "Zoo Story – Ja 76", 61-62; surrealism for unreal times, 59
Hogg, Donald, 17, 64
Holiday, Billie, 202
Hopkins, Gerard Manley, 54, 98, 199
Hopkinson, Slade, "The Mad Woman of Papine", 169, 203
Hossay, 328-329
Hudson, Melanie, "I Will Always Be There For You", 320; "Cry My Beloved Country", 320
Hughes, Ted, *Crow*, 63
Interior descent into self, Fola in *Season of Adventure*, 19, 52, 69, 72-73, 75-78, 81, 82-92, 162; Mark Kennedy in *Of Age and Innocence*, 19, 21, 24, 31, 70, 74, 90
Iwer George, "Rough Neck", 305, 306
Jai, Rikki, "Another Bakr Will Come", 305
James, C.L.R., 13, 35, 117, 267; *Mariners, Renegades and Castaways*, 115
Jarvis, J. Antonio, *Bamboula Dance*, "Bamboula Dance", 158-160
Jayson (John Perez), "Soldiers We Are All", 320
Jazz aesthetic in Caribbean writing, 50, 55, 158, 166, 195, 200, 204-205, 208, 224, 225, 238, 261
Jeremiah (prophet), 238, 254
John, Errol, *Moon on a Rainbow Shawl*, 43
Johnson, Linton Kwesi, 38, 60, 172, 271, 274; *Dread, Beat and Blood*, 56, 67; "Reggae for Radni", 171; "Reggae fi Dada", 172; as Poet and the Roots, 56; "Street 66", 49; on "bass-culture", 171
Jones, Jim and People's Temple massacre, 273

Juvenal, as influence on Walcott, 47, 67
Kafka, Franz, 20, 64
Keane, Shake, 157, 158; "Calypso Dancers", 18, 36, 66; "Shaker Funeral", 25-26, 27-28, 30, 36, 65; *One a Week with Water*, 35; "Per Capita per Annum", 58, 67, 177
Keats, John, 246
Keens-Douglas, Paul, 35; "Sugar George", 38, 175; "Jus Like Dat", 167
Kelshall, Jack, 164, 274
Kenny J (Kenrick Joseph), "Say a Prayer for T & T", 304
King Fighter (Shurland Wilson), "Indian Party", 313
King Lear, 96, 310, 326
King, Johnny, "Nature's Plan", 287, 288, 291, 316
Kingsley, Charles, 110
Kitchener, Lord, 169, 176, 279, 281, 306, 314, 317; as defender of calypso as entertainment, 279-280; former singer of political commentary in "Black Power", "No Freedom", "Jericho", 279; as loyal supporter of PNM, 279-280; "Spree Simon", 38; "Take Your Meat Out Me Rice", 173; "Not a Damn Seat", 280, 284; "Soca Corruption", 280, 284, 301, 311; "Town Burning Down", 312
L'Ouverture, Toussaint, 245, 247, 253
Lady B (Beulah Bobb), "Move the Camera", 308; "Hostages", 310
Lamming, George, 10, 14, 18, 21, 24, 94, 100, 105, 113, 114, 125, 180, 202, 233, 266; *In the Castle of My Skin*, 19, 175; *The Pleasures of Exile*, 19; *Season of Adventure*, 10, 52, 161, **68-93**: Africa and Haiti in, 18, 71; possession in, 69-71, 74-78; the outsider in, 71-74; the colonised Black person in, 78-81; mulatto crisis in, 82-84; the seeker in, 84-86; the medium/communicator in, 86-88; resistance in, 88-91; self-and-other in, the writer's note, 91-93; *Of Age and Innocence*, 10, 18, 20-24, 70, 245; *Natives of My Person*, 106, 115; *Water with Berries*, 19; "The Negro Writer and His World", 21
Lawrence, D.H., 234, 236, 263
Layne, Lancelot, "Blow Way", "Bringing Off", "Ghetto", 175
Legba, 45, 72, 77, 85, 86, 87, 140, 145, 173, 188, 189, 227, 237, 331, 332
Liston, Melba, 204, 215
Living and Dead, dialogue between, rituals of reverence and reparation, 69, and see Ceremony of Souls
Loas, 17, 18, 56, 57, 72, 73, 85, 90, 188, 229, 237, 245, 253, 254, 255, 256, 258; and see Legba, Ogun, Xango
Lord Pretender (Ulric Farrell), "Black Power", 292
Lovelace, Earl, 37, 266; *The Dragon Can't Dance*, 24; *The Wine of Astonishment*, 160
Lucie-Smith, Edward, 116
Luta (Morel Peters), 292, 316, 323, 324; "Think Again", analysis of the failings of education system connected to the 1990 explosion, 321, 322, 324, 327; "Change Your Attitude", 321
Maestro (Cecil Hulme), "The Poor Man", 322
Mais, Roger, 30; *Brother Man*, 34; as archetype, 236, 237, 252; *The Hills Were Joyful Together*, 168; "All Men Come to the Hills", 168
Malik, Abdul (Delano De Couteaux), 164, 165; "Pan Run I & II", 32, 38, 65, 168, 175; "Fireflies... for Beverly", 170; "Instant Ting", 172
Malik, Michael, aka Michael X, aka Michael De Freitas, 268, 276
Mansoor affair, 307
Marley, Bob, 51, 63, 262, 270; and the Wailers, 56; "War", 55; "One Love", 55
Maroonage, 121, 160, 250, 253, 254
Marquez, Garcia, Gabriel, 9, 99, 100
Martial, (and Walcott), 47
Mastertone (Anthony Salloum), "2001", 304, 306
Matthews, Marc, "Eleven O'Clock Goods Train", 35, 66, "Rass Pan", 175
Maxwell, Marina, 45
Mayer, John, 65, 157

Mayers, Richard "Nappy", "Bring Back the Old Time Days", 317
McAndrew, Wordsworth, 35, 161, 164, 273
McBurnie, Beryl, 50
McCleod, Errol (OWTU), 301
McNeill, Anthony, 62, 162, 165; *Credences at the Altar of Cloud*, 14; "For the D", 7, 11, 170; *Reel from the "Life Movie"*, 22, 63, 142; "Ode to Brother Joe", 61; "Strange My Writing to You", 177; Walcott on, 163
McTurk, Michael ("Quow"), 166
Meeks, Brian, 271
Melville, Herman, 68; *Moby Dick*, 115
Mendes, Alfred, 35
Merchant (Dennis Franklyn Williams), "Pain", 297
Michaelangelo, 261
Mighty Striker (Percival Oblington), 291
Mighty Swallow, "Don't Stop the Party", 314
Mighty Trini (Robert Elias), "Animal Farm", 305, 320
Millenarian Christianity, 30, 235
Minshall, Peter, *Rat Race, Danse Macabre, Santimanitay*, 309, 330
Modernism, Modernist aesthetics, 10, 15, 19, 20, 21, 22, 24, 32, 33, 34, 35, 45, 57, 63, 101, 143, 157, 165, 166, 196, 200, 204, 234
Modernity, 63, 149, 150, 200, 233, 261
Moral degeneration and moral awakening, themes of, 33, 49, 60, 76, 84, 93, 113, 117, 127, 132, 146, 153, 167, 175, 242, 277, 278, 280, 282, 285, 286, 306, 310, 312, 320, 324
Mordecai, Pam, 166, 205, 268; "Southern Cross", 170
Morris, Mervyn, 6, 11, 267; *The Pond, Shadow Boxing*, 22; "Valley Prince", 38
Morrison, Toni, *Song of Solomon*, 30
Mukdar (group and journal), 117, 118
Mulatto figures and tropes in Caribbean writing, 19, 55, 75, 111, 159, 160, 162, 164, 245
Murray, David, "Flowers for Albert", 199
Music, relationship to literature, literature about music (see also calypso, reggae),17, 18, 30, 36, 37, 39, 41, 43, 51, 55, 56, 71-72, 73, 79, 89, 90, 107, 130, 136, 157-158, 162, 164, 166, 171, 175, 177, 178, 184, 194, 195, 196, 200, 204, 205-207, 208, 244-245, 258
Muslimeen attempted coup (1990), 306, 307, 308, 309, 311, 316, 317, 324, 326, 328, 329, 332
Mutabaruka, "A Sit Dung Pun De Wall", 169, 172, 173, 271
Muttoo, Henry, 35
Naipaul, Shiva, on Jonestown, 273
Naipaul, V.S., 86, 94, 121, 123, 251, 267; from wit to confessional absurdism, 35; influence of calypso, 37; existentialist characters, 61, 90, 98, 107; resemblances to Ellison and possible influence, 107-109; on small countries and powerlessness, 97; the exploration of Hindu-ness, 97, 98, 100-101, 105; on the grotesque in, 99; formal experiment in or lack of, 100, 105; on death of gods in, 101; style in, 101-102; Conrad & Naipaul, 102-106; travel and journalism, 103; asceticism as writer, 106; displacement in, 109-110; literary ancestry sought among racist English visitors, 110-111; the overlap between fiction and non-fiction in writing, 112; differences in reception of VSN between metropole and Caribbean, African and Indian, 113, 115-116; critical responses to Rohlehr's view of Naipaul, 116; on Naipaul as blamer of the victim, 113-115; VSN's rejection of Indian chauvinism, 118; on sources of VSN's concept of mimicry, 118-120; accuracy and penetration in diagnosis, 122-123; *Miguel Street*, 35; *The Mystic Masseur*, 99; *A House for Mr Biswas*, 35, 97, 116; *The Middle Passage*, 103, 110; *The Mimic Men*, 20, 33, 35, 97, 98, 107, 115, 217; "Christmas Story", 32; "One Out of Many", 32, 61, 100; "Tell Me Who to Kill", 32, 61; *Guerrillas*, and absence of possibility,

96, 100, 122, 270; "The Killings in Trinidad", 270; *In A Free State*, 102, 104; *The Loss of Eldorado*, 114

Nam, concept of as a Brathwaite coinage, 50, 51, 53, 193, 223, **229-230**, 231, 232, 238, 240, 241, 251, 253, 256

Nanny Nanahemmaa, 244, 254

NAR (National Alliance for Reconstruction), perceived as associated with big business, 286, 291, 292; calypsonians commentary on tasks, failures and achievements, **293-295;** 296, 297, 298, 300, 301, 302, 303, 304, 305, 306, 308, 309, 310, 311, 314, 315, 319, 323, 323, 324

Narain, Harry, 268

Nebeker, Helen, *Jean Rhys: Woman Passage*, 216

Neruda, Pablo, 45

Nettleford, Rex, 14, 162; the NDTC, and dance forms, "Desperate Silences", "Kumina", "Two Drums for Babylon", 50, 51;

Nietzsche, Friedrich, 41

Niney (the Observer), "Blood and Fire", 55

Nyabinghi, 244, 245

O'Halloran, Johnnie and Sam P. Wallace and political corruption, 281, 282, 286

Ogotemelli, 230, 257, 265

Ogun family, 18, 24, 31, 53, 187, 207, 214, 217, 237, 238, 252, 253, 255, 256, 258, 259, 262

Oral and scribal, 10, 15, 16, 17-21, 25, 31, 32, 33, 34, 35, 36, 38, 39, 40, 44, 45, 46, 47, 49, 52, 63, 119, 152, 156-159, 162-167, 173, 176, 259

Orange Lane fire (Jamaica) 270, 271

Organizer (Leydon Charles), "Who Is Your Leader", 306, 308, 309, 311, 317

Orisha religion, see also loas, Ogun, Shango, Legba

Orr, Eastlyn, "People Where You Goin", 318

Pantin, Raoul, 39, 66

Parker, Charlie ("Bird"), 200, 202, 205

Patterson, Orlando, Alexander Blackman in *An Absence of Ruins*, 20, 61

Paz, Octavio, 45; *The Other Mexico:*
A Critique of the Pyramid, 37

Pearse, Andrew, 43, 162

Penguin (Seadley Joseph), 291, "The Devil", 38, 174, 291; "TELCO Poops", 301

People's National Congress (Guyana), 126

Perse, St. John, 45, 171

Persons of letters in Caribbean, involved in multiple art forms, 13-14

Pierre, Lennox, 162

Pink Panther (Eric Taylor), "For the Good Times", 296, 305

Pirenne, Henri, the Pirenne thesis, 242

Plain Clothes (Clinton Moreau), "Chambers Done See", 287

Plumb, Charles, 47, 48, 67

Plummer, Denyse, 320; "A Nation Forges on", 295, "Let the Flowers Bloom Again", and criticism of racist stereotypes of video, 318-319; "Don't Cry La Trinite", and Christian iconography, 319, 320; "Well We Are Here to Stay", 320

Pope, Alexander, 47

Possession, as personal state, as communal ritual, as dialogue between living and dead; between instinct and knowledge; drum and music as avenue to possessed state, 10, 18, 22, 25, 31, 35, 68, **69-70**, 72, 74-78, 81, 82-83, 86, 88, 206, 237, 238

Prince Buster, "Judge Dread", 153

Prophecy and the oracular, 15, 23, 25, 33, 70, 75, 238, 252, 253, 259, 277, 278, 302

Protector (Michael Leggerton), "We Talking Change", 293, 302; "Satan", 301

Queh-Queh, 157

Questel, Victor, 10, 33, 45, 57, 129, **144-155**, 166, 167, 199; biography, 144-145; research on Walcott, 144-145; personal and communal themes, 146-147; images of entrapment, 147; severity of vision, 148-149; portraits of domestic and political life in *Hard Stares*, 148-149; poetry as integrative, 150-151; family portraits, 151-152; political satires,

152-154; poems of ironic reconciliation, 154-155; punning and wordplay in, 168-169; *Near Mourning Ground*, 150; "Two Choices", 59; "Scarecrow", 145-146; "Ash Wednesday", 146; "Wreck", 146, 147, 177; "Sea Blast", 146-147, 151; "Coconut", 147-148; "Father", 151; "Downbeat", 167, 168, 169; "Pan Drama", 168; *Hard Stares*, ; "The Eye Explodes", 149; "Hard Stares", 149; "Dirt", 149; "Absence", 149; "Playroom", 149; "Downstairs", 149-151; "Numb", 151; "Pa", 151-152; "Severity", 152, 154; "Judge Dreadword", 152-153; "Footfalls", 153; "A Prime Minister's Address", 153-154; "Calm", 155
Quetzalcoatl, 260
Rajah (Dhanni-O-Gopal), "Is We", 323
Rao, Raja, 16
Rapso, 174, 176
Rastafarians, 49, 166, 171, 250, 277; in Brathwaite's work, 34, 187, 191, 237; destruction of Pinnacle settlement, 50, 161; Rastafarian ideas in Hippolyte's work, 57, 61-62
Reed, Ismael, neo-Hoodo aesthetic, 18
Reggae, 22, 30, 35, 36, 38, 49, 50, 53, 55, 56, 59, 63, 157, 164, 169, 171, 172, 174, 184, 268, 271, 292
Relator (Willard Harris), 174; "Deaf Panmen", 38, 168; "China Syndrome", 283; "Take a Rest", 290
Revelation, Book of, 235, 244, 252, 264, 330
Rhys, Jean, 32, 216, 217, 219, 220, 223, 267; *Voyage in the Dark*, 212, 213; *Wide Sargasso Sea*, 217, 218
Richmond, Angus, 268
Riddles and runes, 32, 35, 137, 138, 157
Risden, Winnifred, 197
Ritual in religion and drama, 16, 17, 18, 19, 24, 27, 30, 36, 45, 69, 70, 71, 76, 83, 89, 148, 161, 171, 211, 217, 238, 310, 327, 329
Roach, Eric, 160, 165, 275; hostility to Afrocentrism and oral poetry, 160; "I am the Archipelago", 32; "Hard Drought", 171; "Transition", 177
Roach, Max, *Lift Every Voice and Sing*, 18

Robber Talk, 35, 44
Robinson, A.N.R., as scapegoat, **297-298, 301-302**; and alleged obeah, 301; 310, 321, 324, 325
Robinson, Douglas, *American Apocalypses*, 234
Robinson, Neville, 275
Rocksteady, 50, 171
Rodney, Walter, 48, 126, 152, 153, 165, 169, 208, 244, 271, 274,
Rohlehr, Gordon, *Pathfinder*, 51
Romeo, Max, "Babylon Burning", "Jordan River", 55
Rudder, David and Charlie's Roots,8; "Power and the Glory", 295, 330; "Hoosay", 311, **326-333**; best of the 1990 calypsos, sees Bakr as the dark side of Trinidad, 326; complexity of metaphor and use of Islamic iconography in song, 327, 329; Bakr as offering instant fake salvation, 328; polluted ritual and corruption of ideals, 329; visionary apocalypse in, 331; "Outta Hand", 313; "Permission to Mash up the Place", 313; "Madness", 313-315; "One More Mr Officer", 315; "1990", 315; "I Will Always Be There for You", 320; "Fire in the Laager", 315, 328; "Victory is Certain", 315
Ryan, William, *Blaming the Victim*, 113
Salkey, Andrew, 267; *A Quality of Violence*, 18, 34, 68; "Maurice", 171
Salmon, C.S., 111, 124
Sartre, Jean-Paul, 238; *Nausea*, 20
Satire, 30, 37, 44, 47, 48, 49, 57, 58, 100, 101, 109, 111, 114, 115, 122, 152, 158, 174, 176, 177, 195, 197, 203, 243, 266, 280, 282, 292, 301, 303, 325
Scott, Dennis, 14, 45, 50, **51-55**, 60, 162, 165, 266, 270; *An Echo in the Bone*, 14, 18, 52, 68; *Dog*, 53, 55, 271; *Uncle Time*, 22, 51, 52, 167; *Dreadwalk*, 22, 51, 53, 55, 60, 67, 169; "Apocalypse Dub", 34, 55, 59; "No Sufferer", 51; "Nightwalk", 52; "Neighbours", 52; "Lemonsong", 52-53, 55; "More Poem", "Third World Blues", 55, 56; dialogue between Self and Other, 53-54

Self and Other, dialectic of, 25, 53-54, 55, 60, 61, 69, 75, 82, 91, 148, 241
Selvon, Samuel, 35, 37, 105, 267
Senghor, Leopold, 25, 65
Senior, Olive, *Talking of Trees* and *Summer Lightning*, 169
Sewell, W.G., *The Ordeal of Free Labour*, 111, 112, 124
Shadow, Mighty (Winston Bailey), "Bass Man", 47, 170; "Judgement Day", 292; "Tempo", 306
Shango (see also Xango), 24, 31, 161, 187, 191, 217, 220, 237, 238, 252, 253, 255, 256, 259
Sharma, P.D., "Government Memorandum", 177
Sherlock, Philip, "Pocomania", 25, 28
Short Pants (Llewellyn McIntosh), 318; *Things Goin' Thru Mih Mind*, 279-280; "The Law is an Ass", 283
Shorty, Lord (Garfield Blackman), "Money is No Problem", 279
Shouters (Spiritual Baptists), 25 161
Simpson, George, 162
Singing Francine (Francine Edwards), 268
Ska, 50, 171
Slavery, 36, 47, 70, 71, 77, 84, 109, 110, 111, 186, 187, 189, 211, 214, 215, 228, 230, 231, 234, 246, 247, 249, 258, 271, 289
Smith, Bessie, 216
Smith, Ian, 53, 67
Smith, Keith, 326
Smith, Mikey, 165, 172, 173, 196, 202, 208, 271; "Mi Cyaan Believe It", 168-169, 202
Sniper (Mervyn Hodge), "Portrait of Trinidad", 38, 175
Soca (See also David Rudder), 11, 277, 281, 282; "Soca Corruption", 282, 285, 302, 307, 308, 311, 312, 316, 317, 325, 330
Sparrow, Mighty (Singer Francisco), 40, 174, 268, 325; abandonment of PNM, 282; "Drunk and Disorderly", 37; "Get the Hell Outa Here", 37; "Slave", 40; "Ah Digging Horrors", 277, 278; "We Like It So", "Capitalism Gone Mad", 279; "The Bomb", 280, 312; "Prophets of Doom", 282-283, 286, 296, 303; "Sam P", 284-285; "Sedition", 296; "We Can Make it Easy If We Try", 305; "Abu Bakr Take Over", 306
Spiritual autobiography, 31, 32
Spoiler, Mighty (Theophilus Phillip), 39, 41, Walcott's fictive character and the actual calypsonian, 46, 48-49; "My Shadow", 46; "Twin Brother", 46; "Magistrate Try Yourself", 46; "Lost memories", 46; "Sleep Walkers", 46; "Cat Brain", 46; "Fountain of Youth", 46, 174
St John the Divine, 68, 175, 253
St Omer, Garth, 20; *Shades of Grey*, 203
Steelband, 24, 35, 38, 41, 42, 89, 176, 309, 332; connection to African drumming and revolt, 71, 82
Stewart, John, *Last Cool Days*, 32
Sudama, Trevor, and "Club 88", 308
Sugar Aloes (Michael Osouna), "The Judge", and "My Decision", 283; "The Argument", 297; "Public Advice", 298; "The Judge", "My Decision", 298, 305, 306
Suicide, the toll of writers, 275
Sullivan, Arthur, 47
Summit of People's Organisations (SOPO), 324
Sunsum, concept of, 189, 190, 193, 212
Superblue (Austin Lyons), "Get Something and Wave", 312, 321
Swift, Jonathan, 49
Terror (Fitzgerald Henry), "Madness", 268, 278
The Tempest: characters and archetypes: Caliban, 19, 70, 177, 187, 191, 214, 229, 249, 250, 266, 274; Prospero, 70, 177, 187, 191, 203, 214, 215, 216, 217, 218, 243, 249, 256, 261, 274; Ariel, 333; Sycorax, 214, 215, 221, 243; Miranda, 19
Thomas, Dylan, 200; "The Force That Drives the Green Fuse", 199; "Fern Hill", 221
Thomas, G.C.H., *Ruler in Hiroona*, 32
Thomas, J.J., 111, 124
Tobago Crusoe (Orthneil Bacchus), "Productivity", 286
Toomer, Jean, 25; *Cane,* 18, 64, 68

Tosh, Peter, 271
Trade Winds, on Jonestown, 273, 274
Trinidad: responses to state of the nation, 11, 37, 48, 49, 148, 174-176, 277-279, 290, 291, 293, 296, 299, 304, 306-307, 310, 312, 313, 317, 319, 322, 326; Trinidad in 1980s-90s, 14, 48, 122, 270, 275, 287, 289, 295-297, 300, 309-310, 327, 332-333; cultural resources and values, 34, 38, 39, 41, 43, 168; Walcott residence in, 39-45, 48; calypsos and political opposition, 59, 174; historical and contemporary censorship of African-Creole culture, 59, 71, 89, 161, 164; cultural diversity in, 157-158; (See also Muslimeen attempted coup)
Trollope, Anthony, 110, 111
Twain, Mark, *King Leopold's Soliloquy*, 115
Underhill, Edward, 111, 112, 124
U-Roy, 171
Valentino, Brother (Anthony Emrold Phillip) 174, 289, 295; "Dis Place Nice", 37, 174, 278; "Barking Dogs", 37; "Recession", 287, 288; "No Revolution", 297
Vallejo, Cesar, 45
Villon, Francois, 44, 48
Virgil, 23, 68
Voiceprint, 10, 156-179
Walcott, Derek, 9, 13, 38, 55, 66, 101, 144, 162, 267; duality of personas: Shabine and Spoiler and voices, 19, 33-34, 46, 112, 292; Walcott and calypso, 39, 40, 45, 46; arrival in Trinidad, 39-41; on carnival as theatre, 41-42, 44; quarrel with Errol Hill, 42-43; on Kabuki and Noh theatre as models, 42; Walcott's failure with *Batai*, 43; classical allusions in, 43; attitudes to "serious" and "folk", 44; "The Muse of History", as reversal of position, 44-45, 163-164; critique of "oral" poets, 45-46, 163; own movement towards orality in style, 166; synthesis of Old World nihilism and New World "primalism", 45; abusiveness towards "African revivalists" and Black Power, 162-163, 235; satirical models, 47-48; wordplay, 129; as mulatto of culture, 162-163; fear of historical consciousness, 236; Plays: *Drums and Colours*, 39; *Dream on Monkey Mountain*, 14, 19, 59, 61, 235, 292; *Ti-Jean and His Brothers*, *The Charlatan*, 41; *Joker of Seville*, 46; *O Babylon*, 46; *Marie Laveau*, 46; *Pantomime*, 59; Poetry: "Tales of the Islands", 167; "Poopa Da was a fete", 167; "The Schooner *Flight*", 46, 65, 176, 292; *Another Life*, 60; *Sea Grapes*: "The Spoiler's Return", 41, 46, 47-49, 59, 176; *The Star-apple Kingdom*, 33; "Mass Man", 168; "Codicil", 177; "Gib Hall Revisited", 203; interviews, 39, 40; Criticism: "What the Twilight Says", 39, 235; "Popular Poets are Now Severely Tested", 39; "Our Poetry in Song", 40; "Cheers for the Insincere Clown", 40;
Walke, Olive, 162
Walmsley, Anne, 12
Warner-Lewis, Maureen, "Odomankoma Kyerema Se", 212, 225
Watchman (Wayne Hayde), 284, 285; "Positive Vibrations", 297, "Attack with Full Force", 296, 311, 317, 324; "Leader of the Opposition", 311
Whitman, Walt, 45, 63
Whylie, Marjorie, 205
Williams, Aubrey, 8, 9
Williams, Denis, 45, 234; Lionel Froad in *Other Leopards*, 19
Williams, Eric E., 8, 38, 44, 115, 119, 120, 121, 124, 151, 278, 279, 286, 287, 290, 291, 293, 295, 296, 301, 324, 325; *Capitalism and Slavery*, 115; *From Columbus to Castro*, 119
Williams, N.D. (Wyck), *Ikael Torass*, 20, 203, 268
Word-play and punning, 38, 147, 148, 149, 168, 176, 217, 316
Wordsworth, William, 137, 181; *The Prelude*, 32; "The Leechgatherer", 140
Working People's Alliance, 125
Xango, 9, 232, 251, 256, 257-258, 259-263, 265
Yaa Asantewa, 215, 216
Yeats, W.B., 8, 42; "Sailing to Byzantium", 7, 11, 193, 207; "Cast a Cold Eye", 148